ASSET
MANAGEMENT
TOOLS AND STRATEGIES

ASSET MANAGEMENT

TOOLS AND STRATEGIES

B L O O M S B U R Y

pp. 19–24, "Passive Portfolio Management and Fixed-Income Investing"
   copyright © Andrew Ainsworth
pp. 37–42, "Venture Capital Funds as an Alternative Class of Investment"
   copyright © Michael D. McKenzie and Bill Janeway
pp. 85–95, "Risk Management Revisited" copyright © Duncan Hughes

First published in 2011 by
Bloomsbury Information Ltd
36 Soho Square
London
W1D 3QY
United Kingdom

A CIP record for this book is available from the British Library.

Standard edition   Middle East edition
ISBN-10: 1-84930-021-6   ISBN-10: 1-84930-022-4
ISBN-13: 978-1-84930-021-6   ISBN-13: 978-1-84930-022-3

Project Director: Conrad Gardner
Project Manager: Ben Hickling
Assistant Project Manager: Sarah Latham

Cover design by Suna Cristall
Page design by Fiona Pike, Pike Design, Winchester, UK
Typeset by Marsh Typesetting, West Sussex, UK
Printed in the UK by CPI William Clowes, Beccles, NR34 7TL

Contents

Asset Management: Tools and Strategies

Contents

QFINANCE

Contributors

Andrew Ainsworth is a lecturer in the finance discipline at the University of Sydney Business School. He received a bachelor of economics degree with first-class honors from the University of Western Australia, and a master of finance and PhD from the University of New South Wales. He has previously worked at the Reserve Bank of Australia. His current research interests include investments, the role of information in fixed income and equity markets, ex-dividend trading behavior, and market microstructure.

Keith Black is associate director of curriculum, CAIA Association, Massachusetts, USA. He was formerly an associate of Ennis Knupp + Associates, a member of the opportunistic strategies group, advising foundations, endowments, and pension funds on their asset allocation and manager selection strategies in the alternative investment space. His professional experience prior to this includes commodities derivatives trading at First Chicago Capital Markets, stock options research and trading for Hull Trading Company, building stock selection models for Chicago Investment Analytics, and teaching finance at the Illinois Institute of Technology. He has earned the Chartered Financial Analyst (CFA) and the Chartered Alternative Investment Analyst (CAIA) designations. Black is the author of the book *Managing a Hedge Fund*.

Kevin Burrows is a senior investment analyst and portfolio adviser for the Nedgroup range of funds of funds, which totals approximately US$600,000,000. His areas of primary responsibility include fixed-income, event-driven, distressed debt, and global macro-strategies, where he performs extensive and in-depth manager search and due diligence for initial investment and on an ongoing basis. He is involved in all aspects of the Nedgroup fund products through his participation on the investment committee. Burrows graduated with a BA in economics from Yale University and holds an MPhil in finance from Cambridge University. Kevin holds both the CFA and CAIA professional designations.

Mark Camp is director of institutional liquidity funds for Henderson Global Investors, where he is responsible for marketing a comprehensive range of such funds. He was formerly a business development manager for AIM Global money market funds, part of the Amvescap Group. Camp joined the Amvescap Group soon after its inception and made a significant contribution to getting money market funds accepted for regulatory purposes for the insurance and public sectors. Before that, he worked for over 10 years in the UK insurance market with banking and investment responsibilities.

Moorad Choudhry is managing director, head of business treasury, global banking and markets at Royal Bank of Scotland, UK. He was formerly head of treasury at Europe Arab Bank in London, prior to that head of treasury at KBC Financial Products, and has worked at JP Morgan Chase, ABN Amro Hoare Govett, and Hambros Bank. Dr Choudhry is visiting professor at the Department of Economics, London Metropolitan University, visiting research fellow at the ICMA Centre, University of Reading, and a fellow of the Securities and Investment Institute. He is on the editorial board of the *Journal of Structured Finance*.

Tom Coyne has been a chief investment strategist at the Index Investor since 2000. He received a BS in economics from Georgetown University and MBA from Harvard University. He began his career at Chase Manhattan Bank in South America, and for many years specialized in turnaround and growth consulting at the MAC Group in London and Bristol Partners in San Francisco. He has also been both the CFO and CEO of a publicly traded environmental technology company in Canada.

Aswath Damodaran is a professor of finance at the Stern School of Business at New York University, where he teaches corporate finance and equity valuation. He also teaches on the TRIUM Global Executive MBA program, an alliance of NYU Stern, the London School of Economics, and HEC School of Management. Professor Damodaran is best known as author of several widely used academic and practitioner texts on valuation, corporate finance, and investment management. He is also widely published in leading journals of finance, including the *Journal of Financial and Quantitative Analysis*, *Journal of Finance*, *Journal of Financial Economics*, and the *Review of Financial Studies*.

Emma Du Haney is senior fixed-income product specialist on the fixed-income team at Insight Investment. Previously she worked at Henderson Global Investors as investment director. Her focus now is Insight's developing client base outside the United Kingdom, especially in Europe. Emma has over 20 years of fixed-income experience in both fund management and product specialist roles. Before Henderson she spent most of her career at Credit Suisse Asset Management.

Rainer Ender is managing director of Adveq. Before joining Adveq in 2001, he was an underwriter for alternative risk transfer at Zurich Reinsurance Company. From 1997 to 2000 he was a manager in the financial risk management practice at Arthur Andersen. He also served for several years on the board of DTS, a regulated derivatives trader in Switzerland. Dr Ender holds an MSc in physics and a PhD in natural sciences from the Swiss Federal Institute of Technology (ETH), and he is a CFA charter holder.

Javier Estrada, professor of financial management at Barcelona-based IESE Business School, set the cat among the pigeons with his ground-breaking research, *Black Swans and Market Timing: How Not to Generate Alpha.* Published in 2008, this revealed that investors who seek to time the market are unlikely to reap rewards. His research focuses on risk, portfolio management, investment strategies, emerging markets, and insider trading. The founding editor of the *Emerging Markets Review*, he also has several visiting professorships in Scandinavia and Latin America. His first degree, a BA in economics, was from the National University of La Plata in Buenos Aires, and he has an MSc and PhD from the University of Illinois at Urbana-Champaign.

Martin S. Fridson is a former managing director of Merrill Lynch & Co. Inc. and was a member of *Institutional Investor*'s All- America Fixed-Income Research Team. He is the author of *It Was a Very Good Year*, *Investment Illusions*, and *Financial Statement Analysis*. He serves on the board of the Association for Investment Management and Research. According to the *New York Times*, Fridson is "one of Wall Street's most thoughtful and perceptive analysts." The Financial Management Association International named him its financial executive of the year in 2002. In 2000 Fridson became the youngest person ever inducted into the Fixed Income Analysts Society Hall of Fame.

James Gifford is executive director of Principles for Responsible Investment (PRI) and has been guiding the initiative since its inception in November 2003. He was also a member of the Global Reporting Initiative working group that developed the environmental sector supplement for the finance sector. As well as leading the PRI, he has recently completed a PhD at the Faculty of Economics and Business, University of Sydney, on the effectiveness of shareholder engagement in improving corporate environmental, social, and corporate governance performance. He has degrees in commerce and law from the University of Queensland, and a master's in environment management from the University of New South Wales.

Martin Gold is a senior lecturer at the Sydney Business School, University of Wollongong, having joined academia after a successful career in the investment industry. He is an experienced funds manager and investment analyst who has held senior analytical and managerial positions in financial institutions and investment research firms. Dr Gold coauthored *Corporate Governance and Investment Fiduciaries* (Thomson Lawbook Co., 2003), and he has also published a number of articles on innovative investment products and the related fiduciary obligations of fund managers and pension fund trustees.

Raj Gupta is research director of the Center for International Securities and Derivatives Markets (CISDM) at the University of Massachusetts, Amherst. He is also a visiting faculty at Clark University and has taught finance at the University of Massachusetts, Amherst. Gupta is assistant editor for the *Journal of Alternative Investments* and has published articles in the *Journal of Portfolio Management*, *Journal of Alternative Investments*, *Journal of Investment Consulting*, *Journal of Trading*, *Alternative Investment Quarterly*, *IMCA Monitor*, and the *Journal of Performance Measurement*. He is a frequent speaker at industry conferences on topics such as performance measurement, asset allocation, and risk management. He holds a PhD in finance from the University of Massachusetts, Amherst.

Christopher Holt is head of industry relations in the Americas for the Chartered Alternative Investment Analyst Association, sponsors of the CAIA designation. He is also the founder of AllAboutAlpha.com, a leading alternative investment website focusing on academic research and industry trends. Prior to this he was head of institutional sales for JC Clark, a $400 million Canadian hedge fund manager, and spent a decade in the management consulting industry with various firms, including Ernst &

Young. During this time he worked as both a consultant and a research director, providing counsel to major clients in the financial services and telecom sectors. For 10 years he was also a consultant to the annual meetings of the World Economic Forum in Davos, Switzerland. Holt has an MBA from Duke University and holds the CAIA designation.

Duncan Hughes has 25 years' experience in the City of London in specialties ranging from fund management to investment banking. During his career he has held senior roles at NM Rothschild & Sons and Threadneedle Asset Management, and recently he has focused on private equity and corporate financing and structuring with specialist boutiques. He is a guest lecturer in finance at London Metropolitan University and the London Financial Academy, and he is author of the book *Asset Management in Theory and Practice*. He is also a managing director of Global Analytics, an international financial training and consultancy firm. Hughes won the Chartered Financial Analysts (CFA) Institute's prize for statistics and financial mathematics in 1994 and he now sits on the Institute's UK examination panel.

Antoine Hyafil is the Deloitte professor of finance and energy at HEC and a former dean of the faculty at the HEC School of Management, Paris. He has been on the visiting faculty at the Sloan School of Management, MIT, and at INSEAD in Singapore. He teaches both intermediate and advanced courses in corporate finance, and he has taught executives in Brazil, Bahrain, China, Lebanon, Lithuania, India, Japan, Poland, Russia, and the United States. More recently, he has been commissioned to develop a portfolio of courses linking financial and strategic issues in the field of energy within the context of climate change economics. Professor Hyafil has been an officer of the First National Bank of Chicago and an academic in residence with Merrill Lynch Investment Banking Department.

Bill Janeway is senior adviser at Warburg Pincus. He received his doctorate in economics from Cambridge University, where he was a Marshall scholar. He was valedictorian of the class of 1965 at Princeton University. Prior to joining Warburg Pincus in 1988, where he was responsible for building the information technology practice, he was executive vice president and director at Eberstadt Fleming. Janeway is a director of Nuance Communications, O'Reilly Media, and Wall Street Systems, and he is a member of the board of managers of Roubini Global Economics.

He is also chairman of the board of trustees of Cambridge in America, co-chair of Cambridge University's 800th anniversary capital campaign, and a member of the board of managers of the Cambridge Endowment for Research in Finance. Janeway is a member of the board of directors of the Social Science Research Council (SSRC), the board of governors of the Institute for New Economic Thinking, and the advisory boards of the Bendheim Center for Finance (Princeton University) and the MIT Sloan Finance Group.

Joachim Klement is a partner and chief investment officer at Wellershoff & Partners, Zurich, Switzerland. He specializes in investment management, asset allocation advice, and the impact of personal values and investor psychology on investment decisions. He particularly emphasizes the impact of emotions on investor behavior and financial markets and helps wealth managers, asset managers, and family offices improve their investment processes and client services. Before joining Wellershoff & Partners, Klement spent six years at UBS Wealth Management in Zurich, first as an investment consultant for institutional clients and then as head of asset allocation strategy and head of equity strategy. He graduated from the Swiss Federal Institute of Technology (ETH Zürich) with a degree in mathematics and from the University of Hagen, Germany, with a degree in finance. Additionally, he is a CFA charter holder and a CFP® certificant.

Theo Kocken, founder and CEO of the Cardano Group, graduated in business administration (Eindhoven) and econometrics (Tilburg) and gained his PhD at Vrije Universiteit (VU), Amsterdam. From 1990 on he headed the market risk departments at ING and Rabobank International. In 2000 he started Cardano, a specialized organization that supports end users such as pension funds and insurance companies around Europe with strategic derivatives solutions and portfolio optimization. Cardano, now with over 60 employees, has offices in Rotterdam and London. Kocken is coauthor of various books and articles in the area of risk management. In 2006 he wrote *Curious Contracts: Pension Fund Redesign for the Future*, in which he applied embedded option theories as a basis for pension fund risk management and redesign.

Satya Kumar is an associate at Ennis Knupp and manages consulting assignments for several retainer and project clients. Prior to joining Ennis Knupp in 2004, he served as a research associate involved in risk management and quantitative strategy development with a proprietary options trading firm. Kumar holds a BComm degree from the University of Madras and earned a MS degree in finance from the Illinois Institute of Technology. He is a CFA charterholder and a member of CFA Institute and the CFA Society of Chicago. He is also an associate member of the Institute of Chartered Accountants of India.

Gene C. Lai is Safeco distinguished professor of insurance and chairperson of the Department of Finance, Insurance, and Real Estate at Washington State University. His publications have appeared in many journals, including the *Journal of Risk and Insurance*. Professor Lai has won numerous best paper awards, including one from the Casualty Actuarial Society. He serves as a coeditor for the *Journal of Insurance Issues* and as associate editor for many other journals, including the *Journal of Risk and Insurance*. He is vice president of the American Risk and Insurance Association (ARIA).

Michael D. McKenzie is a professor of finance and the chair of discipline at the University of Sydney, Australia, and a research associate at the Centre for Financial Analysis and Policy, Cambridge University, England. During his time as an academic he has published numerous books and journal articles on a wide range of topics. His main research interests encompass the areas of risk management, market volatility, price discovery, and market microstructure analysis. Prior to joining academia McKenzie was a treasury analyst for Deloitte Touche Tohmatsu, and he currently works as a consultant with the Midwine Financial Risk Management Consulting group, Australia, which specializes in the areas of strategic asset allocation and financial risk management.

Arun Muralidhar is cofounder and chairman of AlphaEngine Global Investment Solutions (AEGIS) and its parent company, Mcube Investment Technologies. Muralidhar earned an undergraduate degree in economics in 1988 from Wabash College in Indiana. After gaining a PhD in managerial economics at the Sloan School of Management he joined the World Bank, where he rose to become head of investment research for the bank's pension fund. He has also worked as managing director and head of currency research at JP Morgan Investment Management and FX Concepts.

Sanjay Muralidhar, cofounder and CEO of AlphaEngine Global Investment Solutions (AEGIS) and its parent company, Mcube

Investment Technologies, is devoted to helping clients to make better investment decisions and improve returns. Muralidhar earned an undergraduate degree in accounting in 1984 from Bombay University and an MBA from the University of Pennsylvania. He has worked in senior finance positions at Bristol-Myers Squibb, Reader's Digest, and iVillage.

Graham Partington is currently an associate professor at the University of Sydney. He has extensive experience in research and teaching at universities around the world and has designed several very successful degrees in finance. He is coauthor of four textbooks and many research papers, including prize-winning work. His particular research interests lie in dividends, valuation, and the cost of capital, and he provides consulting advice in these areas. From 2002 to 2008 he was education director of the Capital Markets Cooperative Research Centre, where he ran one of the world's largest and most successful PhD programs in capital markets research.

David Pitt-Watson is chair and founder of Hermes Focus Funds, the first shareholder activist fund of any large institution in the world. Over the last ten years these funds and Hermes' other stewardship activities have catalyzed change at some of Europe's largest companies and have been instrumental in many initiatives in the field of responsible investment. Following an early career at 3i and McKinsey & Company, Pitt-Watson was cofounder and ultimately managing director of Braxton Associates Ltd, which became the strategic consulting arm of Deloitte & Touche. In that role he had 17 years' experience of boardroom decision-taking and corporate transformation. A graduate of Oxford and Stanford universities, Pitt-Watson was visiting professor of strategic management at Cranfield School of Management from 1990 to 1995.

Luc Renneboog is a professor of corporate finance at Tilburg University, the Netherlands. Before joining Tilburg, he taught at the Catholic University of Leuven and at Oxford University. Dr Renneboog graduated with a BSc/MSc in management engineering from the University of Leuven, followed by an MBA from the University of Chicago, a BA in philosophy from Leuven, and a PhD in financial economics from the London Business School. He has also been a visiting researcher at the London Business School, HEC Paris, and Venice University. He is a widely published author, with research interests are corporate finance, corporate governance, mergers and acquisitions, and the economics of art.

Gerasimos G. Rompotis is a senior auditor at KPMG Greece and also a researcher at the Faculty of Economics of the National and Kapodistrian University of Athens. His main areas of research cover the evaluation of mutual fund managers' selection and market timing skills, the performance of exchange-traded funds, calendar effects on the performance and volatility of equity investments, and intervaling effects on the systematic risk of ETFs. His work has been published in a number of industry journals such as the *Journal of Asset Management*, the *Guide to Exchange Traded Funds and Indexing Innovations* issued by Institutional Investor Journals and the *International Research Journal of Finance and Economics*, including the European conferences.

Amarendra Swarup is a partner at Pension Corporation, a United Kingdom-based pension buyout firm, where he oversees alternatives and the thought leadership program. Previously he was at an AAA-rated hedge fund of funds based in London, He is closely involved in both the alternatives community and the wider financial industry. Swarup is a CAIA (Chartered Alternative Investment Analyst) charter-holder and sits on the CAIA examinations council, the editorial board of AllAboutAlpha.com, and the CRO committee of the ABI (Association of British Insurers). He holds a PhD in cosmology from Imperial College, London, and MA (Hons) in Natural Sciences from the University of Cambridge. He has written extensively for a range of media and academic publications on diverse topics including alternatives, cosmology, macroeconomic issues, pensions, asset–liability management, and risk management. He is currently a visiting fellow at the London School of Economics, where he is working with the Department of Management on Pensions Tomorrow, a research initiative looking into the economic, sociopolitical, and financial aspects of pensions and longevity.

Simon Taylor is a University Lecturer in finance at Cambridge University's Judge Business School. His main areas of research include how capital markets monitor and influence company's decision-making and methods of valuation used by equity research analysts. Taylor spent nine years as an equity analyst at a number of investment banks, including BZW, JP Morgan, and Citigroup, where he was involved in several major equity transactions and takeovers. In 2001 he became deputy head of European equity research at JP Morgan, where he was responsible for the technical and quantitative research teams and for the technology, media, and telecoms sectors. Taylor joined Judge Business School in 2007 where he is the Director of the new Cambridge Master of Finance degree.

Steve Wallace joined the Chartered Alternative Investment Analyst (CAIA) Association as associate director of industry relations in June 2008 and is based in England. Prior to joining the CAIA Association he managed client relations for several UK firms—most recently with an emerging market equity hedge fund as well as ING Wholesale Banking and Société Générale Corporate & Investment Banking. In addition, he spent seven years working in the private wealth management sector in Australia, primarily in investment strategy for high net worth individuals at firms, including the private bank division of National Australia Bank and AXA Australia.

Chendi Zhang is assistant professor of finance at Warwick Business School. His main areas of research include corporate finance, behavioral finance, ethical/social investments, and emerging economies. He is junior extramural fellow of the Center for Economic Research, Tilburg, the Netherlands, and was previously lecturer in finance at the University of Sheffield. He has also held positions as consultant/researcher at the World Bank and the International Finance Corporation (IFC), Washington, DC. Dr Zhang has published in academic journals such as the *Journal of Corporate Finance* and the *Journal of Banking and Finance*. He holds a PhD in financial economics from Tilburg University, the Netherlands.

Guofu Zhou is professor of finance at Olin Business School, Washington University. His teaching and research interests include asset pricing tests, asset allocation, portfolio optimization, Bayesian learning and model evaluation, econometric methods in finance, futures, options, and derivatives, the term structure of interest rates, and the real option valuation of corporate projects. Before joining Olin Business School in 1990, Zhou studied at Duke University for his PhD in economics and MA in mathematics, at Academia Sinica for an MS in numerical analysis, and at Chengdu College of Geology for a BS.

Best Practice
Investments

Booms, Busts, and How to Navigate Troubled Waters by Joachim Klement

EXECUTIVE SUMMARY

- We review the typical anatomy of financial market bubbles and subsequent crashes.
- We show that financial innovation has often triggered exuberant market developments, leading to unjustified market optimism and catastrophic losses for many investors.
- We emphasize the role that psychology and behavioral biases play in market dynamics before, during, and after a crash.
- We provide tips on how to navigate volatile markets more effectively in the inevitable bubbles and crashes of the future—inevitable because of the very nature of investor psychology and financial markets.
- Assess the auditing and monitoring process for effectiveness.

A BRIEF HISTORY OF BUBBLES AND CRASHES

For many, the tech bubble of the late 1990s is probably the most prominent example of a stock market boom and bust. Figure 1 shows the exuberance in the Nasdaq Composite stock market index, which includes a significant proportion of technology and telecommunications stocks, compared to the S&P500 Index of the 500 large-cap stocks from traditional sectors like industrials, transportation, utilities, and financials. As the internet and information technology spread throughout society, investors became ever more optimistic about the growth prospects and profit potential of companies involved in IT.

But irrational exuberance, as former Fed Chairman Alan Greenspan called it, is not a phenomenon of the information age. It has taken hold of financial markets time and again throughout history. Table 1 summarizes a selection of stock market slumps after periods of irrational exuberance in the United Kingdom and the United States since 1800. Two observations stand out: Bubbles and crashes are not rare, reoccurring at intervals of 10 to 30 years, and the subsequent market declines typically eliminate from 15% to 50% of the peak market value. Assets such as commodities, sovereign bonds, and currencies have also frequently shown signs of irrational euphoria followed by a severe correction.

THE ANATOMY OF A CRASH

A closer examination of asset price bubbles reveals that the behavior of markets often follows a common pattern that comprises at least four stages:

Figure 1. The tech bubble at the end of the 1990s. (Source: Bloomberg and UBS Wealth Management Research as of July 25, 2008)

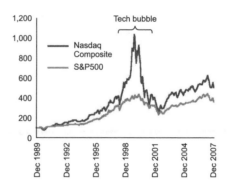

Innovation

A common ingredient in market bubbles, innovations are often based on concepts that are difficult for a lay person to understand, like the information technology boom, or the biotech bubble at the end of the 1990s. Investors cannot assess the true potential of an innovation for a company's earnings growth or productivity. Innovation in a favorable economic environment increases company earnings, but these initial successes may ultimately have limitations that may be unknown to investors. Since no historical evidence is available about possible risks, market participants may underestimate risks and project excessively high initial growth rates, ignoring the inherent limitations of growth for a new technology.

Investments • Best Practice

QFINANCE

Table 1. Selected UK and US stock market booms and busts since 1800.
(*Source*: M. Bordo, 2003, UBS Wealth Management Research, as of July 25, 2008)

UK boom and bust events			
	Boom (stock market increase, %)	Correction	Decline from peak (%)
Latin America mania	1822–1824 (+78%)	1824–1826	–37.3%
American boom	n.a.	1835–1839	–23.4%
Railroad boom	1840–1844 (+52%)	1844–1847	–34.1%
European financial crisis	n.a.	1874–1878	–31.0%
Roaring twenties	1920–1928 (+137%)	1928–1931	–60.3%
Housing boom	1931–1936 (+110%)	1936–1940	–50.1%
Go-go years	1965–1968 (+67%)	1968–1970	–18.9%
Tech boom	1994–2000 (+89%)	2000–2002	–24.8%

US boom and bust events			
	Boom (stock market increase, %)	Correction	Decline from peak (%)
Railroad boom	n.a.	1853–1859	–50.6%
Railroad boom	1875–1881 (+51%)	1881–1885	–26.7%
Rich man's panic	1899–1902 (+30%)	1902–1904	–16.3%
World financial crisis	1903–1906 (+52%)	1906–1907	–19.4%
Roaring twenties	1920–1929 (+168%)	1929–1932	–73.4%
Post-war slump	1941–1945 (+90%)	1946–1949	–10.8%
Go-go years	1965–1968 (+31%)	1968–1970	–15.7%
Tech boom	1994–2000 (+130%)	2000–2002	–27.7%

Exuberance

In a second stage, the presumed benefits of innovation and a new economic era are increasingly overestimated. Prices of stocks or houses continue to rise steadily and markets tend increasingly to ignore risks. Often, risks are only acknowledged after they materialize in the real world. This is the time when euphoria begins and investors clamor to get into the market "because prices can't go down" and "this time it's different", or "this is a new era." High profits attract new investors, and this in turn leads to higher returns as cash pours into these markets. A lack of liquidity in the markets may lead to further exuberance when demand becomes much bigger than potential supply. Especially in illiquid assets like houses, short-term demand can drive prices far from fundamentally justified values.

Crash

The positive feedback loop cannot last forever. At some point fundamental forces lead to a trend reversal. The result is often a rapid and steep decline in asset prices as the bubble bursts and the market crashes. The consequent loss in wealth can lead to lower consumption or investments in the real economy and can even destabilize the financial system. The effects can include recessions, or banking and currency crises as we witnessed in 2008. Here, a lack of liquidity can increase the fall in asset prices when sellers want to unload their investments at any price and illiquid investments may have

to be sold at the worst possible time. In the financial crisis of 2008 it was the forced selling by hedge funds, private equity funds, and other investors that partially contributed to the sell-off of stock markets in the second half of 2008.

Regulation

A crash frequently is followed by increased regulation to prevent similar events from happening again. It is interesting to note that as a result of regulation and the lessons learned from a market crash, the exact same events are indeed very unlikely to recur and financial market stability is increased. But, as time passes, the positive effects of regulation fade. Market participants tend to forget about the causes and consequences of past bubbles. Who today considers the lessons of the go-go years of the 1960s, or even remembers them? Every generation can repeat the mistakes of previous generations, as is confirmed by the emergence of bubbles roughly every 20 to 30 years.

A BEHAVIORAL FINANCE VIEW OF THE CURRENT HOUSING CRISIS

We recognize several behavioral biases when reviewing the US housing bubble and the current credit crisis:

- *Selective perception:* House prices tend to be overestimated, and people buying houses as an investment tend to believe that house prices always increase. Information pointing at an overdue correction was ignored and the focus was on affirming news.

- *Herding behavior:* Investors who initially were skeptical about innovative structured credit products started buying them because everyone seemed to be investing and returns were higher than from traditional bonds.
- *Anchoring:* When assessing the risk of losses, past house price corrections were used as an anchor value for possible future corrections. The higher risk of subprime mortgages and the impact of the new mortgage structures were not properly considered, while the possibility of sharper corrections than seen in the past was also grievously underestimated.
- *Loss aversion:* In early 2007, when the first signs of losses from subprime mortgages appeared, mortgage-related structured products incurred minor losses. Even investors who were concerned about a further decline in the housing market held their positions to avoid selling at a loss. This bias also applies to investors who have not sold any stocks since the market peak in July 2007.
- *Cognitive dissonance:* Once an investment incurs a big loss, we tend to blame the wrong investment decision on someone else. Among those blamed for the credit crisis and its losses in affected assets are the mortgage originators, investment banks, real estate speculators, rating agencies, and regulators. We note that investors who were willing to invest in products they did not fully understand simply because they hungered for additional yield are usually not blamed for bubbles and the subsequent crises."

HEED THE WARNING SIGNS

It is extremely difficult to predict when a bubble will burst. Sometimes it is even impossible to judge if there is a bubble at all. We identify some warning signs that can signal excessive exuberance:

- Bubbles are frequently fueled by the procyclical nature of credit supply: Credit increases when the economy booms and vanishes once risks emerge, thus intensifying the bust. When financing becomes very cheap or "free"—that is, nominal interest rates are close to inflation rates—overinvestment is sure to follow. Market participants grow less careful when selecting investments and fuel an evolving boom. Ask yourself: Is the cost of financing unusually cheap? Is credit being used to finance investments, or has some new form of leverage even become the latest innovation?
- By definition, a bubble involves an unsustainable pattern of price changes or cash flows. If returns have been good for a few years, and are possibly even accelerating, ask yourself if this is sustainable. If not, you are in a bubble. If your reaction is that higher returns with lower risks are possible due to some new financial innovation, again, look for a bubble. Financial innovation can never make risks disappear—it can merely redistribute them. If it seems that total risks are lower, the financial innovation is probably opaque or poorly understood at best, and you might be taking on more risk than you thought.
- Have you seen a friend get rich? Are you considering trying something similar? Once nonprofessional investors start putting money where high returns have become self-evident, the bubble is probably well on its way. The emotions we feel when returns are stellar in a market we are not in are nicely described by Charles P. Kindleberger: "There is nothing as disturbing to one's well-being and judgment as to see a friend get rich."[1] Unfortunately, these emotions can mislead, enticing us to enter a bubble at a late stage.

MAKING IT HAPPEN

Even if we recognize a bubble, we often are unable to judge how long prices will keep rising. Also, staying out of a booming market is frustrating. So how should we behave if we have identified a possible bubble? Here are some useful principles:

- Don't sell everything when you identify a bubble—you can take the ride as prices go up. That does not mean that we think we can time the markets, and that one has to be able to know when markets top out to ride the bubble. We think that one can stay invested in a bull market but that one should always have a safety net ready that limits the downside risks of a potential investment—even though this might typically come at additional cost or limited upside potential. For example, the booming asset will take up an ever larger share of your portfolio as it grows in value faster than the rest of your portfolio. It is essential to regularly adjust your exposure to this asset by selling a certain share. Decide on a target allocation, say 5% of the portfolio, and regularly rebalance your portfolio to this target once prices have risen. This also locks in profits.

QFINANCE

- If an asset or market has rallied for, say, more than three years, consider investing with downside protection, for example, through protective put options.
- Don't try to get the timing right. Just as around 75% of licensed car drivers think their driving skills are better than average, investors also tend to believe that they can judge market changes better than the rest. History has shown that the largest inflows into markets occur just before the bubble bursts. Emotions and behavioral biases tend to make investors poor market-timers.
- Limit losses through stop-loss orders. This is particularly useful for stocks; however, stop-loss orders can be ineffective in a market crash. Once a bubble bursts, prices often fall sharply as buyers flee the market. Whereas large-cap stocks are usually kept liquid by market makers, small-cap stocks, emerging markets, corporate bonds, derivatives, funds, and structured credit products can turn illiquid overnight. Not being able to sell a position is a real risk in a crisis and investors should consider this when allocating funds to such investments. One remedy here can be guaranteed stop-loss orders, where available. In this case stop-loss limit prices are guaranteed by the broker at the cost of a somewhat higher spread for the transaction. When investing in fixed-income products, a buy-and-hold perspective is recommended.
- Seize opportunities that open up during a crash. Crashes create opportunities through mispricing, and when credit becomes scarce, promising opportunities can arise for investors with spare liquidity.
- Buy only what you understand.

A FINAL WORD

Bubbles appear again and again, and it is extremely difficult to know when one will burst. Our desire to be part of the chase, and our jealousy when seeing others gain, often make us poor investors in times of exuberance. Most of the time, we know a bubble only after it bursts— to our detriment.

However, exuberance works both ways. After a bubble bursts, anything that fueled the bubble is broadly condemned and, once again, underlying fundamentals are ignored. Looking at the credit crisis, we see that the useful innovation of securitization was poorly understood. On the other hand, sudden sell-offs often result in mispricing that can offer significant investment opportunities. The lesson from behavioral finance is probably best reflected in the words of Warren Buffett: "Be fearful when others are greedy and greedy when others are fearful."

MORE INFO

Books:

Kindleberger, Charles P., and Robert Aliber. *Manias, Panics, and Crashes: A History of Financial Crises*. 5th ed. Hoboken, NJ: Wiley, 2005.

Mackay, Charles. *Extraordinary Popular Delusions and the Madness of Crowds*. Radnor, PA: Templeton Foundation Press, 1999.

Nofsinger, John R. *The Psychology of Investing*. 3rd ed. Upper Saddle River, NJ: Prentice Hall, 2007.

Plous, Scott. *The Psychology of Judgment and Decision Making*. New York: McGraw-Hill, 1993.

Shiller, Robert J. *Irrational Exuberance*. 2nd ed. New York: Doubleday, 2006.

Website:

Behavioral finance resources: www.behaviouralfinance.net

NOTES

1 Kindleberger and Aliber, 2005.

Investing Cash: Back to Basics by Mark Camp and Emma Du Haney

EXECUTIVE SUMMARY

- Have regard to risk and security when deciding where to invest.
- A guarantee is only as good as the giver. There is no such thing as an absolute guarantee.
- When investing cash:
  - use internal resources if there is a fully functioning professional treasury;
  - use your clearing bank or custodian;
  - use a specialized investment manager;
  - use suitable pooled funds (money market funds), perhaps through a treasury portal.
- Money market funds offer different yields and returns. Before investing, prioritize between yield, security, and liquidity, and carry out detailed due diligence.
- Simplicity and transparency are key factors.
- The current crisis has highlighted the importance of liquidity and credit.

LESSONS FROM RECENT EXPERIENCE IN FINANCIAL MARKETS

It has become crystal clear that cash must be treated as a separate asset class. This means taking care when considering how, and with whom, cash should be held and invested.

It is equally clear that risk is a very relevant factor for cash. Institutional investors have discovered in the past year that so-called safe cash investments have not been as secure as they thought. For many years, investors have ignored the fundamental principle that extra yield is associated with extra risk. It is now clear that the especially attractive rates paid by Icelandic banks came with significant additional risk.

In times of plenty we tend to overlook or downplay risks and concentrate on the rewards. All we tend to think about is who is top of the league table so that I can maximize my interest income. What can be all too easily forgotten is that the return *of* your money is always more important than the return *on* your money.

A flight to quality, or perceived safety, can quickly become an unstoppable tsunami that can take the good with the bad; witness the ever-lengthening queue outside Northern Rock (a British bank) last September, and the subsequent effect on confidence in all British banks. Everyone now wants a guarantee, and an absolutely safe investment.

What does "guarantee" itself mean? We now know that it is only as good as the counterparty that gives it. Having to worry about counterparty risk is something most of us thought was the thankless and purely box-ticking task of compliance officers, or the credit committee. Now we know better. It must be stressed that it is very unusual for an institutional investor to receive a specific guarantee on a cash placement, except to the extent that a bank, or investment product, receives overt support from a relevant authority that one trusts.

What no one wants to say is that, ultimately, there is no absolute guarantee. This may seem more obvious now, after a year in which we have seen that AAA credit ratings do not guarantee security, and that even a government guarantee is only as good as the economic strength of the country that gives it.

The whole financial world is built on confidence, and if that is fatally cracked then the whole pack of cards can come down, with disastrous economic consequences for us all. That is why all the major governments and central banks, in both West and East, finally acted as decisively as they did toward the end of 2008, coughing up some US$6.75 trillion to save the world. This is equivalent to some 10% of the entire US$65 trillion global economy (CIA World Factbook 2007), and has been used to recapitalize banks, buy up toxic assets (including subprime-related assets), make loans to financial institutions, and give state guarantees to get the wholesale markets moving again. Even with the size of this unprecedented rescue, risks remain in the financial system according to a recent Bank of England financial stability report.

SO WHAT CHOICES DOES A TREASURER HAVE WHEN INVESTING CASH?

Very large treasury operations. The very largest holders of cash can afford to run a well-resourced internal treasury, including a fully functioning cash desk. Aside from the major banks, however, such entities are few in number, as you have to be investing very large amounts on a daily basis to do this properly.

Treasuries with small or intermittent balances. At the other end of the scale, if one has cash balances that arise only intermittently, or if they are less than US$1.5 million, leaving them with your main clearing bank(s) (having done appropriate due diligence and negotiated the best available rates) is probably the best approach.

Netting and pooling are a must. It is assumed that any treasurer will have already maximized any pooling, netting, and aggregating possibilities, across currencies if necessary, as these always offer the best value operationally and economically—and usually in terms of security too.

For treasuries in the middle ground the main strategic options are as follows.

1. Utilize Internal Resources

This has been an attractive option in the past, often because it is considered a low-cost option. But what are the risks involved with this approach? Even if one hires a good cash specialist, where is the backup if he or she falls under the proverbial bus? Where is the backup for the credit specialist? It is no longer good enough to rely solely on the credit rating agencies, or review the agreed counterparty list once a year. Instrument and counterparty credit ratings are just one of the guides to utilize, and they can, and should, be challenged from time to time. Certainly, just calling your friendly money broker from time to time for advice cannot now be considered best practice.

2. Outsource to a Specialist Provider/
Treasury Portal

The bank. The first option is to see what your clearing bank, or custodian (if relevant), can provide, especially if cash can be automatically swept on a daily basis. The problem here is risk concentration with just one, or only a handful, of counterparties. A good example of this type of situation is a hedge fund with a single prime broker. Not only does the fund have a serious risk with the prime broker as the derivative counterparty, but the cash margin/collateral would typically be held with the same party, doubling the counterparty risk. Before the Bear Stearns and Lehman Brothers troubles, the main global prime brokers were considered too big to fail; this is not the position now.

Investment manager. If an institution has large and relatively stable cash balances to

invest, then an investment manager can be approached to run a segregated cash mandate. The advantage of this approach is that you get to choose the investment manager, and you can also specify the investment parameters and benchmark, and in that way control risk. Invested cash should also be held with a third-party custodian, thus ring-fencing the assets from the investment manager. The downside is that it is a relatively cumbersome and expensive process to set up in the first place, and it is not very flexible. A serious bespoke cash investment manager will usually require a large minimum investment balance (US$150 million plus), and/or minimum fees. Frequent redemption, or movements generally in the mandate, will not be welcomed, as they can materially affect investment strategy and performance. Such arrangements best suit long-term investment cash, and not volatile cash investment.

Pooled funds. Money market funds have been invaluable to many corporate and institutional treasurers in recent years; freeing them from the task of spreading their funds around the various banks. However, money market funds come in many guises, and, as some investors have found to their cost, some of these funds have invested in assets that have proved to be far from low risk.

Treasury portals. Use of portals is extensive in the United States, and brings operational efficiencies if one is a multi-fund user. Such portals are now available in Europe.

MONEY MARKET FUNDS

Let's remind ourselves why money market funds became so attractive. They now account for some 40%, or US$4 trillion, of all cash held in the United States. This reflects a 25% rate of growth over the last 12 months, as investors have generally seen SEC registered (Rule 2a-7) money market funds as a safe haven, in spite of a few funds exhibiting obvious stress that has required promoter support, and the well-publicized failure of both "The Reserve" and the "Lehman Funds". However, what this overall growth disguises is a clear move by US institutional investors away from traditional so-called "prime" funds, to US Treasury and government-backed security money market funds, even though the yields on such funds are very low, and even went negative for a short period.

This trend has been much less noticeable with European-domiciled money market funds, although there are now a small number of euro-denominated government securities, and one sterling government fund that has been recently launched. Demand for these new funds has largely been from European subsidiaries of US multinationals, and it remains to be seen whether such funds catch on with European institutional investors.

European money market funds now account for some €420bn (US$500 billion) equivalent in the three main currencies, and this includes around £100bn (US$145bn) plus of sterling funds.[1] The last decade has seen a very rapid growth for such funds, and although there are recent signs that growth has checked among institutional investors, it seems that high net worth investors are now taking up any slack as they move out of enhanced funds that have contracted sharply or been closed down.

However, Not All Cash Funds Are the Same

Typically, "liquidity" or "treasury-style" funds are managed to a short-dated benchmark such as 7-day Libid (London Interbank bid rate). They offer daily liquidity, carry AAA ratings, and have a constant net asset value (or stable pricing). First of all, they offer diversification—by issuer, instrument, and maturity—and to a greater degree than most institutions could achieve on their own.

Other variants of money market funds, often called cash plus or enhanced cash funds, would typically be managed to 3-month Libor (London Interbank offered rate) or similar, have two-day or longer settlement, and a variable net asset value (i.e. daily market pricing). Such funds can carry an AAA rating, but often they are lower rated. Their attraction is that they should carry a higher yield or return, because they can invest further out along the money market curve (given different benchmark and settlement requirements), and can invest in a wider range of credit instruments, including derivatives and asset-backed paper. All this depends on the extent to which they are "enhanced."

It may seem obvious now, but going forward investors will need to decide what their priorities are from an investment perspective. Security, liquidity, and yield should all be part and parcel of a money market fund, but there has to be a trade-off between yield and the first two. With the credit ratings agencies somewhat discredited, it is all the more important to seek out a professional manager who has the resources to carry out detailed credit analysis on names and instruments.

It is also worth confirming that an offshore fund is run under the IMMFA (Institutional Money Market Funds Association) Code of Practice, as this is a useful "kite mark" to have. IMMFA currently has over 20 active members, and reads like a Who's Who for the money market fund industry.

Going forward, simplicity is also going to be key. Historically, floating-rate instruments, asset-backed securities, medium-term notes and repos may have seemed ideally suited to a money market portfolio. That has proved costly for some, particularly as far as liquidity is concerned. For a pure liquidity fund, the only really acceptable instruments are deposits with reputable counterparties, certificates of deposits (CDs) issued by solid bank names, and short-dated government issued debt. Conventional floating-rate notes or CDs may play a part in some funds, but for those with liquidity as priority, the poor secondary market in these instruments needs to be factored in. The commercial paper market, meanwhile, has all but dried up, removing it as an investible option for many funds.

CURRENT ISSUES IN THE CASH WORLD

Finally, a few comments about the current state of the interbank markets. Liquidity has become a huge issue amid the ongoing financial crisis. Even instruments such as CDs with well-rated banks, which would normally be completely liquid, have become difficult to trade—indeed, the market has even been shut at times. In the United States, the Federal Reserve has recently announced that it is now giving Rule 2a-7 (treasury-style) money market funds access to the Fed window to provide them with liquidity to meet outflows, especially if these are abnormally large. The Bank of England is now committed to providing a similar facility and the European Central Bank may do something similar. A further plan to support funds is to set up a deposit insurance scheme for retail investors similar to that for bank deposits.

As a defensive move, in late September 2008 most funds increased their overnight liquidity (in sterling it was probably in the region of £20–30 billion, or US$30–45 billion), and this dislocated the interbank markets even more, exacerbating the gap between overnight rates and Libor rates. However, this exercise came at a cost to performance, especially for those funds with a higher proportion of less liquid securities like floating-rate notes and commercial paper, whose managers' therefore felt that the funds they managed had to hold an even greater proportion in overnight investments, at a time when overnight rates were collapsing.

Sterling and Euro money market funds generally seem to have weathered the storm for now, but of late the disparity between different fund performances has been much greater than usual, as has the gap against their respective fund benchmarks. This is an area worth exploring, as it can tell you a lot about how the fund has been managed and what issues have arisen. It will be interesting to see how funds cope with the recent downturn in interest rates globally.

Usually funds are at their most competitive when interest rates are falling.

It is clear that Regulators both in the US and Europe will be reviewing whether, and how, money market funds should be specifically regulated. Watch this space, but in the meantime expect funds to be much more conservatively managed and operated.

MAKING IT HAPPEN

- It is important to have a clear strategy and credit procedures.
- The days of do it yourself are probably numbered, unless you can gear up to run a fully functioning, professional cash desk.
- Your bank, custodian, or financial adviser should be the first port of call.
- Longer term cash can always be placed in a segregated mandate with a specialist cash investment manager.
- There is now a viable choice of pooled funds, as long as you do the appropriate due diligence and get comfortable with the fund and the provider's credentials.
- Treasury-style money market funds can provide professional cash management at low cost with a smoothed return, and give the operational flexibility that is essential for working cash balances. Portals can offer operational advantages for the multi-fund user.
- You do have a choice, and best practice demands careful consideration of all the available options.

MORE INFO

Book:

Corporate and Institutional Money Market Funds in Europe. 4th ed. London: Treasury Today, 2008.

Articles:

Treasury Management International (tmi). Issue no. 167 (July/August 2008), "Seeking investment returns." Online at: tinyurl.com/6xltcbr

Websites:

Association of Corporate Treasurers (ACT): www.treasurers.org
Fitch Ratings: www.fitchratings.com
Institutional Money Market Funds Association (IMMFA): www.immfa.org
Treasury Management International (tmi) online: www.treasury-management.com
Treasury Today, publisher and provider of treasury info: www.treasurytoday.com

Investing in Structured Finance Products in the Debt Money Markets by Moorad Choudhry

EXECUTIVE SUMMARY

- A number of structured finance investment products are available in money markets that offer investment options for cash-rich investors..
- Products include asset-backed commercial paper, total return swaps, and collateralized committed repo liquidity lines.
- The returns available for cash-rich investors differ according to asset credit quality, with higher yields on lower-rated assets.
- Returns also differ by product type.
- Investors should assess the liquidity of an instrument type as well as its credit risk.

INTRODUCTION

The application of synthetic securitization and structured finance techniques in debt capital markets has made a range of asset classes available to investors who would not otherwise have access to them. Thus banks, fund managers, and cash-rich corporate institutions can choose from a wide variety of investment options for their funds. This article introduces a sample of money market products that present alternatives for the investment of surplus funds. In each case we consider the basic product structure, and we look at the different yields across products.

The global credit and liquidity crunch in 2007–08 resulted in a widespread "flight-to-quality" as investors became excessively risk-averse. Yield spreads widened considerably and certain asset classes and products were no longer viable. We review here only instruments that remain practical products for both investors and borrowers. The products considered are:

- Asset-backed commercial paper;
- Total return swap funding, or synthetic repo;
- Collateralized committed repo liquidity lines.

ASSET-BACKED COMMERCIAL PAPER

The application of securitization technology in the money markets has led to the growth of short-term instruments backed by the cash flows from other assets, known as "asset-backed commercial paper" (ABCP). Securitization is the practice of using the cash flows from a specified asset, such as residential mortgages, car loans, or commercial bank loans as backing for an issue of bonds. In the case of ABCP the assets are funded in the commercial paper market. The assets themselves are transferred from the original owner (the "originator") to a specially created legal entity known as a "special purpose vehicle" (SPV), so as to make them separate and bankruptcy-remote from the originator. In the meantime, the originator is able to benefit from capital market financing charged at a lower rate of interest than that earned by the originator on its assets.

Figure 1 illustrates a generic securitization transaction for the debt capital markets, issuing asset-backed securities (ABS). The originator has set up the SPV, which then buys the assets from it. The SPV funds itself in the debt capital markets by issuing ABS.

Figure 1. Securitization structure

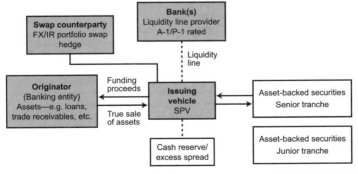

Investments • Best Practice

Generally securitization is used as a funding instrument by companies for three main reasons: It offers lower-cost funding than traditional bank loan or bond financing; it is a mechanism by which assets such as corporate loans or mortgages can be removed from the balance sheet, thus transferring the default risk associated with those assets to investors; and it increases a borrower's funding options. For investors it offers a class of assets that would not otherwise be available to them directly, thus widening their return options and potentially diversifying the sources of risk in their portfolio. Equally, issuing ABCP enables an originator to benefit from money market financing that it might otherwise not have access to, perhaps because its credit rating is not sufficiently strong.

When entering into securitization, an entity may issue term securities against assets into the public or private market, or it may issue commercial paper via a special purpose legal entity known as a "conduit." These conduits are usually sponsored by commercial banks. ABCP trades as a money market discount instrument. Investors purchase it from a number of ABCP dealers who work on behalf of the conduit. The return available on ABCP is a function of the credit rating of the issuer, which is dependent on the credit quality of the underlying assets. Conduits often pay a fee to be backed by a line of credit, known as a "liquidity line," which is supplied by a bank. The credit quality and standing of the liquidity bank also drive the credit rating of the conduit.

The assets that can be funded via a conduit program are many and varied; to date they have included:

- trade receivables and equipment lease receivables;
- credit card receivables;
- auto loans and leases;
- corporate loans, franchise loans, and mortgage loans;
- real-estate leases;
- investment grade-rated structured finance bonds, such as asset-backed securities (ABS).

Figure 2 illustrates a typical conduit structure for ABCP issued to the US and European commercial paper markets. (The difference in yields available on ABCP rated A1/P1 compared to bank-issued commercial paper of the same rating is illustrated in Table 2. The higher yield on ABCP reflects investor perception of the higher associated credit risk.)

REPO AND SYNTHETIC REPO

A repo is a transaction in which one party sells securities to another, and at the same time and as part of the same transaction commits to repurchase those securities on a specified date at a specified price. The seller delivers securities and receives cash from the buyer. The cash is supplied at a predetermined rate of interest—the repo rate—which remains constant during the term of the trade. On maturity, the original seller receives back collateral of equivalent type and quality, and returns the cash plus repo interest. Although legal title to the securities is transferred, the seller retains both the economic benefits and the market risk of owning them. This means that the seller will suffer loss if the market value of the collateral drops during the term of the repo, as the seller retains beneficial ownership of the collateral. The buyer in a repo is not affected in profit/loss account terms if the value of the collateral drops.

Figure 2. Typical conduit structure for ABCP issuance

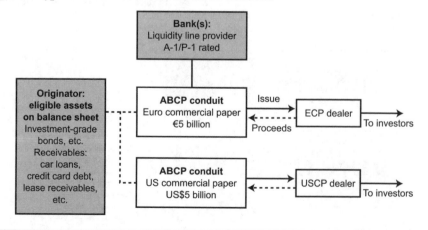

Best Practice • Investments

The repo market is a vital element of the global capital and money markets. The market experienced substantial growth during the 1990s and is now estimated to account for up to 50% of daily settlement activity in non-US government bonds worldwide; this is a phenomenal figure. Repo, from "sale and *repurchase agreement*," is closely linked to other segments of the debt and equity markets. From its use as a financing instrument for market-makers to its use in the open market operations of central banks, and its place between the bond markets and the money markets, it integrates the various disparate elements of the marketplace and allows the raising of corporate finance across all sectors.

Across the world, including financial centers in the North American, European, and Asia-Pacific region, repo is a well-established investment product, utilized by fund managers, hedge funds, corporate treasuries, and local authorities. The practicality and simplicity of repo means that it can be taken up even in capital markets that are still at an emerging stage as well as by a wide range of participants.

What we have described is in effect a secured loan, but one with added flexibility for use in a variety of applications. Market participants enter into a classic repo because they wish to invest cash, for which the transaction is deemed to be *cash-driven*, or because they wish to finance the purchase of a bond or equity that they have bought. Alternatively, they may wish to borrow a stock that they have sold short, which is known as a "reverse repo." However the reverse repo trader is also lending cash. So the trade might be cash-driven or *stock-driven*. The first and most important thing to state is that repo is a secured loan of cash, and it is categorized as a money market yield instrument. Note that every repo is also a reverse repo, depending on which counterparty viewpoint one looks at the transaction from.

Repo market-makers, which include the large money-center banks, make two-way prices in repo in the major currencies. This means they will trade both repo and reverse repo, lending and borrowing cash, against either receiving or supplying collateral, according to customer need. A generic type of collateral, such as government bonds, is known as "general collateral" and refers to a trade in which any specific bond that fits the general collateral type can be supplied as collateral.

Repo is traded under a standard legal agreement termed the Global Master Repurchase Agreement (GMRA). Such an agreement executed once between two parties governs all subsequent trades between them.

Plain Vanilla Repo

Let us say that the two parties to a repo trade are Bank A, the seller of securities, and Bank (or corporate entity) B, which is the buyer of securities. On the trade date the two banks enter into an agreement whereby on a set date, the "value" or "settlement" date, Bank A will sell to Bank B a nominal amount of securities in exchange for cash. The price received for the securities is the market price of the stock on the value date. The agreement also demands that on the termination date Bank B will sell identical stock back to Bank A at the previously agreed price; consequently, Bank B will have its cash returned with interest at the agreed repo rate.

The basic mechanism is illustrated in Figure 3.

Figure 3. Classic repo transaction for 100-worth of collateral stock

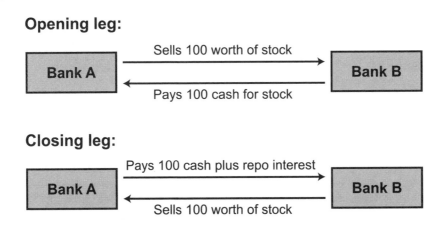

Investments • Best Practice

Synthetic Repo Via the Total Return Swap

Synthetic repo, undertaken for the purposes of funding a portfolio or investing against a credit-linked instrument, is common in the market. The repo is in the form of a total return swap (TRS), which is classified as a credit derivative; however, when traded for funding or stock borrowing purposes it is identical in economic terms to a classic repo.

A TRS has similarities to an interest rate swap in that it consists of two payment legs, one the "total return" and the other an interest payment linked to Libor. As a credit derivative, a TRS enables a market participant to access the total return on an asset such as a bond without actually buying it. The return is in the form of the bond's coupon and any capital appreciation during the term of the trade. For an existing investor that is already holding a bond, entering into a TRS enables it to transfer the credit risk associated with the bond to the TRS counterparty.

TRS contracts are used in a variety of applications by banks, and are discussed in detail by Choudhry (2004). When used for funding purposes, a TRS is more akin to a synthetic repo contract. To illustrate this application, we describe here the use of a TRS to fund a portfolio of bonds, as a substitute for a repo trade. This is shown at Figure 4, where counterparty A is the investor lending funds and receiving a Libor-based return. The counterparty to the trade is investing cash against a credit-linked return, which, depending on the credit quality of the linked assets, may be substantially above Libor.

Consider a bank that has a portfolio of assets on its balance sheet for which it needs to obtain funding. These assets are investment grade-rated structured finance bonds such as credit card ABS

and investment grade-rated convertible bonds. In the repo market, it is able to fund these at Libor plus 200 basis points. That is, it can repo the bonds out to a bank or non-bank financial counterparty, and will pay Libor plus 200 bps on the funds it receives.

Assume that for operational reasons the bank cannot fund these assets using repo. Instead it can fund them using a basket TRS contract, provided that a suitable counterparty can be found. Under this contract, the portfolio of assets is "swapped" out to the TRS counterparty, and cash is received from the counterparty. The assets are therefore sold off the balance sheet to the counterparty, which may be a corporate treasury or an investment bank. The corporate or investment bank will need to fund this itself—it will either be cash-rich or have a line of credit from another bank. The funding rate the investor charges will depend to a large extent on the rate at which it can fund the assets itself. Assume that the TRS rate charged is Libor plus 220 bps—the higher rate reflecting the lower liquidity in the basket TRS market for non-vanilla bonds.

Assume that at the start of the trade the portfolio consists of five euro-denominated ABS bonds. The parties enter into a three-month TRS, with a one-week interest rate reset. This means that the basket is revalued at one-week intervals. The difference in value from the last valuation is paid (if higher) or received (if lower) by the lender to the borrowing bank; in return the borrowing bank also pays one-week interest on the funds it received at the start of the trade. The bonds in the reference basket can be returned, added to, or substituted. So if any stocks have been sold or bought, they can be removed or added to the basket on the reset date.

Figure 4. Total return swap as a synthetic repo

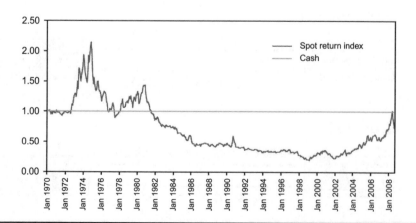

Example of a TRS

Table 1 shows a portfolio of five securities that were invested in via a TRS trade between a bank and a non-bank, cash-rich financial institution, which is the investor. The trade terms are shown below.

Trade date	January 8, 2009
Value date	January 12, 2009
Maturity date	April 13, 2009
Rate reset	January 19, 2009
Interest rate	2.445% (one-week euro Libor fix of 2.225% plus 220 bps)
Market value of reference basket	€100,002,300.00

At the start of the trade, the bonds in the basket are swapped out to the lender, who pays the market value for them. On the first reset date, the portfolio is revalued and the following calculations are confirmed:

Old portfolio value	€100,002,300.00
Interest rate	2.445%
Interest payable by borrower bank	€47,542.76
New portfolio value	€105,052,300.00
Portfolio change in value	€ +5,050,000.00
Net payment: borrowing bank receives	€ +5,002,457.24

The existing bonds had not changed in price; however, a new security was added to the portfolio and there has been a week's accrued interest, thus increasing the portfolio's market value. This trade has the same goals and produced the same economic effect as a classic repo transaction on the same basket of bonds. The investor is lending three-month floating money, and is receiving a higher return than from the repo market in the same securities. The cash flows are shown in Table 1.

START OF LOAN
Portfolio additions	€0.00
Loan amount	€100,002,300.00
Interest rate (Libor + 220 bps)	2.445000%

Roll-over
PAYMENTS
Interest
Rate	2.445000%
Principle	€100,002,300.00
Interest payable	€+47,542.76

Performance
Portfolio additions	€5,000,000.00
Accrued interest	€50,000.00
Price movements	€0.00
New portfolio value	€105,052,300.00
Old portfolio value	€100,002,300.00
Performance payment	€+5,050,000.00

Net payment

Borrower receives from bank/investor	€+5,002,457.24

NEW LOAN
New loan amount	€105,052,300.00
New interest rate	1-week euro Libor + 220

Table 1. TRS trade ticket, showing portfolio value at start of trade, interest cash flows, and value at end of trade

TRS TICKET					
1-week euro Libor	2.225%				
Name	Currency	Nominal	Price	Accrued	Consideration
ABC Telecoms 6.25%	Euro	15,000,000	98.00	0.000000	14,700,000.00
SAD Bros 7.50%	Euro	12,000,000	105.00	0.000000	12,600,000.00
DTI 5.875%	Euro	37,000,000	108.79	0.000000	40,252,300.00
Bigenddi 8.25%	Euro	15,000,000	78.00	0.000000	11,700,000.00
BanglaBeat plc 9%	Euro	50,000,000	41.50	0.000000	20,750,000.00
Jackfruit Funding ABS	Euro	5,000,000	100.00	0.000000	5,000,000.00
(addition to basket at roll-over)					
				Portfolio value at start:	100,002,300.00
				Portfolio value at rollover:	105,002,300.00

COMMITTED LIQUIDITY LINE FUNDING

The standard bank liquidity line is a standing credit facility set up for a borrower that may be drawn on at any time. Lines are usually reviewed on an annual basis, so they represent a maximum 364-day facility. A structure offered by banks to clients that desire longer-term funding is the "evergreen" committed line, which is in theory a 364-day tenor but which is formally "renewed" on a daily basis. This enables the borrower to view the line as longer-dated funding because it is always 364 days away from maturity. Liquidity credit facilities attract a Basel regulatory capital weighting if they are committed to the client. It is common for any borrowings on the line to be collateralized. This turns the liquidity into a committed repo line.

A liquidity facility is an avenue for a bank to invest surplus cash and carries two charges:
- the standing charge, usually calculated as a fixed fee in basis points and payable monthly or quarterly in advance;
- the actual borrowing cost (an interest rate charge) when the line is drawn on.

The standing fee is a function of the credit quality of the borrower. A recent development, widely used by ABCP vehicles, has been the replacement of part or all of the liquidity line with a "committed repo" facility (or committed TRS facility), which carries with it a lower fee and thus saves on costs. Under the committed repo a bank will undertake to provide a repo funding facility using the vehicle's assets as collateral. Thus, in the event that commercial paper cannot be repaid, the vehicle will repo out its assets to the repo provider, enabling it to meet maturing commercial paper obligations.

YIELD MATRIX

The different products available in money markets mean that there is a range of risk-reward profiles for investors to consider. Table 2 illustrates the variation in yields available in US dollars during January 2009. Investors expect a different return profile for different credit ratings, with higher yields on lower-rated assets. This is confirmed in Table 2. The rates in the table also confirm that returns differ for different instrument types, with a greater yield offered by TRS funding of AAA-rated structured finance securities than by repo of the same collateral.

Structured finance instruments are an alternative investment option for cash-rich long-only investors in the money markets, and in certain cases they can offer a higher return for the same theoretical credit risk. This often reflects liquidity factors, which should be factored into any investment analysis.

MAKING IT HAPPEN

Commercial and retail banks all have dedicated repo, commercial paper, and corporate banking desks that provide investment products for other banks as well as cash-rich investors. Investors may contact their correspondent bank in the first instance.

Those wishing to invest in structured finance instruments should consider the following:
- Their risk/reward profile, from both a credit-rating perspective and a value-at-risk perspective.
- The exposure to underlying assets, and how the value of their investment changes with changes in value of the underlying assets.
- The range of yields available, and why identically rated assets should have different credit spreads.
- Reviews of yields, such as those published by Bloomberg.

Investing in Structured Finance Products

Table 2. US dollar lending rates against different instrument types, January 2009.
(*Source*: Bloomberg; market counterparties)

Instrument	1-month	3-month	1-year
Bank commercial paper			
A1-P1	0.50%	0.95%	
A2-P2	1.95%	3.56%	
Asset-backed commercial paper			
A1-P1	0.75%	1.30%	
Repo			
US Treasury	0.25%	0.30%	
AAA MBS*	0.85%	2.35%	
Total return swap			
AAA MBS*	0.95%	2.50%	
Liquidity line†			
A1 borrower			
Standing fee	20 bps		
Borrowing fee	Libor + 100 bps		
A2 borrower			
Standing fee			50 bps
Borrowing fee			Libor + 220 bps

* Triple-A rated mortgage-backed securities. † This is a one-year committed liquidity line, drawn against investment grade-rated collateral.

MORE INFO

Books:
Bhattacharya, Anand K., and Frank J. Fabozzi (eds). *Asset-backed Securities*. New Hope, PA: Frank J. Fabozzi Associates, 1996.
Choudhry, Moorad. *Structured Credit Products: Credit Derivatives & Synthetic Securitisation*. Singapore: Wiley, 2004.
Choudhry, Moorad. *Fixed Income Markets: Instruments, Applications, Mathematics*. Singapore: Wiley, 2005.
Choudhry, Moorad. *Bank Asset and Liability Management: Strategy, Trading, Analysis*. Singapore: Wiley, 2007.
Fabozzi, Frank J., and Steven V. Mann (eds). *Securities Finance: Securities Lending and Repurchase Agreements*. Hoboken, NJ: Wiley, 2005.
Fabozzi, Frank J., Steven V. Mann, and Moorad Choudhry. *The Global Money Markets*. Hoboken, NJ: Wiley, 2002.
Martellini, Lionel, Philippe Priaulet, and Stéphane Priaulet. *Fixed-income Securities: Valuation, Risk Management and Portfolio Strategies*. Chichester, UK: Wiley, 2003.

Websites:
Bloomberg on rates and prices: www.bloomberg.com
Investopedia on structured finance: www.investopedia.com/terms/s/structuredfinance.asp
YieldCurve market research: www.yieldcurve.com

Best Practice • Investments

QFINANCE

Passive Portfolio Management and Fixed-Income Investing by Andrew Ainsworth

EXECUTIVE SUMMARY

- Fixed-income securities are an important asset class that adds considerable diversification benefits to a portfolio.
- The passive strategy known as stratified sampling allows investors to achieve benchmark returns while controlling risk and transaction costs.
- This approach can be utilized in a tactical asset-allocation strategy, as it allows for relatively quick changes in portfolio allocations.
- Stratified sampling allows for active bets to be integrated into the portfolio by tilting weights in response to forecasted returns.
- The use of back-testing will ensure that actual outcomes align with expectations by adequately controlling benchmark risks.

INTRODUCTION

An allocation of investment to fixed-income assets is an important component of any diversified investment strategy. The fixed-income asset class comprises a variety of debt instruments that include government bonds, corporate bonds, municipal bonds, mortgage-backed securities, inflation-indexed debt, and convertible bonds, among others. With such a large number of securities available from which

to construct a portfolio, this article reviews the stratified sampling method of replicating the returns of a benchmark portfolio in fixed-income securities. This method is of use to investors who are undertaking both active and passive portfolio management approaches.

Figure 1 shows the daily total returns of the S&P 500 and the MSCI World equity indices as well as fixed-income indices covering a broad-based global benchmark, global high yield, and

Figure 1. Total returns of selected fixed-income and equity indices ($US), 2002–12. For key to fund names, see Table 1. (*Source*: Datastream)

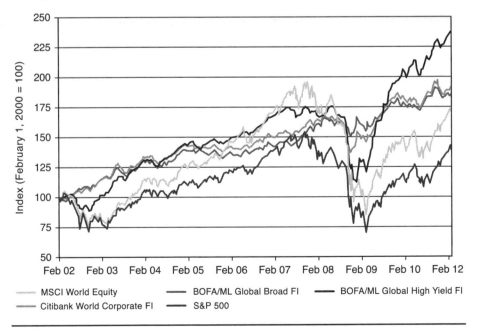

Table 1. Correlation coefficients of monthly returns for the indexes in Figure 1, February 2002 to February 2011. (*Source*: Datastream)

	MSCI World Equity	S&P 500	BOFA/ML Global Broad FI	BOFA/ML Global High Yield FI	Citibank World Corporate FI
MSCI World Equity	1.000	0.973	0.264	0.755	0.466
S&P 500	0.973	1.000	0.166	0.705	0.357
BOFA/ML Global Broad FI	0.264	0.166	1.000	0.346	0.877
BOFA/ML Global High Yield FI	0.755	0.705	0.346	1.000	0.622
Citibank World Corporate FI	0.466	0.357	0.877	0.622	1.000

BOFA/ML: Bank of America Merrill Lynch; FI: fixed income

world corporate debt between February 2002 and February 2012. The impact of the financial crisis is clearly evident in the figure. Interestingly, an investment made in February 2002 in either of the fixed-income indices would be worth more today than either of the equity benchmarks. In terms of risk, the standard deviation of monthly returns is considerably higher for the two equity indices—around 16%. The global broad-based index and the world corporate index have values of 6–7%. An important benefit of including fixed income in a portfolio is the diversification benefit. The correlation coefficients between the five indices are given in Table 1. The global high-yield index is more highly correlated with the equity indices than the other fixed-income indices. Either way, it is clear that fixed income should be included in a diversified portfolio.

RISKS OF INVESTING IN FIXED INCOME
Despite the lower standard deviation of returns, the recent events of the financial crisis have shown that significant risks are involved in investing in fixed-income securities. As with any financial security, expected returns will vary with risk. Before constructing a portfolio of fixed-income securities, it is important to understand the risks that an investor faces when investing in such securities.

- *Interest rate risk.* There is an inverse relationship between the level of interest rates and bond prices. However, the prices of some bonds are more sensitive to changes in interest rates and are therefore exposed to greater interest rate risk. Reinvestment risk is also related to interest rate risk, as coupon payments received are reinvested at an uncertain interest rate.
- *Credit risk.* This is the risk that the issuer of a bond may not make periodic coupon payments or pay back the full amount of principal at maturity. Credit rating agencies (Standard & Poor's, Moody's, and Fitch IBCA) provide ratings on the creditworthiness of bond issuers. These credit ratings allow investors to differentiate between bonds on the basis of the rating agencies' assessments that an issuer will default and not meet its obligations.
- *Liquidity risk.* This represents the chance that you will not be able to trade the desired quantity of a specific security when you want to trade. Bonds that are more liquid are cheaper to trade. A prime example of liquidity risk is that which occurred in certain collateralized debt obligations and mortgage-backed securities during the financial crisis.
- *Inflation risk.* The chance that inflation will erode the value of investments.
- *Sovereign risk.* This is related to credit risk as it represents the chance that a foreign government will not repay its debts. As the recent sovereign debt crisis has highlighted, it is an important consideration for investors in Portugal, Ireland, Greece, and Spain.
- *Currency risk.* This represents the risk that a domestic investor may purchase a bond that is denominated in a foreign currency. A domestic investor faces uncertainty about the domestic currency value of the coupons and the principal paid in foreign currency.
- *Call risk.* Certain bonds may allow the issuer to call the issue before maturity. This adversely impacts the investor as it introduces uncertainty as to the stream of future cash flows and limits the price appreciation of the security. Generally, these bonds are called when interest rates are low, creating reinvestment risk. Prepayment risk affects mortgage-backed securities and is related to call risk. It reflects the uncertainty surrounding the timing of cash flows to the holders of securitized loans that depend on the mortgage repayments of mortgage holders.

In order to realize a return that is in line with expectations, it is necessary for an investor to adequately monitor and manage these risks.

ACTIVE VERSUS PASSIVE MANAGEMENT

Investors in fixed-income assets essentially have two choices as to how to construct their portfolio. First, active management attempts to outperform a selected benchmark index, such as the Barclays Capital US Aggregate Bond Index. In order to outperform the index, an investor needs to either exercise superior security selection or time the market by entering the market before prices rise and exiting the market before prices fall (ignoring coupon payments). Passive portfolio management, on the other hand, aims to provide an investor with a return that matches a selected benchmark index.

There is continued debate in both the industry and academic literature on whether active portfolio management is superior to passive portfolio management. The findings from the most recent academic studies show that in some instances active funds outperform passive funds. However, the fees charged by active funds are higher and they generally erode the additional return they provide. Chen, Ferson, and Peters (2010) show that, after controlling for timing ability, funds outperform benchmarks before fees and costs, but underperform when fees and costs are taken into account. Boney, Comer, and Kelly (2009) find perverse market timing ability for high-quality corporate bond funds. An earlier study by Blake, Elton, and Gruber (1993) found that active funds that performed well in the past did not exhibit continued outperformance in the future. However, there is recent evidence from Huij and Derwall (2008) that past performance predicts future performance.

Thus, the jury is still out on whether an active or passive approach to bond portfolio management is preferable. Active strategies can provide higher returns than the benchmark, but an investor needs to consider the additional risks they are taking and any additional fees charged. All in all, the choice between active and passive investment styles in fixed-income assets is based on the investor's ability to provide consistent returns above the benchmark after fees. If they are unable to do this, then adopting a passive approach that seeks to provide returns consistent with a benchmark index is a wise decision.

Active managers may also make use of a passive approach for a number of reasons. If they believe that the underlying signals that drive the performance of their active strategy are currently not strong enough, an alternative is to match their portfolio to the index to avoid introducing risk and potentially letting performance deteriorate.

A passive approach is also of use if investors are engaging in tactical asset allocation. By building a portfolio that replicates the benchmark return without the need to hold all the constituents of the index, investors can be nimble in response to changes in forecasts of returns across asset classes. Enhanced indexing is another benefit, as it allows for an additional return pickup if an investor has some information about future returns that would allow them to slightly outperform the benchmark.

Finally, an important question to be addressed is whether the investor has the skill in a specific area to undertake active management. Consider an investor who specializes in European corporate debt. It may be prudent for investments in other sectors, such as US mortgage-backed securities, to be based on a passive approach rather than actively trading in mortgage-backed securities and attempting to outperform the benchmark.

CHOOSING A BENCHMARK INDEX

The first decision an investor should make is what benchmark they should target. There are a vast number of fixed-income benchmarks to choose from: Barclays Capital, Merrill Lynch, JP Morgan, and other investment banks all offer benchmark bond indices for investors to track and benchmark their performance against. These bond indices can track the performance of the global bond market, or focus on different sectors of the bond market: US Treasury, corporate, mortgage-backed securities, municipal, inflation-indexed, high-yield, Eurodollar, etc. They can also focus on different geographical areas, such as the United States, Asia, or Europe, and their specific sectors.

The primary concern regarding choice of index is to select a benchmark that has the desired risk and return profile of the investor. For example, investing in emerging market high-yield debt is going to be considerably more risky than investing in US Treasury securities (ignoring currency risk). Certain benchmarks can be selected to avoid exposure to certain risks altogether. For example, if a US investor does not want to be exposed to currency risk in their fixed-income portfolio, they should choose a US bond index. Similarly, if an investor wanted to remove inflation risk, they should select an inflation-indexed benchmark that invests only in inflation-protected securities, such as Treasury Inflation-Protected Securities (TIPS). The nature of the liabilities will also impact the choice of benchmark and could well indicate that a passive approach is unsuitable. Instead, a liabilities-based strategy such as cash flow matching would be more appropriate.

PORTFOLIO CONSTRUCTION

A number of different methods for constructing passive bond portfolios exist: tracking error minimization, factor-based replication, and derivatives-based approaches (see references in the More Info section for a more detailed discussion). One relatively straightforward method of building a portfolio designed to achieve benchmark returns is to use a stratified sampling (or cell-matching) technique. This method allows an investor to control the risk factors which they deem most important in determining returns in the bond market. This approach can be used irrespective of the scale of the portfolio and is flexible enough to be incorporated into an active portfolio management process.

After targeting a benchmark index, an investor then chooses risk factors that they think are important in determining benchmark returns. For example, an investor might choose duration (a measure of interest rate risk), credit ratings, and call risk as being important determinants of bond returns. The investor would then divide the benchmark into a number of different cells based on these three factors. If they partition the index into short, medium, and long duration; AA and above, BBB+ to AA−, and BBB and below;

and callable and noncallable debt, they would get a total of $3 \times 3 \times 2 = 18$ cells. The investor then determines the percentage of market value that is contained in each cell. They would then purchase at least one bond from each cell, allocating their capital in proportion to the index weights.

One benefit of this approach is that it allows the investor to incorporate subjective forecasts in their portfolio. They can adjust the weight in each cell, relative to the benchmark index, if they believe that certain factors will provide outperformance. For example, if an investor thinks that interest rates are likely to decrease, then long-duration bond prices will increase by a greater amount than short-duration bonds. As a result, they could take an overweight position in the long-duration cells, compared to the benchmark weights, and an underweight position in the short-duration cells. They may also be underweight the callable bond cells, relative to the benchmark weights, to minimize the adverse impact of bonds being called when interest rates fall.

An important step in forming a passive portfolio is to undertake back-testing of the portfolio based on the choice of cells. This will ensure that unwanted results from omitting an important risk factor do not occur. It will also allow for a better understanding of the trade-off between achieving benchmark returns and minimizing the number of bonds held in the portfolio.

CASE STUDY

Let us consider the Barclays Capital US Aggregate Bond Index. The index has more than 8,000 constituents, which is clearly too many bonds to hold in a portfolio. First and foremost, a substantial number of these bond issues would be illiquid and very expensive to trade in. By using stratified sampling, it is possible to achieve benchmark returns without holding a large number of bonds in the portfolio.

An investor may decide that maturity and credit risk are the three important risks that they need to take into account. The benchmark can be divided based on the time until maturity of the bonds— short, medium, and long; and credit ratings—AAA, AA, A, and BBB. The investor would obtain a grid like the one in Table 2, with a total of 12 cells.

Table 2. Credit rating

Maturity	BBB	A	AA	AAA
Short	1%	8%	9%	18%
Medium	3%	6%	12%	14%
Long	2%	4%	7%	16%

In this instance, the simplest approach would be to choose 12 bonds and allocate the portfolio investments in proportion to the market value weights in each cell for the index. With only 12 bonds in the portfolio, additional diversification benefits may accrue by including several bonds from within each cell. As mentioned above, a back-testing approach would shed light on what might be a reasonable number of bonds to include in the portfolio. The investor may also want to partition the index based on the various sectors of the market—Treasury, government-related, corporate, and securitized—to increase the number of cells from which to choose bonds.

ADVANTAGES AND DISADVANTAGES OF STRATIFIED SAMPLING APPROACH

What are the advantages of pursuing a stratified sampling approach to passive portfolio construction? First, it is straightforward and easy to understand. It matches the risk profile of the index, and therefore the return generated. By reducing the number of bonds in the portfolio and selecting the liquid bonds in each cell, transaction costs can also be reduced. From an asset allocation perspective, the use of stratified sampling makes it relatively easy to adjust holdings in response to changes in forecasted returns. The stratified sampling approach also avoids problems associated with statistical models that rely on historical correlations. After the financial crisis it is clear that these correlations are not always stable. In addition, bonds mature and exit the benchmark index (unlike the case of equity securities), and it can be difficult to estimate correlations on a security that has just been issued.

One disadvantage of the stratified sampling approach is that the investor has discretion as to the number and type of risk factors to focus on, and the number of partitions to divide the index into. Investors face the risk that an omitted risk factor may be a significant driver of index performance. As mentioned above, back-testing of various combinations of risk factors and partition size will

alleviate concerns. There is a trade-off between the number of cells chosen and the costs associated with the strategy. An increase in the number of cells will improve the ability of the portfolio to match the index more closely; however, transaction costs are likely to rise. An additional consideration for investors is that passive strategies need to be monitored and rebalanced regularly so that the actual return does not deviate from the benchmark.

CONCLUSION

Fixed-income assets represent an important component of a diversified investment portfolio. Although debate on the relative merits of active versus passive portfolio management in fixed-income securities has not reached a resolution, indexing can play a significant role in an investment portfolio. Stratified sampling is a method of achieving benchmark risk and return while reducing transaction costs. It can also be incorporated into a tactical asset allocation process, as it allows investors to be more nimble in altering their portfolios. A further benefit of the stratified sampling approach to index replication is that it allows for active bets to be easily incorporated by altering weights in each cell relative to the benchmark weight. Investors using a stratified sampling approach should undertake back-testing to ensure that actual outcomes align with expectations.

MAKING IT HAPPEN

- Pick an appropriate benchmark and identify the risk–return profile that you are targeting.
- Assess whether you have the skills to undertake active management in a given sector of the bond market.
- Determine the risk factors that you consider important in determining the returns of the benchmark index.
- Undertake back-testing of the stratified sampling approach. Compare different combinations of risks (interest rate, credit risk, etc) and assess the performance of the strategy based on the number of cells chosen.
- Monitor your portfolio and rebalance regularly as the index weights in each cell will change over time.

Investments • Best Practice

MORE INFO

Books:

Fabozzi, Frank J. *Bond Markets, Analysis, and Strategies*. 7th ed. Boston, MA: Pearson, 2009.

Martellini, Lionel, Philippe Priaulet, and Stéphane Priaulet. *Fixed-Income Securities: Valuation, Risk Management and Portfolio Strategies*. Chichester, UK: Wiley, 2003.

Articles:

Blake, Christopher R., Edwin J. Elton, and Martin J. Gruber. "The performance of bond mutual funds." *Journal of Business* 66:3 (July 1993): 371–403. Online at: www.jstor.org/stable/2353206

Boney, Vaneesha, George Comer, and Lynne Kelly. "Timing the investment grade securities market: Evidence from high quality bond funds." *Journal of Empirical Finance* 16:1 (January 2009): 55–69. Online at: dx.doi.org/10.1016/j.jempfin.2008.06.005

Chen, Yong, Wayne Ferson, and Helen Peters. "Measuring the timing ability and performance of bond mutual funds." *Journal of Financial Economics* 98:1 (October 2010): 72–89. Online at: dx.doi.org/10.1016/j.jfineco.2010.05.009

Huij, Joop, and Jeroen Derwall. "'Hot hands' in bond funds." *Journal of Banking and Finance* 32:4 (April 2008): 559–572. Online at: dx.doi.org/10.1016/j.jbankfin.2007.04.023

Websites:

The Index Investor: www.indexinvestor.com

Investing in Bonds: www.investinginbonds.com

QFINANCE

Funds of Hedge Funds versus Single-Manager Funds by Steve Wallace

EXECUTIVE SUMMARY

- The process you undertake when selecting a FoHF is very different to that when selecting a portfolio of single managers.
- A decision on which to use, FoHF or single manager, is generally dependent on two primary factors: the monetary size of your investment allocation, and the resources at your disposal.
- The extra fee layer imposed when utilizing a FoHF structure is, in general, to pay for the resources used to source and select managers in addition to providing the investment vehicle.
- It is important to get a match between the mandate you have and that on which the FoHF is based.
- There are a number of factors that need to be considered in addition to those mentioned above when deciding whether to use a FoHF or collection of single managers; it is not a black and white decision.

INTRODUCTION

Funds of hedge funds (FoHFs) have caused heated debate over the years no matter which side of the fence you are on. The main issue this debate revolves around has two parts:

- *Fees*—that is, fees charged at the underlying manager level and then again at the FoHF level.
- *Control*: Accepting that you don't have the internal expertise and must pass control of the underlying fund selection to a FoHF manager can be difficult for some. They would rather have control even though they may not achieve the result they hoped for rather than hand over control for a result that isn't of their own making—regardless of the outcome.

The first step in choosing between FoHF or single manager should be to look inside the firm for the knowledge, expertise, and experience required to source and select the underlying managers. In this article I will be looking at elements of the decision to invest either in a basket of single managers or in a FoHF product.

A DEFINITION

A FoHF, as the name implies is a fund which invests in a collection of hedge funds. The collection of funds is constructed in an effort to provide risk/return characteristics that achieve its mandate. Before I go any further it should be noted that a FoHF does not only apply to hedge funds; it is a portfolio construction process that is also utilized by long-only products, i.e. FoFs (funds of funds).

The basic premise of a FoHF is that a portfolio can be constructed in such a way as to generate a rate of return with lower volatility than may otherwise be the case if the investor constructed the portfolio himself, dependent of course on the investor (as I will discuss in the next section).

As such, the FoHF manager is saying that it has the ability to source, research, and select funds which, when brought together to form a portfolio, can satisfy the investor's investment mandate while reducing volatility.

Probably the two most often mentioned risks that a FoHF aims to reduce are manager risk and downside risk, which are in any event inextricably linked. Manager risk is reduced by the simple fact that more than one is involved in the product, thereby reducing the risk to that element of your portfolio which a single manager could bring. In other words, purely by having more managers in your portfolio you reduce the risk to your portfolio of any one of them failing, whether this be operationally, performance-wise, or in terms of strategy. The other primary risk that FoHFs aim to reduce is downside risk; arguably, one of the main benefits of a FoHF is not that it will "shoot the lights out" in terms of performance but that it will manage the downside risk.

INVESTOR TYPES

Generally investors have certain characteristics that will encourage them to opt for a FoHF rather than a single manager, and vice versa. Of course, in addition to this are emotive factors related to fear, control, and, perhaps, misplaced confidence in one's abilities.

Generally speaking, the greater the monetary value of the portfolio, the more likely an investor will go down the single-manager route. However, this leaves out one crucial element: the ability to select managers and construct a portfolio using a blend of managers to achieve a return target while minimizing risk.

Looking at Figure 1 we can draw certain conclusions as to the likelihood that—or more importantly whether—an investor should favor a FoHF strategy or a single-manager strategy when allocating to hedge funds.

The x-axis represents the ability of the investor to source and select individual managers. The "source" part is an important element as there are literally thousands of different funds that one can invest in, but the ability to get hold of a list of funds that you wish to consider further is an important part of the process and one that should not be taken for granted. The "select" element ties in the research part of the process as well. This is where you have managed to acquire a list of appropriate funds and are able to research them to the level of a hedge fund research professional. I use the prefix "hedge fund" in front of "research professional" as the kind of due diligence one applies to hedge funds, whatever the strategy, is very different to that required for long-only funds.

I have labeled the y-axis as the monetary size of the investment that the investor is seeking to allocate to hedge funds. The smaller this is, the less likely you will be able both to invest in the number of single managers necessary to satisfy diversification needs and meet minimum investment requirements.

Figure 1. Factors influencing choice between FoHF and single-manager strategies

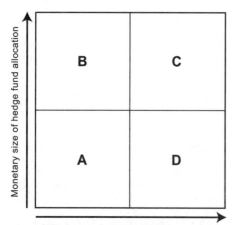

Ability to source and select single managers

Obviously, the descriptions of each of the four boxes illustrated in the diagram above are not mutually exclusive—there will be overlap, and other components will come into the decision; I have taken two of the primary drivers purely to discuss.

A: This is where not only is the size of the

allocation to hedge funds low, but the investor also may not have sufficient ability to source and select single managers.

B: This is where problems can occur: the size of the allocation is high, so on first inspection the situation lends itself to a selection of single managers. However, on the x-axis the ability to source and select managers remains relatively low. Therefore, investors who fall into this box should really look to increase their expertise before allocating to single managers.

C: This area of the diagram clearly is where the single-manager route makes sense. Here a large allocation of funds is matched by a strong ability to source and select single hedge fund managers.

D: This area represents the investor who may have a strong ability as per C above to build a portfolio of single-manager hedge funds to satisfy allocation requirements but who may not have the funds needed to satisfy the minimum investment requirements of certain funds, which will limit his choice.

ADVANTAGES AND DISADVANTAGES
Below I have listed some of the main advantages and disadvantages of each option when allocating to hedge funds. Note that this is by no means an exhaustive list.

FoHFs
Advantages
- Professionally selected underlying hedge fund managers.
- Reduced volatility.
- Manager diversification.
- Ease of access.
- Low minimum investment requirements (i.e. to invest in one FoHF the minimum investment would in most cases be less than the aggregate minimum investments of say 20 single-manager funds).
- Ability to negotiate fees.

Disadvantages
- Not bespoke.
- May not fit within the overall portfolio as well as specifically selected single managers.
- Additional layer of fees means the performance return needed to break even is higher. However, it should be noted that the investor is getting something for this extra fee level in terms of expertise at manager selection, provision of the FoHF structure, and so on. What value this translates to is dependent on the investor's situation.

Single managers
Advantages
- Bespoke portfolio.
- Ability to dovetail the hedge fund allocation into the overall portfolio.
- Transparency of the overall portfolio.

Disadvantages
- Cost of human intellectual property required to build a professional portfolio of single managers.
- Investment required to ensure an appropriately diversified hedge fund portfolio.
- Overconfidence in one's own ability, or that of one's team, to select single managers.
- Potential for large losses by any one manager to significantly and negatively impact your portfolio if not constructed properly.

MAKING IT HAPPEN

One of the points that is often made concerns a FoHF's ability to invest in up and coming hedge funds that will generate significant returns as they grow from start-up. This comes back to ability as not all FoHFs are in a position, from the standpoint of expertise and knowledge, to invest in emerging hedge funds as this calls for a much more complicated due diligence process.

If you are a novice to hedge funds, the risk to the value of one's portfolio by investing in such funds, whether they are single managers or a FoHF, is high. It should also be noted that if you do decide to access hedge funds via a FoHF this absolutely does *not* mean that you can abdicate responsibility completely. There is a whole other area of FoHF due diligence that comes into play here. The best way to proceed is to go back to first principles—i.e. to ask yourself what was the rationale for investing in hedge funds in the first instance.

Once you have that in place, you can ask yourself the next question: What is the best way for me to access hedge fund investment opportunities? This is linked with the question whether you have the knowledge required either to invest in a FoHF or to put together a portfolio of single-manager hedge funds. If you don't, there are a number of ways of gaining that knowledge or gaining access to it, whether it is by educating yourself by going through the Chartered Alternative Investment Analyst program, discussion with peers, use of hedge fund advisory consultants, or other means.

That will then guide you in the choice between the single-manager and FoHF paths, although, as mentioned earlier, if you have the experience to construct a portfolio utilizing single-manager hedge funds but not enough funds to gain diversification benefits, it would be foolhardy to invest in single managers

MORE INFO

Books:
Anson, Mark J. P. *Handbook of Alternative Assets*. 2nd ed. Hoboken, NJ: Wiley, 2006.
Ineichen, Alexander M. *Asymmetric Returns: The Future of Active Asset Management*. Hoboken, NJ: Wiley, 2007.
Jones, Chris. *Hedge Funds of Funds: A Guide for Investors*. Chichester, UK: Wiley, 2007.
Lhabitant, François-Serge. *Handbook of Hedge Funds*. Chichester, UK: Wiley, 2006.

Websites:
Alternative Investment Management Association (AIMA): www.aima.org
Chartered Alternative Investment Analyst (CAIA) Association: www.caia.org
EDHEC-Risk Institute: www.edhec-risk.com
Hedge Fund Matrix: www.hedgefundmatrix.com
Hedge Fund Standards Board: www.hfsb.org

QFINANCE

Hedge Fund Challenges Extend Beyond Regulation by Kevin Burrows

EXECUTIVE SUMMARY

- The loss of liquidity and its impact on hedge fund performance.
- Redemption issues and their impact on future practice.
- Management challenges and sector performance.
- The threat from alternatives to hedge funds.
- How the crash changed the rules of the game.
- The dilemma of a global regulator.

INTRODUCTION
Victim Rather than Villain

The hedge fund sector has been vilified by some politicians, both in Europe and in the US, as if it were a significant contributor to the banking collapse and subsequent global recession. In reality, the hedge fund industry was very much a victim of the banks during the latter half of 2008, and there are some significant litigation actions pending, in which hedge funds are suing investment banks for alleged misdealings in their collateralized debt obligation (CDO) products and credit default swap (CDS) transactions.

However, potential misdealings aside, it is clear that the dreadful performance turned in by many hedge funds in 2008 was precipitated not just by stock market and property price collapses, but also by the total loss of liquidity in all risky markets, a direct consequence of the massive deleveraging by banks. At the same time as they were reducing the size of their balance sheets, numerous banks closed or drastically slimmed down their proprietary trading desks, leaving hedge funds with no bidders for any instrument that had any degree of complexity about it.

Adding insult to injury, many banks forcibly withdrew previously agreed lines of credit to hedge funds, forcing any hedge fund manager running a leveraged strategy to liquidate their positions as fast as possible. Finally, their clients, disappointed by the lack of "absolute returns" that they were implicitly promised by the hedge funds, became extremely nervous, and many decided to turn their investments back into cash, even though they often had nowhere to put the cash (as banks themselves posed a risk for any significant cash holding), and had no clear alternative investment strategy in sight.

THE IMPACT OF REDEMPTIONS

Faced with the perfect storm of poor performance and severe redemption pressure, hedge fund managers were forced to close funds or suspend redemptions, in order to protect values for those investors remaining with the fund. What the sector experienced during 2008, in other words, was less a performance issue, with strategies failing to work, than a bank run caused by their liquidity mismatch. Money that fund managers thought was "sticky money" (i.e., money that would stay with the fund for the medium term, and so give the fund's investment strategy a chance to work) turned out to be "on demand" money that investors urgently wanted returned to them.

It did not appear to matter, in these circumstances, whether the hedge fund was invested in assets that the investors could expect to be highly liquid, such as equities or government bonds, or whether the fund had a very illiquid strategy, such as asset-based lending, where there was effectively no liquidity or secondary market for those loans. In the latter situation, if a significant proportion of the investors run for the exit at the same time, the fund management has very few options. They can either halt redemptions or run the risk of paying out all of the remaining liquidity at the expense of those opting to stay. Or they can simply liquidate the fund.

MANAGEMENT CHALLENGES AND SECTOR PERFORMANCE

In reality, the way the hedge fund sector as a whole managed the difficult circumstances that characterized the second half of 2008 and the opening months of 2009 was highly commendable. As a generalization, portfolios were managed in a way that protected the interests of as many investors as possible. As a fund-of-funds manager, we were often on the phone to our hedge fund managers saying that, on behalf of our investors, we did not want the fund attempting to pay out all redemptions by liquidating the portfolio at fire-sale prices, as that hurts everyone. We wanted to see redemptions frozen and value preserved.

What the hedge fund sector has learned from this whole experience is that there is a definite price to pay for liquidity, or the lack of it. Investors clearly value the ability to convert their investment back into "cash at hand" in a reasonably short time frame. That ability has a significant value, so in future we will see that option priced into the contract between investor and fund. Moreover, for investment strategies that are largely liquid, the dealing terms will be forced to become more liquid to match the underlying instruments. As a consequence, we will see more monthly dealing hedge funds, with perhaps only a month's notice or even less for withdrawals. We will also witness the continued development of many more daily dealing UCITS III type funds, trading in long-only and long-short strategies, in response to this new-found desire on the part of the investor community for highly liquid products. (The caveat to this, as we shall see in a moment, is that in the current investing environment, it is not clear that hedge fund managers have that much more added value to offer, even in this new format, versus passive investments such as an exchange-traded fund or ETF, where the units can be traded at any time, and where the unit charges are vastly lower than hedge fund fees.)

While the near-liquid funds move to highly liquid redemption terms, strategies that legitimately need a longer investment period to realize their returns, such as distressed debt and structured credit, will move their terms to something more akin to a private equity structure, with anywhere from a two-to-five-year lock-up, and no option for investors to get their money out early. The "middle ground," which used to be comprised of hedge funds with 90-day exit clauses, but where the strategy was, in reality, rather more liquid that this conveys, will come under huge pressure to improve its liquidity terms. It will not be possible for managers to seek to hold assets just to control them; rather, they will have to match the liquidity terms of the clients to the liquidity terms of the assets. That will be a very significant change for the industry.

THE THREAT FROM ALTERNATIVES TO HEDGE FUNDS
The resolution of the liquidity mismatch is only one of a number of changes that the sector is

going to have to deal with. Another challenge, which ironically arises naturally from the current dislocation of the markets, is that a large number of investment opportunities today do not require a hedge fund strategy to generate very acceptable levels of return. This is a point that is hard to overemphasize in terms of its potential impact on the sector—at its moment of maximum client distrust, the hedge fund industry must contend with the fact that many of the best returns available today may lie outside of their hedged strategies.

As an example, take the present dislocation in convertible bonds. An investor today can buy long-only convertible bonds, and be satisfied to simply earn the market beta (which is to say, the performance delivered by the market itself, rather than any outperformance, or alpha, delivered by the skill of the hedge fund manager). That beta has a very good chance of delivering a return on a mixed portfolio of investment-grade and high-yield bonds, in excess of 10–12%. Faced with those levels of expected return, there is little incentive for an investor to seek to gain another 3% by investing with a hedge fund manager promising 15% returns with the traditional hedge fund fee structure of 2/20 (2% management fee and 20% performance fee), but which also comes with all the liquidity, regulatory, and potential fraud risks that hedge fund investing entails. What this means is that it has become much more difficult for hedge fund managers to justify their alpha fee than it was in an era where market beta was delivering very low single-digit returns.

Two further areas of competition for hedge funds, apart from the fact that investors can build their own long-only portfolios with relative ease, come from ETFs, and from the synthetic hedge fund replicators now being offered by the likes of Goldman Sachs, State Street, and Merrill Lynch.

There is now a substantial body of research on hedge fund performance that suggests that about 80% of a hedge fund manager's income stream can be attributed to "alternative beta" factors rather than to management skill. Alternative beta factors refers to market risk characteristics such as equity risk, term structure, credit risk, small cap equity, and emerging markets equity, as well as nonlinear returns such as trend-following strategies. It is now possible to replicate a significant part of hedge fund returns through investing in an appropriately designed futures, ETF and/or options strategy. As they are using liquid instruments as their building blocks, these replicators have no hedge fund fee structure associated with it, and provide complete liquidity, full transparency, no fraud risk, and the opportunity for investors to trade in and out as they require.

Of course, it is true that there are limits to how much of a good hedge fund manager's strategy can be replicated in such structures, and the remaining 20% of manager alpha cannot be captured through these products. However, just as ETFs are taking market share from the actively managed long-only fund industry, I believe the hedge fund replicators now being developed by the former investment banks, among others, will attract sizeable flows of pension fund money that would, in the past, have gone directly into hedge funds.

HOW THE CRASH CHANGED THE RULES

What all this amounts to is that, quite apart from the coming wave of regulation that hedge funds are going to have to deal with, the rules of the game have already changed as a result of the crash. While they were evolving anyway, as they do whenever an industry matures, the market meltdown of 2008 has definitely speeded up this process.

One such change we were seeing just before the crash was a convergence between the active managers in the long-only space, now that the UCITS III rules allow them to take short positions in some circumstances, and hedge funds. This has put a further strain on hedge fund fees, as investors are only willing to pay above-average fees if it gives them access to real investment skill that they cannot tap into at a lower fee structure. Asset allocators (funds of funds, pensions, endowments, etc.) are becoming much more skilled at separating their beta market exposure from their alpha (the value added brought through skill), putting real pressure on hedge fund managers to prove that what they are providing is not simply a leveraged market return. Sophisticated investors are quite capable of leveraging their own positions; they do not need a hedge fund manager to do that for them. So, if on careful analysis a hedge fund's perceived outperformance over the relevant benchmark turns out to be simply a return due to leverage, then that is no longer going to be accepted as the creation of genuine alpha through investment skill.

It is now becoming quite widely recognized just how much the performance of some hedge fund strategies owed simply to leverage. However, ETFs have been created that are leveraged two to five times, which investors can access directly if they want leveraged plays, so that game by the

hedge funds has gone. One must also recognize that leverage was a strategy for a buoyant market where liquidity and credit was cheap. Similarly, if the hedge fund strategy was based largely on short-selling, there are short-leveraged ETFs that investors can now use. Again, this is yet more pressure on hedge fund managers to demonstrate to investors just where their alpha performance comes from. Much has been said about the scalability or otherwise of hedge fund strategies. As successful hedge funds attract a flood of investor money, it inevitably pushes them towards a multi-strategy approach to be able to deploy a large amount of capital effectively. With real skill this can continue to be effective, so another dynamic in the market is that we see the larger, more established and institution-like hedge funds becoming multi-strategy funds, while at the same time the smaller, more niche funds, with assets under management of £100–250 million, are seeking to limit their growth. As managers are paid based on the amount of assets under management, remaining small takes real discipline, but the penalty for not doing so is poorer performance if you grow larger than the opportunity set in which you are investing.

As an added dynamic, there is tremendous pressure on politicians and regulators to "do something," so more regulation now looks certain. However, the irony of this is that the market itself has forced hedge funds to become much more transparent and open, anyway. Following the Madoff fraud, no hedge fund manager can expect to operate an opaque structure on a "trust me" basis.

AN INTERNATIONAL COLLEGE OF REGULATORS?

There are real dangers, however, lying in wait for regulators as they seek to move into the hedge fund space. What would the shape of such regulation look like? One view seems to be favoring the formation of an international college of regulators who would somehow have oversight across the highly complex investment strategies and positions of some 3,000–7,000 hedge funds around the world. The data requirements necessary to enable such oversight are absolutely huge. If one remembers that the individual investment banks themselves did not know or understand what was on their own balance sheets, and it took some of them many weeks with an army of staff to begin to put some numbers to their exposures, it is well-nigh impossible to see how a single regulatory body could have meaningful oversight of the risk exposures of the entire financial industry.

Investments • Best Practice

And if it saw what it deemed to be too much risk, how would it address this? By sending a mass email to everyone saying "cut all X exposures by Y percent?" Or would they focus on just the largest funds, thereby giving smaller funds a competitive advantage in the market?

CONCLUSION

Any intervention by a global regulator would be likely to have a tremendous distorting effect in the market. As hedge fund managers live and breathe market distortions, gaming the regulator to produce distortions would become a very viable strategy in its own right. Political rhetoric is easy. Implementing meaningful regulation for a sector that has already become vastly more transparent to investors is much harder. Is the additional gain in transparency and stability that is being sought really worth the huge effort and expense that would be entailed, remembering that the current crisis was precipitated by loose credit standards and the bursting of an asset bubble, events in which hedge funds were only a minor player? These are questions regulators will have to ponder as they look to extend their sway over the hedge fund sector.

MORE INFO

Article:

Andrew Baker. "Shorting—An essential endangered hedge." *Financial Times* (June 8, 2008). Online at: tinyurl.com/62xgb7w

Websites:

Alternative Investment Management Association (AIMA): www.aima.org

"Majority of hedge fund assets under management now from institutional investors" (AIMA press release): tinyurl.com/6gn89yb

Ethical Funds and Socially Responsible Investment: An Overview by Chendi Zhang

EXECUTIVE SUMMARY

- Ethical funds, also known as socially responsible investment (SRI) funds, have experienced rapid growth around the world. Issues such as global warming, corporate governance, and community involvement have gained significant attention from governments and investors.
- Maximization of stockholder value often conflicts with the interests of other stakeholders in a firm. Corporate social responsibility (CSR) plays a role in reducing the costs of such conflicts.
- Empirical research shows that the following components of CSR are associated with higher stockholder value: good corporate governance, sound environmental standards, and care of stakeholder relations.
- Existing studies hint, but do not unequivocally demonstrate, that SRI investors are willing to accept suboptimal financial performance to pursue social or ethical objectives.
- Given the growing social awareness of investors and the increasingly positive regulatory environment, we expect SRI to continue its growth and relative importance as an asset class.

THE RISE OF SRI

Ethical funds, often also called socially responsible investment (SRI) funds, integrate environmental, social, and governance (ESG) considerations, or purely ethical issues, into investment decision-making. SRI has experienced a phenomenal growth around the world. According to the Social Investment Forum, the professionally managed assets of SRI portfolios in the United States, including retail and, more importantly, institutional funds (for example, pension funds, insurance funds, and separate accounts), reached US$2.7 trillion in 2007, or approximately 11% of total assets under management in that country. The European SRI market is also growing rapidly. In 2007, SRI assets in Europe amounted to €2.7 trillion, representing 17% of European funds under management (European Social Investment Forum).

Although ethical investing has ancient origins that were based on religious traditions, modern SRI is based more on the varying personal, ethical, and social convictions of individual investors. Issues such as environmental protection, human rights, and labor relations have become common in the SRI investment screening process. In recent years, a series of corporate scandals has turned corporate governance and responsibility into another focal point of SRI investors. Hence, criteria such as transparency, governance, and sustainability have emerged as essential in SRI screening.

Over the past decade, a number of national governments in Europe have passed a series of regulations on social and environmental investments and savings. For instance, the United Kingdom was the first country to regulate the disclosure of the social, environmental, and ethical investment policies of pension funds and charities. The Amendment to the 1995 Pensions Act requires the trustees of occupational pension funds to disclose in the Statement of Investment Principles "the extent (if at all) to which social, environmental and ethical considerations are taken into account in the selection, retention and realization of investments." This has contributed considerably to the growth of the SRI industry.

SHOULD COMPANIES BE SOCIALLY RESPONSIBLE?

Finance textbooks tell us companies should maximize the value of their stockholders' equity. In other words, a company's only responsibility is a financial one. In recent years, corporate social responsibility has become a focal point of policymakers (and the public), who demand that corporations assume responsibility toward society, the environment, or stakeholders in general. SRI investors thus aim to promote socially and environmentally sound corporate behavior. They avoid companies that produce goods which may cause health hazards or exploit employees (negative screening), whether in developed or developing countries. They select companies with sound social and environmental records, and with good corporate governance (positive screening). In general, SRI investors expect companies to focus on social welfare in addition to maximizing value.

At the heart of the SRI movement is a fundamental question: Is a firm's aim to maximize *stockholder* value or *social* value (where social value is defined as the sum of the values generated for all stakeholders)? Classical economics (for example, Adam Smith's "invisible hand" and the social welfare theorems) states that there is no conflict between the two goals: In competitive and complete markets, when all firms maximize their own profits (value), resource allocation is optimal and social welfare is maximized. However, modern economic theory also tells us that in some circumstances, namely when some of the assumptions of the welfare theorems do not hold, profit-maximizing behavior does not necessarily imply social welfare-maximizing outcomes. One of such circumstances is the existence of externalities that arise when the costs and benefits of an agent's action are affected by the actions of other (external) agents in the economy. Jensen (2001) gives a simple example of externalities, where a fishery's catch is impaired by the pollution of an upstream chemical plant.[1] When the chemical plant maximizes its profit by increasing pollution (as the costs of pollution are not borne by the chemical plant), the fishery downstream suffers through catching fewer fish and social welfare—which in this case is equal to the sum of the profits of the two stakeholders—is not maximized.

In practice, the maximization of stockholder value often conflicts with the social welfare criterion represented by the interests of all stakeholders of a firm, including employees, customers, local communities, the environment, and so forth. By maximizing stockholder value, firms may not take care of the interests of other stakeholders. Economic solutions to the externality problem are based on the principle of internalizing externalities, for example, by imposing regulations (such as quotas, or taxes on pollution) and creating a market for externalities (such as the trading of pollution permits). Furthermore, in continental European corporate governance regimes, a stakeholder approach is more common than in Anglo-Saxon countries.

STOCKHOLDER VALUE VERSUS STAKEHOLDER VALUE

One of the main arguments in favor of CSR and the stakeholder model is that it is consistent with stockholder value maximization. For instance, by anticipating and minimizing the potential conflicts between corporations and society, CSR plays a role in reducing the cost of conflicts. CSR may soften competition in product markets and lead to higher firm value, signal a firm's product quality and improve reputation, and help to attract motivated employees.

Critics of stakeholder value maximization argue that CSR, and the stakeholder theory, have problems in terms of accountability and managerial incentivization. According to the stockholder value concept, managers are expected to invest in a project if its expected return exceeds the cost of capital. In the stakeholder value story, managers are asked to balance the interests of all stakeholders to the point that aggregate welfare is maximized. Still, the stakeholder theory does not define how to aggregate welfare and how to make the trade-off between stakeholders. If the social value of firms can be maximized, society will by definition benefit. However, the question is whether this goal is achievable and how economic efficiency and managerial incentives are affected by the maximization of stakeholder value (including social and environmental value).

Furthermore, CSR and the stakeholder model are also subject to Friedman's (1962)[2] arguments: Companies should only care about profits and, therefore, their stockholders, while governments deal with the provision of public goods and the existence of externalities. If CSR lowers firms' profits due to compromises with stakeholders, firms should not implement CSR strategies as it is more efficient if they charge lower prices and allow consumers to make their own charitable contributions based on personal social and ethical values. This critique also has important implications for SRI: If SRI underperforms conventional portfolios, it would be more efficient for SRI investors to invest in better-performing conventional funds and use part of the returns to comply with their personal convictions by donating money to good causes.

PORTFOLIO CONSTRAINTS AND MARKET (IN)EFFICIENCIES

SRI applies various screening processes to retain stocks complying with specific CSR criteria on social, corporate governance, environmental, and ethical issues, which imposes a constraint on the investment universe available to non-SRI investors. SRI screens may therefore limit the diversification possibilities, and consequently shift the mean–variance frontier toward less favorable risk–return tradeoffs than those of conventional portfolios. In addition, believers in the efficient market hypothesis argue that it is impossible for SRI funds to outperform their conventional peers. Screening portfolios based on public information such as CSR issues cannot generate abnormal returns.

Ethical Funds and Socially Responsible Investment

However, it is also possible that SRI screening processes generate value-relevant information which is otherwise not available to investors. This may help fund managers to select securities and consequently generate better risk-adjusted returns than conventional mutual funds. In this case, investors may do (financially) well while doing (social) good, i.e. investors earn positive risk-adjusted returns while at the same time contributing to a good cause. For instance, empirical research on CSR shows that portfolios constructed with reference to corporate governance, environmental, and social criteria may outperform their benchmarks.

A key assumption underlying the above hypothesis is that the stock markets misprice information on CSR in the short run. For instance, they may undervalue the costs of litigation that may have to be met by socially irresponsible corporations, while socially responsible firms may be better protected against such costs. As a result, SRI may outperform conventional funds in the long run. This outperformance hypothesis is also at odds with the efficient market hypothesis. If SRI screening processes do generate value-relevant information, conventional portfolio managers could easily replicate the screens, and the performance edge of SRI over conventional investments should then diminish.

The question as to whether SRI creates stockholder value is ultimately an empirical one. Empirical findings on the performance of SRI are mixed. Although there is little evidence that the average performance of SRI funds in the United States and the United Kingdom is different from that of conventional funds, SRI funds in many continental European and Asia-Pacific countries underperform their benchmarks.[3] Existing studies hint, but do not unequivocally support, that investors are willing to accept suboptimal financial performance if their personal values on social responsibility are satisfied.

CASE STUDY
Calvert Social Investment Fund

Calvert is one of the largest families of SRI mutual funds in the United States. Social investment research analysts at Calvert examine corporate performance in the following broad areas, in addition to financial criteria:

- Governance and ethics: Including disclosure of policies and procedures, board independence and diversity, executive compensation, and attention to stakeholder concerns.
- Workplace: Including labor diversity, labor relations, and employee health and safety. Calvert monitors the quality of policies and programs, compliance with national laws and regulations, and proactive management initiatives.
- Environment: Focusing on corporate environmental performance, responsiveness to incidents, and compliance with environmental regulations.
- Product safety and impact: Selecting companies that produce safe products and services, in accordance with federal consumer product safety guidelines.
- International operations and human rights: Avoiding investment in companies that have a record of serious and persistent human rights problems or that directly support governments that systematically deny human rights.
- Indigenous peoples' rights: Avoiding companies that have a pattern and practice of violating the rights of indigenous peoples around the world.
- Community relations: Investing in companies that have built solid relationships with the local communities in which they operate.

CONCLUSION

SRI has experienced rapid growth around the world, reflecting investors' increasing awareness of social, environmental, and governance issues. In recent years issues such as global warming, the Kyoto Protocol, corporate governance, and community investing have gained significant attention from governments and investors around the world. In addition, governments in Western countries have taken many regulatory initiatives to stimulate SRI. Given the growing social awareness of investors and the increasingly positive regulatory environment, we expect SRI to continue its growth and relative importance as an asset class.

MAKING IT HAPPEN

In order for CSR/SRI to become a workable concept, the following key issues of performance yardsticks should be considered:

- Do you adopt the stockholder value maximization criterion or the stakeholder value maximization criterion? Even if you opt for the stockholder value criterion, it is important to consider the welfare of all stakeholders (employees, community, environment, etc.) as firm behavior induces important externalities. The long-run market value of a firm cannot be maximized if any important stakeholders are mistreated.
- Is corporate social/environmental performance measurable? A lack of precisely formulated corporate goals and measures in respect of CSR/SRI may destroy firm value in the long run. The long-run value of a firm remains the single most important performance measure for management. Maximizing long-run firm value is consistent with maximizing social welfare.
- Are you seeking a competitive advantage for your company by implementing CSR/SRI strategies? Empirical research shows that the following components of CSR are associated with higher stockholder value: good corporate governance, sound environmental standards, and care of stakeholder relations.
- Are investors willing to pay a price for CSR/SRI? If SRI underperforms conventional funds, it could be more efficient for SRI investors to invest in better-performing conventional funds and use part of the returns to comply with their personal convictions by donating money to good causes.

MORE INFO

Book:

UNEP Finance Initiative. *Values to Value: A Global Dialogue on Sustainable Finance.* United Nations Environment Programme, 2004.

Article:

Renneboog, Luc, Jenke Ter Horst, and Chendi Zhang. "Socially responsible investments: Institutional aspects, performance, and investor behavior." *Journal of Banking and Finance* 32:9 (September 2008): 1723–1742. Online at: dx.doi.org/10.1016/j.jbankfin.2007.12.039

Websites:

Association for Sustainable and Responsible Investment in Asia: www.asria.org
European Social Investment Forum (Eurosif): www.eurosif.org
Social Investment Forum: www.socialinvest.org

NOTES

1 Jensen, Michael C. "Value maximization, stakeholder theory, and the corporate objective function." *Journal of Applied Corporate Finance* 14:3 (Fall 2001): 8–21. Online at: dx.doi.org/10.1111/j.1745-6622.2001.tb00434.x

2 Friedman, Milton. *Capitalism and Freedom.* 40th anniversary ed. Chicago, IL: University of Chicago Press, 2002.

3 Renneboog, Luc, Jenke Ter Horst, and Chendi Zhang. "The price of ethics and stakeholder governance: The performance of socially responsible mutual funds." *Journal of Corporate Finance* 14:3 (June 2008): 302–322. Online at: dx.doi.org/10.1016/j.jcorpfin.2008.03.009

Venture Capital Funds as an Alternative Class of Investment by Michael D. McKenzie and Bill Janeway

EXECUTIVE SUMMARY

- Venture capital funds became prominent during the dot.com/telecom boom period, which has distorted investors' perceptions of this class of asset.
- Venture funds are extremely risky and illiquid, and the evidence suggests that the average fund does not outperform public equity. Further, their supposed diversification benefits are most likely overstated.
- The funds that do well are typically large, run by managers who are very experienced, and most of the alpha comes from only a handful of projects that generate large payoffs.
- The future direction of the venture industry is toward funding large-scale projects, which are typically not a good fit of the venture capital funding model. Thus, potential investors need to be very cautious when considering this type of investment.

AN INTRODUCTION TO VENTURE CAPITAL

The modern venture capital industry began after the Second World War, when the first venture funds were created to commercialize technology that had been developed during the war.[1] A formal trade association was created in 1974 with the formation in the United States of the National Venture Capital Association (NVCA). However, venture capital was still a relatively small and esoteric investment sector, with fewer than 100 firms and less than US$500 million under management.

The mid-1990s, however, saw a remarkable change as an unprecedented volume of funds flowed into the venture capital industry on the back of the dot.com/telecom boom. This resulted in the industry becoming one of the largest asset categories in the alternative investments industry. Figure 1 presents the total capital under management for US venture funds, and the phenomenal growth rate of 45% in 1998, 58% in 1999, and 54% in 2000 is vividly illustrated. The bursting of the internet bubble, however, put an end to this meteoric rise, and the recent trend has been one of consolidation across the industry. In 2009, there were 794 venture capital firms in existence managing US$179.4 billion across 1,188 funds.

Figure 1. Capital under management for US venture funds. (*Source*: NVCA, 2010, p. 10.)

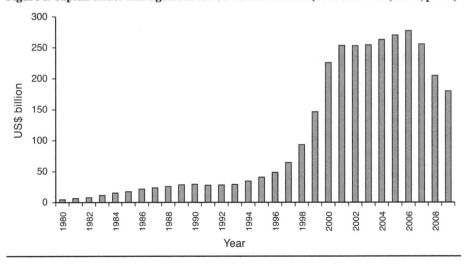

As professional venture capital evolved, it adopted the limited partnership form, which was designed (1) to protect passive sources of funds from losing more than the portion of their committed capital actually drawn down and invested, and (2) to reward the active venture managers with compensation contingent on investment success. The central character in a venture fund is the general partner (GP), who establishes a fund by seeking a financial commitment from various investors, who are referred to as limited partners (LPs). The GP's compensation takes the form of a management fee, defined as a percentage (typically 2% of committed capital), and a "carried interest" in the profits of the fund (typically 20%). Note that, at this stage, LPs are only required to commit to the fund (typically for a period of 10 years) and no money is actually invested. The year in which the fund is established is referred to as the fund vintage year, and funds typically range in size from as little as $10 million to more than $1 billion.

Having established the fund, the GP will then set about identifying suitable investment opportunities. Venture opportunities may be as early in their process of generation as a sole entrepreneur with an idea, or they may be as mature as a well-established organization seeking growth capital. This process of identifying opportunities is the primary role of the GP and, anecdotally, for every 100 opportunities, only 10 will be given serious consideration, and then only one investment will be made.[2]

Historically, venture capital investing in the United States has been concentrated in the information and communications technology (ICT) and the life sciences/healthcare sectors. Nowadays, venture funds invest in a wide variety of industries: for example, in 2009 the sectors most favored were biotechnology (20% of venture capital investments), software (18%), medical devices and equipment (14%), industrial/energy (13%), media and entertainment (7%), and IT services (6%).[3] A fund may choose to specialize in a particular sector, or, alternatively, it may be a general venture fund that has no restrictions on the scope of its investment activities. It is interesting to note that specialist venture funds have been found to outperform general venture funds, which is to be expected given that, unlike traditional fund managers, GPs typically engage in direct oversight of companies in which they invest. Consequently, industrial knowledge and relevant contacts are of paramount importance to successful venture investing.

Venture funds may also invest at various stages in the development of the company. For example, "seed funding" is provided to an entrepreneur to prove a concept (9% of venture capital investments in 2009 were to pure start-ups); "early-stage funding" is provided to companies which have products that are in testing or pilot production (26% of venture capital investments in 2009); "expansion funding" is where working capital is provided to a company, which may or may not be profitable, for the purposes of expansion (31% of investments in 2009); and "later-stage funding," where capital is provided to a company that has established itself in the market, is typically cash-flow positive (but not necessarily profitable), and is growing at a consistent rate (33% of investments in 2009). As a general rule, the latter stages of investment are lower risk and so have lower expected returns. While some funds may choose to specialize in funding particular stages of financing, others may have no preference.

It is worth noting that, much like other segments of the fund management industry, venture capital funds-of-funds also exist. These funds-of-funds seek to lessen the risk from this type of investment by diversifying across a number of venture capital funds.

Venture capital funds typically have a stipulated "investment period"—usually four to five years—during which full management fees are paid, with these fees generally reducing after the investment period has elapsed. Whenever an investment decision is made, the GP will draw down the needed funds from the capital committed by the LPs. There is no requirement that all of the committed funds be called over the life of the fund—if suitable investments cannot be identified, the GP will not invest. However, a venture capitalist who is unable to find suitable investments is unlikely to raise a subsequent fund.

The return to the LPs from their investment in the venture fund comes in the form of periodic distributions. These distributions are the result of the GP creating liquidity in their investments either through outright sale of the investee company or through a successful initial public offering (IPO). In the former case, the distribution may take the form of either cash or liquid securities (if the acquiring company used such securities as the medium for the transaction). In the latter case, shares of the investee company are typically distributed to the limited partners, although the timing and number of distributions will necessarily

Best Practice • Investments

reflect the liquidity and performance of the shares.

THE PERFORMANCE OF VENTURE CAPITAL FUNDS

One key generalized fact about the performance of venture funds is that venture investing is a high-risk activity. As a general rule, only one in six companies ever goes public and one in three is acquired.[4] Thus, GPs expect only a small number of their investments to generate a return, while the majority will fail.

To understand why such a large number of investments fail, consider a simple example of the venture investment process (Table 1). Assume that there are eight different facets of the venture investment process that go together to produce a successful investment. Further, assume that the GP involved with the company has a good track record, such that it has an 80% probability of achieving success against each of these facets, or criteria. Probability theory tells us that there is only a 17% chance of success, and if we reduce three of the probabilities to 50%, the combined chance of success falls to only 4%. Of course, the real world is far more complex than depicted in this simple example, but the point remains.

Table 1. The probability that a venture investment will be successful. (*Source*: Zider, 1998)

Individual event	Probability
1. Company has sufficient capital	80%
2. Management has sufficient skills	80%
3. Product development proceeds as planned	80%
4. Input sourcing proceeds as planned	80%
5. No change in market competition	80%
6. Demand is forecast correctly	80%
7. Pricing is forecast correctly	80%
8. Patents are issued and enforceable	80%
Combined probability of success	17%

The high probability of failure in any individual investment explains why successful venture capital funds tend to be heavily capitalized. In simple terms, it is necessary to have sufficient capital to invest in a variety of different projects such that, on average, at least some of them will succeed and the gains from the few winners will exceed the losses from the losers. By way of example, the American Research and Development Corporation initially invested US$70,000 in Digital and received a distribution of US$355 million following its IPO in 1968. This equates to an annualized rate of return in excess of 100% per year and accounted for half of the company's profits over its 26-year life.

This is not to say that a "shot gun" approach to venture investing works best—in fact, quite the opposite is true, as there is a high degree of persistence in venture fund returns (unlike almost every other class of managed fund). This means that managers who do well in the past will most likely continue to do well as they are better networked and more knowledgeable about the segment of the market they operate in.

A controversial question is whether venture investments provide a level of performance that justifies their risk and illiquidity. A general index of performance for the venture capital investment industry is provided by Sand Hill Econometrics (Figure 2). The incredible performance of the venture industry during the dot.com/telecom boom is clearly evident in the data, as is the subsequent bursting of the bubble. For the purpose of comparison, the S&P 500 as well as the Nasdaq indexes are also included.[5] Across the entire period over which the index is available, the average annualized return for the index over the period December 1991 to March 2010 is 20.3%, while the return to the S&P 500 was only 6.8% and 10.7% for the Nasdaq, respectively.

As noted earlier, funds in the venture industry are extremely heterogeneous. Rather than looking at industry-wide measures of performance, a more satisfactory approach is to examine the performance of individual funds. The most commonly used database for this purpose is provided by Thomson Venture Economics, which has data for individual funds. Although the early literature on this issue generally found that venture funds outperform public equity, the Thomson database has inherent problems when used to benchmark performance that stem from self-reporting of the data and survivorship bias. After correcting for sample bias and accounting values, the average fund performance was found to change from over- to underperformance of −3.83% per year with respect to the S&P 500.[6]

Figure 2. Venture capital, S&P 500 and Nasdaq indexes. (*Source*: Sand Hill Econometrics and Datastream. The Sand Hill All Industries index is presented)

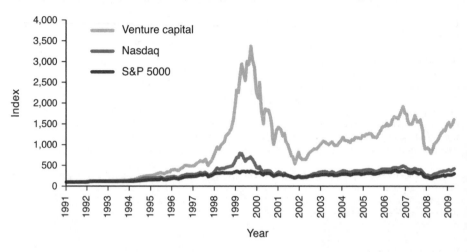

GPs prefer to exit an investment through an IPO, as exit valuations for listed companies are higher than those of buyouts. For example, a $1 investment in a firm that goes public was found to provide an average cash return of $1.95 beyond the initial investment, while an acquisition yields a cash return of only 40 cents.[7] In fact, Metrick (2007, p. 100) goes so far as to argue:

"Without a doubt, the most important driver of VC investment is the existence of a lucrative market to exit these investments. ...The most profitable exits are achieved through initial public offerings."

This is an interesting point as, if the conditions in the IPO market exert an influence on venture fund performance, public and private equity returns may not be independent. This is potentially an important issue, as summarized by Gompers and Lerner (2004, p. 354), who state:

"...many institutions...have increased their allocation to venture capital...in the belief that the returns of these funds are largely uncorrelated with the public markets."

The available empirical evidence on this issue does find evidence of the existence of such a relationship. In the last 30 years, for example, the median venture fund produced an internal rate of return (IRR) of 76% when the IPO market was hot (i.e. during the 1983 Q4, 1986 Q3, 1993 Q4, 1996 Q2 and 2000 Q1 periods), which is substantially higher than the median return in a neutral (24%) and poor (9%) IPO market.[8] Thus, clear evidence of a link between the public equity market and the performance of venture funds is

found, which suggests that the diversification benefits of this class of alternative investment may be significantly overstated.

THE VENTURE CAPITAL INDUSTRY: LOOKING FORWARD

To understand the future of the venture capital industry and where the profitable investment opportunities are to be found, one needs to gain an appreciation of which sectors the venture capital industry serves well and those it does not.

The history of venture investing suggests that venture capitalists have *successfully* invested in a narrow band of the spectrum of technological innovation—more specifically, ICT and biotechnology. The latter, however, comes with a caveat as biotechnology is arguably a failure when measured by cash generation (Pisano, 2006, p. 117):

"[F]rom1975 to 2004...[w]hile revenues have grown exponentially..., profit levels essentially hover close to zero throughout the life of the industry. Furthermore, the picture becomes even worse if we take the largest and most profitable firm, Amgen, out of the sample. Without Amgen the industry has sustained heavy losses throughout its history.... [T]he analysis includes no privately held firms, almost all of which lose money. Therefore, the data presented here are just for the most profitable part of the industry...."

Venture capitalists, however, have been notably *unsuccessful* in materials science and other "high-tech" areas. The key difference is that in the case of ICT, the US Department of Defense funded the enabling science, from semiconductor physics through computational logic, and also supported movement down the operational learning curve to reliable and efficient manufacturing both as an investor and as a customer. Similarly, the National Institutes of Health have funded the research base for the biotechnology industry. The search for relevant, commercially attractive applications of novel materials, however, is a very extended process, as demonstrated by the history of engineered polymers ("plastics"): commercial success was the result of billions of dollars and decades of experimentation on the part of DuPont and General Electric.

These observations do not bode well for the industry, as venture investments in the energy, nanotechnology, and green-technology sectors are likely to be the most common type of opportunity presented to investors in the future. These investments will be seeking considerable capital funding (investments are likely to be measured in billions rather than millions of dollars), with promises of big returns. Unfortunately, none are a good fit to the venture capital funding model since the science is immature, the exposure to competitive commodity pricing pressure from conventional energy sources is acute, and the capital required for economically meaningful deployment is massive.

Venture capitalists can play a useful role in funding distributed research and development for established companies and launching lightweight web start-ups. However, the industry is still considerably overcapitalized for these purposes, even taking into account the recent fall in funds under management (see Figure 1), which means that many funds will simply not be able to access the right type of investments.

CONCLUSION

The venture capital industry initially focused on exploiting technologies that had been fostered by government funding of basic science and engineering in the ICT and biotechnology sectors. Its success was amplified by the dot. com/telecom bubble of the late 1990s, which led to a considerable sum of investment funds being diverted into the industry in a very short time. The maturation of the ICT sector, however, means that there are only a limited amount of good ideas available to invest in at any given time, effectively forcing many GPs to invest in projects that are not well suited to the venture model.

Thus, the potential venture fund investor needs to tread carefully. Venture fund returns are highly positively skewed, as the industry is dominated by a small number of well-connected and highly experienced GPs who consistently outperform the rest of the industry. To invest outside of this select group means that you are likely to find your money tied to a fund whose performance is, at best, more in keeping with that of public equity.

MAKING IT HAPPEN

A potential investor in the venture sector is likely to be overwhelmed by the substantial number of funds available to choose from. To be successful, the investor must choose wisely, and the foundation of a successful foray into venture fund investing relies on understanding the key components that go into making a successful venture capital firm. Specifically, successful GPs:

- tend to specialize in a particular segment of the investment universe;
- have a good track record of past successes;
- run large funds that allow them to gain exposure to a range of opportunities, in the expectation that many will fail;
- focus on distributed research and development for big start-up companies and launching lightweight web start-ups, which are the types of investments best suited to venture investing.

Without these elements in place, an investor is likely to lock his or her money up for a considerable period of time and at the end of it all receive a return that is akin to that of public equity.

MORE INFO

Books:

Gompers, Paul, and Josh Lerner. *The Venture Capital Cycle*. 2nd ed. Cambridge, MA: MIT Press, 2004.

Metrick, Andrew. *Venture Capital and the Finance of Innovation*. Hoboken, NJ: Wiley, 2007.

National Venture Capital Association (NVCA). *2010 NVCA Yearbook*. Arlington, VA: NVCA, 2010. Online at: tinyurl.com/5wkwz9o

Pisano, Gary P. Science Business: *The Promise, the Reality, and the Future of Biotech*. Cambridge, MA: Harvard Business School Press, 2006.

Article:

Zider, Bob. "How venture capital works. The discipline of innovation." *Harvard Business Review* 76:6 (November–December 1998): 131–139. Online at: hbr.org/1998/11/how-venture-capital-works/ar/1

Websites:

National Venture Capital Association (NVCA): www.nvca.org

Sand Hill Econometrics: www.sandhillecon.com

Thomson Venture Economics: www.alacrastore.com/research/thomson-financial-venture-economics

NOTES

1 American Research and Development Corporation and J.H. Whitney & Company were both founded in 1946 and were the first modern venture capital funds (the latter is still active in the industry). Prior to this, wealthy individuals and family trusts were the main source of this type of development capital.

2 NVCA, 2010, p. 7.

3 NVCA, 2010, p. 12.

4 NVCA, 2010, p. 8.

5 Note that both the S&P 500 and the Nasdaq have been reindexed to start at a value of 100, the same starting value as the Sand Hill index.

6 See Phalippou, Ludovic, and Oliver Gottschalg. "The performance of private equity funds." *Review of Financial Studies* 22:4 (April 2009): 1747–1776. Online at: dx.doi.org/10.1093/rfs/hhn014

7 See Ross, Peter W., and Susan Isenstein. *Exiting Venture Capital Investments*. Wellesley Hills, MA: Venture Economics, 1988.

8 See McKenzie, Michael D., and William H. Janeway. "Venture capital funds and the public equity market." *Accounting & Finance* (forthcoming). Online at: dx.doi.org/10.1111/j.1467-629X.2010.00373.x

The Role of Commodities in an Institutional Portfolio by Keith Black and Satya Kumar

EXECUTIVE SUMMARY

- Institutional investors, including public and corporate pension plans, endowments, and foundations, are rapidly increasing the portion of their assets allocated to commodity investments.
- Investments in commodity futures may improve the reward-to-risk ratio for investment portfolios, as the low correlation between commodity futures and equity and fixed-income investments reduces portfolio volatility.
- Over long periods of time, investments in commodity futures have a risk–return profile similar to that of stocks, which means that there can be substantial gains or losses in any given month or year.
- Commodity futures have a positive correlation with inflation, which can be attractive for pension plans that are required to pay inflation-adjusted benefits to their beneficiaries.
- The best way for institutional investors to access the commodity markets is by identifying skilled and active managers in the futures markets. Investing in commodity index funds, physical commodities, or equity securities are suboptimal solutions.

THE CASE FOR COMMODITIES

The case for commodities is based largely on their historical tendency to offer returns that exhibit a low correlation with those of stock and bond market indices. Although commodities may be volatile, their low correlation with traditional investments can result in a significant diversification benefit. Table 1 shows the correlation between two commodity indices—the Standard & Poor's GSCI (S&P GSCI) and the Dow Jones–AIG Commodity Index (DJ-AIG)—and traditional investments and inflation indices since 1991. Over the last 18 years, a small allocation to investments in commodity futures would have substantially reduced portfolio volatility.

Historically, investments in commodity futures have offered their strongest returns during times of below-average returns from traditional stock and bond market investments. Figure 1 shows the performance of commodity futures sorted by the return of the Wilshire 5000 stock market index during the period.

From 1991 to the third quarter of 2008, the Wilshire 5000 index declined by an average of −8.2% during the 20% of calendar quarters with the largest stock market declines. During these quarters of sharp stock price corrections, the S&P GSCI averaged a total return of 4.0%, while the Dow Jones–AIG Commodity Index returned 2.1%. In the second quintile, in calendar quarters when the stock market return was 0.0%, commodity indices earned their highest returns, at 6.1% and 4.8%. Each commodity index experienced its largest gains during times of below-average stock market returns. Conversely, the only periods in which the commodity indices consistently experienced losses were those in which the stock market indices posted their largest gains.

Figure 2 tells a similar story, comparing the returns of commodity indices with those of the Lehman Brothers Aggregate Bond Market Index. In the 20% worst quarters for bond markets, the Lehman Aggregate returned −1.0% and inflation-linked bonds (TIPS) fell by 0.6%. During these quarters of weak bond markets, the commodity indices offered their highest returns: 5.4% for the S&P GSCI, and 3.5% for the DJ-AIG.

Historically, commodities have served in a defensive role, as commodities have earned

Table 1. Correlation matrix for two commodity indices with traditional investments and inflation indices, January 1991 to September 2008

Correlation with	S&P GSCI	DJ-AIG
DJ Wilshire 5000 Index	0.04	0.10
Lehman Aggregate Bond Index	0.03	0.02
Consumer Price Index (CPI)	0.18	0.15
Treasury Inflation-Protected Securities (TIPS)	0.16	0.17

their highest return in times of weak stock and bond prices. Should these correlations persist in the future, a small allocation to commodities may serve to reduce portfolio risk by increasing returns in times of falling stock and bond prices.

Figure 1. Performance of commodity futures sorted by return of Wilshire 5000 Stock Market Index, 1991 to third quarter of 2008

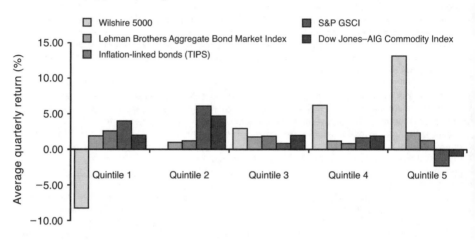

Figure 2. Comparison of commodity index returns with returns of Lehman Brothers Aggregate Bond Market Index

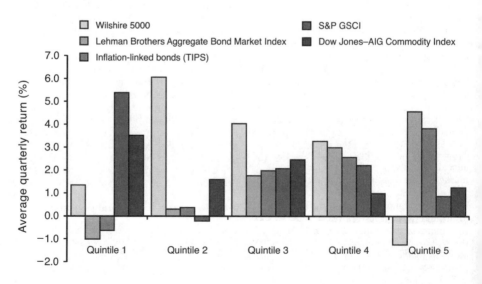

CASE STUDY

Commodity Stocks versus Commodity Futures

Some investors have chosen to implement their views on commodity prices by investing in equity securities. The prices of these stocks may be somewhat correlated with those of commodity futures. Metals firms include, for example, Alcoa, and Anglo American, while agricultural firms include Archer Daniels Midland. In the energy sector, stocks such as Exxon-Mobil, Chevron, and ConocoPhillips may be used as a proxy for crude oil. These three companies alone make up 4.6% of the market capitalization of the Wilshire 5000 index. The energy sector as a whole comprises 11% of the US stock market, and another 4% is made up by metals, food, chemicals, and other materials companies. Given that most investors already have a large allocation in equity securities, an additional allocation to commodity-linked equities may not be the best way to express a view on commodity prices.

As an example, consider that the price of a stock is the product of the earnings per share (EPS) and the stock's price/earnings multiple (P/E). When commodity firms have not hedged their output in the futures market, the profits of a firm (i.e. EPS) will be highly correlated with the prices of the commodities it produces. These profits give the firm a desirable commodity market exposure (beta), such that this portion of the stock price is responsive to changes in commodity prices. However, each firm also has a P/E ratio, which can vary with the level of the stock market. This introduces a potentially undesirable stock market beta into the commodity portfolio. This sensitivity to stock prices is unwelcome, as a key reason for investing in commodities is to experience returns that are uncorrelated with those of equity markets. In fact, commodity stocks are likely to underperform commodity futures during times of high inflation. When inflation and commodity prices are rising, stock prices are typically declining. Should the price/earnings ratio of commodity stocks decline in a bear market, the investor may not realize the anticipated benefit of the commodity firm's profits in terms of stock price appreciation. Commodity futures are a more direct way to earn the diversifying benefits of commodity investments without increasing the stock market risk of the overall portfolio.

In the first quarter of 2008, energy stocks and commodity futures indices moved in opposite directions. Even though oil prices were increasing (commodity beta) and commodity futures indices rose as much as 18% in the quarter, the stock market was decidedly negative. Energy stocks fell 8% during the quarter, as the US stock market declined nearly 10% in the quarter. While energy stocks had a higher return than the broader market, there remained a large gap between the performance of commodity stocks and commodity futures.

Though energy, metals and agricultural commodities are well represented in the futures markets, there are other commodities for which futures markets do not currently exist. Markets such as those for water, coal, steel, chemicals, and renewable energy can only be accessed by investors through equity securities. Firms that produce capital goods needed for exploration and production, or to maintain ownership, of commodities in these sectors represent a relatively small part of the equity market, and futures contracts are not available. Although investment in commodities through stocks in the energy, metals, and agricultural sector is not advocated, investors who desire exposure to these other commodity markets may do so using stocks.

COMMODITY FUTURES INDICES

The two most commonly used commodity futures indices are the S&P GSCI and the Dow Jones–AIG Commodity Index. Table 2 shows the allocation of each index to various commodity markets. Note that the energy markets represent 76% of the GSCI. In contrast, the DJ-AIG index intentionally limits exposure to any single sector to around 33%. Investors may prefer the DJ-AIG index to gain a potential improvement in the risk–reward tradeoff, as the overweight given to energy commodities in the GSCI has historically resulted in higher volatility without a corresponding boost in returns. Since 1991, the GSCI has earned an average total return of 7.1% with a standard deviation (volatility) of 18.4%, while the DJ-AIG averaged an annual return of 8.1% with a lower standard deviation of 12.3%. Earlier, Table 1 showed that the two commodity indices share similar correlations with traditional stock and bond investments and inflation.

The total return to a commodity futures index consists of three components: spot return, roll return, and yield. The spot return is the return to an investment in physical commodities. The roll return is earned in the process of passively trading (rolling) futures contracts as they mature and must be replaced. The yield is the interest earned on a short-term fixed-income investment

Table 2. Composition (%) of S&P GSCI and DJ-AIG indices as of September 30, 2008

Commodity sector	S&P GSCI	DJ-AIG
Energy	76.0	35.1
Precious metals	2.2	10.2
Industrial metals	6.2	17.8
Agriculture	12.0	28.4
Livestock	3.6	8.5

that is pledged to the futures exchange in order to maintain the collateral required to back the futures investments. Table 3 breaks down the total returns from spot, roll, and yield.

Figures 3 and 4 show some interesting characteristics of the returns on owning physical commodities. Most notably, spot commodity markets have underperformed inflation and cash over long periods of time: while the GSCI spot index earned an annual return of 4.8% since 1970, cash returned 5.6% and the US Consumer Price Index (CPI) increased by 4.6% per year over the same period. Commodity price increases have not exceeded the rate of inflation over long periods of time. As new natural resources are discovered, production technologies improve, and research advances in areas such as crop engineering and alternative energy, commodity prices tend to

decline in real (after-inflation) terms.

How, then, could commodities futures have offered a total return since 1970 rivaling that of equities if the ownership of physical commodities does not offer a return that exceeds inflation? The answer is in the roll return and the collateral yield, as shown in Figure 3. (The roll return is approximated by the difference between the excess return and the spot return of the GSCI.) The roll return and collateral yield can only be earned when investing in commodity futures. The return on commodity futures investments, then, has significantly exceeded that of a direct investment in physical commodities over the last 37 years. An extended discussion of roll yield, and the relationship to contango and backwardation term structures in the futures markets, can be found in Black and Kumar (2008).

Table 3. Decomposition of S&P GSCI returns, 1970 to September 2008

	Annualized return (%)
S&P GSCI Total Return Index	11.8
S&P GSCI Spot Return Index	4.8
S&P GSCI Excess Return Index	5.3
Roll return	0.5
Three-month Treasury Bill yield	5.6

Figure 3. Ratio of cumulative wealth normalized to cash, 1970 to September 2008

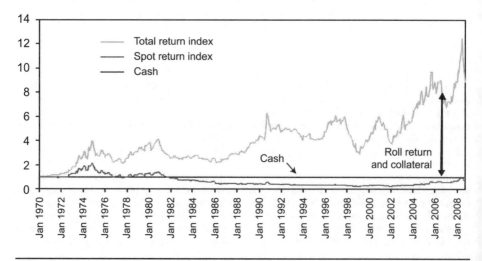

The Role of Commodities in an Institutional Portfolio

Best Practice • Investments

Figure 4. Ratio of cumulative wealth of spot returns normalized to cash, 1970 to September

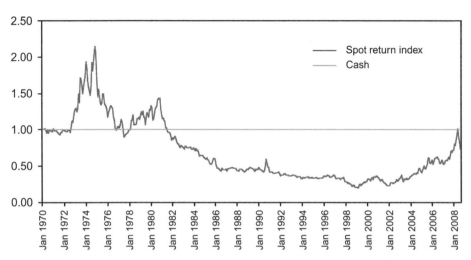

Not every investor will choose to make use of commodities in their portfolio. It can be difficult to value commodities, as their characteristics don't neatly follow classical valuation models. Commodities do not generate a cash flow, so they can't be valued using discounted cash flow methodologies. Because commodities have a near-zero correlation to equity indices, their beta is also near zero, which disallows use of the capital asset pricing model. Variables such as political strife and weather can have a significant impact on both long- and short-run commodity prices. These exogenous variables are extremely difficult to predict, and they create systemic risks that are not priced in traditional return forecasting models.

ACTIVELY MANAGED COMMODITY FUNDS

Active management has a number of advantages over allocating assets to a commodity index fund. There are several ways in which an active commodity manager can add value relative to an investment in a commodity index. Should a manager demonstrate skill in these areas, an allocation to its managed commodity product can be supported.

First, an active commodity manager should have an intimate understanding of the shape of the futures curves in a variety of commodity markets. Commodity index funds require that investors hold long positions in the near-dated contract, regardless of the shape of the futures curve and the size of the positive or negative roll yield. Active managers, however, have significant

flexibility in their selection of contract. For example, although the front-month contracts in a given market may be priced to result in roll losses, later-dated contracts, perhaps at a 12-month maturity, may be priced in such a way that investors may earn a profit from the roll. This flexibility can significantly increase the potential for a return from the futures roll. In a case where the entire futures curve for a given commodity is in contango, causing negative roll yields, an active manager may choose to reduce or eliminate exposure to that commodity. Commodity index programs also have a stated timing when they are required to roll from the front month to the later-dated futures contract. When managers follow a mechanical strategy, such as rolling 20% of their position in each of the fifth through ninth business days of the calendar month, other traders in the market become aware of the roll requirement and change their prices to maximize the market impact of that trading program. Active managers will choose to roll their positions at a date other than that of the index rolls, which can significantly reduce the market impact of their trading.

Second, commodity index investors are required to hold a certain portion of their assets in each futures market, regardless of the fundamental drivers of the spot commodity price. Active commodity managers should be able to show skill in their analysis of the supply and demand dynamics in each market. Ideally, the active manager will implement a long position only in markets where demand is likely to grow faster than supply, while avoiding or selling

QFINANCE

short in markets with less favorable supply–demand dynamics. While index investors only take long positions in commodity markets, active managers may choose to take no position or a short (negative) position in commodity markets where their analysis predicts a low probability of price increases.

Given the significant opportunities to enhance the returns from spot returns and roll investments in the futures markets, active managers who show skill in these areas may be viewed as an attractive investment opportunity. While active managers may choose to maintain significant short positions in certain commodity markets, funds that maintain a long bias in each of the major market sectors, including energy, metals, and agriculture maximize the diversification effect of the commodities investment. For commodities to play their role as a portfolio diversifier, the fund needs to maintain long positions during times of commodity price increases.

CONCLUSION

Over the last 18 years, commodities have served as an excellent portfolio diversifier. Because of the historical tendency for commodity futures to have a high correlation with inflation, they typically offer higher returns than stocks, bonds, and even Treasury Inflation-Protected Securities during times of market stress. Commodities tend to be a defensive asset class and, as such, tend to underperform during bullish equity markets. Should these trends continue, investors can reduce their portfolio risk by allocating a small portion of their portfolio to commodity futures.

MAKING IT HAPPEN

- Examine your investment portfolio to determine the potential value added by an allocation to commodity futures investments.
- Should you determine that commodities would improve the risk–return tradeoff of your portfolio, begin your search for an actively managed portfolio that can add value above an index fund investment.

MORE INFO

Books:

Fabozzi, Frank J., Roland Füss, and Dieter G. Kaiser (eds). *The Handbook of Commodity Investing*. Hoboken, NJ: Wiley, 2008.

Till, Hilary, and Joseph Eagleeye (eds). *Intelligent Commodity Investing: New Strategies and Practical Insights for Informed Decision Making*. London: Risk Books, 2007.

Articles:

Erb, Claude B., and Campbell R. Harvey. "The strategic and tactical value of commodity futures." *Financial Analysts Journal* 62:2 (March/April 2006): 69–97. Online at: dx.doi.org/10.2469/faj.v62.n2.4084

Gorton, Gary B., and K. Geert Rouwenhorst. "Facts and fantasies about commodity futures." *Financial Analysts Journal* 62:2 (March/April 2006): 47–68. Online at: dx.doi.org/10.2469/faj.v62.n2.4083

Journal of Indexes. November/December 2008. issue, "Inside commodities." Online at: tinyurl.com/6jjrspe

Reports:

Black, Keith. "The role of institutional investors in rising commodity prices." Ennis Knupp & Associates, June 2008. Online at: tinyurl.com/5uc9xjv [PDF].

Black, Keith, and Satya Kumar. "The role of commodities and timberland in an institutional portfolio." Ennis Knupp & Associates, February 2008. Online at: tinyurl.com/6cewjk3

Websites:

Dow Jones–AIG Commodity Indexes: www.djindexes.com/aig
Standard & Poor's: www.standardandpoors.com

Corporate Covenant and Other Embedded Options in Pension Funds by Theo Kocken

EXECUTIVE SUMMARY

- The various contingent claims in a pension fund, such as the parent guarantee (corporate covenant) or conditional indexation, can be valued with the same techniques that are used to value options on stocks.
- An application to a real life pension case shows how risk absorption by employers and beneficiaries varies widely, depending on such variables as asset allocation and rating of the sponsor.
- This valuation technique is an indispensable tool for improving pension fund risk management, redesigning pension contracts, and supporting Chief Financial Officers in their decision-making process with regard to mergers or acquisitions.
- Assess the auditing and monitoring process for effectiveness.

INTRODUCTION

Pension funds in their defined benefit (DB) form and the alternative structures that have evolved over time are among the most complex risk-sharing institutions ever created, not least because they involve many stakeholders (such as employers, retirees, and employees), all of whom assume different risks.

The employers assume some of the risks by, for example, being obligated to replenish any shortfall in the pension fund. The pensioners and actives assume some of the risk via, for example, partial (instead of full) compensation for inflation.

Unlike with a corporate balance sheet, where it is clear who owns the equity (and hence takes the highest risk and first loss accordingly) and who owns senior debt, there is little agreement on ownership within pension funds. In fact, there is little knowledge about the risks assumed by each stakeholder. Usually, risk is measured for the pension funds as a whole and is typically expressed in terms of the risk of funding shortfall. However, this does not equal the risk that each of the stakeholders may face.

A better quantification of the risks that the various parties assume, which would enable more effective risk management, would prove very valuable. It could be used to negotiate pension contracts and to agree on any entitlements that stakeholders may have to the potential upside (surplus) in the pension fund. As a further illustration, Chief Financial Officers (CFOs) are interested in the specific share of risk that they assume—and the value of those risks— when acquiring a firm with a DB pension fund. With the knowledge provided by the embedded option technique, the CFO could assess what kind of policy measures applied to the pension fund would result in acceptable risks when a target firm—including the firm's obligation to the pension fund—is acquired.

The single most objective way of dealing with multi-stakeholder risk situations that arise in pension funds is the embedded options approach. The risks various stakeholders assume in a pension fund are formulated in terms of options—contingent claims—which stakeholders have written to the pension fund. These options have a certain value that can be determined by employing the same techniques as are applied in the financial markets to price financial options. Since most of the variables relevant to the pension fund have a basis in financial markets (riskless assets such as government bonds, risky assets such as equity and corporate bonds, and interest rate-related liabilities), this is an approach that provides reliable market-consistent values.

Determining the value of these embedded options can be well worth the effort. As will be shown in the analysis below, the contingent claims that stakeholders have in pension funds can easily exceed 20% or 30% of total liabilities in a pension fund. Considering that the estimated value of, for instance, the joint liabilities of UK and Dutch pension funds alone already exceeds 2,000 billion euro, the value of the embedded options is at least hundreds of billions of euros.

IDENTIFYING THE VARIOUS EMBEDDED OPTIONS

To start with, some of the most significant embedded options identified in pension funds are discussed. One of the most important embedded options the employer writes to the pension fund is the so-called parent guarantee, also known as the sponsor covenant. This is the guarantee to support the pension fund in case of funding shortfalls. This option depends on, among other factors, the exact trigger levels at which the parent will pay, as well as (from the perspective of the pension fund) the development of the default probability of the parent company over time.

Two important options that the beneficiaries write to the pension fund are the indexation option and the pension put.

The *indexation option* is the right the pension fund has to waive indexation in case of, say, an insufficient funding level.[1] In case of a very low funding ratio, this implies that the beneficiary's maximum value loss compared to full indexation is roughly the expected inflation multiplied by the duration of his contract.

The *pension put* is the occurrence of a joint "default" event (i.e. a deficit of the pension fund's funding and at the same time a default of the sponsor). Such a joint event will imply write-offs of the pension entitlements, which is defined as the "payout" of the embedded option. The value of the option depends on, among other things, the (assumptions made with respect to) default probability as a function of time, recovery rates, and correlation between financial markets and the default probability.

Many pension funds have additional embedded options, such as the option to increase contributions (paid by employers and often also partially by the employees) in case of a low funding ratio.[2] And in exceptional cases, such as BAE Systems' pension fund, even longevity options are written by active employees to the pension fund, allowing the fund to reduce pension entitlements in case of an unanticipated rise in longevity. Many other embedded options are implicitly present in pension funds, although the set described above covers the majority of options in DB funds.

The embedded options described above can be explicitly calculated using market-consistent valuation. The values of the embedded options in this article are measured using arbitrage-free option pricing techniques and assuming complete markets. Monte Carlo simulations are used because of the complex nature of the options. It is outside the scope of this essay to discuss these valuation techniques and their underlying assumptions in further detail, since literature is abundant.[3]

APPLICATIONS

How can we use this information to improve risk management and pension design?

The methodology can be applied in many different decision-making situations, among which are:

- evaluating the impact of policy adjustments in a pension fund on the various embedded options and, if necessary, trying to steer with different policy instruments (asset allocation, contribution rate policy, etc.) to make the changes acceptable to all stakeholders;
- actively hedging the complex interest rate and inflation risks that arise from conditional or capped indexation;
- determining the economic value employers should pay into a pension fund when they want to retreat as risk takers in the pension fund and transfer the risks to the beneficiaries;
- determining the entitlements of the different stakeholders to a potential future surplus in the pension fund, in proportion to the risks they assumed;
- determining the claim a pension fund has on a corporate when considering a merger.

CASE STUDY

The following case is based on a Dutch risk-sharing pension fund with a sponsor that provides the guarantee to the nominal pension obligations, beneficiaries who accept conditional indexation as well as the possibility of a default by the employer (translated into the pension put described above). The contribution rate is fixed to simplify the case.

For expository reasons, the pension fund case applies a simple asset allocation of 50% risk-free government bonds and 50% equity investments. The funding ratio equals 100.[4] The values in the table are expressed as a percentage of the value of the liabilities at $t = 0$. The sponsor's debt is assumed to be BB-rated. Table 1 gives values of embedded options for three different kinds of risk sharing. The second column from the left shows a situation with beneficiaries assuming no risk at all: The sponsor has provided a guarantee and is assumed to be default-free (or a pension protection vehicle such as the PBGC in the United States or the PPF in the United Kingdom exists that in its turn is assumed default-free). In this column, the beneficiaries are entitled to full inflation indexation of their liabilities under all scenarios. They simply bear zero risk. In the third column, the BB rating of the sponsor is taken into account, putting slightly more risk on the

50

beneficiaries' plate through the pension put. In the fourth column, beneficiaries are confronted with the potential default of the employer as well as indexation cuts in situations of low funding ratios.

Table 1. Values of the embedded options for different kinds of risk sharing (% liability value)

Type of pension fund	Full indexation + default-free sponsor	Full indexation + "default-risk" sponsor	Conditional indexation + "default-risk" sponsor
Parent guarantee (sponsor covenant)	29.7%	28.6%	17.8%
Pension put Indexation option	- -	4.8% -	3.1% 11.3%
Sponsor share (as percentage of total risk)	100%	86%	55%

What does this information tell us? First of all that for this specific situation, the parent guarantee has a value that is close to 30%, in case the possibility of default of the parent is excluded. While this specific result reveals a significant level of risk, it should be noted that it may vary from fund to fund, depending on many factors such as the funding ratio and volatility of the assets. However, it is interesting to see the impact of corporate default risk, and especially explicit risk-sharing such as the possibility of indexation cuts. In the case at hand, the beneficiaries assume almost half of the risks (45%) by accepting conditional indexation and the default risk of the sponsor.

The option values depend on various parameters, such as the composition (and hence the volatility) of the asset mix and the credit rating of the sponsoring company. Table 2 provides some insight on the effect of asset allocation on the embedded option values, with lower equity (higher bonds) and higher equity (lower bonds) allocations.[5] Table 3 provides insight on the effect of variations in credit rating on the option values.

Table 2. Option values (% of liability value) as a function of asset mix composition

Type of option	Equity % in total assets		
	30%	50%	70%
Parent guarantee	15.2	17.8	22.7
Pension put	2.5	3.1	3.8
Indexation option	12.3	11.3	10.4
Sponsor share (as percentage of total risk)	51%	55%	61%

Table 3. Option values (% liability value) as a function of employer's credit rating

Type of option	Employer's credit rating		
	CCC	BB	A
Parent guarantee	8.7	17.8	21.3
Pension put	10.0	3.1	0.3
Indexation option	12.1	11.3	11.0
Sponsor share (as percentage of total risk)	28%	55%	65%

Table 2 reveals that more risk-taking in the pension fund in this case requires that more additional risk be assumed by the employer, by comparison with the beneficiaries, both in absolute and in relative terms. Table 3 explains the importance of credit risk and its effect: If the employer has a low credit rating, the amount of risk beneficiaries are taking is higher in embedded option value terms than the risk assumed by the employer. This picture is completely reversed in the case of a supporting employer with a high credit rating.

Table 4. Option values (% liability value) as a function of actual funding ratio

Type of option	Current (nominal) funding ratio		
	80%	100%	120%
Parent guarantee	34.0	17.8	9.1
Pension put	3.4	3.1	2.6
Indexation option	13.4	11.3	6.4
Sponsor share (as percentage of total risk)	67%	55%	50%

Investments • Best Practice

Many other variables determine the value of these options, a key one being the actual funding ratio. Table 4 compares the various option values at different funding ratios.

It is clear from Table 4 that at very low funding levels, far below fully funded status, the risk assumed by the corporate is relatively high by comparison with the beneficiaries' risk absorption. This is due to the fact that the indexation option cannot increase that much with lower funding levels (you can only lose your indexation, irrespective of the shortfall level), where the corporate sponsor has to complete the entire shortfall.

MAKING IT HAPPEN

Implementing the embedded option approach requires various adjustments in the asset and liability management (ALM) models applied by the pension fund. The main steps are:

* The ALM model used should be able to cope with risk-neutral scenarios. Though this may be quite a tedious exercise, a first rough indication can be obtained by setting the risk premia in the system to zero.
* The various option payoffs need to be recognized in the ALM model. Usually this can be achieved via simple adjustments, since all the relevant variables (funding ratio, level of indexation) are available in the model.
* The present value of the risk-neutral payoffs in the previous steps represents the embedded option value.

The reading suggestions below provide some support in executing these steps.

MORE INFO

Books:

Bodie, Zvi. "Pension guarantees, capital adequacy and international risk sharing." In Broeders, Dirk, Sylvester Eijffinger, and Aerdt Houben (eds). *Frontiers in Pension Finance.* Cheltenham, UK: Edward Elgar, 2008; pp. 243–257.

Kortleve, Niels, Theo Nijman, and Eduard Ponds. *Fair Value and Pension Fund Management.* Oxford: Elsevier, 2006.

Reports:

Hoevenaars, Roy Peter Maria Mathieu. "Strategic asset allocation and asset liability management." PhD thesis. Maastricht University, 2008. Online at: arno.unimaas.nl/show.cgi?fid=9679 [PDF].

Kocken, T. "Curious contracts: Pension fund redesign for the future." PhD thesis. Free University of Amsterdam, 2006.

Website:

Though not much literature is available online, the Social Science Research Network (SSRN) sometimes provides good help on this topic. Visit www.ssrn.com and search for "embedded options." Most applications are related to guarantees in life insurance contracts, bonds, etc., but it may prove useful given the similarities with pension funds' embedded options.

NOTES

1 Different kinds of embedded options exist related to indexation. The example given here relates to indexation conditional to the level of the funding ratio, as applied in the Netherlands. In the United Kingdom, indexation cuts are linked to the inflation level itself (indexation is capped at a certain level, for example 2.5% or 5%), though introducing "Dutch-type" conditional indexation is high on the United Kingdom's political pension agenda as well.

2 And often also the option to reduce contribution rates in case of a high funding ratio.

3 For the assumptions underlying the case in the text, see Kocken (2006).

4 Discounted against the nominal swap curve.

5 The credit rating of the sponsor in Table 2 is BB; the funding ratio is again 100%.

Understanding the Role of Diversification
by Guofu Zhou

Best Practice • Investments

EXECUTIVE SUMMARY

- Diversification is a way to reduce risk by investing in a variety of assets or business ventures.
- Systematic risk is not diversifiable, while idiosyncratic risk can be reduced or even eliminated.
- Portfolio diversification depends on risk-aversion and time horizon, and the portfolio mix must be rebalanced periodically.
- Overdiversification/"diworsification" can occur under certain conditions. Business diversification relies on endogenous opportunities, whose value depends on how flexibilities such as timing and expansion options are managed.

INTRODUCTION

To diversify is to do things with variety in order to improve well-being. Diversification is thus a common and fundamental concept in both daily life and business. However, the practice is primarily known as a way of reducing risk by investing in a variety of assets or business ventures. Buying one utility stock in the East coast and one in the West will minimize local shocks, while maintaining roughly the same return as buying either of the two alone. A shop at a resort selling both umbrellas and sunglasses clearly will have a less variable income whether a sunny or a rainy day comes up.

To obtain the optimal strategy of diversification, the risk must be defined and the associated investment opportunities modeled. In addition, the utility or investor's risk tolerance and investment horizon must be specified. In terms of asset allocation and portfolio choice, the risk is usually defined as the standard deviation of the portfolio return. This measures the variability of the return relative to the expected value of the return. Given a fixed level of expected return, the strategy that generates the minimum variance is preferred. To achieve this, the optimal diversification among the assets will usually be required. The risk tolerance of an investor determines the trade-off between return and risk, as well as the level of risk to take.

MODERN PORTFOLIO THEORY

Without a formal framework, *naive diversification* calls for an allocation of an equal amount of money across N assets, and thus it is also known as the $1/N$ rule. This rule goes back to as early as the fourth century, when Rabbi Issac bar Aha suggested: "One should always divide his wealth into three parts: a third in land, a third in merchandise, and a third ready to hand." Naive diversification is clearly not optimal in general. For example, when investing in a money market and a stock index, few investors will allocate 50% to the money market.

In 1951 Markowitz published his famous portfolio theory, which provides the optimal portfolio weights on a given N risky assets (stocks) once the expected returns, covariances, and variances of the assets are given, along with the investor's risk tolerance, in a quadratic utility function. The resulting optimal portfolio is a full diversification with money invested in all of the risky assets. The benefits of diversification depend more on how the assets perform relative to one another than on the number of assets you want to invest. The more the assets do not behave alike—that is, the lower the correlations among them—the more the risk can be minimized by holding the right mix of them.

The optimal portfolio is not risk-free. It is simply the one that has the minimum risk among all possible portfolios of the assets for a given a level of expected return. For any asset, one can decompose its total risk into two components, systematic/market-wide risk and idiosyncratic risk. The optimal portfolio has only market risk, because idiosyncratic risk is diversified away. As a result, there is no point in taking any idiosyncratic risk. But market risk is unavoidable. Intuitively, the return on a suitable portfolio of all stocks in the market has only the market risk, and will not be affected by bad news from some companies, which is likely to be offset by good news from others. However, a war, a national disaster, or a global crisis will likely affect the entire portfolio in one direction.

With leverage, the optimal portfolio can theoretically be designed to obtain any desired level of expected return by taking certain necessary risk. The greater the desired expected return on the optimal portfolio, the higher is

QFINANCE

53

the risk. Without borrowing and short selling, the diversified portfolio must have an expected return between the highest and the lowest of the asset expected returns. However, the risk is often much smaller than the lowest risk of all the assets.

An efficient portfolio is one that offers either the highest expected return for a given level of risk or the lowest level of risk for a given expected return. The efficient frontier represents that set of portfolios that has the maximum expected return for every given level of risk. No portfolio on the efficient frontier is any better than another. Depending on the investor's risk tolerance, the investor chooses theoretically one, and only one, efficient portfolio on the frontier.

The investment opportunity set is static in the mean–variance framework underlying the Markowitz portfolio theory. As investment opportunities change over time, many argue for *time diversification*—that the risk of stocks diminishes with the length of the investment horizon. While this is debatable, the benefit of diversification across assets, and much of the mean–variance theory, carry through into dynamic portfolio choice models with changing investment opportunities. However, due to incomplete information (such as parameter and model uncertainties), trading costs (such as learning and transaction costs), labor income, and solvency conditions, it can be optimal theoretically to *underdiversify*—to not invest in all assets. Diversification purely for the sake of diversification can cause unnecessary diversification or *overdiversification*, to end up *diworsification* i.e. worsening off from bad diversification.

CASE STUDY

A Stock Investment

Consider an investment in General Motors, or IBM, or the diversified S&P500 Index for 50 years from 1957 to 2007. Examined at a monthly frequency, and based on all the 50 years of data, the estimated expected return on the three assets are 1.12%, 0.84%, and 0.69% per month, and the estimated monthly standard deviations are 7.01%, 7.59%, and 4.13%, respectively. IBM has the highest expected return, with return per unit of risk of 0.16. Although the market has the estimated lowest expected return, its return per unit of risk is higher, 0.17. On the risk-adjusted basis, the market is the best of the three.

In practice, good firms like IBM are not easy to identify ex ante. If one randomly picks a single stock, the average expected return is almost the market return but with much higher risk. The same is true if one randomly chooses a small group of stocks. In fact, back in 1957, IBM, GM, and Eastman Kodak were all blue chip stocks in the famous Dow Jones Index. Eastman Kodak has long gone from the index, and GM it seems is on the verge of being the next to go, with its value drops of more than 75% up to October, 2008. In addition, many firms have gone bankrupt, merged, or been bought over the years. Hence it is important to hold a diversified portfolio and to manage it over time.

BUSINESS DIVERSIFICATION: REAL OPTIONS

With competition, the margin of any business diminishes over time. It is therefore vital for a company to make constant innovations and take on good growth opportunities. All of these activities are closely related to diversification. To enhance existing businesses, a company can diversify geographically in its production and R&D, and diversify vertically to take on more of the functions of the businesses previously run by others. While this increases efficiency and reliability, it also increases the risk exposure of the existing business. A company can, however, diversify horizontally by making new products and opening new markets.

Business diversification is, however, much more complex than stock investment diversification. First, the diversification possibilities are not obvious and have to be studied and developed with resources. Second, the risk and return on a new business are endogenously determined by how it is managed. Third, the benefits of diversification may not show up at the start. This is because existing businesses can be weakened when both management and financial resources are switched to diversification. Also, the new business will typically experience higher risk since the firm's management has less experience in running it.

Business diversification is almost always sequential. For any project, there are usually many embedded options, such as when to start, whether to expand, and how to switch. Optimal exercise of the options can enhance the value significantly, and so they should be analyzed carefully. Various risk management practices in a company can also be viewed as diversification whereby, to reduce risk, investments are made in financial assets or derivatives to offset the occasional negative payoffs of businesses. However, business diversification can be counterproductive if funds are inefficiently allocated across divisions, if division managers are self-interested, or if the conglomerates, created through mergers of already inefficient firms perhaps, remain inefficient. In addition, diversification typically provides consistent performance with less upside surprises. Academic research finds a *diversification discount*—that a diversified firm usually trades at a discount relative to a comparable matched portfolio of single-segment firms.

MAKING IT HAPPEN

For asset investments, while money managers can apply modern portfolio theory to diversify the risk with a desired level of return, individual investors can make use of the theory indirectly by investing in portfolios managed by the money managers. In practice this can be done via mutual funds and exchange traded funds. Large and wealthy investors can diversify even more with alternative asset classes such as hedge funds, collectibles (like art works), and exotic investment vehicles sold by large banks. They can diversify over various investment styles, managers, and brokerage accounts. For businesses, diversification means putting managerial and financial resources from your primary business into other opportunities. A small investment in strategic planning and diversification can pay off handsomely later. Vertical diversification may be the first to be started, though horizontal vehicles can be pursued at the same time. Diversification can increase the risk of the existing business but reduce the total risk exposure of the firm. However, the various flexibility options in diversification, such as timing and switching, must be valued carefully and managed efficiently to obtain the maximum diversification benefit.

CONCLUSION

For asset investments, diversification is an effective tool in reducing the risk of investments in stocks, bonds, and other securities. Utilizing the correlation structure among the assets, idiosyncratic risk can be reduced or even eliminated. For businesses, diversification is a strategic decision. It is vital for a firm's long-term value creation to identify and manage growth opportunities. Diversification is an important way to manage these opportunities well, reducing risk and ensuring success.

MORE INFO

Books:

Bodie, Zvi, Alex Kane, and Alan J. Marcus. *Investments*. 8th ed. New York: McGraw-Hill, 2009.

Campbell, John Y., and Luis M. Viceira. *Strategic Asset Allocation*. Oxford: Oxford University Press, 2002.

Markowitz, Harry M. *Portfolio Selection: Efficient Diversification of Investments*. Hoboken, NJ: Wiley, 1991.

Reports:

Liu, Hong. "Portfolio insurance and underdiversification." Working paper. November 29, 2008. Online at: ssrn.com/abstract=932581

Tu, Jun, and Guofu Zhou. "Being naive about naive diversification: Can investment theory be consistently useful?" Working paper. .July 2008. Online at: ssrn.com/abstract=1099293

Website:

Guofu Zhou's references on diversification: tinyurl.com/5rwk2kw [PDF].

When Form Follows Function: How Core–Satellite Investing Has Sparked an Era of Convergence by Christopher Holt

Best Practice • Investments

EXECUTIVE SUMMARY

- Core–satellite investing involves the separation of portfolios into a passively managed "core" (conforming to a strategic asset allocation framework) surrounded by actively managed "satellites" made up of active long-only funds and alternative investments.
- While this structure yields operational benefits, it stops short of its full potential as a portfolio construction rubric since it deals only with superficial labels (asset classes). Instead, institutional investors are beginning to think in terms of alpha (skill-based) returns and beta (index-based) returns.
- The separation of *alpha* and *beta*, regardless of their source, is a more accurate way to view core–satellite investing.
- This bifurcation has recently led to major changes in the way some pension portfolios are managed and in the way that asset managers service their clients. Asset classes once treated as separate or distinct are now converging into one integrated alpha/beta paradigm.
- Though challenges remain, there is little doubt that core–satellite investing has unleashed a wave of change that is reshaping asset management.

INTRODUCTION

"It is the pervading law of all things organic and inorganic...that form ever follows function."

Nineteenth century Chicago architect Louis Sullivan famously observed that a building's design must follow from its functional use. The same might be said about the design of modern portfolios and their management entities (pensions, endowments, asset managers, etc.). After emerging over the past decade as a simple portfolio management rubric, core–satellite investing is leading to a wholesale reengineering of the investment management function.

Core–satellite investing can generally be described as the separation of beta-centric (core) investing from alpha-centric (satellite) investing. However, the term has become stretched and overused. Today, "core" often refers to any number of passive asset classes and even to actively managed mandates. But a more literal definition of core as pure beta and satellite as pure alpha helps to shed light on one of the most significant underlying trends in asset management today—*convergence*.

HISTORY

Prior to modern portfolio theory little effort was made to distinguish between active and passive investing. All investing was simply seen as *active*. Then, in the 1960s, the capital asset pricing model (CAPM) revealed that security

and portfolio values could be expressed in terms of two distinct concepts: beta and alpha.

Still, the CAPM remained primarily an analytical technique until the 1990s, when index mutual funds and, soon afterwards, exchange-traded index funds (ETFs) provided investors with an efficient way to invest in the market passively. Advocates of the efficient markets hypothesis saw ETFs as a way to rid themselves of the scourge of active management. But, as evidenced by the continuing interest in mutual funds, many investors were not willing to give up on active management altogether. They wanted both active and passive returns, and they wanted them in a flexible and interchangeable format.

Alternative investments (hedge funds, private equity, real estate, infrastructure, and commodities), it turned out, were the ideal complement to these pure beta funds since their returns had a very low correlation with markets. Thus, a combination of a passively managed ETF and an actively managed alternative investment could be made essentially to approximate a traditional actively managed portfolio. And so the institutional example of core–satellite investing, "portable alpha," was born.

Portable alpha generally refers to a more efficient construction of sponsor portfolios that involves access to market returns (beta) synthetically via futures or swaps, and access to manager skills (alpha) separately, usually via

QFINANCE

57

an allocation to a hedge fund. Separating these two sources of returns provided institutional investors with greater flexibility than ever before.

In response to this trend, the asset management industry began to bifurcate into providers of "high alpha" and "cheap beta." As one industry supplier put it at the time:[1]

"The separation of Alpha from Beta is expected to shift profit away from traditional long only active funds toward the extremes of unconstrained Alpha-generating investing (more volatile pools, such as certain types of hedge funds and private equity) and passive investing (index funds, exchange-traded funds and certain types of derivatives)."

CONVERGENCE WITHIN INSTITUTIONAL PORTFOLIOS

By placing the major components of the strategic asset allocation in the "core" and more active alpha-generating investments in the "satellite," institutional investors gained flexibility and achieved cost reductions (Figure 1). For example, transitions between active managers (in the satellite) could be executed without incurring the costs of liquidating the core or hiring a transition manager. Also, by removing the benchmark constraint from satellite managers,

they are free to implement a greater portion of their investment ideas.

While innovative, this view of core satellite investing still relied on traditional asset class labels (large cap, small cap, hedge fund, etc.), and not on the underlying characteristics of these mandates identifying them as alpha or beta.

Since their introduction in 1949, hedge funds had been viewed by investors as a separate and distinct asset class. But by the early years of the 21st century, the separation, manipulation, and recombination of alpha and beta had begun to attract the interest of large institutional investors. These investors saw alternative investments as *alpha delivery vehicles* first and foremost.

Innovative public pension plans such as Sweden's AP7 (see case study) went a step further, ignoring labels such as "traditional" and "hedge fund," and reoriented their portfolios and organizations along the lines of alpha and beta *regardless of their respective sources.*

As a result, asset classes that have been managed separately are now converging into one business model whose salient parts are alpha and beta, not "traditional" and "hedge fund.

Figure 1. A "converged" approach to asset management combines aspects of both the traditional and alternative investment models

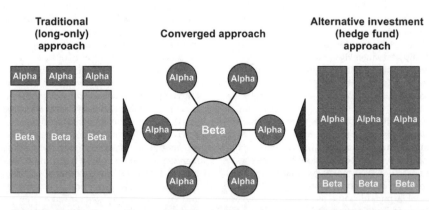

Traditional (long-only) approach	Converged approach	Alternative investment (hedge fund) approach
• Fees based on assets under management; • Hierarchical structure; • Stable investment theses; • Robust operations; • Well-evolved risk management systems; • Mature regulatory environment.	• Hybrid fee structures; • Matrix organizational structure; • Retooled operational environment; • Robust yet highly extensible risk management systems; • Quickly evolving regulatory environment.	• Fees based primarily on performance; • Flat structure; • Often long or short same names/theses; • Nascent operations; • Evolving risk management systems; • Weak regulatory environment.

CONVERGENCE WITHIN THE GREATER ASSET MANAGEMENT INDUSTRY

Faced with the headwind of a bull market between 2003 and 2007 and targeting the huge assets under management by traditional asset managers, many hedge funds launched long-biased (even long-only) funds during the past decade.

At the same time, traditional asset managers began to buy hedge fund companies, clearly attracted by their relatively high fees. In 2005, there were 30 major M&A transactions involving alternative investment managers.[2] The next year, the number doubled to 60, then rose again to 76 in 2007. These transactions rose from 20% of the total transaction volume for all asset management deals in 2005 to 32% only two years later.

By 2007, both hedge fund managers and long-only managers saw so-called "130/30" funds as a fertile middle ground between their two business models. Estimates of the potential size of this converged market quickly ranged up to US$2 trillion.[3]

Throughout this time, many mutual fund companies also launched long-short or market-neutral funds and marketed them alongside traditional mutual funds. Although these funds tended to underperform *bona fide* hedge funds, they *outperformed* their traditional mutual fund peers. Researchers attributed this to the more flexible investment strategies used by these so-called "hedged mutual funds."[4]

Today, most major traditional asset management firms run some form of hedge fund. And while many hedge fund companies have not yet launched separate long-only funds, researchers agree that hedge funds themselves have become increasingly correlated with markets—a form of *de facto* convergence.

KEY IMPLEMENTATION CHALLENGES

Convergence has now become the defining trend in the traditional investment management sector. The need to develop a convergence strategy is nowhere more apparent than within the executive suites of traditional investing's entrenched leadership. As the head of one US$800 billion asset management firm told the *Financial Times*:[5]

"On one side, you have exchange-traded funds and, on the other, you have [private equity firm] Blackstone and the hedge funds. It leaves firms like ours, traditional long-only buy-side firms, needing to make some very tough decisions."

Recent market calamities have required many financial institutions to sell off their asset management divisions to raise capital. Doing so

has only accelerated the forces that are driving hedge funds and long-only funds into each others' arms. But although we are well on our way to a "converged" industry, many business model challenges remain.

Some key implementation challenges are described below.

Fee Convergence

Chief among these challenges are the conflicting fee models used by traditional and alternative managers. According to a study by McKinsey & Company, the average hedge fund fee paid by an institutional investor in 2007 was 174 bps. The average fee paid for a domestic (US) equity mandate was 40 bps.[6]

But, beneath the surface of the posted fee rates, convergence is slowly but surely occurring. One study of US equity funds, for example, revealed that while the posted fees for many leading mutual funds were approximately 1% per annum, the effective fee per unit of active management was actually many times higher. If the beta portion of returns was assumed to be replicated by a low-cost ETF, the fees *per unit of active management* were 5% or more. Thus, a hedge fund with a 2% management fee, a 20% performance fee and a low market correlation could easily have the same fee as a traditional mutual fund.[7]

Cultural Convergence

In part due to this contrasting fee model, traditional asset managers have often faced challenges getting (traditionally higher-paid) hedge fund managers to work alongside (traditionally lower-paid) long-only managers.

Portfolio Management Convergence

Hedge fund managers are quick to say that short selling requires a skill set not readily available in a traditional long-only organization. Whether or not this is true, the management of two parallel funds with dramatically different fee structures can raise potential conflicts of interest for portfolio managers. For example, managers can have an incentive to allocate profitable trades to the fund with the performance fee.

But although such conflicts may exist, researchers have discovered that mutual funds managed alongside hedge funds actually perform better than mutual funds managed on their own. The opposite was not found to be true, however. Hedge funds managed alongside mutual funds perform on par with those managed alone.[8]

Operational Convergence

Due in part to industry consolidation, some hedge

fund managers have now become so large that their administrative and operational capabilities eclipse those of many mid-sized mutual fund companies. Well over half of the world's hedge fund assets are now managed by companies with at least three billion dollars of assets under management. Many of these firms are diversified financial institutions with many tens of billions of dollars in assets under management.

The varied success of hedge fund initial public offerings (IPOs) has revealed the importance of converged business models. As one M&A advisory firm put it:[9] "Public market investors like the growth story that alternative asset managers present, but they also want to see characteristics more akin to the broadly diversified fund managers they trust."

Risk Management Convergence

Hedge funds emerged from an environment of less regulation and proportionately less risk management infrastructure than traditional funds. Cognizant of this, institutional hedge fund investors are often more likely to demand complex risk analysis and exposure reporting from hedge funds than they do from their traditional managers.

Regulatory Convergence

Regulators such as the US Securities and Exchange Commission have long sought to bring hedge funds under the same regulatory umbrella as traditional investment advisers (although its efforts have been punctuated by intermittent setbacks).

The reports published by the President's Working Group on Financial Markets[10] in the United States and the Hedge Fund Working Group[11] in the United Kingdom make it clear that increased regulation—whether government-sponsored or self-imposed—is on its way. Short position disclosure requirements implemented by several regulators in October 2008 have simply added an exclamation mark to this trend.

Summary

This is only a brief list of the business issues arising from convergence in the asset management industry. Convergence will play out in unpredictable ways over the next decade as the investment management industry undergoes a fundamental realignment. This will require institutional investors, hedge funds, and traditional managers to retool their capabilities, to reorganize their structures, and to reinvent themselves. The new organizational form that emerges from the convergence of alternative and traditional investing will have characteristics associated with both models.

What began as a simple framework for organizing a portfolio has sparked a revolution in the way institutional investors and asset managers manage both their portfolios and their organizations. As Louis Sullivan declared, form has once again followed function.

CASE STUDY

Sweden's AP7 Pension Fund

At the end of 2007, Sweden's national pension system managed approximately US$190 billion. The system comprises seven separate "buffer" funds. Funds one through six manage assets for the system's defined benefit program, while the seventh (AP7) is the default fund for the system's defined contribution plan. About one third of the system's assets are managed in the defined contribution plan, with AP7 managing slightly more than US$14 billion.

Traditionally, the AP7 fund sought beta returns in the form of passive mandates in mature (informationally efficient) markets such as US large-cap equities and alpha returns in the form of active mandates in informationally inefficient markets such as Asian equities. Alpha was also sought via a separate and distinct class for hedge funds and private equity.

But in 2005, after poor performance from its traditional active managers, AP7 decided to restructure the fund in order to "improve the alpha opportunities for traditional long only portfolios." Vice-president Richard Grottheim described the program in AP7's 2007 annual report:[12]

"Separating the alpha management (active management) from the beta management (index management) has been discussed for years in the fund industry and among academics. But few have ever tried it in practice. At the AP7 Fund we decided three years ago to test this approach in our internal management of our equities portfolio."

In 2008 Grottheim and his colleagues described some of the challenges they faced and benefits they saw by implementing such a program:[13]

• *Organizational change*: Management described the most significant change as being a "complete specialization approach in the daily investment operation."

Core–Satellite Investing Has Sparked an Era of Convergence

- *Risk measurement*: While AP7 measured the risk of long-only managers using tracking error, this was not possible for pure alpha managers with no apparent benchmark.
- *Portfolio management*: Alpha managers were provided with no net capital, only a "notional amount" used as a baseline for risk measurement. As a result, AP7 management found it difficult to communicate and gain approval for the approach from traditional managers.
- *Fees*: AP7 also found it difficult to agree on an appropriate fee structure. There were no actual assets under management (AUM) amount for calculating management fees, and many had never charged performance-based fees before.
- *Benefits*: According to senior management, the change from traditional long-only portfolios to alpha/beta management has yielded several benefits for both investors and AP7:
- *Expanded universe:* The fund is now able to "search for skilled managers wherever they exist, even in asset classes outside the strategic allocation."
- *Fewer investment constraints:* Unlike in traditional long-only mandates, "unnecessary constraints are removed allowing the full insight of active managers to be reflected in portfolio positions."
- *Fee transparency:* Separating alpha returns from beta returns let AP7 "capture the full economies of beta management and pay active management fees that reflect a manager's skill and ability to add value." While the total fees charged for alpha managers were higher than traditional active managers, they were lower than true hedge funds.

MORE INFO

Books:

Callin, Sabrina. *Portable Alpha Theory and Practice: What Investors Really Need to Know.* Hoboken, NJ: Wiley, 2008.

Dorsey, Alan H. *Active Alpha: A Portfolio Approach to Selecting and Managing Alternative Investments.* Hoboken, NJ: Wiley, 2007.

Reports:

Engstrom, Stefan, Richard Grottheim, Peter Norman, and Christian Ragnartz. "Alpha–beta-separation: From theory to practice." Working paper. May 26, 2008. Online at: ssrn.com/abstract=1137673

Hubrich, Stefan. "An alpha unleashed: Optimal derivative portfolios for portable alpha strategies." Working paper. January 8, 2008. Online at: ssrn.com/abstract=1015327

Miller, Ross M. "Measuring the true cost of active management by mutual funds." Working paper. August 2005. Online at: ssrn.com/abstract=746926

Thomas, Lee R. "Engineering an alpha engine." PIMCO, February 2004. Online at: tinyurl.com/6a4jt24 [PDF].

NOTES

1 IBM Institute for Business Value. "The trader is dead, long live the trader! A financial markets renaissance." 2006. Online at: tinyurl.com/64u7vn5 [PDF].

2 Defined as "minority transactions, recapitalizations and IPOs" (Phillips, 2008; see note 9).

3 Tabb Group. "Asset flows move from long-only equities to hedge funds and active-extension funds in heightened search for alpha, says TABB Group." September 19, 2007. Online at: tinyurl.com/5wroon3

4 Agarwal, Vikas, Nicole M. Boyson, and Narayan Y. Naik. "Hedge funds for retail investors? An examination of hedged mutual funds." Working paper. June 2007. Online at: ssrn.com/abstract=891621

5 Brewster, Deborah. "Equity fund outflows bring need to adapt." Financial Times (April 27, 2008). Online at: tinyurl.com/68d7y52

6 McKinsey & Company. "The U.S. asset management industry: Smooth sailing gives way to choppy seas." September 2008. Online at: tinyurl.com/5r9e9ll [PDF].

7 Miller, 2005.

8 Nohel, Tom, Zhi Jay Wang, and Lu Zheng. "Side by side management of hedge funds and mutual funds." Working paper. March 2008. Online at: ssrn.com/abstract=1107675

9 Phillips, Benjamin F. "All shook up: M&A and capital markets activity in global fund management, 2007." Putnam Lovell, February 2008. Online at: tinyurl.com/6fgrvrg

10 Asset Managers' and Investors' Committee: www.amaicmte.org

11 Hedge Fund Working Group: www.hfwg.co.uk

12 "Sjunde AP-fonden annual report 2007." Online at: tinyurl.com/6ea54zh [PDF].

13 Engstrom, 2008.

The Role of Short Sellers in the Marketplace by Raj Gupta

EXECUTIVE SUMMARY

- This article examines the role of short-sellers in the marketplace. The process of short-selling involves three major participant groups: the lenders, the agent intermediaries, and the borrowers.
- First, the history of short-selling is discussed briefly. This includes the enactment of the Securities Exchange Act of 1934, the adoption of the uptick rule following concentrated short-selling in 1937, and the relaxation of that rule in 2007.
- Next, the short-sale process is discussed. Five categories of short positions are identified. These categories include general collateral, reduced rebate, reduced rebate and fail, fail only, and buy-in.
- Third, the borrowers are identified and their activities are discussed. These borrowers include hedge funds, mutual funds, ETF counterparties, and option market-makers.
- Fourth, the lenders are identified and their motivations for lending are discussed. The primary lenders include mutual funds and pension funds.
- Fifth, historical statistics on the universe of lendable securities and the percentage of loaned equities are presented. A dramatic increase in the level of loaned securities is observed for the period 2006 to the second quarter of 2008 followed by significant declines in the third and fourth quarters of 2008. Since then, the level of loaned securities has gradually increased by 12%.
- Finally a brief review of the academic literature on short-selling is conducted.

INTRODUCTION

The term "short-selling" or "shorting" is used to describe the process of selling financial instruments (such as equities or futures) that the seller or holder does not actually own but borrows from various sources. If the value of the instrument declines, the short-seller can repurchase the instrument at a lower price and cover the loan. Short-sellers have long played the crucial role of price discovery in financial markets. If short-selling were not allowed, traders with negative views of certain stocks would at best avoid those stocks. However, short-selling allows them to generate returns based on their views if they are correct, hence making short-selling an important aspect in price discovery. Companies in certain countries where short-selling is not allowed may also list on the exchanges of countries where it is allowed. After the crash of 1929, the US Congress created the Securities and Exchange Commission (SEC) by enacting the Securities Exchange Act of 1934. Following an inquiry into the effects of concentrated short-selling during the market break of 1937, the SEC adopted Rule 10a-1. Rule 10a-1(a)(1) stated that, subject to certain exceptions, a listed security may be sold short:

- at a price above the price at which the immediately preceding sale was effected ("plus tick"); or

- at the last sale price if it is higher than the last different price ("zero-plus tick").

This implied that short sales were not permitted on minus ticks or zero-minus ticks, subject to narrow exceptions. The operation of these provisions was commonly described as the "tick test." Both the New York Stock Exchange (NYSE) and the American Stock Exchange (Amex) had elected to use the prices of trades on their own floors for the tick test. In 2007, the Commission voted to adopt amendments to Rule 10a-1 and Regulation SHO that removed Rule 10a-1 as well as any short sale price test of any self-regulatory organization (SRO). In addition, the amendments prohibited any SRO from having a price test. The amendments included a technical amendment to Rule 200(g) of Regulation SHO that removed the "short-exempt" marking requirement of that rule.

On July 15, 2008, the SEC issued an emergency order related to short-selling securities of 19 substantial financial firms,[1] which took effect July 21, 2008. This order stated that any person executing a short sale in the publicly traded securities of 19 financial firms, using the means or instrumentalities of interstate commerce, must borrow or arrange to borrow the security or otherwise have the security available to borrow in its inventory prior to executing the short sale. On September 19, 2008, the SEC, acting in concert with the UK Financial Services Authority, took temporary emergency action[2] to prohibit short-selling in 799 financial companies to protect the integrity and quality of the securities market and strengthen investor confidence. This ban was lifted on October 8, 2008.

In this article we will examine the role of short-sellers. The profile of short-sellers includes hedge funds and other speculators, proprietary desks of bank holding companies, options market-makers, and, in recent years, mutual funds that execute 1X0/X0 strategies. We will discuss the academic literature on short sales, illustrate the short-sale process, examine the role of various participants in the process including lenders such as mutual funds and pension funds, agent intermediaries such as prime brokers, and borrowers such as hedge funds, mutual funds, and options market-makers, and we will present statistics on the universe of lendable and loaned securities. We find that the level of securities loaned versus the total universe of lendable securities increased dramatically during the period 2006 to the second quarter of 2008, followed by significant declines in the third and fourth quarters of 2008.

THE SHORT-SALE PROCESS

There are generally three groups of players in the short-sale process. The groups are securities lenders, securities borrowers (short-sellers), and agent intermediaries.

Securities lenders: Securities lenders are institutions with securities portfolios of sufficient size to make securities lending worthwhile. Generally these institutions include mutual funds, insurance companies, pension funds, and endowments. The lending activities of these groups are discussed in greater detail later.

Securities borrowers: Securities borrowers are institutions that engage in short-selling either as part of their trading strategies or to hedge their risk exposures. These institutions include hedge funds, mutual funds, ETF counterparties, and option market-makers. We will examine these groups in detail in the next section.

Agent intermediaries: Agent Intermediaries are institutions that facilitate the lending and borrowing of securities. These institutions may include custodian banks, broker-dealers, and/or prime brokers. We will examine the functions of these groups later.

Figure 1. The short-sale process

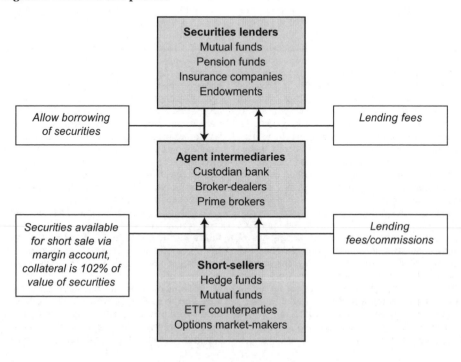

The process illustrated in Figure 1 works well if there are plenty of shares available to borrow. However, one must consider another possibility: What if shares desired for borrowing purposes are unavailable? Several academic articles have examined impediments to the short-selling process. Evans, Geczy, Musto, and Reed (2009) group short positions from an unnamed options market-maker into five categories: general collateral, reduced rebate, reduced rebate and fail, fail only, and buy-in. These categories as defined in their database as follows:

- *General collateral* indicates that a stock has been loaned at the normal rebate rate, i.e. the stock is easy to borrow.
- *Reduced rebate* indicates that the rebate rate is below the general collateral rate, i.e. the stock is special.
- *Reduced rebate and fail* indicates that some shares have been borrowed at a reduced rebate and that the market-maker failed to deliver some shares that were sold short.
- *Fail only* indicates that the market-maker failed to deliver any of the shares in this short position.
- *Buy-in* indicates that the counterparty of the short-sale transaction is forcing delivery on some or all of the shares in the short position.

One would expect a significant majority of short positions to fall into the general collateral category. More than 90% of the short positions in the database used by Evans *et al.* (2009) fell into that category.

THE KEY SHORT-SELLERS

In this section we will examine the key short-sellers. While certain participants may engage in short-selling by virtue of their trading strategy, others may engage in short sales to hedge their risk exposures (see Figure 1 for an illustration of the short-sale process). We will examine in detail each of these groups below.

Hedge Funds and Other Speculators

Several hedge fund strategies employ shorting stocks as part of their strategy. In the case of convertible arbitrage, the arbitrageur generally takes long positions in convertible bonds and sells short the underlying stock. In the case of equity strategies, managers may use fundamental or quantitative analysis to sell stocks short. Long/short equity strategies generally comprise the bulk of the hedge fund universe both in terms of assets under management as well as number of funds. In the case of merger arbitrage, managers sell short the acquiring company, while short-biased strategies engage in short-selling of seemingly overvalued stocks.

Bank Holding Companies

Prior to the recent requests by Goldman Sachs and Morgan Stanley to change their status to bank holding companies, investment banks borrowed stock for their proprietary trading desks.[3] However, these and other banks will continue to borrow stock for their proprietary trading desks and other functions.

Short and Ultra-Short Exchange-Traded Funds

In recent years, several exchange-traded funds have been established that offer either the inverse or twice the inverse of the returns on a certain index. These exchange-traded funds are generally referred to as short-ETF or ultra-short ETF. The funds generally achieve their short exposure using derivatives such as swaps. Although these funds generally do not short underlying stocks, they retain the ability to do so if necessary.

ETF Counterparties

One of the primary instruments that the short- and ultra-short exchange-traded funds described in the previous section use to achieve their exposures is swaps. The counterparty in the swap transaction may choose to hedge its exposures by shorting stocks.

Mutual Funds

In recent years several firms have launched 1X0/X0-type funds. Generally, the equities owned by the fund equal 1X0% of its net asset value, while the equities shorted equal X0% of the fund's net asset value. Although the vast majority of 1X0/X0-type funds are offered through separate accounts, there are several mutual funds that are available to the public.

Option Market-Makers

Options market-makers short-sell securities on a regular basis for hedging purposes. They are, however, exempt from locating shares before short-selling.

THE KEY EQUITY LENDERS

In this section we will examine the key lenders. These institutional lenders include mutual funds, pension funds, insurance companies, and endowments (see Figure 1 for an illustration of the short-sale process). Generally, the lending activities take place through an intermediary agent such as a custodian bank or broker-dealer.

These intermediary agents pool securities from various lenders who are unable to lend securities directly. Most broker-dealers combine their security-lending activities with their prime-brokerage operations. We will examine each of these groups next.

Mutual Funds

The US mutual fund industry managed around US$12 trillion in assets as of year-end 2007. Stock mutual funds accounted for 54% of the total mutual fund industry. In light of the actions of the SEC relating to the banning of short sales on the securities of 799 financial firms, two major mutual funds, Vanguard Group Inc. and State Street Corp., imposed additional restrictions that halted the lending of their shares.[4] However, lending fees received by mutual funds can be substantial and permanent restrictions may impact revenues.

Pension Funds

Equities form a major component in the asset allocation of defined contribution (DC) plans. According to Pensions & Investment online,[5] more than 50% of assets in corporate DC plans are allocated to equities, while significant percentages are allocated by public and union DC plans as well. Defined benefit plans have a significant percentage of assets allocated to equities as well. Pension funds participate significantly in the equity-lending market.

The reasons for lending securities include not only the offsetting of custody and administrative costs but also the generation of revenue. The infrastructure to support securities lending varies from lender to lender. Lenders sometimes impose credit restrictions. As noted earlier, certain lenders imposed restrictions on borrowing activities in light of the SEC rules prohibiting short-selling.

SUMMARY DATA ON SHORT SALES

In previous sections we examined the various aspects of the short-sale process and the key players. In this section we will look at the data on short sales. Figure 2 presents statistics on total lendable equities worldwide. The data were obtained from the Risk Management Association.[6]

The universe of lendable equities (or lendable assets, represented on the left axis in Figure 2) denotes the total dollar value of equities available for lending worldwide. These include North American, European, and Pacific-rim equities (including Australia) along with other equities not included in the aforementioned categories. The figures are reported as aggregate assets without consideration of client- or bank-imposed guidelines. The universe of loaned

Figure 2. Universe of lendable (left axis) versus loaned (right axis) equities worldwide

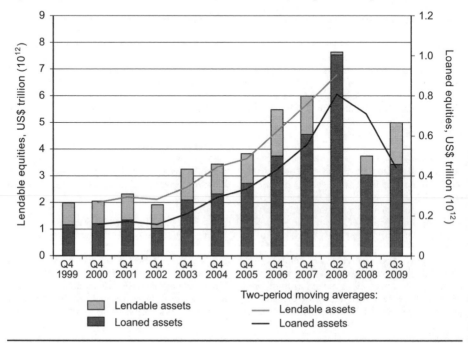

Best Practice • Investments

assets (right axis in Figure 2) represents the total dollar value of equities loaned worldwide.

One of the interesting aspects is the growth in the universe of lendable assets from around US$2 trillion in 1999 to more than US$7 trillion at the end of the second quarter of 2008. Expectedly, the universe shrank between 2001 and 2002 and then experienced a steady increase.

The level of loaned assets worldwide has followed a similar pattern. However, the level of loaned assets experienced a dramatic increase, from less than US$600 billion at the end of 2006 to over US$1 trillion at the end of the second quarter of 2008. The numbers definitively capture the sentiments of short-sellers leading up to the third and fourth quarters of 2008.

The significant increases in the levels of loaned equities in the years 2006–2008 suggest a negative outlook on the stock market on the part of certain traders. In fact, the first signs of the subprime debacle can be traced back to early 2007. Stock prices of bond insurers such as Ambac and MBIA recorded their all-time highs in early 2007 before declining precipitously to 15-year lows in 2008, losing more than 90% of their value. The stock prices of erstwhile investment banks such as Bear Stearns and Lehman Brothers also followed similar patterns before the former merged with JP Morgan and the latter filed for bankruptcy. Further, Fannie Mae, Freddie Mac, American International Group (AIG), Merrill Lynch, Citigroup, Wachovia, and American Express among many others also witnessed precipitous declines in the value of their equities. These numbers, as well as media reports, suggest that short-biased traders such as certain hedge funds correctly predicted the decline of these companies, thus generating enormous capital appreciation for their investors (such as pension funds, endowments, and foundations). The two-period moving average lines show this more explicitly.

In Figure 3 we explore levels of lendable assets for North America, Europe, and the Pacific Rim. Not surprisingly, North American and European equities represent a significant portion of the total dollar value of lendable equities worldwide. In Figure 4 we explore levels of loaned assets for the same regions. Again, the total dollar value of loaned North American and European equities represents a significant portion of the universe.

By the end of 2008 the level of loaned equities dropped to around 408 billion dollars, a fall of almost 60%. Numerous factors contributed to this decline, including the meltdown of equity markets, the ban on short-selling of financial stocks, and the self-imposed restrictions on stock lending by various financial institutions. It is also interesting to note that the levels of loaned assets have gradually increased to around 458 billion dollars as of the third quarter 2009, an increase of around 12%.

Figure 3. Universe of lendable equities in North America, Europe, and the Pacific Rim

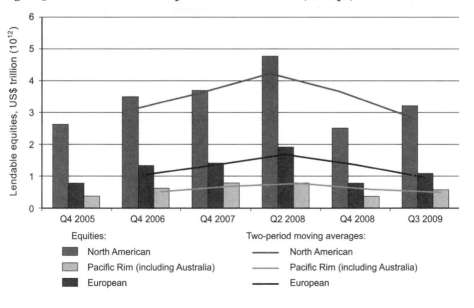

Figure 4. Universe of loaned equities in North America, Europe, and the Pacific Rim

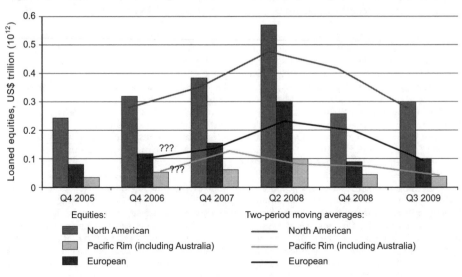

LITERATURE REVIEW

A plethora of academic articles have examined various aspects of short-selling. In this section we will examine some of these articles and their contribution to the literature.

Seneca (1967) examined the net effects of large short positions using data between 1946 and 1965 and found that short sales acted as a predictor of stock prices. Baron and McDonald (1973) explored the risk–return patterns of reported short positions. Using data from the NYSE over the period 1961–1966, they found that stocks with more idiosyncratic risk had higher short interest. Brent, Morse, and Stice (1990) examined the increase in short interest over the period 1974–1986. They found that stocks with convertible securities, options, and high betas tended to have more shares held short. Further, Figlewski and Webb (1993) examined the effects of options on short sales. Using data from the Center for Research in Security Prices (CRSP) and Interactive Data Corp. (IDC) over the period 1969–1985, they found that options facilitated short-selling.

More recently Geczy, Musto, and Reed (2002) have examined short-selling costs and constraints. Using data from an unnamed custodian bank over the period 1998–1999, they found that short-selling frictions appear strongest in merger arbitrage. Bris, Goetzmann, and Zhu (2007) investigated the relation between short sales and market efficiency

in world markets. Using data from various investment banks[7] over the period 1990–2001, they found that markets where short-selling is prohibited display significantly less negative skewness. Boehmer, Jones, and Zhang (2008) considered whether short-sellers are informed. Using data from CRSP and the NYSE over the period 2000–2004, they found that short-sellers are well informed and contribute to efficient stock prices. Diether, Lee, and Werner (2008) studied the trading strategies used by short-sellers. Using data from various exchanges for 2005, they found that short-sellers in both NYSE and NASDAQ stocks increased their short-selling activity after periods of positive returns. Finally Evans, Geczy, Musto, and Reed (2009) explored whether options market competition tends to oligopoly as stocks become difficult to short. Using data from a large options market-maker over the period 1998–1999, they found that market-makers profit when they fail to deliver stock.

CONCLUSION

In this article we examined the role of short-sellers in the marketplace. We showed that the process of short-selling involves three major participant groups: the lenders, the agent intermediaries, and the borrowers. We discussed the history of short-selling, including the enactment of the Securities Exchange Act of 1934, the adoption of the uptick rule in

1937, and the relaxation of that rule in 2007. We then discussed the short-sale process and identified five categories of short positions. Further, we discussed the profile of borrowers and lenders and provided historical statistics on the percentage of lendable securities and loaned equities. We observed a dramatic increase in the level of loaned securities between 2006 and the second quarter of 2008, followed by a dramatic decline by the fourth quarter of 2008. Finally, we presented a brief review of the academic literature on short-selling.

MORE INFO

Articles:

Boehmer, Ekkehart, Charles M. Jones, and Xiaoyan Zhang. "Which shorts are informed?" *Journal of Finance* 63:2 (April 2008): 491–527. Online at: dx.doi.org/10.1111/j.1540-6261.2008.01324.x

Brent, Averil, Dale Morse and E. Kay Stice. "Short interest: Explanations and tests." *Journal of Financial and Quantitative Analysis* 25:2 (June 1990): 273–289. Online at: dx.doi.org/10.2307/2330829

Bris, Arturo, William N. Goetzmann, and Ning Zhu. "Efficiency and the bear: Short sales and markets around the world." *Journal of Finance* 62:3 (June 2007): 1029–1079. Online at: dx.doi.org/10.1111/j.1540-6261.2007.01230.x

Diether, Karl B., Kuan-Hui Lee, and Ingrid M. Werner. "Short-sale strategies and return predictability." *Review of Financial Studies* 22:2 (February 2009): 575–607. Online at: dx.doi.org/10.1093/rfs/hhn047

Evans, Richard B., Christopher C. Geczy, David K. Musto, and Adam V. Reed. "Failure is an option: Impediments to short selling and options prices." *Review of Financial Studies* 22:5 (May 2009): 1955–1980. Online at: dx.doi.org/10.1093/rfs/hhn083

Figlewski, Stephen, and Gwendolyn P. Webb. "Options, short sales, and market completeness." *Journal of Finance* 48:2 (June 1993): 761–777. Online at: www.jstor.org/stable/2328923

Geczy, Christopher C., David K. Musto, and Adam V. Reed. "Stocks are special too: An analysis of the equity lending market." *Journal of Financial Economics* 66:2–3 (November–December 2002): 241–269. Online at: dx.doi.org/10.1016/S0304-405X(02)00225-8

McDonald, John G., and Donald C. Baron. "Risk and return on short positions in common stocks." *Journal of Finance* 28:1 (March 1973): 97–107. Online at: www.jstor.org/stable/2978171

Seneca, Joseph J. "Short interest: Bearish or bullish." *Journal of Finance* 22:1 (March 1967): 67–70. Online at: www.jstor.org/stable/2977301

Websites:

Australian Securities Lending Association (ASLA): www.asla.com.au

High short interest stocks: www.highshortinterest.com

International Securities Lending Association (ISLA): www.isla.co.uk

NASDAQ short interest: www.nasdaqtrader.com/asp/short_interest.asp

Pan Asia Securities Lending Association (PASLA): www.paslaonline.com

Risk Management Association (RMA): www.rmahq.org/RMA

Securities Industry and Financial Markets Association (SIFMA): www.sifma.org

ShortSqueeze.com: www.shortsqueeze.com

NOTES

1 These companies include BNP Paribas Securities Corp. (BNPQF or BNPQY), Bank of America Corporation (BAC), Barclays PLC (BCS), Citigroup Inc. (C), Credit Suisse Group (CS), Daiwa Securities Group Inc. (DSECY), Deutsche Bank Group AG (DB), Allianz SE (AZ), Goldman Sachs Group Inc. (GS), Royal Bank ADS (RBS), HSBC Holdings PLC ADS (HBC and HSI), JPMorgan Chase & Co., (JPM), Lehman Brothers Holdings Inc. (LEH), Merrill Lynch & Co., Inc. (MER), Mizuho Financial Group, Inc. (MFG), Morgan Stanley (MS), UBS AG (UBS), Freddie Mac (FRE), and Fannie Mae (FNM).

2 For more information see www.sec.gov/news/press/2008/2008-211.htm

3 The US House of Representatives on December 11, 2009, passed a 1,279-page Bank Reform bill (Financial Stability Improvement Act of 2009) that seeks to prohibit proprietary trading if it puts the firm's safety and soundness at risk. See "Winners and losers in the Bank Reform bill." *Wall Street Journal* "Dear Journal" blog (December 11, 2009). Online at: tinyurl.com/6f89h7c. To become law, the bill would have to pass the Senate, which would be a tall order.

4 See "2 mutual fund firms act to halt short sales." *Boston Globe* (September 23, 2008). Online at: tinyurl.com/4yze4w

5 For more information see www.pionline.com

6 For more information see www.rmahq.org/RMA

7 The term "investment bank" ceased to exist in 2008 when the last two remaining investment banks, Goldman Sachs and Morgan Stanley, asked the Federal Reserve to be converted to bank holding companies following the failures of Bear Stearns and Lehman Brothers and the announcement of the merger of Merrill Lynch with Bank of America.

How Stockholders Can Effectively Engage with Companies by James Gifford

EXECUTIVE SUMMARY

* The executive director of the United Nations-backed Principles for Responsible Investment shares his experience of working with and researching stockholders who actively engage with the companies in which they invest.
* He argues that the effectiveness of such engagement is driven by 12 key factors. These include the business case behind a stockholder request, the values of the target company managers, the assertiveness and persistence of the stockholder, and the policy environment in which the engagement takes place.
* Above all, the most influential factor may be whether the company itself wants to change.

INTRODUCTION

How many social workers does it take to change a light bulb? One. But the bulb has got to *want* to change. This is also the theme of this essay on stockholder engagement—the practice of investors seeking to influence corporate behavior for the better.

Institutional investors are increasingly engaging in dialog with companies for the purpose of improving some aspect of a company's environmental or social impact, corporate governance, or strategic performance. This practice is widely known as "stockholder engagement." As of early 2009, the UN-backed Principles for Responsible Investment (PRI), which contain commitments to active ownership, had over 470 signatories representing more than US$18 trillion in assets under management. Surveys of these signatories show that more than half engage in dialog with companies, either directly or as part of broader investor collaborations, to influence corporate behavior.

If stockholders want to influence corporate behavior, the company has got to *want* to change. Unless the stockholder has a large stake in a company, they are simply one of many stakeholders in the firm. If the stockholder wants the company to change, the company's managers must be convinced that it is in the best interests of the company to do whatever it is the stockholders are asking.

THE ESSENTIALS OF EFFECTIVE ENGAGEMENT

So what makes for successful engagement? There are 12 key factors that stockholders should consider when seeking to influence a company.

The Values of the Company's Managers Should Be Broadly Aligned with the Premise of the Investors' Request

When an investor engages in a dialog with a company, each of the participants in the conversation must understand from where the other is coming. They should not be too far apart. If, for example, there is a CEO who simply doesn't believe that climate change exists, then it is likely that a request to enhance disclosures of greenhouse gas emissions will fall on deaf ears. If the company's managers are on an entirely different wavelength, it may be wise to expend resources elsewhere, or focus on a topic where the differences are not so great. That said, these companies may well be those where management is so out of touch that it is causing severe damage to the company's prospects. In such cases, the stockholder needs to weigh up the costs and benefits of a long and protracted effort to get the message through.

Strong Business Case

Stockholders need to present a very strong business case, ideally backed up by some kind of evidence. There are many issues that companies have not considered in detail, and in many cases companies are unaware of best practices followed by peers in their industry. The stronger the business case for companies to do something differently, the more likely they are to recognize that the investor has a point.

Assertiveness and Persistence

The UK government-commissioned Myners Report stated that "merely meeting senior management and expressing polite reservations about strategy is not sufficient if it is not effective." CalPERS' legendary 1990s CEO Dale Hanson stated that "kinder, gentler, is not working" when referring to the fund's escalation of activism by its stockholders. But again, assertiveness needs to be appropriate, as the company has got to *want* to change, and if a stockholder is too assertive, it may lead to greater resistance by the company.

Persistence is another important attribute that contributes to effective stockholder engagement. Companies are often slow-moving beasts, and paradigms take time to change. Stockholders need to hang in there for the long term, as engagements can take up to three years to bear fruit. For example, a group of US funds, including Domini and Calvert, successfully encouraged Gap to release its first social responsibility report after two years of dialog.

Building Coalitions with Other Stockholders and Stakeholders
One investor alone, even if it is a large pension fund, has limited capacity to engage with a company. Many large funds hold thousands of companies in their portfolios. It is important that, to promote changes in company behavior, stockholders work together to pool resources and influence. Many investors have the same concerns about particular companies or sectors. In addition, it is more efficient for companies to have a deeper and more comprehensive dialog with well-informed representatives from a group of investors, than having the same superficial conversation with many different stockholder representatives.

There are also opportunities for stockholders to collaborate with other stakeholders, such as NGOs and public policy-makers. Again, it is important that these collaborations are constructive and not seen as ganging up on the company. In many cases, NGOs can provide considerable expertise to companies about managing complex sustainability issues, and many of these organizations work with companies on a routine basis. For example, Insight Investment teamed up with the World Wide Fund for Nature (WWF) to conduct a benchmark of UK-listed house building companies, a process which led to the establishment of the Next Generation benchmark, a multi-stakeholder initiative supported by the house building sector itself.

Going Public
There is no doubt that in certain circumstances it can be useful for a stockholder to up the ante and go public with his or her concerns about a company's behavior. However, this should be a last resort, because forcing a company to do something in reaction to negative publicity or embarrassment is not a recipe for long-term buy-in by the company, which is what the

stockholder really wants. Again, the company has got to *want* to change.

Alignment with the Interests of the Company, and Being Internally Consistent
For a company to *want* to change, the managers have to feel that the stockholder genuinely has its interests at heart. There may be many points of disagreement, at least initially, but if the company and the stockholder both share a common commitment to the company's long-term success, it will make the engagement much more constructive.

Stockholder organizations also need to be internally consistent. The equities analysts in a fund management organization are often not closely linked with the ESG (environmental, social, governance) people, and they send mixed signals to companies. For example, in their discussions with companies the analysts, may be focusing on short-term financial factors, while the ESG or governance people are talking about longer-term ESG or structural issues. The stockholder organization needs to ensure that it is joined up internally and is sending consistent signals to those companies with which it interacts.

Supportive Political and Policy Environment
If stockholders mirror the political and policy environment, they are more likely to gain a positive response from companies. Regulators are the most powerful stakeholders in a firm. Where there is regulatory momentum on an issue, or clear indications from public policy-makers that they would like companies to move in a certain direction, this provides fertile ground for stockholders to give companies a push along. There is also a very persuasive argument for companies to be well ahead of the regulatory curve.

Make Sure that Your People Are Credible, Senior, Experienced, and Knowledgeable
Company managers know more about their companies than anyone else. Stockholder representatives need to have the expertise and knowledge to add value to the conversation with the company.

Use of Voting and Stockholder Resolutions
Voting against management and filing stockholder resolutions at company AGMs is another tool in the stockholder engagement toolbox. Companies will go to some lengths to avoid embarrassing votes against management or the filing of stockholder resolutions. But again, stockholder resolutions should be used as a last resort as, being seen as hostile acts, they

How Stockholders Can Effectively Engage with Companies

can undermine the legitimacy of stockholders in the eyes of the company.

Societal Legitimacy

It is helpful, though not essential, that the issue on which the investor is engaging is also one that has strong support within the community. It is more likely that a company will recognize the importance of addressing an issue where there is some momentum for change, and it is likely that regulation, NGO pressure, or consumer pressure will emerge in the future.

An Implicit or Explicit Threat of Divestment?

Companies spend significant resources on investor relations, presumably because they value the marginal buyer or seller of their stock. If a stockholder is a large one, a threat of divestment can increase a company's motivation to work with that stockholder to address the issue of concern.

However, divestment is a two-edged sword, and once a stockholder has sold out, it no longer has a relationship with that company. That said, a number of pension funds, such as the Norwegian Government Pension Fund, continue their discussions with divested companies, keeping open the possibility of reinvesting.

Does Size Matter?

It would seem intuitive that large investors would have a greater ability to influence companies. However, while this might be true to an extent, it does not mean that small investors cannot be very influential. For example, Calvert, a US-based sustainable and responsible investment (SRI) fund, played an important role in encouraging Dell to implement a computer take-back and recycling scheme. This was because Calvert brought with it significant experience on these issues and became a trusted adviser to Dell on this process. Dell also saw Calvert as a key stakeholder with which it could have a constructive relationship.

CASE STUDY

Collaborative Stockholder Engagement

Morley Fund Management (now Aviva Investors) led a collaborative engagement in 2008 focused on the UN Global Compact, a set of ten principles of corporate responsibility. Working closely with the UN-backed Principles for Responsible Investment, a coalition of 20 investors representing approximately US$2.13 trillion in assets was developed. The coalition sent letters to company chief executives focused on adherence to the disclosure requirement of the UN Global Compact, which is known as a Communication on Progress (or COP).

Without adequate reporting on progress, signing up by companies to the Global Compact's ten principles represents little more than a statement of good intentions. While an engagement focused on reporting is only a part of the process of improvement advocated by the UN Global Compact, it represents the most obvious initial area in which investors have the most potential leverage and influence.

Depending on whether the company was a leader or a laggard in meeting this COP disclosure requirement, the coalition either welcomed good practice or challenged the company to achieve full participant status. In total, the investors wrote to the CEOs of 103 companies in more than 30 different countries, with 25 companies receiving the group's congratulations, and 78—the laggards—being asked to improve their adherence to the Compact. The engagement resulted in over 32% of the companies identified as laggards subsequently submitting a communication on progress and improving their involvement with the UN Global Compact.

The success of the exercise also played a part in stimulating the launch in October 2008 of the "Seoul Initiative"—a collaboration among 52 PRI signatories asking almost 9,000 listed companies to join the UN Global Compact.

CONCLUSION

Some of the factors identified above are related to the legitimacy of the investor and their case in the eyes of the company (specifically, the credibility of the stockholder representatives, the business case, and the political support for an issue). Some of the factors are power-related, that is, they seek to force the company to do something it doesn't want to do (going public and filing stockholder resolutions). If investors want the company to *want* to change, they should focus on those approaches that build legitimacy and good relationships with the company and only use the power-oriented tools when all else fails.

And what if the company simply doesn't want to change? If the issue is crucial to the stockholder, then there needs to be a willingness to dig in over the long term, build coalitions with other stockholders, make public statements, file stockholder resolutions, and, where necessary, take legal action to ensure that stockholders' interests are protected.

MORE INFO

Books:

Davis, Stephen, Jon Lukomnik, and David Pitt-Watson. *The New Capitalists: How Citizen Investors Are Reshaping the Corporate Agenda*. Watertown, MA: Harvard Business School Press, 2006.

Hebb, Tessa. *No Small Change: Pension Funds and Corporate Engagement*. Ithaca, NY: Cornell University Press, 2008.

Kiernan, Matthew J. *Investing in a Sustainable World: Why Green is the New Color of Money on Wall Street*. New York: AMACOM, 2008.

Krosinsky, Cary, and Nick Robins (eds). *Sustainable Investing: The Art of Long Term Performance*. London: Earthscan, 2008.

Sullivan, Rory, and Craig Mackenzie (eds). *Responsible Investment*. Sheffield, UK: Greenleaf Publishing, 2006.

Websites:

Principles for Responsible Investment (UNEP Finance Initiative and UN Global Compact): www.unpri.org

Responsible Investor: www.responsible-investor.com

Social Investment Forum: www.socialinvest.org

UNEP Finance Initiative: www.unepfi.org

UN Global Compact: www.unglobalcompact.org

Money Managers by David Pitt-Watson

EXECUTIVE SUMMARY

* Money managers invest trillions of dollars on behalf of millions of individuals.
* Investments primarily involve the holding and trading of shares.
* Money managers that own equities have a powerful role in the governance of companies, should they choose to exercise it.
* Active stockholders can be of great influence on how, and by whom, companies are managed.

A VAST AND DIVERSE INDUSTRY

Money managers (also known as fund managers or investment managers) manage money on behalf of other people. In most Western countries more than half the population will, directly or indirectly, have a money manager working for them. The managers find suitable investments, and are usually given the discretion by clients to make investments on their behalf.

It is usually the client who owns the investment and takes the risk that it will do well or badly. Therefore placing money with a money manager is different from putting it in a bank account. The bank offers a given return on your money, and it takes the risk on any loan or investment it may make.

The biggest money managers are household names; often they are part of banks or insurance companies. Examples are Fidelity, Vanguard, Barclays Global Investors, Nippon Life, Generali, Allianz, AXA, and Legal and General. Each of these companies manages hundreds of billions, and sometimes over a trillion dollars of people's savings. They have both individual clients and large institutional clients, such as pension funds, who will in turn represent many thousands of savers.

There are literally hundreds of money managers. Sometimes one money manager will use the funds they have under management to invest in another money manager's fund if they feel that gives them access to particular investment skills. And each may offer scores of different funds, each one designed to attract the savings of a particular type of investor.

Money managers invest in all sorts of things, from property to commodities, from government bonds to exchange rate futures. But their largest investments are in the shares and bonds issued by large companies, typically publicly traded companies, whose securities can be easily bought and sold should the need arise.

Money managers are hugely significant in large and developed capital markets. More than 80% of public company shares in the United Kingdom are owned through money managers.

In the United States, Japan, and much of Continental Europe, the figure is around 70% and growing.[1]

SOME HISTORY AND CONTEXT

The growth of these financial giants is a comparatively modern phenomenon. In the early days of the Industrial Revolution most companies were both owned and managed by the founders and their families. Over the generations these families had less interest in management and wished to realize the value of their stockholding. One way to do so was to sell some of their shares on the stock market. And being quoted on the stock market had other advantages, in particular, access to a large pool of capital for companies needing finance.

Thus was born the significant stock markets that have now developed in most modern economies.

However, to manage investment in these companies requires a degree of expertise. First, to choose appropriate companies in which to invest. Second, to manage the administration of the various financial transactions that companies undertake, from paying dividends, to rights issues, share splits and repurchases, voting, and other rights given to stockholders.

By the 1950s, money managers had emerged as separate entities, often out of brokerage or other advisory businesses. However, the greatest fillip to their growth came with the development of the private pensions industry and its decision to invest in company securities, including company shares. In most developed capital markets in the 1950s, money managers might have held 15–30% of a company's shares—today it is nearer to three-quarters.[2]

Further, money managers have expanded globally as their investors have sought global investment opportunities. In most European countries, upwards of 40% of shares are owned by foreign investors, usually through a multinational money manager.

The development of an honest and ethical money management industry requires considerable regulation, oversight, and professionalism. After all, these people control trillions of dollars of other people's savings. In most jurisdictions, strict rules are applied on the custody of securities held on behalf of others. Investment mandates make specific rules on what sort of investments and risks can be taken, and regulators insist on systems for the management of conflicts of interest. Nevertheless such conflicts do occur, and they continue to raise issues for the money management industry.

WHAT MONEY MANAGERS DO

So what does a typical money manager do? This, of course, depends on the particular investment mandate they have been given. They may, for example, specialize in Japanese company equities, or in US government bonds, and so on.

However, the usual process of deciding how, say, a pension fund will be managed would be as follows:

- First, the fund will allocate its investments among different types of asset, to maximize return while minimizing risk. So money may be allocated to bonds, equities, property, and other more specialized asset classes.
- Each of these investments has particular characteristics. A bond will give a certain financial return, provided that it is held for its entire life. An equity will give a less certain return but may yield more over the long term, and it is less likely to have its value eroded by inflation.
- Often, a significant investor will choose a specialized money manager for each asset class.
- Usually the money manager will be set a benchmark against which their performance will be judged. So a US equities manager may be compared to the performance of the US stock market. They aim to outperform this benchmark, usually by buying shares which they believe to be cheap, and selling them when they feel they are relatively expensive.

A whole industry of brokers and information providers has grown to serve this trading. Accountants prepare financial statements on company performance. Credit rating agencies decide whether or not a bond is likely to default. Others provide information on the management, the governance, or the social and environmental performance of companies.

In turn, fund managers often specialize in increasingly arcane and complex products, usually with the aim of beating the benchmark.

In the fund management world, the average return achieved by the market is known as the beta return. Any additional return is known as the alpha return. Hence, fund managers are focused on seeking the alpha.

EQUITY FUND MANAGEMENT

For most CEOs or boards of companies which are not in crisis, the most significant fund manager is likely to be the one that owns the equities, or shares, in their company. It is therefore worth reviewing some of the different styles of equity fund manager.

The classic mandate is that of the active fund manager. Their aim is to spot companies whose share price is low or high relative to what the money manager believes the ultimate value will prove to be. Active fund managers therefore have a great interest in gaining insight into a company in advance of other investors. In doing this they have to avoid receiving insider information. This is information that is known to people who have access to privileged company information but not known or readily knowable to all stockholders. To avoid abuse of one stockholder by another, it is against the regulations to trade shares if you are "inside" (i.e. in receipt of insider information). However, there are many sources and combinations of sources that active funds use to help them outperform. These can vary from long-term analysis of a company's prospects, to short-term predictions of a company's announcements, and the likely reaction to them. Some managers use quantitative models of a company's behavior, and complex statistics, to try to predict whether its share price is likely to rise or fall. Since it is the trading of shares which determines the price, this often means that money managers try to guess how other money managers are likely to behave.

Some active fund managers seek mandates that encourage them to take significant risks. Others will make only marginal bets to ensure that their performance is never too bad. The latter are known as closet tracker funds.

During the 1970s, researchers studied active fund managers to see whether they were able to beat the market. They discovered that the success of those who did beat the market could be attributed to luck as much as to skill. For that reason, many investors decided that they would stop hiring managers to buy and sell shares and instead hire them to track the market, or the market index. These funds, known as index tracker funds, now account for a significant part of the equity market.

In the last 10 to 15 years, the growing sophistication of derivatives markets has opened new possibilities for fund managers. Rather than simply investing in a security (long-only investing), they can invest in options to buy or sell, or contracts for difference. They can borrow a share and sell it on, so that they will benefit if the share price goes down (known as shorting). Or they can go long in some stocks and short in others, which they believe will allow them to maximize the value of their research into companies and hedge the risk that all company stocks will rise or fall. Such sophisticated investment strategies are often undertaken by hedge funds.

By owning a share in a company, a fund manager also becomes entitled, in most jurisdictions, to vote for who will be on the board of directors and on other issues where there is a need to protect owners' interests. Overt use of these powers lies behind the growth of stockholder activist funds. These invest in companies where they think the management is not creating value as it ought, and they seek to use stockowner powers to bring about a change in the management, the strategy, or the finances of the company.

DIFFERENT TYPES OF EQUITY MANAGER

Money managers have developed different legal forms or vehicles through which to carry out their work. One simple form would be to create a segregated account to handle an investor's funds. Or they may suggest that the investor puts their money in a pooled account. In different countries there are different vehicles through which fund managers operate, often in response to legal and taxation rules. These can include pension and life insurance funds, open- and closed-end funds, mutual funds, and others. More recently there has been a huge growth in exchange-traded funds, which reflect the value of a particular market or index and can be bought or sold at a price reflecting that index.

Depending on their investment philosophy and their mandate, fund managers have a different influence on company management. Active fund managers, who trade shares, determine the share price of a company. If this falls too low it may well attract another company wishing to make a bid. Even if no bid is forthcoming, the failure of a company to maintain a strong return for its stockholders will reflect very badly on management.

Active stockholders are very concerned with the news flow of the company. They will aim to meet the management of the company on a regular basis following company profit announcements. A large company may send their CEO to 50 or more private meetings with money managers following the annual profit announcement. Often their analysts will build complex models of the company's finances and be keen to test assumptions. However, their response to poor management by the company is more often to sell the shares than to agitate for change. Index tracking managers, on the other hand, have few resources to quiz companies. Their strategy will be to hold the shares provided that the company forms part of the index.

Activist stockholders are a different breed. They are keen to influence management decisions. Sometimes this is done in private discussion, but often companies find that their discussions with activists have been leaked to the press, since this is one way that a stockholder, who holds only a limited amount of the company's equity, can put pressure on management.

INFLUENCE ON COMPANY MANAGEMENT

Different fund managers will therefore seek to influence company behavior in different ways, depending on the mandate they have been given by their investors. We have already discussed active and activist managers. Passive managers take only modest interest in day to day performance, but may be more interested in longer-term issues of governance and corporate social responsibility. Some hedge funds may even be in the position where it is in their economic interest for a company to do badly—for example if they are "short" the shares.

Many directors also complain that, since fund managers are often measured on short-term performance, they encourage companies to take action that will cause a short-term rise in the share price but which will damage the company in the longer term, by which time the money manager may have sold his stake. Whatever the truth of these criticisms, it is clearly against the interests of the company and its continuing stockholders to sacrifice a good long-term future for short-term gain.

Directors should also be aware that money managers have multiple sources of information about their companies, from brokers, voting agencies, credit rating agencies, accountants, and many other providers of information. Therefore, as well as briefing money managers who own their shares, they also need to put considerable effort into briefing others who will opine on company performance.

MAKING IT HAPPEN

Finance directors should remember that it is their role to ensure that the company strategy creates value for stockholders. If money managers trust this to be the case, and they enjoy equal access to information about the company, this will usually stand a company in good stead. In dealing with investors, companies will discover managers keen to learn about their company. Finance managers may wish to enquire about the style of the manager's investments, and hence their motivation in investing.

Finance directors are often one of the principle points of contact for money managers. If their company is well run, and if they give appropriate ownership information, they are likely to find relations good. However, if information is unreliable, or inconsistent, or if the company is ill managed, this can cause enormous problems. After all, it is the stockholders for whom the company should be run, and in most countries it is the stockholders who decide who should be on the board of directors.

MORE INFO

Book:

Davis, Stephen, Jon Lukomnik, and David Pitt-Watson. *The New Capitalists: How Citizen Investors Are Reshaping the Corporate Agenda*. Boston, MA: Harvard Business School Publishing, 2006.

NOTES

1 Davis, Lukomnik, and Pitt-Watson, 2006, p. 4*ff*.   2 *Ibid*.

Best Practice
Analysis

Viewpoint: Investing in a Volatile Environment: A Black Swan Perspective
by Javier Estrada

INTRODUCTION

Javier Estrada, who is Professor of Financial Management at Barcelona-based IESE Business School, was a tennis coach in his native Argentina before moving to live and work in Spain in 1993. He set the cat among the pigeons in global investment circles with his ground-breaking research, "Black swans and market timing: How not to generate alpha," which conclusively revealed that investors who seek to time the market are unlikely to reap rewards. His research focuses on risk, portfolio management, investment strategies, emerging markets, and insider trading. The founding editor of *Emerging Markets Review*, he holds visiting professorships in Scandinavia and Latin America. As wealth management adviser at Sports Global Consulting, Estrada advises professional sports-players on their investments. His favorite football team is Club Atletico River Plate. A fan of hard-rock bands, including Queen, Kansas, and Led Zeppelin, he plays electric guitar in his spare time. His first degree, a BA in economics, was from the National University of La Plata in Buenos Aires, and he also holds MSc and PhD degrees from the University of Illinois at Urbana-Champaign.

HEALTHY EATING AND INVESTING

We all know that eating properly is essential for our health. Most of us are aware that certain types of food are good for us while others are best avoided. We are also aware of the trade-off between the desirable long-term goal of being fit and healthy and the pain associated with denying ourselves foods that we really like. We also know that patience and discipline are required.

What does healthy eating have to do with investing, you may well ask? Arguably, there are plenty of similarities. Anyone who has gone into a bookstore in search of a book on healthy eating will have been confronted by rows and rows of books, each outlining a different miracle diet.

Anyone looking for a book on investing has a similar experience. Shelf after shelf bulges with with books outlining "high-return, low-risk" strategies. Each gives the impression that all we need do is to follow the indicated path to instant riches. If only life were as easy! If it was, I would not be writing these lines and you would not be reading them—we would probably both be enjoying the Caribbean sun.

A BALANCED DIET

Most of us recognize that eating healthily is going to require a long-term commitment and the making of certain sacrifices (we must kiss goodbye to all those tasty 600-calorie blueberry muffins), and that there is no such thing as a painless shortcut. The same applies to investing.

In reality, the only way to generate high long-term investment returns is to endure some risks in the short term, with the associated pain that comes from sleepless nights as our portfolio value bounces about. There is no such thing as a "high-return, low-risk" strategy. Sadly, the same "no pain, no gain" rule applies both to eating and to investing.

And yet, when it comes to investing, many investors are seduced by "get rich quick" schemes. They often get blinded by the lights of easy money and delude themselves into thinking that gain can be achieved without pain.

For the purpose of this article, I would like to group the investment strategies people are offered into two types: in one group are the "exciting" active investment strategies, which usually promise high returns but claim to achieve them with little or no risk; in the second group are the more boring and conservative passive strategies, which usually promise no gain without pain.

The two approaches can be evaluated from several standpoints, not all of which lead us to the same conclusions. I will evaluate them here through the prism of my own recent research into the so-called "black swans" in financial markets.

BLACK SWANS

A black swan is an event that has three main attributes: First, it is an outlier, lying outside the realm of regular expectations because nothing in the past can convincingly point to its occurrence; second, it carries an extreme impact; and third, despite being an outlier, plausible explanations for its occurrence can be found after the fact, thus giving it the appearance of being both explainable and predictable. In summary, a black swan has three characteristics: rarity, extreme impact, and retrospective predictability.

The black swan perspective of investing is based on three main ideas. The first is that an extremely small number of trading days have a disproportionate impact on long-term investment performance—this is an empirical fact. The second is that, although being invested on the good days and not invested on the bad days would yield extraordinary returns, investors are extremely unlikely to get the timing right. And third, because attempts to time the market are doomed to fail in the long term (in fact, their main consequence is likely to be higher transaction costs), investors are better off holding a properly diversified investment portfolio for the long term.

A PATH TO POVERTY?

Curiously, this is exactly the same recommendation that is put forward by advocates of the efficient market theory of investment. However, the black swan perspective assumes neither market efficiency nor normally distributed returns. Instead, it argues that return distributions have very fat tails and are therefore far from being normal. It also argues that mistakenly assuming that returns are normally distributed can lead to a massive destruction of wealth, as it leads investors to underestimate risk substantially.

Let's first examine the facts. My own research (Estrada, 2008) reveals that a tiny number of days can have an exceptional impact on long-term portfolio performance.

Across 15 developed markets, being out of the market on the ten days when the biggest stock market rallies occurred would have resulted in portfolios being 51% less valuable than if the money had been passively invested. Not being invested in these markets during their ten worst days would have resulted in portfolios being 150% more valuable than a passive investment would have been.

Given that these ten days represent less than 0.1% of the days in the average developed market I considered, the conclusion is obvious: A negligible proportion of days determines a massive creation or destruction of wealth, and the odds of successfully and consistently predicting the right days to be in and out of the market are nil.

In emerging markets, a tiny number of days have an even bigger impact on portfolio performance. My own research (Estradra, 2009) reveals that across 16 emerging markets, missing the ten best

days would have resulted in portfolios being 69% less valuable than if the money had been passively invested. Not being invested on the ten worst ten days would have resulted in portfolios being 337% more valuable than a passive investment would have been. Given that ten days represent 0.15% of the days in the average emerging market I considered, the conclusion is again stark: The probability of successfully and consistently getting the timing right is negligible.

At times of high stock market volatility, like those we experienced during 2008, investors are often tempted to try and take advantage of large daily swings. In such turbulent times many investors attempt to capture outsized returns by frequently jumping in and out of the market, or from one market to another. But investors who engage in this sort of active trading, particularly in a volatile environment, are largely relying on luck rather than on a sound financial strategy.

Investors should bear in mind that the odds are heavily stacked against them; they should also remember that, while the additional transaction costs of their active trading strategy are certain, outsized returns are, at best, a hope.

I run a program on portfolio management for individuals (as opposed to institutions) that aims to give unsophisticated investors some basic tools with which to manage their savings. In this program I tell participants about the two "sad truths" of financial markets. I call them sad truths because these are two statements that most investors would prefer were false. Unfortunately, however, both are true.

PATIENCE IS A VIRTUE

The first statement is that the higher the required return, the greater must be the exposure to risk. The second is that the higher the exposure to risk, the longer must be the investment horizon. Deep inside, participants know that these statements are true, but a part of each of them would prefer to go on believing in painless shortcuts.

In the program, I also tell participants that they should stop focusing on forecasting. I give them many reasons why they should forget about trying to second-guess the market, which stock to buy or sell, or which currency is going to appreciate. I give them plenty of reasons why they should start focusing on asset allocation instead. As with the "sad truths," they instinctively know this advice to be right, but more often than not their next question is whether I think the dollar is going to appreciate or the market is going to fall. Oh, well...

Some investors may well question the wisdom of being passively invested in an environment such as that in 2008, when markets displayed exceptional levels of volatility and were apparently going nowhere but down. But hindsight is 20:20. It is very easy to say now that we should have cashed out at the beginning of 2008, but it did not look that obvious at the time. Trends, in fact, are not obvious until they are well in place. Black swans are unpredictable, and we only know when one has hit us after the event.

As mentioned at the beginning, eating healthily and investing have much in common; in both, the long-term goal is desirable, but the "getting there" is the problem. Most investors know what they have to do along the way; most

know that pain is a part of the process; most know that patience and discipline are essential; and yet most are tempted into shortcuts ("miracle diets" or "high-return, low-risk" strategies), even though they probably recognize that these may ultimately be dead ends. When it comes down to healthy eating or investing, there is simply no gain without pain.

Black swans do exist, both in the natural world and in the financial markets. Those in nature are just a curiosity, but those in financial markets have critical implications for investor behavior. Volatile markets invite investors to engage in a losing game. And yet, at the end of the day, black swans render market timing a goose chase.

MORE INFO

Books:

Estrada, Javier. *Finance in a Nutshell: A No-nonsense Companion to the Tools and Techniques of Finance*. Harlow, UK: FT Prentice Hall, 2005.

Mandelbrot, Benoit B., and Richard L. Hudson. *The (Mis)Behavior of Markets. A Fractal View of Risk, Ruin and Reward*. London: Profile Books, 2005.

Taleb, Nassim Nicholas. *The Black Swan. The Impact of the Highly Improbable*. New York: Random House, 2007.

Articles:

Estrada, Javier. "Black swans and market timing: How not to generate alpha." *Journal of Investing* 17:3 (Fall 2008): 20–34. Online at: dx.doi.org/10.3905/joi.2008.710917

Estrada, Javier. "Black swans in emerging markets." *Journal of Investing* 18:2 (Summer 2009): 50–56. Online at: dx.doi.org/10.3905/joi.2009.18.2.050

Best Practice • Analysis

QFINANCE

Risk Management Revisited
by Duncan Hughes

EXECUTIVE SUMMARY

- Traditional risk management techniques have failed the asset management industry in recent years as portfolios have been unable to deliver sustainable returns throughout the economic cycle.
- The world, and consequently the factors affecting investment portfolios, has shown itself to be more complex and therefore less predictable than has been assumed to date, and particularly with regard to the impact of human behavior on investment returns.
- The requirement for contingency planning for risks that we cannot know about ex ante requires a sea change in the industry's approach to risk management.
- Effective liquidity planning and protection of portfolios against clear secular risks, such as inflation, must form a core part of a robust risk management approach.

INTRODUCTION

Risk management has taken centre stage in many commercial organizations in recent years, but it is in the financial services industry that it has assumed the greatest prominence, particularly since the subprime crisis and the ensuing credit crunch of the late "noughties." Major banks and asset management firms now boast a chief risk officer (CRO) sitting alongside the chief financial officer (CFO) and other executives on the main board. While this innovation could be viewed as rather shutting the stable door after the horse has bolted, it nonetheless demonstrates a renewed commitment to risk management, which has traditionally been viewed as a synonym for "business prevention." This previous sentiment was clearly demonstrated in an infamous incident involving the then CEO of the Halifax Bank of Scotland Group (HBOS)—who was also the deputy chairman of the United Kingdom's Financial Services Authority (FSA) before he was forced to resign—who fired the group's risk manager at the height of the subprime boom in 2005 for challenging the bank's cavalier approach to risk management.[1,2]

The focus on overhauling risk management in financial services gained considerable impetus from the publication of official critical reviews, such as the Turner Review[3] by the FSA, which, although primarily concentrating on the banking sector, nonetheless calls into question the fundamental tenets on which risk analysis in the asset management industry have traditionally based. While those of us who have lived through a series of greed/fear cycles in financial markets over the last 25 years or so may be forgiven for cynically anticipating that any new prudent risk management measures will quickly be discarded if and when markets begin to rally, it is likely that the subprime crisis and its aftermath will result in a lasting philosophical change in the risk management paradigms employed by asset managers.

The statistically convenient and mathematically elegant models previously used in risk modeling must give way to more heuristic and empirically effective approaches to analysis that reflect the realities of the world of investment and are better able to allow for the idiosyncratic and, at least partially, stochastic behavior of financial markets. Economics is a social, not a pure, science, unlike pure mathematics or physics, and consequently cannot be modeled in the same way. The effect of collective human behavior that influences all economic indicators is exacerbated in financial markets, which are more strongly and immediately influenced by the emotions of greed and fear. Any analysis of risk that does not encompass the impact of human behavior in financial markets (or "behavioral finance" as it is generally called) is probably dangerously incomplete.

THE TRADITIONAL APPROACH TO RISK MANAGEMENT—A CRITIQUE
Underlying Statistical Framework

The basic tenets underlying the risk management policies and techniques that are generally employed in financial markets make perfect theoretical sense. Risk is usually equated

Figure 1. Standard Normal distribution and 95% confidence interval

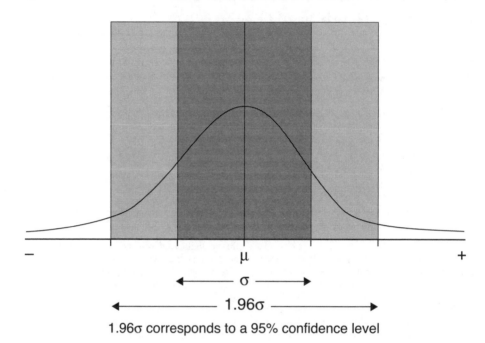

μ

← σ →

← 1.96σ →

1.96σ corresponds to a 95% confidence level

to volatility, the idea being that the greater the variance an investment exhibits from an expected or mean return, the greater is its risk. Similarly, the idea of portfolio diversification resonates with most of us given our mothers' advice not to put all our eggs in one basket. Although the mathematics and statistical techniques required for optimal portfolio construction look impressively complex, it has become clear that these techniques, and the models on which they are based, have been ineffective in protecting investors from the risks that they faced.

The devil, as ever, is in the detail. In order to get to the root of the problem, we must first critically evaluate the statistical models that underlie risk analysis. First, let us examine the measure of volatility that is generally used, i.e. standard deviation. Standard deviation purports to provide us with a measure of how much a variable—for our purposes, the value of an investment—will vary from its mean, or expected, value, μ. From standard deviation, σ, we can readily calculate "confidence intervals," which are a measure of the probability of

the actual outcome falling within a given tolerance of the expected value. Thus, for a risk tolerance of one standard deviation, we are "confident" that the actual outcome will fall within the given range 68% of the time. If we have less risk tolerance, we might insist that the actual outcomes fall within a given range 95% or 99% of the time (roughly corresponding to two and three standard deviations, respectively; see Figure 1). So far, so good: we can prescribe the level of risk that we want to assume and select investments that meet the required statistical criteria.

The problem is, however, that standard deviation does *not* at all adequately describe the possible actual outcomes of financial markets. Technically, standard deviation is the second moment of a probability density function (where the mean, or expected, return is the first moment). There are, however, two further moments of probability density functions (moments could be seen as being analogous to the four dimensions of space and time), these being skewness and kurtosis (Figures 2 and 3).

Figure 2. Third moment: skewness

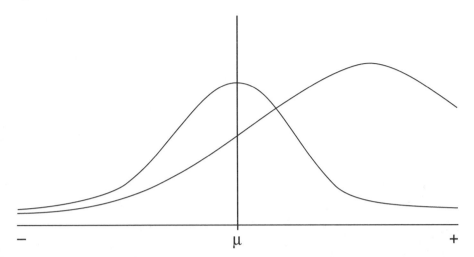

Figure 3. Fourth moment: kurtosis

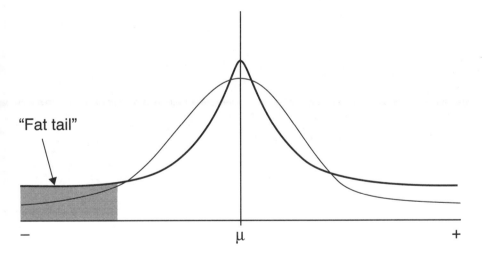

"Fat tail"

Different financial markets exhibit different, but not generally neutral, levels of skewness and kurtosis. Most notably, many financial markets have probability density functions with "fat tails" (technically, leptokurtosis). Crucially, this implies that financial markets have many more extreme outcomes than that predicted by the use of standard deviation alone and the underlying assumption of the normal distribution that a two-moment model dictates (indeed the normal distribution is expressed in statistical shorthand as $N(\mu,\sigma^2)$ where μ represents the distribution's mean, expected value, and σ represents its standard deviation). Some markets tend to exhibit skewness, where either more of the actual observed outcomes fall above (positive skewness) or below (negative skewness) the expected return. A notable example of this phenomenon is senior credit instruments, which deliver an actual return that is more often higher than the expected return due to their generally extremely low incidence of default. The key here is that the use of standard deviation alone has the *hidden assumption* of zero skewness and neutral kurtosis (technically, mesokurtosis) in the expected distribution of actual returns.

If we now turn to the question of portfolio diversification, the key underlying statistic here is correlation, which is the degree to which one variable, or investment for our purposes, moves in line with another investment. In forming a portfolio, optimization techniques minimize the degree of intra-portfolio correlation given the constraint of a given number of investments. Modern portfolio theory tells us that we should have as many different investments in our portfolio as possible, since each additional investment will increase the robustness of the portfolio through increased diversification. The apogee, according to modern portfolio theory, is the "market portfolio," which contains every conceivable asset, since we should seek to squeeze every last drop of correlation benefit from the available asset pool.

$$\rho_{X,Y} = \text{cov}(X, Y) \div \sigma_X \sigma_Y$$

This states that the correlation of investments X and Y is the quotient of the covariance between the returns of X and Y over the sum of the standard deviations of X and Y individually.

From this formula we can once again see the specter of standard deviation at the feast. As before, this condemns the correlation coefficient, ρ, to being a two-dimensional (or, strictly, two-moment) measure, ignoring the real-life facets of skewness and kurtosis in investment returns. The implication is that the benefits hoped for from diversification may be severely undermined.

None of the above is beyond the grasp of most market practitioners (skewness is, after all, nothing more than a description of the position of the mode relative to the mean in a probability function), so the question is, why have financial markets persisted with the use of these models, particularly when they have consistently proved themselves to be inadequate? The answer may lie in the sheer convenience of standard deviation-based measures: everyone can understand the idea of standard deviation and the confidence intervals that can be derived from the normal distribution which it describes. However, the fact remains that models which "stop" at the

second moment of standard deviation, ignoring the third and fourth moments of skewness and kurtosis, are as limited as a description of our physical world would be if we tried to describe it using only length and breadth and ignored dimensions of height and time.

Although it is unclear what should replace this framework in the analysis of financial markets (and it clearly needs to be replaced), it is nonetheless imperative that the assumptions described above, which implicitly underlie any analysis carried out using it, must be recognized. The overreliance and overconfidence in these models has, I believe, been a significant factor in the general empirically disappointing performance of asset portfolios, particularly in their inability to weather the all-too-frequent financial storms to which they are subjected.

Information and Other Issues

In addition to the inappropriateness of the statistical models on which investment analysis has been based to date, the received wisdom of risk management has also included other flaws and oversimplifications. One clear, and frankly gross, oversimplification is the assumption that risk is somehow homogenous and that, for example, equity investments relating to firms in Argentina or Sri Lanka can be analyzed using the same type of framework as for those stocks included in the S&P 500 index of the largest publicly quoted firms in the United States. One of the principal reasons why this approach is asinine is that the cohort of investors interested in various securities markets are different, both in their behavior and in their investment horizons and objectives. Similarly, the use of standardized techniques for the analysis of "alternative" investments such as private equity and hedge funds is fatuous at best, but more likely extremely dangerous.

Other issues include myopia, which has been proposed as an explanation for the historical outperformance of equities over bonds,[4] but which more generally manifests itself in a lack of focus on the "big picture." Asset managers are overwhelmed by information presented to them 24/7 by a plethora of sources such as CNN, Bloomberg News, broker research, and daily newspapers. This information overload can dangerously obscure the secular themes which generally represent the greatest knowable (and therefore manageable) risks to an asset portfolio over the intended investment horizon. Depending on a particular portfolio's objectives, these themes might include those shown in Table 1.

Table 1. Secular themes as sources of long-term portfolio risk

Secular Theme	Implication	Risk
Aging of G7 population	Lower demand for equities	Equity markets become moribund
Polarization of wealth	Lower consumer spending	Economic growth falters
Domination of "big oil"	Higher oil prices	Inflation
Global population explosion	Food shortages	Inflation
Globalization	Greater competition	Reduction of "lives" of businesses
Environmental concern	Higher cost of doing business	Inflation Lower equity returns

NEW DIRECTIONS IN RISK MANAGEMENT

Decomposition of Risk

A first step in the robust analysis of the risk of an investment is to break down the risks into sensible (and honest) categories. Particularly in the ambit of asset management—where investments are considered within the context of an overall portfolio, and an important consequent dynamic is their behavior with respect to the other constituents—homogeneous factors (such as the securities market and liquidity) need to be separately identified from heterogeneous factors (such as branding and management). As will be discussed subsequently, we also need to build in tolerance for those risk factors that cannot be known at a given point in time, but which may become important or dominant.

Behavioral Finance

From an academic perspective, the worlds of psychology and financial economics definitively came together in a meaningful way in 1979 with the publication of Kahneman and Tversky's seminal paper on "prospect theory,"[5] which introduced empirical evidence that a subject's attitude to loss is very different to that toward a similar gain (essentially, that subjects felt a loss considerably more than they felt a gain). This contradicts the standard utility theory assumption that underlies expected behavior in microeconomics and it is therefore an important refinement. This differential is illustrated by the asymmetric value function shown in Figure 4.

To emphasize the point, the value function relating to financial markets differs from the utility function that is generally used in microeconomics in two ways: first, the function is asymmetric, i.e. the behavior exhibited with regard to a gain (being "risk-aversion", i.e. preferring a definite gain) is different to that

Figure 4. An asymmetric value function

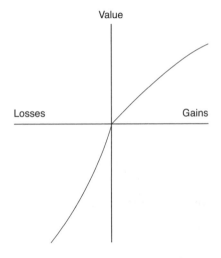

exhibited for a loss (being "loss-aversion", i.e. preferring to take risk to avoid a loss). Second, the value function described above illustrates far more extreme reactions to losses or gains than that exhibited by standard utility functions—particularly with regard to losses, where there is no tolerance for a small loss and experiments have shown that subjects will risk suffering a significantly larger loss to avoid a definite smaller loss. Further groundbreaking empirical research was carried out by De Bondt and Thaler[6] in 1985, which clearly demonstrated that investors and traders overreact to both good and bad news.

Bringing these discoveries back to our probability distributions from the first section, we can see a psychological rationale for the "missing" third and fourth moments of the probability distribution observed in financial markets. These are shown in Figure 5.

Figure 5. Behavioral impact on market returns profile

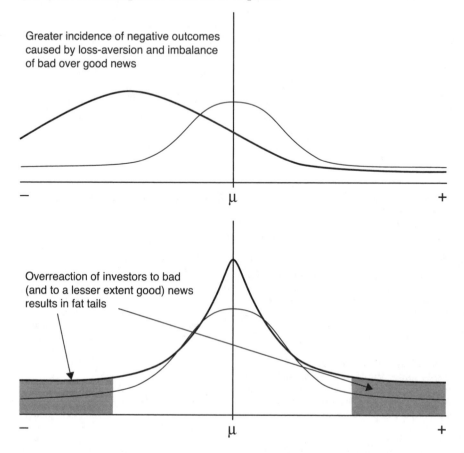

Behavioral finance is a burgeoning field and deserves fuller treatment than that provided here. Table 3 provides a brief summary of some important concepts that go beyond the familiar "greed and fear" paradigm.

In summary, these phenomena cannot be ignored when considering the behavior of financial markets. A logical consequence of all of these differing, and often conflicting, individual behaviors is that the aggregate behavior of the market may well just be too complex to model at all accurately.

For an interesting (and more complete) treatment of behavioral finance, see Shiller (2004).[8]

Epistemology
Although all aspects of epistemology—broadly speaking the study of knowledge and the justification of beliefs—are of interest (particularly when considered in conjunction with the psychological phenomena discussed above), from the perspective of financial markets it is the scope and limitations of knowledge that are of most interest.

The key issue is that there are events that will occur in the future that we *cannot* know about now. These "black swans," as Nassim Taleb famously describes them,[9] can be as devastating as they are unpredictable. From the perspective of our models of potential outcomes, the most

Table 3. Major theoretical frameworks in behavioral finance

Theory	Concept	Implication
Prospect theory	Subjects have a different approach to managing gains than to managing losses	Negative skewing of investment return profile
Allais paradox	Subjects react inconsistently with standard utility theory when presented with option of certainty	Overvaluation of certainty with respect to standard utility theory
Framing	Subjects make different decisions with regard to the same choice depending how the choices are framed	Unpredictability of investor behavior because dependent on each subject's (different) perspective
Anchoring	Subjects base their investment decisions on a fixed reference point, e.g. a previous valuation of a property	Unpredictability of investor behavior because dependent on each subject's (different) reference point
Regret theory	Subjects avoid selling stocks to crystallize a loss	Negative skewing of investment return profile
Wishful thinking bias	Exaggeration of probability of success	Positive skewing of investment return profile
Mental compartments	Individual investors compartmentalize their portfolios into a "risk-averse" part and a "risk-seeking" part. Particularly important where investors have already made (large) gains, q.v. Brian Hunter at Amaranth.[7]	Difficult to predict overall investor behavior because dependent on the compartmentalization approach of each
Representativeness heuristic	Subjects see patterns in random data (e.g. "head and shoulders," etc.)	Groups of market participants "herd" into positions when they "see" these patterns, distorting market returns
Disjunction effect	Subject's inability to make a decision without historical information	Overreliance on historical data

important facets of this phenomenon are as follows.

- The incidence of extreme, unpredictable outcomes is *far* higher than forecast by the normal distribution of returns described above (some of the dramatic events in a short period in 2010–11 are listed below). Thus, the probability density function that we face is more leptokurtic, i.e. has "fatter tails."
- Empirically, more unanticipated bad events are reported than good—e.g. natural and anthropic disasters.[10]
- The probability of these events is rarely, if ever, factored into asset prices and risk models, despite their frequency and consequential impact.

The limitations of knowledge extend not only to what we can know, because situations are too difficult to model and, therefore, to predict (e.g. climate change, the Russian crop fires of 2010, the devastation of Queensland in late 2010/

early 2011, the causes and effects of the strife in the Arab world in early 2011, the Christchurch earthquake of February 2011, and the Japanese earthquake and ensuing tsunami of March 2011). They also affect us at the micro level, in terms of what we are not told: even the largest shareholders in publicly quoted companies can only "see through a glass darkly" into the machinations of corporations through the dimly lit and narrow apertures of shareholders' meetings and infrequent meetings with senior managers. From this perspective, private equity investment is actually less risky, or at least less opaque, since investors usually insist on having a seat on the board of the company in question.

The overwhelming point is that we think that we know more about the future than we actually do—that is, we are consistently overconfident in our predictions of the future and systematically underestimate what can go wrong and by how much it can go wrong.

CASE STUDY
Toyota Motor Corporation
In the analysis of any individual investment, the main challenge for asset managers is to establish an effective paradigm for risk analysis. Whilst some risks will be specific to the company or issuing entity to which a security relates, others will be extraneous to it, and may be common to a number of assets in a portfolio.

Table 2. Examples of risks faced by investors in Toyota

Factor	Example Risks
Automobile manufacture	Oil price increase reduces demand Subject to discretionary spending by consumers Low-cost competition
Japanese equity	Share price falls along with Japanese/global market Lower demand from aging population
Brand	Strong brand undermined by accelerator pedal issues
Management	Traditional Japanese management structure and philosophy could make firm vulnerable to competition from firms that outsource manufacturing

A key point here is that, even in this simple analysis, there is a lot of uncertainty. Although we know that sales of Toyota cars will probably fall if the oil price rises, standard supply and demand analysis may be inadequate and actual demand may well be subject to critical thresholds (e.g. oil at US$200 per barrel, or where it costs a US consumer $100 to fill his or her Toyota with gasoline) as well as other factors. The accelerator pedal issues faced in 2009, which tarnished Toyota's previously premium brand, could not have been known by asset managers who invested in 2008. The risk faced by investors is broadened purely through the membership of Toyota in the Nikkei 225 index, which is a proxy for the Japanese equity market and, more generally, the Japanese economy. Consequently, a natural disaster, such as the earthquake and tsunami of March 2011, that affects Japan will adversely affect an investment in Toyota, irrespective of that event's actual impact on Toyota's business.

It should be clear from this short case study that the risks faced by investors in Toyota cannot sensibly be summarized in one number (e.g. standard deviation)—and, indeed, that not all of the risks can easily be expressed numerically. The dangers are oversimplification, standardization of analysis, and consequent overconfidence. This is particularly so where investors rely on the perceived safety of a firm with a large capitalization that is quoted on a major stock exchange, which, although generally helpful from a liquidity perspective (actually one of the main benefits), is no panacea, and is no substitute for doing one's own research (q.v. Enron, WorldCom).

What we should really be worried about is the risk of loss in a given investment, not necessarily increased volatility (indeed, holders of options warmly welcome increased volatility since it increases their asset's value). Thus, avoiding bad situations in the first place is probably the most effective risk management tool of all. Warren Buffett's approach as a "value" investor has ensured that he has avoided such market collapses as the technology bust of 2001, since the valuations of such stocks were too high for him to consider investment.

FACING UNCERTAINTY AND UNKNOWNS IN THE REAL WORLD
In 2002, the US Secretary of Defense, Donald Rumsfeld, gave one of the most abstruse press conferences in the history of the English language, during which he created his now infamous paradigm of "known knowns," "known unknowns," and "unknown unknowns."

Although it confused the world at that time, it nonetheless creates a useful framework for the analysis of knowledge and the risks that we face. To his three categories I would add the additional class of "unknown knowns," so that our knowledge of the world and its risks is broken down as in Table 4.

Table 4. Risk categories by "knowability"

Category	Meaning	Examples
Known known	Risks we know about now and can predict and quantify with reasonable accuracy now	Current volatility Short-term inflation Secular demographic factors Expected default rates
Known unknown	Risks we know about now, but cannot predict the timing of and/or quantify accurately now	Firm/industry demise Long-term inflation Changes in consumer tastes Actual default rates
Unknown known	Risks we forgot we knew about	Universal banking11 Portfolio correlations in bear markets
Unknown unknown	Risks we cannot know about now	9/11 terrorist atrocity Madoff fraud Arab uprisings 2011

Table 5. Categories of risk and hedging strategies

Risk	Category(ies)	Mitigator(s)/Hedge(s)
Current volatility	Instrument-specific	Diversification
Short-term inflation	Inflation	Commodity hedging
Secular demographic factors	Inflation	Commodity hedging
Expected default rates	Instrument-specific	Diversification
Firm/industry demise	Instrument-specific	Diversification
Long-term inflation	Inflation	Commodity hedging
Changes in consumer tastes	Instrument-specific	Diversification
Actual default rates	Instrument-specific	Diversification
Universal banking[12]	Liquidity	Liquidity planning
9/11 terrorist atrocity	Liquidity Inflation	Liquidity planning Commodity hedging
Madoff fraud	Instrument-specific	Diversification
Arab uprisings 2011	Inflation	Commodity hedging

An honest appraisal of the risks that we face and an acknowledgement that there are risks that we cannot know about ex ante is the first step to better risk management. An important factor in our favor when managing risk is that the *symptoms* of risk (i.e. how any risk affects the value of our portfolio) are far less numerous than the *causes*. This is particularly helpful when trying to deal with the "unknown" risks that we face. In fact, if we look at the examples of known and unknown risks detailed in Table 4 and their potential mitigators and hedges, we can see that the action to be taken is very similar in nature. This is shown in Table 5.

In summary, we should be allowing for more risk than that which currently is clearly predictable. The $64,000 question is, of course, how much more liquidity, inflation hedging, etc., should we be incorporating into our risk management program? Since every portfolio (and its underlying liabilities) is different, it is impossible to generalize. However, in setting the quantum of the portfolio's contingent risk protection and other risk management measures, the following issues must be addressed:

- How can the concentration of risk be reduced?
- How much loss can the asset portfolio bear?
- How likely is it that the portfolio will be able to recover from a significant loss?
- What is the investment horizon (i.e. how long does the portfolio have to recover any losses)?

CONCLUSION

The reality of investment risk in asset management (and other spheres of finance) has proved itself to be more complex and far less prescriptive than the implicit description of risk in the models that were originally conceived by the pioneers of modern portfolio theory. Unfortunately, no clear alternative to the intuitively appealing models centering on standard deviation, confidence intervals, and correlations is immediately apparent, but to continue to rely too heavily on these models in their current form, knowing what we now know about the nature of the modern world and the empirical behavior of investors, is negligently dangerous.

Going forward, knowing more about individual investments and their potential pitfalls, rather than relying on blind diversification, is a good first step. A good second step is greater humility in admitting to ourselves that there are some things we do not know and others that we simply cannot know at any given point. Making additional allowances for these "unknowns" (which will inevitably cause a drag on portfolio returns in the short run) is probably the greatest Rubicon that the asset management industry needs to cross.

MAKING IT HAPPEN
- Understand as much as you can about each investment in your portfolio, but accept that you cannot know everything.
- Understand the known and potential liquidity requirements of your portfolio's liabilities and how these relate to the liquidity of the portfolio's assets.
- Try not to make rash decisions: if you have made considered investment choices for the long term, don't be panicked into changing them when short-term crises arise (which they will).
- Don't rely on numbers alone: any statistics should only support a robust investment proposition that has intuitive as well as logical appeal.

MORE INFO

Books:

Gardner, Dan. *Risk: The Science and Politics of Fear*. London: Virgin Books, 2008.
Shiller, Robert J. *Market Volatility*. Cambridge, MA: MIT Press, 1989.
Taleb, Nassim Nicholas. *Fooled by Randomness: The Hidden Role of Chance in Life and in the Markets*. New York: Texere, 2004.

Report:

Sewell, Martin. "Behavioural finance." Working paper. April 2010. Online at: www.behaviouralfinance.net/behavioural-finance.pdf

Websites:

CFA Institute publications: www.cfapubs.org
EDHEC-Risk Institute: www.edhec-risk.com

NOTES

1 news.bbc.co.uk/1/hi/business/7883409.stm
2 tinyurl.com/b25pre
3 Financial Services Authority. "The Turner review: A regulatory response to the global banking crisis." March 2009. Online at: www.fsa.gov.uk/pubs/other/turner_review.pdf
4 Benartzi, Shlomo, and Richard H. Thaler. "Myopic loss aversion and the equity premium puzzle." *Quarterly Journal of Economics* 110:1 (February 1995): 73–92. Online at: dx.doi.org/10.2307/2118511
5 Kahneman, Daniel, and Amos Tversky. "Prospect theory: An analysis of decisions under risk." *Econometrica* 47:2 (March 1979): 263–292. Online at: www.jstor.org/stable/1914185
6 De Bondt, Werner F. M., and Richard Thaler. "Does the stock market overreact?" Journal of Finance 40:3 (July 1985): 793–805. Online at: www.jstor.org/stable/2327804
7 The case of Brian Hunter at Amaranth during 2005 and 2006 is interesting. Having made a reported US$75–100 million bonus in the previous trading year, the compartmentalization theory would suggest that the excessive risk-seeking behavior exhibited by him in the subsequent trading year (which resulted in losses of Biblical proportions) was due to Hunter having "money in the bank" which he felt he could afford to gamble with.
8 Shiller, Robert J. "Radical financial innovation." Cowles Foundation Discussion Paper No. 1461.

April 2004. Online at: ssrn.com/abstract=537402
9 Taleb, Nassim Nicholas. *The Black Swan: The Impact of the Highly Improbable*. New York: Random House, 2007.
10 Whether this high incidence is "real" or perceived is largely irrelevant; even if the media industry biases reported news to bad events in order to sell more newspapers, the effect on sentiment is the same. The effect of this is that our probability density function is negatively skewed.
11 Universal banking is a business model whereby investment banking and deposit-taking activities are combined one organization. Universal banking was effectively declared illegal in the United States in 1933 (the Glass–Steagall Act, 1933) following the Wall Street crash of 1929, the failure of around 10,000 banks, and the ensuing Great Depression. The Gramm–Leach–Bliley Act, 1999 (GLB), repealed those parts of the Glass–Steagall act that prevented universal banking. GLB was widely blamed for exacerbating the financial crisis of the late noughties. Paul Krugman, the Nobel prize-winning economist, was quoted in the *New York Times* (March 2008) as saying that Senator Phil Gramm was second only to Alan Greenspan (who pumped unprecedented and, perhaps, unnecessary liquidity into the US financial system) in terms of responsibility for causing the crisis.
12 *Ibid.*

Asset Allocation Methodologies
by Tom Coyne

Best Practice • Analysis

EXECUTIVE SUMMARY

- Asset allocation is both a process and a collection of methodologies that are intended to help a decision-maker to achieve a set of investment objectives by dividing scarce resources between different alternatives.
- Theory assumes that asset allocations are made in the face of risk, where the full range of possible future outcomes and their associated probabilities are known. In the real world this is rarely the case, and decisions must be made in the face of uncertainty.
- The appropriate asset allocation methodology to use, in part, depends on an investor's belief in the efficacy of forecasting. Assuming you believe that forecasting accuracy beyond luck is possible, there remains an inescapable trade-off between a forecasting model's fidelity to historical data and its robustness to uncertainty. Confidence in prediction also increases when models based on different methodologies reach similar conclusions. In fact, averaging the results of these models has been shown to raise forecast accuracy.
- The traditional methodology for asset allocation problems is mean–variance optimization (MVO), which is an application of linear programming that seeks to maximize the return for any given level of risk. However, MVO has many limitations, including high sensitivity to input estimation error and difficulty in handling realistic multiyear, multiobjective problems.
- Alternative techniques include equal weighting, risk budgeting, scenario-based approaches, and stochastic optimization. The choice of which to use fundamentally depends on your belief in the predictability of future levels of risk and return.
- Although they are improving, all quantitative approaches to asset allocation still suffer from various limitations. For that reason, relatively passive risk management approaches such as diversification and automatic rebalancing occasionally need to be complemented by active hedging measures, such as going to cash or buying options.

INTRODUCTION

Everyone has financial goals they want to achieve, whether it is accumulating a target amount of money before retirement, ensuring that a pension fund can provide promised incomes to retirees, or, in a different context, achieving an increase in corporate cash flow. Inevitably, we do not have unlimited resources available to achieve these goals. We often face not only financial constraints, but also shortages of information, time, and cognitive capacity. In many cases, we also face additional constraints on how we can employ available resources to achieve our goals (for example, limits to the maximum amount of funds that can be invested in one area, or the maximum acceptable probability of a result below some threshold).

Broadly, these are all asset allocation problems. We solve them every day using a variety of methodologies. Many of these are nonquantitative, such as dividing resources equally between options, using a rule of thumb that has worked in the past, or copying what others are doing. However, in cases where the stakes are high, the allocation problem is complicated, and/or our choice has to be justified to others, we often employ quantitative methodologies to help us identify, understand, and explain the potential consequences of different decision options. This article considers a typical asset allocation problem: how to allocate one's financial assets across a range of investment options in order to achieve a long-term goal, subject to a set of constraints.

THE CORE CHALLENGE: DECISION MAKING UNDER UNCERTAINTY

All investment asset allocation methodologies start with two core assumptions. First, that a range of different scenarios could occur in the future. Second, that investment alternatives are available whose performance will vary depending on the scenario that eventually develops. A critical issue is the extent to which a decision-maker believes it is possible to accurately predict future outcomes. Traditional finance theory, which is widely used in the investment management industry, assumes that both the full range of possible outcomes and their associated probabilities are known to the

QFINANCE

97

decision-maker. This is the classic problem of making decisions in the face of risk.

However, when you dig a bit deeper, you find that this approach is based on some questionable assumptions. The obvious question is: how can a decision-maker know the full range of possible future outcomes and their associated probabilities? One explanation is that they understand the workings of the process that produces future outcomes. In physical systems, and even in simple social systems, this may be true. But this is likely not to be the case when it comes to investment outcomes. Financial markets are complex adaptive systems, filled with positive feedback loops and nonlinear effects caused by the interaction of competing strategies (for example, value, momentum, and passive approaches) and underlying decisions made by people with imperfect information and limited cognitive capacities who are often pressed for time, affected by emotions, and subject to the influence of other people. An investor can never fully understand the way this system produces outcomes.

Even without such causal understanding, an investor could still believe that the range of possible future outcomes can be described mathematically, based on an analysis of past outcomes. For example, you could use historical data to construct a statistical distribution to describe the range of possible future outcomes, or devise a formula for projecting a time series into the future. The validity of both these approaches rests on two further assumptions. The first is that the historical data used to construct the distribution or time-series algorithm contain sufficient information to capture the full range of possible future outcomes. The second is that the unknown underlying process that generates the historical data will remain constant, or only change slowly over time. Over the past decade, we have seen repeated evidence that in financial markets these two assumptions are not true, for example in the meltdown of the Long Term Capital Management hedge fund in 1998, the crash of the technology stock bubble in 2001, and the worldwide financial market panic in 2008. In these cases, models based on historical data failed to identify the full range of possible outcomes, or to accurately assess the probability of the possible outcomes they identified. People will live with the consequences of these failures for years.

This is not to say that skilled forecasters do not exist, however. They certainly do. Unfortunately, it is usually easier to identify them with the benefit of hindsight (which also helps to distinguish between skill and luck) than it is to pick them in advance.

This discussion leads to an important conclusion. In the real world, asset allocators must make decisions not in the face of *risk*, but rather under conditions of true *uncertainty*, in which neither the full range of possible future outcomes nor their associated probabilities are fully known in advance. This has two critical implications. First, there is an inescapable trade-off between any forecasting model's fidelity to historical data and its robustness to uncertainty. The more carefully a model is backtested and tightly calibrated to accurately reproduce *past* outcomes, the less likely it is to accurately predict the future behavior of a complex adaptive system. Second, confidence in a forecast increases only when models based on differing methodologies (for example, causal, statistical, time-series, and judgmental forecasts) reach similar conclusions, and/or when their individual forecasts are combined to reduce the impact of their individual errors. In short, decision-making under uncertainty is much harder than decision-making under risk.

Asset Allocation: A Simple Example

Let us now move on to a more concrete, yet still simple, example to illustrate some key issues that underlie the most common asset allocation methodology in use today. Our quantitative data and results are summarized in the following table:

	Asset A	Asset B
Year 1 return	1%	3%
Year 2 return	5%	7%
Year 3 return	9%	20%
Year 4 return	5%	–5%
Year 5 return	1%	8%
Sample arithmetic mean	4.2%	6.6%
Standard error of the mean	1.5%	4.1%
Sample geometric mean	4.1%	6.3%
Sample standard deviation	3.3%	9.1%
Covariance of A and B	0.12%	
Correlation of A and B	0.41	
Asset weight	40%	60%
Expected arithmetic annual portfolio return	5.6%	
Expected portfolio standard deviation	6.1%	
Expected geometric annual portfolio return	4.9%	

Best Practice • Analysis

Our portfolio comprises two assets, for which we have five years of historical data. In line with industry norms, we will treat each data point as an independent sample (i.e. we will assume that no momentum or mean-reversion processes are at work in our data series) drawn from a distribution which includes the full range of results that could be produced by the unknown return-generating process. As you can see, the sample mean (i.e. arithmetic average) annual return is 4.2% for Asset A and 6.6% for Asset B. So it is clear that Asset B should produce higher returns, right? Wrong. The next line of the table shows the standard error for our estimate of the mean. The standard error is equal to the sample standard deviation (which we'll discuss below) divided by the square root of the number of data points used in the estimate (in our case, there are five). Assuming that the data come from a normal distribution (that is, one in the shape of the bell curve), there is a 67% chance that the true mean will lie within plus or minus one standard error of our sample mean, and a 95% chance that it will lie within two standard errors. In our example, the short data history, along with the relatively high standard deviation of Asset B's returns, means that the standard errors are high relative to the sample means, and we really can't be completely sure that Asset A has a higher expected return than Asset B. In fact, we'd need a lot more data to increase our confidence about this conclusion. Assuming no change in the size of the standard deviations, the size of the standard error of the mean declines very slowly as the length of the historical data sample is increased—the square root of 5 is about 2.2; of 10, about 3.2; and of 20, about 4.5. Cutting the standard error in half—that is, doubling the accuracy of your estimate of the true mean—requires about a fourfold increase in the length of the data series. Considering that 20 years is about the limit of the available data series for many asset classes, you can see how this can create problems when it comes to generating asset allocation results in which you can have a high degree of confidence.

The next line in the table, the sample geometric mean, highlights another issue: As long as there is any variability in returns, the average return in a given year is not the same as the actual compound return that would be earned by an investor who held an asset for the full five years. In fact, the realized return—that is, the geometric mean—will be lower, and can quickly be approximated by subtracting twice the standard deviation squared from the arithmetic mean. In summary, the higher the

variability of returns, the larger the gap will be between the arithmetic and the geometric mean.

The following line in the table shows the sample standard deviation of returns for Assets A and B. This measures the extent to which they are dispersed around the sample mean. In many asset allocation analyses, the standard deviation (also known as volatility) is used as a proxy for risk. Common sense tells you that the correspondence between standard deviation and most investors' understanding of risk is rough at best. Most investors find variability on the downside much less attractive than variability on the upside—and they like uncertainty even less than risk, which they can, or think that they can, measure. Also, when it comes to the distribution of returns, it is not just the average and standard deviation that are of interest to investors. Whether the distribution is Gaussian (normal)—that is, it has the typical bell curve shape—is also important. Distributions that are slightly tilted toward positive returns (as is the case with Assets A and B) are preferable to ones that are negatively skewed. Skewness should also affect preference for distributions with a higher percentage of extreme returns than the normal distribution (i.e. ones with high kurtosis). Preference for higher kurtosis should rise as skewness becomes more positive, and fall as it becomes more negative (i.e. as the probability of large negative returns rises). In fact, in our example, Asset B has positive skewness and higher than normal kurtosis (compared to Asset A's lower than normal kurtosis). Hence, some investors might be willing to trade off higher positive skewness and kurtosis against higher standard deviation in their assessment of the overall riskiness of Asset B. This might be particularly true when, as in the case of some hedge fund strategies, the expected returns on an investment have a distribution that is far from normal. However, many asset allocation methodologies still do not take these trade-offs into account, because they either assume that the returns on assets are normally distributed, or they assume that investors only have preferences concerning standard deviation, and not skewness or kurtosis.

Covariance and correlation
Covariance and correlation are two ways of measuring the relationship between the time series of returns on two or more assets. Covariance is found by multiplying each year's return for Asset A by the return for Asset B, calculating the average result, and subtracting from this the product of the average return for

Asset A and by the average return for Asset B— or, more pithily, it is the average of the products less the product of the averages. Correlation standardizes the covariance by dividing it by the product of the standard deviation of Asset A's returns, multiplied by the standard deviation of Asset B's returns. Correlation takes a value between minus one (for returns that move in exactly opposite directions) and plus one (for returns that move exactly together). In theory, a correlation close to zero implies no relationship between the returns on the two sets of returns. Unfortunately, most people forget that correlation only measures the strength of the *linear* relationship between variables; if this relationship is *nonlinear*, the correlation coefficient will also be deceptively close to zero. Finally, covariance and correlation measure the average relationship between two return series; however, their relationship under extreme conditions (i.e. in the tails of the two return distributions) may differ from this average. This was another lesson taught by the events of 2008.

Forming a Portfolio

Let us now combine Asset A and Asset B into a portfolio in which the first has a 40% weight and the second has a 60% weight. The second-to-last row of our table shows the expected arithmetic portfolio return of 5.6% per year. This is simply the weighted average of each asset's expected return. The calculation of the expected standard deviation of the portfolio is more complicated, but it highlights the mathematical logic of diversification. The portfolio standard deviation equals the square root of the portfolio variance. The latter is calculated as follows: [(Asset A weight squared multiplied by Asset A standard deviation squared) plus (Asset B weight squared multiplied by Asset B standard deviation squared) plus (two times Asset A weight multiplied by Asset B weight times the covariance of A and B)]. As you can see, the portfolio standard deviation is 6.1%, which is less than 6.8%—the weighted average of Asset A's and Asset B's standard deviations. The cause of this result is the relatively low covariance between A's returns and B's returns (or alternatively, their relatively low correlation of 0.41). The fact that their respective returns apparently move in less than perfect lockstep with each other reduces the overall expected variability of the portfolio return. However, this encouraging conclusion is subject to two critical caveats. First, it assumes the absence of a nonlinear relationship between A's returns and B's returns that has not been picked up by the correlation estimate. Second, it

assumes that the underlying factors giving rise to the correlation of 0.41 will remain unchanged in the future. In practice, however, this is not the case, and correlations tend to be unstable over time. For example, in 2008, investors discovered that despite relatively low estimated correlations between their historical returns, many asset classes shared a nonlinear exposure to a market liquidity risk factor. When liquidity fell sharply, correlations rose rapidly and undermined many of the expected benefits from portfolio diversification.

Expected Portfolio Returns

The last line in our table is an estimate of the geometric or compound average rate of return that an investor might be expected to actually realize on this portfolio over a multiyear period, assuming that we have accurately estimated the underlying means, standard deviations, and correlations and that they remain stable over time (all questionable assumptions, as we have noted). As you can see, it is less than the expected arithmetic annual return. Unfortunately, too many asset allocation analyses make the mistake of assuming that the arithmetic average return will be earned over time, rather than the geometric return. In the example we have used, for an initial investment of $1,000,000 and a 20-year holding period, this difference in returns results in terminal wealth that is lower by $370,358, or 12.5%, than the use of the arithmetic average would have led us to expect. This is not a trivial difference.

ASSET ALLOCATION: ADVANCED TECHNIQUES

The basic methodology we have just outlined can be used to calculate asset weights that maximize expected portfolio return for any given constraint on portfolio standard deviation (or other measure of risk, such as value-at-risk). Conversely, this approach can be used to minimize one or more portfolio risk measures for any given level of target portfolio return. These are all variants of the asset allocation methodology known as mean–variance optimization (MVO), which is an application of linear programming (for example, as found in the SOLVER function in an Excel spreadsheet). Although MVO is by far the most commonly used asset allocation methodology, it is, as we have shown, subject to many limitations.

Fortunately, there are techniques that can be used to overcome some, if not all, of the problems highlighted in our example. We will start with alternatives to the MVO methodology,

Best Practice • Analysis

and then look at alternative means of managing errors in the estimation of future asset class returns, standard deviations, covariances, and other model inputs.

Alternative Approaches to Portfolio Construction

The simplest alternative to MVO is to allocate an equal amount of money to each investment option. Known as the $1/n$ approach, this has been shown to be surprisingly effective, particularly when asset classes are broadly defined to minimize correlations (for example, a single domestic equities asset class rather than three highly related ones, including small-, mid-, and large-cap equities). Fundamentally, equal weighting is based on the assumption that no asset allocation model inputs (i.e. returns, standard deviations, and correlations) can be accurately forecast in a complex adaptive system.

Another relatively simple asset allocation methodology starts from the premise that, at least in the past, different investment options perform relatively better under different economic scenarios or regimes. For example, domestic and foreign government bonds and gold have, in the past, performed relatively well during periods of high uncertainty (for example, the 1998 Russian debt crisis and the more recent subprime credit crisis). Similarly, history has shown that inflation-indexed bonds, commodities, and commercial property have performed relatively well when inflation is high, whereas equities deliver their best performance under more normal conditions. Different approaches can be used to translate these observations into actual asset allocations. For example, you could divide your funds between the three scenarios in line with your subjective forecast of the probability of each of them occurring over a specified time horizon, and then equally divide the money allocated to each scenario between the asset classes that perform best under it.

When it comes to more quantitative asset allocation methodologies, research has shown that—at least in the past—some variables have proven easier to predict and are more stable over time than others. Specifically, relative asset class riskiness (as measured by standard deviation) has been much more stable over time than relative asset class returns. A belief that relative riskiness will remain stable in the future leads to a second alternative to MVO: risk budgeting. This involves allocating different amounts of money to each investment option, with the goal of equalizing their contribution to total portfolio risk, which can be defined using either standard deviation or one or more downside risk measures (for example, drawdown, shortfall, semi-standard deviation). However, as was demonstrated by the ineffective performance of many banks' value-at-risk models during 2008, the effectiveness of risk budgeting depends on the accuracy of the underlying assumptions it uses. For example, rapidly changing correlations and volatility, along with illiquid markets, can and did result in actual risk positions that were very different from those originally budgeted.

The most sophisticated approaches to complicated multiyear asset allocation problems use more advanced methodologies. For example, rather than a one-period MVO model, multiperiod regime-switching models can be used to replicate the way real economies and financial markets can shift between periods of inflation, deflation, and normal growth (or, alternatively, high and low volatility). These models typically incorporate different asset return, standard deviation, and correlation assumptions under each regime. However, they are also subject to estimation errors not only in the assumptions used in each regime, but also in the assumptions made about regime continuation and transition probabilities, for which historical data and theoretical models are quite limited.

Rebalancing Strategies

Multiperiod asset allocation models can also incorporate a range of different rebalancing strategies that manage risk by adjusting asset weights over time (for example, based on annual rebalancing, or maximum allowable deviations from target weights). When it comes to identifying the best asset allocation solution for a given problem, these models typically incorporate sophisticated evolutionary search techniques. These start with a candidate solution (for example, an integrated asset allocation and rebalancing strategy), and then run repeated model simulations to assess the probability that they will achieve the investor's specified objectives. An evolutionary technique (for example, genetic algorithms or simulated annealing) is then used to identify another potential solution, and the process is repeated until a stopping point is reached (which is usually based on the failure to find a better solution after a certain number of candidates have been tested or a maximum time limit is reached). Strictly speaking, the best solutions found using evolutionary search techniques are not *optimal* (in the sense that the word is used in

QFINANCE

the MVO approach)—meaning a unique solution that is, subject to the limits of the methodology, believed to be better than all other possible solutions. In the case of computationally hard problems, such as multiperiod, multiobjective asset allocation, it is not possible to evaluate all possible solutions exhaustively. Instead, much as for real life decision-makers, stochastic search models aim to find solutions that are robust—ones that have a high probability of achieving an investor's objectives under a wide range of possible future conditions.

ESTIMATING ASSET ALLOCATION INPUTS

A number of different techniques are also used to improve the estimates of future asset class returns, standard deviations, correlations, and other inputs that are used by various asset allocation methodologies. Of these variables, future returns are the hardest to predict. One approach to improving return forecasts is to use a model containing a small number of common factors to estimate future returns on a larger number of asset classes. In some models, these factors are economic and financial variables, such as the market/book ratio, industrial production, or the difference between long- and short-term interest rates. Perhaps the best known factor model is the CAPM (capital asset pricing model). This is based on the assumption that, in equilibrium, the return on an asset will be equal to the risk-free rate of interest, plus a risk premium that is proportional to the asset's riskiness relative to the overall market portfolio. Although they simplify the estimation of asset returns, factor models also have some limitations, including the need to forecast the variables they use accurately and their assumption that markets are usually in a state of equilibrium.

The latter assumption lies at the heart of another approach to return estimation, known as the Black–Litterman (BL) model. Assuming that markets are in equilibrium enables one to use current asset class market capitalizations to infer expectations of future returns. BL then combines these with an investor's own subjective views (in a consistent manner) to arrive at a final return estimate. More broadly, BL is an example of a so-called shrinkage estimation technique, whereby more extreme estimates (for example, the highest and lowest expected returns) are shrunk toward a more central value (for example, the average return forecast across all asset classes, or BL's

equilibrium market implied returns). At a still higher level, shrinkage is but one version of model averaging, which has been shown to increase forecast accuracy in multiple domains. An example of this could be return estimates that are based on the combination of historical data and the outputs from a forecasting model.

When it comes to improving estimates of standard deviation (volatility) and correlations, one finds similar techniques employed, including factor and shrinkage models. In addition, a number of traditional (for example, moving averages and exponential smoothing) and advanced (for example, GARCH and neural network models) time-series forecasting techniques have been used as investors search for better ways to forecast volatility, correlations, and more complicated relationships between the returns on different assets. Finally, copula functions have been employed with varying degrees of success to model nonlinear dependencies between different return series.

CONCLUSION

In summary, although they are improving and becoming more robust to uncertainty than in the past, almost all quantitative approaches to asset allocation still suffer from various limitations. In a complex adaptive system this seems unavoidable, since their evolutionary processes make accurate forecasting extremely difficult using existing techniques. This argues strongly for averaging the outputs of different methodologies as the best way to make asset allocation decisions in the face of uncertainty. Moreover, these same evolutionary processes can sometimes give rise to substantial asset class over- or undervaluation that is outside the input assumptions used in the asset allocation process. Given this, relatively passive risk management approaches such as diversification and rebalancing occasionally need to be complemented with active hedging measures such as going to cash or buying options. The effective implementation of this process will require not only paying ongoing attention to asset class valuations, but also a shift in focus from external performance metrics to achieving the long-term portfolio return required to reach one's goals. When your objective is to outperform your peers or an external benchmark, it is tempting to stay too long in overvalued asset classes, as many investors painfully learned in 2001 and again in 2008.

MAKING IT HAPPEN

* Using broadly defined asset classes minimizes correlations and creates more robust solutions by reducing the sensitivity of results to deviations from assumptions about future asset class returns, which are the most difficult to forecast.
* Equal dollar weighting should be the default asset allocation, as it assumes that all prediction is impossible.
* However, there is considerable evidence that the relative riskiness of different asset classes is reasonably stable over time and therefore predictable. This makes it possible to move beyond equal weighting and to use risk budgeting. There is also evidence that different asset classes perform better under different economic conditions, such as high inflation or high uncertainty. This makes it possible to use scenario-based weighting.
* Techniques such as mean–variance optimization and stochastic search are more problematic, because they depend on the accurate prediction of future returns. Although new approaches can help to minimize estimation errors, they cannot eliminate them or change the human behavior that gives rise to bubbles and crashes. For that reason, all asset allocation approaches require not only good quantitative analysis, but also good judgment and continued risk monitoring, even after the initial asset allocation plan is implemented.

MORE INFO

Books:

Asset Allocation:

Bernstein, William. *The Intelligent Asset Allocator: How to Build Your Portfolio to Maximize Returns and Minimize Risk*. New York: McGraw-Hill, 2001.

Darst, David M. *The Art of Asset Allocation: Principles and Investment Strategies for Any Market*. 2nd ed. New York: McGraw-Hill, 2008.

Fabozzi, Frank J., Petter N. Kolm, Dessislava A. Pachamanova, and Sergio M. Focardi. *Robust Portfolio Optimization and Management*. Hoboken, NJ: Wiley, 2007.

Ferri, Richard A. *All About Asset Allocation: The Easy Way to Get Started*. New York: McGraw-Hill, 2006.

Gibson, Roger C. *Asset Allocation: Balancing Financial Risk*. New York: McGraw-Hill, 2000.

Michaud, Richard O., and Robert O. Michaud. *Efficient Asset Management: A Practical Guide to Stock Portfolio Optimization and Asset Allocation*. 2nd ed. New York: Oxford University Press, 2008.

Swensen, David F. *Pioneering Portfolio Management: An Unconventional Approach to Institutional Investment*. New York: Free Press, 2009.

Forecasting:

Mlodinow, Leonard. *The Drunkard's Walk: How Randomness Rules Our Lives*. New York: Pantheon Books, 2008.

Osband, Kent. *Iceberg Risk: An Adventure in Portfolio Theory*. New York: Texere, 2002.

Rebonato, Riccardo. *Plight of the Fortune Tellers: Why We Need to Manage Financial Risk Differently*. Princeton, NJ: Princeton University Press, 2007.

Taleb, Nassim Nicholas. *The Black Swan: The Impact of the Highly Improbable*. New York: Random House, 2007.

Articles:

There are many academic papers on asset allocation and portfolio construction methodologies. The best single source is www.ssrn.com. SSRN is also a good source for papers on markets as complex adaptive systems by authors including Andrew Lo, Blake LeBaron, Cars H. Hommes, and J. Doyne Farmer.

Analysis • Best Practice

Websites:

In addition to web-based tools based on mean–variance optimization, there are many vendors of more sophisticated asset allocation software. All of the following employ advanced techniques beyond simple MVO:

AlternativeSoft: www.alternativesoft.com

EnCorr: tinyurl.com/6lemmun

New Frontier Asset Allocation Suite: www.newfrontieradvisors.com

SmartFolio: www.smartfolio.com

Windham Financial Planner: www.windhamcapital.com

The Case for SMART Rebalancing
by Arun Muralidhar and Sanjay Muralidhar

EXECUTIVE SUMMARY

- Once investment managers establish a long-term strategic allocation or benchmark, fund managers must decide how to manage the fund's ongoing allocation.
- Daily market movements can result in constant drifts of actual portfolio allocations from the strategic benchmark.
- Traditionally, experts advised "static rebalancing" wherein simple rules bring the allocations back to the benchmark if some allocation limit is breached or some calendar date is reached.
- Static rebalancing strategies are risky, as the investors take an implicit bet to be either long or short an asset without really focusing on the view on the markets.
- While static rebalancing is often better than drift, this article describes how SMART (Systematic Management of Assets using a Rules-based Technique) can be a better tool for investors.
- By using market factors and managing allocations proactively within rebalancing ranges (i.e., no change in overall policy), investors can improve performance and risk management.
- SMART rebalancing is essential for good governance.

BACKGROUND

Every fund manager has to deal with a vexing issue—namely, how to manage the rebalancing process as the returns from this activity impact the total portfolio performance. There is a wealth of information on these strategies, and many papers have been written on this topic.[1] Nersesian (2006) does an excellent job of introducing a process to help determine the ideal rebalancing policy and examine the considerations in selecting the appropriate approach. Most rebalancing policies (periodic, range, or threshold) first focus on minimizing the tracking error or absolute standard deviation of the portfolio as the key measure of risk (either directly or by targeting the highest Sharpe ratio), and then attempt to manage the trade-off relative to the transactions costs that more frequent rebalancing generates.[2]

Many portfolio managers manage their asset allocation decisions by adopting a rebalancing policy which typically involves returning the asset allocation to the target allocation or strategic asset allocation (SAA) at calendar intervals (monthly, quarterly, or annually). Alternatively, portfolio managers may use a "range-based" approach whereby the trigger points or ranges are typically 3–5% from the target, based on the volatility of asset classes. Variations of this approach rebalance to somewhere within these allocation ranges or use periodic cash flows to move the asset allocation of the various assets closer to what a rebalancing action would attempt to do. Often these approaches are a move toward a practical maintenance of the strategic weights, trading off between managing transactions costs and

tracking error relative to the benchmark. These approaches can be called "static rebalancing" because the limits are set. However, the portfolio still drifts within the bands, as most policies are silent about what actions staff should take within the bands. This is demonstrated in Figure 1.

Figure 1. The implicit bet in traditional rebalancing policies

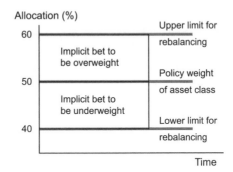

THE ALLURE OF REBALANCING

Rebalancing is attractive because it is simple to understand and to execute, is explicit and transparent, allowing portfolio managers to put in place the exact policy to be followed and be assured that it is being followed, and avoids the appearance of "do-nothing" or "buy-and-hold." Furthermore, discipline provides a decision regime that can be modeled to quantify the historical risk and return profile. Finally, most analyses suggest that a rebalancing policy is better than doing nothing (or letting the portfolio drift), and that has been good enough for most investors.

THE PROBLEM WITH STATIC REBALANCING

Despite the low tracking error relative to their benchmarks, static rebalancing policies can be problematic owing to the large absolute and relative drawdowns (or declines in the value of the fund). Therefore, when US and European equity declined dramatically from 2000 to early 2003, rebalancing would have done little to reduce the pain of the portfolio and would have caused the rebalanced portfolio to plummet as well. While static rebalancing is attractive in up markets, the analogy in down markets would be to tying your leg to the anchor of a sinking ship.

The larger questions that this article addresses in the new rebalancing paradigm are:

- What are the appropriate performance and risk measures in determining the best asset allocation approach? Additional risk measures like the drawdown in the portfolio (maximum decline in the absolute or relative value of the fund), and success ratio (number of months that you outperform the benchmark) are utilized as these better capture the concept of practical portfolio management risk as opposed to standard deviation. After all, a low tracking error relative to a benchmark may be worthless if the fund is bankrupted by a large drawdown in absolute value.
- Is there a better way to manage asset allocation decisions than static rebalancing?
- Can other approaches preserve the advantages that rebalancing policies have, namely the ability to have explicit, transparent, and disciplined asset allocation decisions?

INFORMED OR SMART REBALANCING

The more sensible way to make asset allocation decisions is by a process called "informed rebalancing." Informed rebalancing is simply about making asset allocation decisions among the various assets in a portfolio to take advantage of the higher returns in the attractive assets, while underweighting the less attractive assets commensurately. The case for informed rebalancing was made very successfully in Muralidhar (2007), though McCalla (1997) had hinted at a somewhat different approach. This is done by identifying the factors that affect which assets in your portfolio will perform well and which will perform poorly during any given

regime/cycle/period. This approach, therefore, involves the following steps:

- Identify all the asset allocation decisions being made in the portfolio.
- Develop investment rules to guide the desired asset allocation tilts in the portfolio. These rules will define the assets that should be overweighted or underweighted relative to the target allocation based upon the levels of certain market or economic factors, typically sources from finance or academic journals. These factors will be measures of valuation (whether an asset class is over- or undervalued), economic activity (different economic conditions favor different asset classes), seasonality, momentum, market sentiment (volume, volatility, risk aversion, fund flows, etc.).
- Quantify the historical performance of such an asset allocation approach to understand the risk/return profile of each factor model and possibly fine-tuning the selection of the various factor-based rules to ensure that they meet the investment objectives or constraints.
- Combine many such factor-based rules into a diversified strategy that provides a net indication of the relative attractiveness of each asset class so that risks of making decisions on a single economic factor are mitigated.
- Implement these asset allocation recommendations in a disciplined way (just as one would with static rebalancing). There are a number of ways to carry out such implementation that will be discussed separately.

For simplicity, we term this rules-based systematic approach as SMART rebalancing (systematic management of assets using a rules-based technique).

ADVANTAGES OF SMART REBALANCING

The SAA is normally derived from one of two types of optimization. The first method models assets and liabilities (ALM) to find the long-term asset allocation that has the best chance of meeting the liability (in the case of an individual, this would be the desired retirement income) requirement. The second method uses a mean-variance approach that makes assumptions of future asset returns and risk (often based upon historical performance) and finds an "efficient frontier" asset allocation with the highest return for an acceptable level of risk or the least risk for a given required return.

The attendant shortcomings of these optimizations aside—the most glaring being the need for an assumption of expected return/risk—this allocation is to be interpreted as the target allocation that over a very long period offers the best chance of meeting the fund objectives expressed in return/risk or funding terms. There is nothing in these mean-variance optimizations that reacts to market conditions in intervening periods. Again, to use a sailing analogy, naïve rebalancing is like setting the rudder in the direction of the destination without adjusting for wind direction, tides, or choppy seas, and without considering potentially faster ways of reaching the destination with less risk of drowning. SMART rebalancing, on the other hand, would involve making the appropriate adjustments.

Most importantly, as modern portfolio theory has taught us, the assets included in this portfolio are ideally uncorrelated with each other (or at least have low correlation). The logical extension of this assumption of low correlation is that in any given period (whether determined by market regimes, economic cycles, or calendar periods), some of these assets will perform better than others in the portfolio, and some will outperform their expected returns, while others will underperform these expectations. The static rebalancing approach to asset allocation assumes (or hopes) that these pluses and minuses will even out over time and should not be a concern in the ongoing asset allocation decisions. Moreover, there are many ongoing asset allocations that are necessary as a result of cash flows generated by the portfolio by way of dividends, coupon payments, and contributions, and disbursements to meet ongoing obligations.

SMART rebalancing takes the view that low correlation alone demands that responsible asset managers make asset allocation decisions to position their portfolio for these regimes/cycles/market conditions best and, by doing this well and systematically, can greatly improve the return per unit of risk. After all, most investors expect the same process from their external asset managers/mutual fund managers, and it is logical to demand this same responsibility, process, and governance at one decision level up from the portfolio's managers.

Markets are dynamic and asset returns are going up or down daily, resulting in new changes in the weights of assets changing each day. Many investors feel that if they do not take an explicit decision about an asset weight, they do not have a bet on the markets. However, quite the opposite is true! When applied to the decision on assets that have drifted in allocation above the long-term strategic weight because of strong recent performance, to not rebalance implies a view that this asset will continue to outperform. Similarly, triggering an automatic rebalancing decision to reduce (or increase) the weight on an asset back to its benchmark weight at the end of the quarter because a particular day has been reached, implies a view that this asset will do worse (or better) than other assets. Otherwise, to make such a decision would seem somewhat contradictory. In addition, a rebalancing decision makes the assumption that the benchmark allocation is the most desirable at all times (under all market conditions), and hence managing back to this asset allocation is best for the portfolio regardless of current market conditions. So, all asset managers must realize that every decision—whether to overweight, underweight, or continue to allow assets to drift—is an active decision, whether it is made explicitly or implicitly. In short, all these approaches are tactical in nature, even though they are not labeled as such and are often even cloaked as just the opposite!

CASE STUDY

Analysis of Buy-and-Hold, Static Rebalancing and SMART Rebalancing

A simple case study indicates how a hypothetical portfolio, highlighted in Figure 2, could be managed using such investment rules. We assume a simple portfolio with a strategic investment in four core assets: US Equity (benchmarked to the S&P 500), International Equity (benchmarked to the MSCI EAFE Index), US Fixed Income (benchmarked to the Lehman Brothers Composite Index) and Commodities (benchmarked to the Goldman Sachs Commodity Index). Rules are developed for each set of assets using multiple factors and are combined to create a diversified strategy to manage the allocation across these assets. The performance of this informed rebalancing portfolio is compared with a simple buy-and-hold option and a quarterly rebalanced portfolio. The portfolio target assets and allocation are shown in Table 1.

Analysis • Best Practice

Figure 2. Investment structure of hypothetical US pension fund

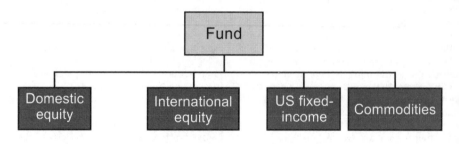

Table 1. Portfolio structure and target allocation

Asset Class	Benchmark	Asset Target Allocation	Range
US Equity	S&P500	31%	2.86%
International Equity	MSCI EAFE	30%	2.92%
Fixed Income	Lehman Brothers US Composite	33%	2.80%
Commodities	GSCI	6%	1.50%

Further, this analysis was backtested over the period from January 1990 through October 2008, so that it covers a few different market regimes, the technology boom of the late 1990s, the subsequent correction of the early 2000s, the subsequent bull market post-2003, and the more recent decline through 2008. We include transactions costs of 20 bps round trip for all assets, though actual experience suggests much lower costs are incurred.

The performance analysis is restricted to a few key metrics in Table 2 in order to facilitate this discussion, but these results are confirmed over a broader set of risk and return parameters.

Table 2. Comparing return and risk of informed rebalancing versus buy-and-hold and quarterly rebalancing

	Buy-and-hold	Range rebalancing	SMART rebalancing
Annualized return	6.2%	6.4%	6.9%
Standard deviation	9.3%	8.6%	8.7%
Return/risk ratio	0.67	0.75	0.79
Maximum drawdown	**-31.9%**	**-33.1%**	-31.7%
Success ratio	51.8%	51.1%	55.3%
Confidence in skill	**31.1%**	**18.7%**	99.9%

As indicated in Table 2, the range rebalancing alternative represents a meaningful improvement over the buy-and-hold strategy and is consistent with most prevailing studies. However, when compared with SMART rebalancing, the only advantage of range rebalancing is a slightly lower standard deviation. However, the lower standard deviation, which is what most professionals use as a proxy for risk, comes at the expense of a 0.5% lower annualized return and therefore a return/risk ratio of 0.67 versus 0.79 for the SMART rebalancing! Notice, though, that this performance and risk advantage comes with very narrow ranges around the strategic asset allocations and hence with ±5% ranges which are more typical, the excess returns and risk management advantages will be much more significant.

More important, in reviewing alternative risk and quality of returns measures—namely *maximum drawdown*, *success ratio*, and *confidence in skill*—the results are more compelling. *Maximum drawdown* measures the maximum decline in the portfolio value during the historical period—to many a more important measure of risk as it is a better indicator of the fund's solvency. This

QFINANCE

statistic is humorously referred to as the "yield to fire," as it measures how much and for how long one can lose money before being fired or bankrupt. The *success ratio* represents the percentage of months that the portfolio outperformed its benchmark (or a comparable passive portfolio with the target allocations held constant), and the *confidence in skill* is a statistical measure of confidenceone could have that these returns were the product of skill as opposed to luck.[3] On all these measures, SMART rebalancing performed much better than the other approaches. While past returns are no guarantee of future returns, essentially SMART rebalancing has the ability to take corrective action to asset allocation within the policy ranges and prevent bad asset allocation decisions from impacting performance and thereby risk.

MAKING IT HAPPEN

The key to this approach is that while it does involve a little more work than implementing (or recommending) a rebalancing policy, it has similar advantages.

- Simplicity. Once the rules are articulated (and typically these are either explained by fundamental arguments, well-researched trends or common intuition) they can be easily followed and implemented. This simplicity also allows investors to track a few key factors consistently and act on them with confidence.
- *Explicitness and transparency*. By definition, this approach requires a clear definition of the market factors (signals) that will be followed, how these will be used to make asset allocation decisions for the fund, and the policy controls operating on this decision-making process (frequency, asset bandwidths, etc.). Investors then will be able to analyze and vet these decisions thoroughly prior to approving them. This then allows them to execute what is now a disciplined and systematic set of decisions.
- *Superiority*. This approach is superior to the static/naïve rebalancing approaches because it recognizes the limitations of the SAA, makes implicit decisions explicit (what gets monitored gets managed), and operates in the area where the SAA is of limited value. Further, it is both responsible and responsive to current information, which is always more relevant and up-to-date than that used as an input for the SAA decision. Implementation of SMART rebalancing is very similar to static rebalancing and would be implemented in exactly the same way that a current rebalancing program would. In our experience, both programs are easily implemented using futures contracts, so this performance is very easy to achieve and hence does not have any impact on the rest of the portfolio.

CONCLUSION

This article has described how the SMART rebalancing approach can meaningfully improve the performance of the investment portfolio. All decisions to change the asset allocation—whether to let the portfolio drift or rebalance on some static policy or to make informed rebalancing decisions—are active asset allocation decisions. Therefore, it is best to make such decisions in an explicit, disciplined, and informed manner by using the various measures that one should constantly be tracking for other investment decisions (economic, valuation, momentum, and market factors). In the current return environment, every bit of performance is needed to meet investment objectives. SMART rebalancing has the advantage of working on the entire asset base, with the added benefit that it can be implemented in addition to other things that may be done in the portfolio.

MORE INFO

Book:

Muralidhar, Arun. *Innovations in Pension Fund Management*. Stanford, CA: Stanford University Press, 2001.

Articles:

Arnott, Robert D., and Robert M. Lovell, Jr. "Rebalancing: Why? When? How often?" *Journal of Investing* 2:1 (Spring 1993): 5–10. Online at: dx.doi.org/10.3905/joi.2.1.5

Arnott, Robert D., and Lisa M. Plaxco. "Rebalancing a global policy benchmark." *Journal of Portfolio Management* 28:2 (Winter 2002): 9–22. Online at: dx.doi.org/10.3905/jpm.2002.319828

Bernstein, William J. "Case studies in rebalancing." *Efficient Frontier* (Fall 2000). Online at: www.efficientfrontier.com/ef/100/rebal100.htm

Buetow, Gerald W., Jr, Ronald Sellers, Donald Trotter, Elaine Hunter, *et al*. "The benefits of rebalancing." *Journal of Portfolio Management* 28:2 (Winter 2002): 23–32. Online at: dx.doi.org/10.3905/jpm.2002.319829

Graham, Benjamin, and David Dodd. "Investment link tutorial: Asset allocation." *Just for Funds* blog (May 26, 2007).

Leland, Hayne E. "Optimal asset rebalancing in the presence of transactions." Working paper. August 23, 1996. Online at: ssrn.com/abstract=1060

Masters, Seth J. "Rules for rebalancing." *Financial Planning* (December 2002): 89–93.

McCalla, Douglas. "Enhancing the efficient frontier with portfolio rebalancing." *Journal of Pension Plan Investing* 1:4 (Spring 1997): 16–32.

Muralidhar, Sanjay. "A new paradigm for rebalancing." *The Monitor* 22:2 (March/April 2007): 12–16. Online at: tinyurl.com/6caxvkr [PDF].

Nersesian, John. "Active portfolio rebalancing: A disciplined approach to keeping clients on track." *The Monitor* 21:1 (January/February 2006): 9–15. Online at: www.imca.org/cms_images/file_545.pdf

Website:

Mcube Investment Technologies: www.mcubeit.com/books_articles.html

NOTES

1 See, for example, Arnott and Lovell (1993), Arnott and Plaxco (2002), Bernstein (2000), Buetow *et al*. (2002), Masters (2002), and Leland (1996).

2 Leland (1996).

3 Muralidhar (2001), ch. 9.

The Changing Role and Regulation of Equity Research by Simon Taylor

Best Practice • Analysis

EXECUTIVE SUMMARY
- Equity research provided by investment banks, broker dealers, and independent researchers has an important influence on share prices.
- Research analysts are a very important constituency for the managers of quoted companies.
- Many major investment banks were accused of publishing biased research during the 1990s stock market boom to win higher-margin corporate finance business.
- Regulatory changes, starting in the United States and copied internationally after 2003, restricted contact between analysts and bankers and prevented analysts being paid on the basis of banking fees.
- Analysts are now more likely to offer unbiased opinions and to be more critical of companies.
- Company managers need to be careful to build good relationships with analysts through clear and consistent publication of information.

WHAT IS EQUITY RESEARCH?
Equity research is the publication by analysts of reports, notes, and emails that offer an investment recommendation on the quoted stock of a company (typically buy, sell, or hold). The recommendation is supported by an investment case, financial forecasts, and a valuation. Reports vary enormously, from short updates of a page or less to substantial documents that analyze whole industries and companies in great detail.

Equity research is also done privately by some buy-side institutional investors and hedge funds, but this is not published externally.

WHO PROVIDES IT AND WHY?
Public equity research is provided by three main types of supplier:
- Integrated investment banks that also offer equity broking and trading services plus a wide range of trading in other financial instruments, capital raising, and advisory services to companies.
- Broker dealers that offer equity broking and trading, but not corporate advisory services.
- Pure research providers.

The largest research departments are those in the global investment banks, which employ several hundred analysts each in a wide range of locations, and cover the majority of the world's liquid stocks. Some cover the less liquid smaller-cap stocks too—though these are often covered by smaller investment banks and broker dealers who specialize in particular sectors (especially technology) or regions (especially emerging or frontier economies). These specialist areas require more local and specific knowledge, which niche providers may be better able to provide.

HOW IS RESEARCH PAID FOR?
Research is normally paid for entirely through commissions charged by equity traders. Research is best thought of as a service rather than a product, and consists of both the written output of analysts and access to the analysts themselves through phone calls, emails, and face to face meetings. The service is provided free at the point of delivery. Reports can be provided at an almost zero marginal cost to a very large number of potential clients. But the analyst's time is far more valuable and is allocated only to those clients who are expected to pay for it.

Payment is made indirectly when the investor puts a buy or a sell trade through the firm for which the analyst works. The investor periodically informs the firm how much of the commission was allocated in compensation for the research service provided (as opposed to the pure cost of executing the trade), and for which analyst in particular. The research manager at the firm can then judge the commercial value of the analyst's service and compensate him or her appropriately.

Pure research providers that do not trade receive a cash payment. Typically this is part of the commission earned by a separate bank or broker dealer, and is paid to the research firm on the instructions of the investor who wishes to use the research. Rarely do investors themselves pay for or commission research on a cash-fee basis.

An analyst's provision of a research service to an investor client is not necessarily or even typically linked to commission received in trading in the stocks on which the analyst provides advice. The process of attributing the

QFINANCE

111

commission received during a year or quarter to the actual service provided by an analyst is therefore complicated, and the data are often poor.

Investment banks also have other motives for publishing research:

- To attract equity capital-raising business. Analyst coverage of a sector may be essential to win IPO (initial public offering) and other equity capital-raising business from companies in that sector. Good research helps to signal that the bank understands the equity markets in those sectors, and that the analyst would likely offer research on a company after its IPO, although the analyst is free to make the shares a "sell."
- To advertise other higher-margin advisory services. Banks seeking to attract companies to use their advisory services, especially in M&A, may see research as a form of advertising; good-quality research may reflect well on the less public capabilities of the firm.
- To promote the general brand and credibility of the bank. Global investment banks in particular wish to be seen as credible commentators on all the main financial markets, products, and matters of the day.

CONFLICTS ARISING FROM INVESTMENT BANKING COVERAGE

The fundamental conflict of interest in any investment bank or other firm that offers services both to investors and to corporate clients is that raising capital involves dealing with the buyer *and* the seller. In an IPO, the bank is contracted to advise the owners of a company how best to sell their equity to investors. A high price is good for the owners, but not for the investors. But the investors are also clients of the firm, and the firm's relationship with the investors is the main justification for their being competent to execute the IPO. Banks deal with this conflict in two ways:

- By segregating information flows behind "Chinese walls," which strictly limits access to nonpublic and proprietary information.
- By segregating incentives: Staff dealing with the investor clients are compensated mainly, if not entirely, by their ability to offer a good service to them; the bankers who deal with the corporate clients are evaluated quite separately and according to how they have served them.

A second potential conflict arises in the publication of research by any broker dealer, including integrated investment banks. The short-term incentive of the firm publishing the research is to maximize commission by inducing

clients to trade as much as possible—to "churn" their portfolios—at the expense of their ultimate investor customers (pension funds, mutual fund investors, etc.). Investment companies are of course mindful of this and, as professionals in the wholesale market, should be able to look after themselves.

THE GLOBAL SETTLEMENT AND OTHER REGULATORY CHANGES IN 2002–2004

In the late 1990s stock markets reached high levels on the back of a general enthusiasm for technology, media, and telecom (TMT) stocks. Many companies were listed on the stock market as IPOs. This business was very profitable for the sponsoring investment banks. When the stock market fell sharply in 2000–2001, many investors became concerned that the research on these companies had been biased and that analysts had knowingly recommended companies they secretly didn't really value.

In 2001, Eliot Spitzer, District Attorney for the State of New York, started an investigation into allegations that analysts at the investment bank Merrill Lynch misrepresented their views because of the investment banking fees in which they would share. Emails were disclosed that led to a wider investigation of all the leading investment banks.

The bankruptcy of Enron in December 2001 led to the passing of the Sarbanes–Oxley Act on July 30, 2002. Among other provisions, it enabled the Securities and Exchange Commission (SEC) to limit the supervision of and compensation decisions concerning analysts to certain officials, essentially excluding corporate financiers from the process. The Act was followed by rule changes by the National Association of Securities Dealers (NASD) and the New York Stock Exchange, which managed the disclosure of conflicts of interest by research analysts.

In February 2003 the SEC introduced analyst certification, whereby analysts individually attested to the independence of their research and recommendations. There followed in April 2003 the Global Settlement, in which ten large investment banks signed a legal contract to undertake to insulate analyst compensation and evaluation from corporate finance influence, among other measures, and to pay a joint fine of US$1.4 billion. The banks were: Bear Stearns, Credit Suisse First Boston, Deutsche Bank, Goldman Sachs, JPMorgan Chase, Lehman Brothers, Merrill Lynch, Morgan Stanley, Salomon Smith Barney, and UBS Warburg.

The key regulatory changes, including the separation of research analysts from the corporate finance business, were copied in rule changes by stock market regulators around the world. For example, in July 2004 the UK regulator—the Financial Services Authority (FSA)—introduced a rule that required firms producing research to tell their clients whether it met the FSA rules on impartiality. In the same year the European Union introduced the Market Abuse Directive, which required full disclosure of conflicts of interest concerning analysts.

CURRENT PRACTICE AND NEAR-TERM PROSPECTS

Research commissioned by the stock market regulators and done by independent academics broadly suggests that the recommendations of analysts are now less likely to be influenced by investment banking considerations. In particular, the distribution of buy and sell recommendations is much less unequal than it was in the late 1990s, when outright sell recommendations were extremely rare on Wall Street. There remain more buys than sells at most banks, but this is likely explained by a combination of analyst optimism and the commercial fact that there are always more opportunities for a buy (anybody can buy) than for sells (only existing holders can sell).

Investment professionals no longer complain about biased or tainted equity research, although they may still doubt the quality or commercial value of much of the research that is produced.

COMPANIES AND EQUITY RESEARCH ANALYSTS

Analysts, no longer facing incentives to be kind about companies with which their corporate finance colleagues do business, are correspondingly able to be more critical of companies. Analysts' opinions influence investors and can raise or lower a company's cost of capital. Companies are well advised to try to keep analysts onside. They are not advised to copy the lawsuit by LVMH (Moët Hennessy Louis Vuitton) against Morgan Stanley in 2002. A French court initially ruled that a Morgan Stanley analyst had allegedly denigrated the company, and fined the bank €30 million. In 2006, the Paris Court of Appeal overturned most of the original findings and canceled the damages.

Any remaining bias in analysts' views results from the desire not to offend a company's management and risk exclusion from corporate events and meetings. But legally companies must disclose material information in a fully public way, so excluding an analyst is either impossible or largely symbolic. Well-established and influential analysts therefore feel emboldened to write candidly about their views of companies and their management, though most are careful to avoid gratuitous offence. Companies can best deal with equity research analysts by being frank, consistent, and helpful.

MAKING IT HAPPEN

* Leaders of stock market quoted companies need to take analysts very seriously because they influence investor perceptions of companies.
* Analysts value transparency, clarity, consistency of disclosure, and as much operating information as can be given without compromising a company's commercial position.
* They also value access to senior management—not just the CFO—and appropriate site visits that provide real information about a company's business.
* Long-term credibility with analysts is built by stating and repeatedly referring to key targets and candid accounts of reasons for failing to hit them. That credibility translates into a lower cost of capital and higher stockholder value.

MORE INFO

Websites:

Most investment banks and brokerages that provide research restrict access to clients, but are normally happy to include companies in their distribution lists and to provide access to their web portals.

Standard & Poor's is a large, independent, nonbank provider of research and has some useful resources on its website. Choose your region and select "Equity Research" from the "Products & Services" dropdown menu: www.standardandpoors.com

A very useful resource on the theory and practice of equity valuation is the home page of Aswath Damodaran of New York University: pages.stern.nyu.edu/~adamodar

Details of the Global Settlement are available at:
www.sec.gov/news/speech/factsheet.htm and tinyurl.com/5uad96y

The Ability of Ratings to Predict the Performance of Exchange-Traded Funds
by Gerasimos G. Rompotis

EXECUTIVE SUMMARY

* Rating of the past performance of securities is considered crucial by investors when they make investment decisions.
* Several rating methods are used in the financial literature and by the investing community to rate the performance of securities.
* Performance is considered to be in some way predictable, and prediction is based on past performance.
* This article empirically assesses the rating of exchange-traded funds (ETFs) and prediction of their performance.
* The methods examined are the Morningstar rating process, the excess return, the Sharpe ratio, and the Treynor ratio.
* The empirical results reveal a high consistency among the rating methods and a sufficient level of predictability of ETF performance.
* ETF performance is persistent over the short term.

INTRODUCTION

Exchange-traded funds, or ETFs, are a relatively new investment product, but they are very important for both institutional and retail investors. ETFs are hybrids of ordinary corporate stocks and open-ended mutual funds which invest in baskets of shares that closely replicate the performance and risk levels of specific broad sector and international indexes. As such, ETFs offer investors a considerable level of risk diversification with just a single transaction. The risk of investing in ETFs can be moderated by choosing non-equity investments such as corporate bonds or treasury bonds, both of which are less risky choices than the most common equity-linked ETFs. Also, fixed-income ETFs, which usually carry low risk, are available for investors along with commodity and real estate ETFs.

ETFs are cheap investment tools because their administrative costs are low. This is reflected in low expense ratios due to their passive investment character, which requires managers simply to follow the tracking indexes and not to develop complicated and high-cost investment strategies. Nevertheless, it should be borne in mind that extremely frequent trading can offset the benefits of low expense ratios. The level of ETF expense ratios varies. In particular, ETFs that track broadly diversified indexes have the lowest expenses, followed by those that track sector indexes and others which invest in international indexes. Beyond managerial costs, ETFs pay commission to brokerage companies.

ETFs provide significant trading flexibility since they offer continuous pricing and the ability to trade throughout the day, unlike most mutual funds, which are traded at the end of the day. Furthermore, ETFs offer opportunities for the implementation of both passive and active trading strategies. The most common investment strategy in ETFs is the passive buy-and-hold strategy, the return of which depends exclusively on market performance. Also, ETFs allow active intraday trading and enable investors to buy and sell, in essence, all of the securities that make up an entire market with a single trade. They therefore provide the flexibility to get into or out of a position at any time throughout the day.

Another significant element of ETFs is the potential for high tax efficiency that they offer, since they tend to generate fewer capital gains than traditional mutual funds. The tax efficiency of ETFs arises from their discrete "in kind" creation/redemption process. ETFs are created in block-sized units of 25,000, 50,000, or 100,000 shares by large investors and institutions. The creator of an ETF purchases and deposits with a trustee a portfolio of stocks that approximates the composition of a specific index. In return for this deposit, the creator receives a fixed number of ETF shares, all of which are then usually traded on a secondary exchange market. The redemption of ETFs follows the reverse direction. Buying and selling of ETF shares usually takes place among shareholders and, as a result, there is no need for the ETF to sell its assets to meet redemptions. This advantageous feature of ETFs restricts the realization of taxable capital gains.

The trading price of ETFs usually deviates from their corresponding net asset value, providing arbitrage opportunities for big investors. If the value of the underlying portfolio of stocks is greater than the ETF price, the institutional investor will redeem the low-priced units of ETF by receiving the high-priced securities. In contrast, if the value of the underlying stocks is lower than the ETF price, the investor will exchange the low-priced securities for a newly created unit of the ETF.

Finally, ETFs are characterized by large liquidity, which contributes to easy and rapid trading near their fair market value and to the narrowness of bid/ask spreads and volatility. The liquidity of an ETF is not related to its daily trading volume but rather to the liquidity of the stocks contained in the index. The high liquidity of ETFs is achieved due to the ability of market-makers, which are usually large brokerage houses, to create and redeem shares of ETFs perpetually in response to market demand.

Because of their success, ETFs have begun to attract significant interest in the finance literature. An issue that so far has not been thoroughly examined is the rating of ETF performance and the ability of ratings to predict future performance. Nevertheless, several companies provide ranking services. The most popular is Morningstar, Inc., which rates ETFs on a scale of one to five stars according to past performance. Here we provide an introduction to ETF performance rating by investigating whether ratings are indicative of future returns. We do so using a sample of 50 Barclays iShares.

PERFORMANCE RATING
Morningstar
We first rate the performance of ETFs by using the Morningstar star rating. We calculate the "Morningstar" return, which is adjusted for expenses such as management fees, 12b-1 fees (annual marketing or distribution fees charged by some mutual funds), custodian fees, and other costs that are deducted from the assets of ETFs. Then we divide average excess return by either the average excess return or the average risk-free rate. The risk-free rate is used when the average excess return is negative or lower than the average risk-free rate. Morningstar return is expressed by the following formula:

$$\text{Morningstar return} = (\text{Expense and load-adjusted return of ETF} - \text{Treasury bill}) \div \max[(\text{Average sample return} - \text{Treasury bill}), \text{Treasury bill}]$$

The risk-free return is used in the dominator of the equation in cases where the average excess return of ETFs is negative or very low.

We then calculate "Morningstar" risk by summing up all the negative average daily excess returns of each ETF and dividing by the number of days in the assessing time period. Morningstar risk is represented by the following equation:

$$\text{Morningstar risk} = \text{Average underperformance of ETF} \div \text{Average underperformance of sample}$$

Finally, the ETF's star rating is calculated by subtracting its Morningstar risk from its Morningstar return. Afterwards, we classify ETFs in five classes, each of which includes 10 ETFs.

Morningstar, Inc., adjusts the returns of funds for expenses such as management fees, 12b-1 fees, custodian fees, and other costs that are deducted from the assets of funds. Return is also adjusted for front-end and deferred loads. However, here we do not need to adjust for expenses and loads because we start out by calculating returns with expense-free net asset values, meaning that we can then treat ETFs as no-load funds and removing the need to adjust for loads.

Excess Return, Sharpe Ratio, and Treynor Ratio
The second performance measure we consider is the average daily excess return of ETFs, which is simply calculated by subtracting a fund's risk-free performance from its return. The third performance measure is the Sharpe ratio. Sharpe ratio is calculated by dividing the average daily excess return of ETFs by the standard deviation of daily excess returns. The last performance measure is the Treynor ratio. This is computed by dividing the average daily excess return of ETFs by their systematic risk. Systematic risk is estimated by the single index market model, where the daily excess return of each ETF is regressed on the excess return of its benchmark.

PERFORMANCE PREDICTION
We examine predictability following regression analysis, represented by the next equation:

$$P_i = \delta_0 + \delta_4 D4_i + \delta_3 D3_i + \delta_2 D2_i + \delta_1 D1_i + u$$

where P_i is the out-of-sample performance of ETFs. Performance is, successively, the Morningstar return, the excess return, the

Predict the Performance of Exchange-Traded Funds

Sharpe ratio, and the Treynor ratio. The control factors of the model are four variables symbolized as D4, D3, D2, and D1, representing the ETFs that receive four, three, two, and one stars, respectively. The class of top-performing ETFs that are assigned five stars is represented by the δ_0 coefficient. This class is the reference group, and hence deltas account for the difference between the top-performing ETFs and other classes.

To estimate the model represented by this equation, we first compute all the performance measures of ETFs in a specific year between 2001 and 2006 and rank them in five classes in descending order. Then, we calculate each of the four types of performance for the subsequent period (2002–07, 2003–07, 2004–07, 2005–07, 2006–07, and 2007). The predictive ability of the model is confirmed when, first, δ estimates are negative and statistically significant and, second, when deltas become more negative as we move from δ_4 to δ_1.

It has been shown in the literature that there is a positive correlation between fund flows and persistence of performance (e.g. Wermers, 2003). Given that investors tend to put more money in mutual funds or ETFs that receive high grades from Morningstar or other agencies, we assume that this new money pushes up prices and returns and therefore that there should be a meaningful relationship between ratings and future performance.

PERFORMANCE PERSISTENCE

We examine persistence by applying simple regression analysis—specifically, cross-sectional regression of ETFs' performance in a given year on their performance in the previous year. The beta coefficient of the model is the indicator of persistence. Positive and significant betas imply persistence, and evidence of persistence strengthens as beta approaches unity. Significant negative beta values reflect inversions of ETF performance, while insignificant betas imply unsystematic variation of performance.

This study is presented in the next section.

CASE STUDY

Barclays iShares

Here we will empirically examine the rating and predictability of ETF performance using a sample of 50 Barclays Global Investors iShares during the period 2001–07. Of this sample, 27 ETFs track domestic broad market or sector indexes (20 and 7 ETFs, respectively), while the other 23 ETFs track the country indexes of Morgan Stanley or other international indexes (21 and 2 ETFs, respectively).

The average estimates of the four performance measures are as follows. The average Morningstar performance is negative and equal to –0.496. The average excess return and Sharpe and Treynor ratios are 0.017, 0.013, and 0.017, respectively.

We evaluate the consistency among the ratings by applying a simple cross-sectional model. Specifically, we regress the rating of ETFs according to method i to the rating of ETFs according to method j. More specifically, we regress the rankings of ETFs (i.e. rankings 1, 2, 3, 4, and 5) and not the actual estimates derived by the Morningstar rating method on the rankings derived by excess return. We repeat the regression for all the pairs of methods used to evaluate the performance of ETFs. The measure of consistency is the beta of the model. Positive beta estimates indicate consistency among ratings. Negative or statistically insignificant betas indicate inconsistency among the ratings. Alternatively, we assess consistency by calculating the correlation coefficients among the rankings obtained using the four methods.

The results, presented in Table 1, reveal high consistency among the performance measures. All betas are positive and significant and approach unity, ranging from 0.910 for the regression between Morningstar and excess return ratings to 0.990 for the pairing of excess return and Treynor ratio. This means that the best performing ETFs receive five stars almost consistently regardless of the rating method. This is also the case for ETFs in the other four classes. Table 2 presents the correlation coefficients among the rankings given by the four methods. Correlation coefficients are all greater than 0.900 and approximate unity, confirming the high consistency among the ranking results. Overall, the results reveal that there is no best method for the rating of ETF performance, and therefore investors (could) consult various alternative methods to make their investment choices based on the available information.

Asset Management: Tools and Strategies

Table 1. Consistency in performance rating

Estimated model	Alpha	t-test	Beta	t-test	R^2	F-stat
Morningstar return = $a_0 + \beta$ (Excess return) + u	0.270	1.360	0.910*	15.206	0.828	231.23*
Morningstar return = $a_0 + \beta$ (Sharpe ratio) + u	0.210	1.193	0.930*	17.530	0.865	307.29*
Morningstar return = $a_0 + \beta$ (Treynor ratio) + u	0.240	1.279	0.920*	16.263	0.846	264.50*
Excess return = $a_0 + \beta$ (Sharpe ratio) + u	0.090	0.773	0.970*	27.644	0.941	764.18*
Excess return = $a_0 + \beta$ (Treynor ratio) + u	0.030	0.444	0.990*	48.621	0.980	2364.06*
Sharpe ratio = $a_0 + \beta$ (Treynor ratio) + u	0.120	0.895	0.960*	23.753	0.922	564.24*

* Indicates statistical significance at the 1% level.

Table 2. Correlation coefficients between performance ratings

	Morningstar	Excess	Sharpe	Treynor
Morningstar	1.000	0.910	0.930	0.920
Excess	0.910	1.000	0.970	0.990
Sharpe	0.930	0.970	1.000	0.960
Treynor	0.920	0.990	0.960	1.000

The regression results for performance prediction are reported in Table 3. To begin with, the average δ_0 estimates are positive for each performance measure. Second, the average δ_4, δ_3, δ_2, and δ_1 estimates are all negative. Informationally, the majority of individual δ_0 in the individual regressions performed for each year of the period are positive and statistically significant, while the majority of δ_4 to δ_1 estimates are negative. Considering the significance of the δ_4 to δ_1 estimates, the results of individual regressions indicate that there is no significant difference between the ETFs included in classes 5 and 4, while there is a definite difference between the top-performing ETFs and medium and low-performing ETFs.

Table 3. Regression results in predicting performance

Variables	δ_0	δ_4 (4-star)	δ_3 (3-star)	δ_2 (2-star)	δ_1 (1-star)	R^2	F-stat
Morningstar return	0.525	−0.147	−0.846	−0.913	−0.438	0.200	1.510
Excess return	0.060	−0.016	−0.032	−0.036	−0.028	0.196	2.874
Sharpe ratio	0.044	−0.006	−0.011	−0.022	−0.011	0.142	2.041
Treynor ratio	0.061	−0.018	−0.033	−0.038	−0.029	0.201	2.957

The results are interpreted as follows: First, the positive δ_0 estimates indicate that the top-rated ETFs display a constant behavior through time. In other words, an ETF that performs well now is likely to perform well in the future. Second, there is no significant difference in the performance of the top-rated and second-rank ETFs. Third, there is evidence that the performance of the medium- and low-rated ETFs is sufficiently predictable, the performance of both these groups being inferior to that of the highly rated ETFs.

The sufficient predictability of ETF returns on the basis of rating in a specific year or period revealed by the results indicates that institutional and retail investors should take into consideration the published ratings of ETFs when they assess their investment choices. However, investors should always bear in mind that returns are not guaranteed and markets can move both up and down. Therefore, ratings are useful but should not be the only criterion in choosing among the bulk of ETFs. Other features, such as risk and expenses, should also be taken into consideration by investors.

Regression results for performance persistence are presented in Table 4. Regarding Morningstar, beta estimates provide evidence for short-term persistence in ETF performance during the periods 2001–02 and 2003–04 but a reversal for 2005–06. Beta estimates for the first two periods are positive and significant, while the beta for the third mentioned period is significantly negative. Considering excess return and Treynor ratio, the results indicate short-term persistence in the periods 2001–02, 2003–04, 2004–05, and 2006–07. The excess return results indicate a reversal of performance during the period 2002–03. With respect to Sharpe ratio, the results reveal performance persistence for all the sub-periods except 2005–06, when performance reversed.

Table 4. Regression results in performance persistence

Period	Alpha	t-test	Beta	t-test	R^2	F-stat
			Dependent variable: Morningstar return			
2001–02	−9.305*	−7.359	0.744*	3.447	0.198	11.883*
2002–03	0.009	0.056	0.001	0.060	0.000	0.011
2003–04	0.000	0.000	0.853**	2.141	0.217	13.318*
2004–05	−0.044	−0.115	0.065	0.207	0.226	6.699*
2005–06	−0.009	−0.051	−0.145**	−2.447	0.176	3.127**
2006–07	−0.487	−0.723	0.077	0.107	0.154	4.187**
			Dependent variable: Excess return			
2001–02	−0.058*	−3.288	0.296*	3.302	0.185	10.904*
2002–03	0.103*	7.968	−0.247***	−1.956	0.168	4.636**
2003–04	−0.004	−0.257	0.538*	4.748	0.320	22.542*
2004–05	−0.009	−1.048	0.530*	2.927	0.242	15.319*
2005–06	0.059*	4.616	−0.044	−0.190	0.291	6.006*
2006–07	−0.017	−1.221	0.588*	2.940	0.153	8.645*
			Dependent variable: Sharpe ratio			
2001–02	−0.034*	−6.139	0.266*	2.936	0.078	4.596**
2002–03	0.124*	13.624	0.377**	2.022	0.168	4.089**
2003–04	0.007	0.299	0.547**	2.392	0.248	15.851*
2004–05	0.005	0.524	0.280***	2.010	0.077	4.039***
2005–06	0.068*	3.317	−0.557*	−4.344	0.367	6.095*
2006–07	−0.006	−0.501	0.298***	1.867	0.068	3.486***
			Dependent variable: Treynor ratio			
2001–02	−0.059*	−8.282	0.302*	3.367	0.191	11.334*
2002–03	0.108*	4.990	−0.197	−0.698	0.141	3.783**
2003–04	−0.007	−0.520	0.565*	5.222	0.362	27.274*
2004–05	−0.009	−1.045	0.529*	2.929	0.243	15.406*
2005–06	0.060*	4.526	−0.031	−0.136	0.300	6.275*
2006–07	−0.017	−1.229	0.584*	2.972	0.155	8.831*

* Statistically significant at the 1% level. **Statistically significant at the 5% level. ***Statistically significant at the 10% level.

Overall, the beta estimates provide sound evidence for persistence patterns in ETF performance at the short-term level. These findings boost the results obtained for the predictability of ETF performance. In other words, persistence may be explained by the performance of either the top or the bottom-rated ETFs. Combining the predictability and persistence of performance, investors may find profitable opportunities by investing in ETFs.

MAKING IT HAPPEN

- ETFs provide investors with a large range of investment choices covering a variety of domestic, regional, international, and global markets. In addition, ETFs are invested in stocks, bonds, commodities, currencies, and fixed-income products.
- The assets of ETFs have shown continuous worldwide growth after their introduction on Amex in 1993.
- ETFs are preferable for both retail and institutional investors due to their trading convenience, low cost, tax efficiency, risk diversification, and portfolio transparency.
- Information on ETF profiles, management, trading processes, return, risk, holdings, and characteristics can be found from a range of sources.
- Investors should consider both the rating of an ETF's past performance and the past performance itself. However, they should bear in mind that past performance does not guarantee future returns.
- Investors should select an ETF after assessing their own investment profile and evaluating both returns and risks.

CONCLUSION

We have investigated the ability of ETF performance ratings to predict the future performance of these funds. We ranked ETFs using the overall Morningstar star rating methodology along with three alternative performance measures: the excess return, the Sharpe ratio, and the Treynor ratio.

First, the results reveal a high level of consistency among the four types of performance measure. In other words, all assign similar ratings to ETFs without significant deviations among them. Going further, regression analysis showed that the performance of ETFs is sufficiently predictable. More specifically, the results show that the highly graded ETFs perform well through time, while low-rated ETFs deliver consistently poor performance. In addition, it was found that there is no significant difference between ETFs assigned five and four stars, respectively.

Considering the predictive ability of each performance measure, the results show that the Treynor ratio produces the most significant results—specifically, it has better predictive ability than the other performance measures. The Morningstar rating has less predictive ability than Treynor ratio and excess return while it is essentially equivalent to Sharpe ratio. Finally, the results provide strong evidence for persistence in the performance of ETFs, at least in the short term.

MORE INFO

Articles:

Blake, Christopher R., and Matthew R. Morey. "Morningstar ratings and mutual fund performance." *Journal of Financial and Quantitative Analysis* 35:3 (September 2000): 451–483. Online at: dx.doi.org/10.2307/2676213

Blume, Marshall E. "An anatomy of Morningstar ratings." *Financial Analysts Journal* 54:2 (March/April 1998): 19–27. Online at: dx.doi.org/10.2469/faj.v54.n2.2162

Khorana, Ajay, and Edward Nelling. "The determinants and predictive ability of mutual fund ratings." *Journal of Investing* 7:3 (Fall 1998): 61–66. Online at: dx.doi.org/10.3905/joi.1998.408470

Reports:

Sharpe, William F. "Morningstar's risk-adjusted ratings." Working paper. January 1998. Online at: www.stanford.edu/~wfsharpe/art/msrar/msrar.htm

Wermers, Russ. "Is money really 'smart'? New evidence on the relation between mutual fund flows, manager behavior, and performance persistence." Working paper. November 2003. Online at: ssrn.com/abstract=414420

Websites:

Morningstar: www.morningstar.com

NASDAQ: www.nasdaq.com
Seeking Alpha's ETF sector page: www.etfinvestor.com

The Performance of Socially Responsible Mutual Funds by Luc Renneboog

Best Practice • Analysis

EXECUTIVE SUMMARY

Socially responsible investment funds employ negative and positive screens to select firms for their portfolios. These screens are based on environmental, social, or ethical criteria.

Trade-off: SRI funds could perform better than conventional ones as SRI funds comprise more carefully and actively selected firms. However, SRI funds could perform worse as the screening reduces the diversification potential which comes at a cost.

SRI performance measurement should involve an asset pricing model that captures investment styles. The Fama–French–Carhart model includes the market, firm size, growth opportunities, and share price momentum. In addition, the performance of SRI funds should be compared with the performance of conventional (non-SRI) funds.

Recent research shows that the performance SRI funds around the world is below the expected performance (measured by, for instance, the Fama–French–Carhart model). Furthermore, SRI funds do not outperform their conventional counterparts.

INTRODUCTION

Over the past decade, socially responsible investment (SRI), frequently also called ethical investment or sustainable investment, has grown rapidly around the world. SRI is a process that integrates social, environmental, and ethical considerations into investment decision making. Unlike conventional types of investment, SRI funds apply a set of investment screens to select or exclude assets based on ecological, social, corporate governance, or ethical criteria, and SRI often engages in the local communities and in shareholder activism to further corporate strategies towards the above aims.

WHAT TYPE OF INVESTMENT SCREENS DO SRI FUNDS EMPLOY?

Table 1 presents a summary of the SRI screens used by ethical funds around the world. Usually, SRI mutual funds apply a combination of the various types of screens. 64% of all socially screened mutual funds in the United States use more than five screens, while 18% of SRI funds use only one social screen (Renneboog, Ter Horst, and Zhang, 2008a). These screens can be broadly classified into two groups: negative screens and positive ones.

Negative Screens

The oldest and most basic SRI strategy is based on negative screening. These filters refer to the practice that specific stocks or industries are excluded from SRI portfolios based on social, environmental, and ethical criteria. A typical negative screen can be applied on an initial asset pool such as the S&P 500 stocks from which the alcohol, tobacco, gambling and defense industries, or companies with poor performance in labor relations or environmental protection, are excluded. Other negative screens may include irresponsible foreign operations, pornography, abortion, poor workplace conditions, violation of human rights, and animal testing. After performing a negative SRI screening, portfolios are created via a financial and quantitative selection. Some SRI funds only exclude companies from the investment universe when these firms' revenues derived from "asocial or unethical" sectors exceed a specific threshold, whereas other SRI funds also apply negative screens to a company's branches or suppliers. A small number of SRI funds use screens based on traditional ideological or religious convictions: for instance, they exclude investments in firms producing pork products, in financial institutions paying interest on savings, and in insurance companies insuring unmarried people.

Positive Screens

SRI portfolios are nowadays also based on positive screens, which in practice boils down to selecting shares that meet superior corporate social responsibility (CSR) standards. The most common positive screens focus on corporate governance, labor relations, the environment, sustainability of investments, and the stimulation of cultural diversity. Positive screens are also frequently used to select companies with a good record concerning

QFINANCE

Table 1. SRI screens. (*Source*: Renneboog, Ter Horst, and Zhang, 2008b)

Screens	Definitions	Pos. or Neg. screen
Tobacco	Avoid manufacturers of tobacco products.	−
Alcohol	Avoid firms that produce/market alcoholic beverages.	−
Gambling	Avoid casinos and suppliers of gambling equipment.	−
Defense/weapons	Avoid firms producing weapons.	−
Nuclear power	Avoid manufacturers of nuclear reactors and firms operating nuclear power plants.	−
Irresponsible foreign operations	Avoid firms with investments in firms located in oppressive regimes such as Burma or China, or firms that mistreat the indigenous peoples of developing countries.	−
Pornography/Adult entertainment	Avoid publishers of pornographic magazines; production studios that produce offensive video and audio tapes; companies that are major sponsors of graphic sex and violence on television.	−
Abortion/Birth control	Avoid providers of abortion; manufacturers of abortion drugs and birth control products; insurance companies that pay for elective abortions.	−
Labor relations and workplace conditions	Seek firms with strong union relationships, employee empowerment, and/or employee profit sharing. Avoid firms exploiting their workforce and sweatshops.	+ −
Environment	Seek firms with proactive involvement in recycling, waste reduction, and environmental cleanup. Avoid firms producing toxic products, and contributing to global warming .	+ −
Corporate governance	Seek companies demonstrating "best practices" related to board independence and elections, auditor independence, executive compensation, expensing of options, voting rights and/or other governance issues. Avoid firms with antitrust violations, consumer fraud, and marketing scandals.	+ −
Business practice	Seek companies committed to sustainability through investments in R&D, quality assurance, and product safety.	+
Employment diversity	Seek firms pursuing an active policy related to the employment of minorities, women, gays/lesbians, and/or disabled persons who ought to be represented amongst senior management.	+
Human rights	Seek firms promoting human rights standards. Avoid firms which are complicit in human rights violations.	+ −
Animal testing	Seek firms promoting the respectful treatment of animals. Avoid firms with animal testing and firms producing hunting/trapping equipment or using animals in end products.	+ −
Renewable energy	Seek firms producing power derived from renewable energy sources.	+
Biotechnology	Seek firms that support sustainable agriculture, biodiversity, local farmers, and industrial applications of biotechnology. Avoid firms involved in the promotion or development of genetic engineering for agricultural applications.	+ −
Community involvement	Seek firms with proactive investments in the local community by sponsoring charitable donations, employee volunteerism, and/or housing and educational programs.	+
Shareholder activism	The SRI funds that attempt to influence company actions through direct dialogue with management and/or voting at Annual General Meetings.	+
Unmarried	Avoid insurance companies that give coverage to unmarried couples.	−
Healthcare/ Pharmaceuticals	Avoid healthcare industries (used by funds targeting the "Christian Scientist" religious group).	−
Interest-based financial institutions	Avoid financial institutions that derive a significant portion of their income from interest earnings on loans or fixed-income securities (used by funds managed according to Islamic principles).	−
Pork producers	Avoid companies that derive a significant portion of their income from the manufacturing or marketing of pork products (used by funds managed according to Islamic principles).	−

renewable energy usage or community involvement. The use of positive screens is often combined with a "best in class" approach. Firms are ranked within each industry or market sector according to CSR criteria. Subsequently, only those firms in each industry which pass a minimum threshold are selected.

Combining Negative and Positive Screens
Negative and positive screens are often referred to as the first and second generation of SRI screens respectively. The third generation of screens refers to an integrated approach of selecting companies based on the economic, environmental, and social criteria comprised by both negative and positive screens. This approach is often called "sustainability" or "triple bottom line" (on account of its focus on people, planet and profit).

Shareholder Activism
The fourth generation of ethical funds combines the sustainable investing approach (third generation) with shareholder activism. In this case, portfolio managers or the companies specialized in granting ethical labels attempt to influence the company's actions through direct dialogue with the management or by the use of voting rights at Annual General Meetings.

DOING WELL BY DOING GOOD?

The fact that SRI funds apply screens that limit the full diversification potential may shift the mean-variance frontier towards less favorable risk–return tradeoffs than those of conventional portfolios. For instance, excluding part of the stock market (firms producing alcohol, tobacco, pornography) may negatively influence the risk–return tradeoffs of SRI funds. By this logic, SRI funds are expected to generate a weaker performance than conventional funds for two reasons. First, SRI funds underinvest in financially attractive investment opportunities, as some of these opportunities are excluded from the investment universe because they do not contribute sufficiently to the SRI objectives of the fund. Second, more intense screening intensity further reduces the investment universe, which may further weaken performance.

However, there are two arguments supporting the alternative hypothesis that states that SRI funds outperform conventional funds. First, sound social and environmental performance signals high managerial quality, which translates into favorable financial performance. Second, social, ethical, and environmental screening

may reduce the high costs that emerge during corporate social crises or environmental disasters. If financial markets tend to undervalue such costs, portfolios based on corporate governance, social, or environmental criteria may outperform their benchmarks.

HOW TO MEASURE THE PERFORMANCE OF SRI FUNDS

The performance of ethical (versus conventional) funds is measured by time-series returns of an equally weighted portfolio of funds. One can evaluate the performance of the fund portfolios on a country basis from a local investor perspective: The country portfolios of mutual funds are in local currency, evaluated against local benchmark factors while using local risk-free interest rates. Alternatively, one can assess fund performance from the perspective of an international investor by using international indices as benchmarks.

A first performance measurement method is based on the capital asset pricing model (CAPM):

$$r_t - r_{f,t} = \alpha_1 + \beta_{MKT}(r_t^m - r_{f,t}) + \varepsilon_t$$

where r_t is the return on an equally weighted portfolio of funds in month t, $r_{f,t}$ is the return on a local risk-free deposit (i.e. the one-month treasury bill rate or the interbank interest rate), r_t^m is the return of a local equity market index, β_{MKT} is the factor loading on the market portfolio, and ε_t stands for the idiosyncratic return. α_1 is Jensen's alpha; if alpha is positive, the funds do better than anticipated, whereas a negative alpha indicates underperformance.

A more robust evaluation method consists of the four-factor model, which includes the market, size, book-to-market, and momentum factors (this is also called the Fama–French–Carhart model). This model controls for the impact of investment styles on performance:

$$r_t - r_{f,t} = \alpha_4 + \beta_{MKT}(r_t^m - r_{f,t}) + \beta_{SMB}r_t^{smb} + \beta_{HML}r_t^{hml} + \beta_{UMD}r_t^{umd} + \eta_t$$

where r_t^{smb}, r_t^{hml}, and r_t^{umd} are the small-versus-big (SMB), high-minus-low (HML) and momentum (UMD) factors, β_{MKT}, β_{SMB}, β_{HML}, and β_{UMD} are the factor loadings on the four factors, and η_t stands for the idiosyncratic return. α_4 is the four-factor-adjusted return of ethical fund portfolios; if this alpha is positive, the funds do better than anticipated by this asset pricing model, whereas a negative alpha indicates underperformance.

More complex asset pricing models that allow for time-varying risk loadings can be implemented, but these are beyond the scope of this article.

Do SRI Funds Outperform?
- Performance measure 1: Is the alpha of the above asset pricing model positive? (Do SRI funds perform better than anticipated by a general asset pricing model that controls for the conventional investment styles?).
- Performance measure 2: Is the alpha of SRI funds higher than the alpha of conventional funds? (Do SRI funds outperform the reference group of conventional, non-SRI, funds?).

THE SRI RETURNS

For all SRI around the world over the period 1992–2003 (see More Info), some striking

results are obtained. SRI funds in all countries on average underperform the stock market index, and SRI funds in all countries on average underperform conventional (non-SRI) funds.

Table 2 shows that:
- a_4 is negative for the SRI funds in all countries. Thus, SRI funds underperform the benchmarks: the market, size, book-to-market, and momentum factors (although it should be noted that some negative returns are not statistically different from zero).
- The conventional funds do not succeed in outperforming the market. The reason is simple: Active funds usually do not succeed in consistently beating the market.
- SRI funds on average underperform conventional funds.

Table 2. SRI fund performance around the world. (*Source*: Renneboog, Ter Horst, and Zhang, 2008a)

		a_4
Europe		
Belgium	SRI	−5.26
	Conventional	−0.78
	Difference	−4.48
France	SRI	−5.96*
	Conventional	−1.87
	Difference	−4.08*
Germany	SRI	−0.62
	Conventional	−1.35
	Difference	0.73
Ireland	SRI	−6.14*
	Conventional	0.55
	Difference	−6.69*
Italy	SRI	−2.82
	Conventional	0.86
	Difference	−3.69
Luxembourg	SRI	−3.34
	Conventional	0.11
	Difference	−3.45
Netherlands	SRI	−4.10**
	Conventional	−2.59*
	Difference	−1.50
Norway	SRI	−4.20
	Conventional	−1.12
	Difference	−3.09
Sweden	SRI	−6.46*
	Conventional	0.51
	Difference	−6.97**

Switzerland	SRI	-3.01
	Conventional	-0.91
	Difference	-2.10
United Kingdom	SRI	-2.22*
	Conventional	-1.14
	Difference	-1.08
North America		
United States	SRI	-3.37*
	Conventional	-2.48*
	Difference	-0.89
Canada	SRI	-5.35*
	Conventional	-2.24*
	Difference	-3.11
Asia-Pacific		
Australia	SRI	-2.59
	Conventional	-0.38
	Difference	-2.21
Japan	SRI	-5.03*
	Conventional	0.81
	Difference	-5.84*
Malaysia	SRI	-2.99*
	Conventional	0.44
	Difference	-3.43
Singapore	SRI	-5.71
	Conventional	0.95
	Difference	-6.66

* Statistical significance

CASE STUDY

In relation to the ethical fund of a major Dutch insurance company, we use the independent services of the Ethical Investment Research Service (EIRIS) to screen the suitability of shares for ethical investment. Shares are also screened by our in-house ethical research team.

Examples of the type of companies not suitable for ethical investment include companies that:

- provide animal testing services or which manufacture or sell animal tested cosmetics or pharmaceuticals;
- have any involvement in intensive farming and that operate abattoirs or slaughterhouse facilities;
- are producers or retailers of meat, poultry, fish, dairy products, or slaughterhouse byproducts;
- manufacture armaments, nuclear weapons, or associated strategic products;
- provide critical services to, or are owners or operators of, nuclear power facilities;
- provide adult entertainment services.

MAKING IT HAPPEN

- Decide whether you are an ethical investor: Do you care about the environment, the social responsibility of firms, human rights, or other social responsibility issues?
- If yes, are you willing to accept a return from an SRI fund that is less than that of conventional (non-SRI) funds?

Analysis • Best Practice

- If yes, choose the type of fund by reading about the SRI of the fund. Select the screens that you deem most important—for instance, investment in producers of alternative
- energy; investment in firms with good human rights record in the developed and developing world; no investment in weapons manufacturers.
- energy; investment in firms with a good human rights record in the developed and developing world; no investment in weapons manufacturers.
- Choose the investment style of the fund: Do they use negative screens or a best-of-class approach on firms that pass the SRI filters?
- Compare the management and load fees of the selected SRI funds.

CONCLUSION

Ethical, social, environmental, or governance considerations influence the stock prices, and investors pay a price for the use of SRI screening by funds. The main reason why SRI investors may be willing to pay such a price for ethics or social responsibility is based on aversion to corporate behavior which is deemed unethical or asocial. Investors of SRI funds may thus explicitly deviate from the economically rational goal of wealth-maximization by pursuing social objectives. SRI funds in many European, North-American and Asia-Pacific countries strongly underperform domestic benchmark portfolios (such as the Fama–French–Carhart factors). When comparing the alphas of the SRI funds with those of matched conventional funds, the SRI returns are lower than those of conventional funds, but there is little statistically significant evidence that SRI funds underperform their conventional counterparts in most countries (exceptions being France, Ireland, Sweden, and Japan).

MORE INFO

Books:

Schepers, Donald. *Socially Responsible Investing*. London: Routledge, 2009.
Vogel, David. *The Market for Virtue: The Potential and Limits of Corporate Social Responsibility*. Washington, DC: Brookings Institution Press, 2006.

Articles:

Renneboog, Luc, Jenke ter Horst, and Chendi Zhang. "The price of ethics and stakeholder governance: The performance of socially responsible mutual funds." *Journal of Corporate Finance* 14:3 (June 2008a): 302–322. Online at: dx.doi.org/10.1016/j.jcorpfin.2008.03.009
Renneboog, Luc, Jenke ter Horst, and Chendi Zhang. "Socially responsible investments: Institutional aspects, performance, and investor behavior." *Journal of Banking and Finance* 32:9 (September 2008b): 1723–1742. Online at: dx.doi.org/10.1016/j.jbankfin.2007.12.039

Report:

Renneboog, Luc, Jenke ter Horst, and Chendi Zhang. "Is ethical money financially smart?" Finance working paper 117/2006. European Corporate Governance Institute, February 2006. Online at: ssrn.com/abstract=887162

Websites:

Social Investment Forum: www.socialinvest.org
Sustainable Investment Research International (SiRi): www.siricompany.com

QFINANCE

Valuation and Project Selection When the Market and Face Value of Dividends Differ
by Graham Partington

EXECUTIVE SUMMARY
The dividends are off the pace
Their value is below their face
So our models we must bend
Towards the valuation end
- When the market and face valuation of dividends differ, the valuation models used for valuing shares and selecting investment projects are likely to result in valuation errors.
- Where valuations are undertaken across different tax jurisdictions, different valuation models may be required.
- Where adjustments are made to discount rates rather than cash flows, this increases the likelihood of error.
- All these problems can be resolved by a simple modification of the standard valuation models.
- The approach, called the q method, provides a convenient and simple valuation model with almost universal application.

INTRODUCTION

Suppose that a company declares a cash dividend of $1, then the face value of the dividend is $1. The market value, which is what that dividend trades for in the market, may, or may not, be the same as the face value. Traditional approaches to valuation, such as the discounted dividend model (see "Using Dividend Discount Models," pp. 231–232) usually assume that the market value and the face value of dividends are the same. When this is not the case you hit problems in valuation and in making investment decisions using traditional capital budgeting techniques.

A common approach to valuing a share is to discount the expected selling price of the share and then add the discounted value of the dividends that you expect to receive before you sell. This approach is the foundation of the discounted dividend model used to estimate the value of shares. The expected price is by definition a market value, but the dividends are at face value. If the market and face value of dividends differ, adding share prices and dividends together is like adding apples and oranges and calling the total apples. The foundation of the discounted dividend model is therefore decidedly shaky if the market value and face values differ.

Whether the face and market values of dividends differ is a much debated question among finance academics, but there is plenty of evidence that they do. One reason for the difference is taxation. If the company gives you a dollar of dividends and then the government

takes away $0.25 in tax, you might well value that dividend at less than a dollar. As it turns out, capital gains taxes also play a role. If instead of paying you $1 of dividends the company keeps that cash in the company, your shares have more asset backing. Consequently your shares are more valuable and you end up paying more gains tax.

The market value of dividends relative to their face value then depends on the relative taxation of dividends and capital gains. In many jurisdictions dividends have a tax disadvantage. This is because returns in the form of price changes are taxed at concessional capital gains tax rates, whereas dividends are taxed as income. In other jurisdictions dividends are tax-advantaged. For example, in imputation tax systems the shareholders receive a refund of corporate tax along with their dividend.

The problem raised by the divergence between the market and face value of dividends also extends to traditional discounted cash flow techniques for capital budgeting (see p. 1099). This is because the use of these techniques is based on their equivalence to the discounted dividend model, as was shown by the Nobel Prize winners Merton Miller and Franco Modigliani.[1]

THE SOLUTION IS q

One solution to the problem is to make the discounted values for prices and dividends consistent by adjusting the discount rate. For example, the capital asset pricing model, or CAPM, a popular model for estimating discount rates, can be extended to allow for differential taxation of dividends and capital gains. The reality, however, is that these after-tax versions of the CAPM have been little used because of the additional complexity that they involve and because of difficulties in implementation. There is a further problem that different models are needed for different tax jurisdictions.

An alternative solution to the problem involves adjusting the cash flow, and it also requires a small change in the definition of the discount rate.[2] This alternative approach is called the q method. The advantage of the q method is that it is both simple and general in its application. It works whether dividends have a tax disadvantage or a tax advantage (as under an imputation tax system). The approach also allows the face value and market value of interest payments to differ. Thus, whatever tax jurisdiction the valuation is being conducted under, the q method can be used without modification. The method also works just as well if the face and market value of dividends differ for reasons other than taxes.

An attractive feature of the q method is that the main adjustment is to the measurement of cash flows. One advantage of adjusting the cash flow is that the adjustment is clearly visible, and therefore executives are alerted to the assumptions that are being made. In contrast, where adjustments are buried in the discount rate, it is often a case of out of sight, out of mind. Cash flow adjustments, therefore, are less likely to lead to errors.

The key to the q method is to let the market do the work and express everything in market prices. To do this it is first necessary to define the return on equity in terms of the expected growth in share prices, R_{price}. This is done as follows:

$$R_{price} = (P^{cum}_{t+1} - P^{ex}_t) \div P^{ex}_t$$

where P^{cum}_{t+1} represents the expected cum-dividend share price in the next period (at time $t + 1$) and P^{ex}_t represents the ex-dividend share price that we observe now (at time t).[3] When prices are in equilibrium, R_{price} is the return that investors require on their investment in the shares. In determining their required return R_{price}, investors will factor in the effect of any capital gains taxes that they may have to pay.

Next, we decompose the expected cum-dividend price into the expected ex-dividend price next period (P^{ex}_{t+1}) and the market value of dividends. The market value of the dividend is obtained by multiplying the face value of the next period's expected dividend (DIV_{t+1}) by q. The q factor is the ratio of the market value of dividends to the face value of dividends. The q factor, just

like the famous Tobin's q, measures the ratio of market value to replacement cost. This is because the cost of replacing the cash paid out as a dividend equals the face value of the dividend. Thus, if the market value of dividends is $0.75 per $1.00 of face value, the q factor is 0.75. The resulting decomposition of the expected cum-dividend price is:

$$P^{cum}_{t+1} = P^{ex}_{t+1} + q(DIV_{t+1})$$

Everything is now expressed in terms of market value. No further adjustments for taxes on dividends or on capital gains are required. This is because the effects of these taxes are fully captured in q and R_{price}. From the two definitions above it is simply a matter of algebra to derive a set of equations for valuation and the cost of capital. We can omit the algebra and go straight to the results.

USING THE q METHOD

We begin with the discounted dividend model for today's ex-dividend price. This looks very like the traditional discounted dividend model except that the dividend is multiplied by q and the discount rate is R_{price}:

$$P^{ex}_t = q(DIV_{t+1}) \div (1 + R_{price})^{t+1} + P^{ex}_{t+1} \div (1 + R_{price})^{t+1} = \sum_{t=t+1}^{\infty} DIV_t q \div (1 + R_{price})^t$$

The term on the extreme right-hand side says that the value of the share is the present value to infinity of future dividend payments expressed in market values. The model is very similar to the standard discounted dividend model, except that the face value of dividends is multiplied by q to get market values and the discount rate is a rate applicable to discounting market values. If q is equal to one, then the model above becomes identical to the standard discounted dividend model.

Turning to capital budgeting, in using the discounted cash flow approach it is traditional to value a project by discounting the unlevered after-tax cash flow of the project using the weighted average cost of capital (WACC). Three modifications are required when the market and face value of dividends differ. First, multiply the unlevered cash flows by q, thus expressing the cash flows in terms of market values. Second, convert the WACC to a discount rate appropriate for discounting market values. This is done by using R_{price} for the cost of equity and multiplying the cost of debt, r_{debt}, by q. Given a corporate tax rate T_c, the resulting equations are as follows:

Best Practice • Analysis

Figure 1. Comparison between old and new shares with different dividend entitlements for Coca-Cola Amatil

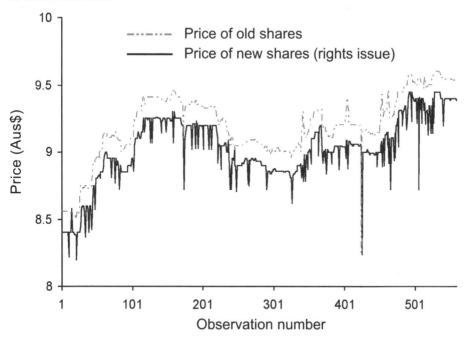

Project value = $\sum_{t=1}^{N}$ (Unlevered after-corporate-tax cash flow)$q \div (1 + WACC)^t$

WACC = (Equity value $\div$ Firm value) R_{price}
+ (Debt value $\div$ Firm value) $r_{debt} (1 - T_c)q$

At first sight the scaling of the cost of debt by q may seem strange.[4] It arises directly from the algebra used to derive the model for project valuation, and an intuitive interpretation is that it captures the tax-effectiveness of debt relative to equity. If q is less than one, this enhances the tax-effectiveness of debt relative to equity, and if q is more than one, this makes debt less tax-effective. If q is equal to one, then both the project value and WACC equations are exactly the same as those used in the traditional approach to capital budgeting.

A third adjustment may be required when computing the increase in company value created by the project (the net present value, NPV.) This adjustment is only needed if the project is financed from retained earnings that could otherwise be distributed as dividends. Let us suppose that the market value of dividends is $0.75 per dollar of face value; then, if the firm

retains $1.00 of earnings rather than paying it as a dividend, investors are only foregoing $0.75 of market value ($q = 0.75$.) Therefore, the firm only needs to earn its cost of capital on $0.75 of value—or, to put it another way, the opportunity cost of retained earnings is $0.75 per dollar of face value retained. Consequently, if the firm retains $1 million to fund a project, the cost in terms of market value is only $750,000.

Given the project value obtained from the valuation equation above, the NPV is computed as:

NPV = Project value – Initial investment

Where part or all of the initial investment is funded from retained earnings, the initial investment needs to be converted to market values. The resulting equation for the NPV becomes:

NPV = Project value – (External finance
+ q × Retained earnings)

When q is less than one, this makes retained earnings an attractive source of finance.

QFINANCE

However, in some jurisdictions, such as countries with imputation tax systems, q can be considerably greater than one. For example, evidence from the German and Australian imputation systems suggests that q can be as high as 1.2, and in some cases higher. In such cases external financing is more attractive than using retained earnings.

One final attractive feature of the q method is that it gives rise to a very simple after-tax version of the CAPM that encompasses the other after-tax CAPMs that have been proposed. Indeed it is so simple that it looks very like the standard CAPM. Given the volatility of the return on a share relative to the overall capital market, measured by beta (β), the risk-free interest rate (r_f), and the q factor for interest payments (q_{debt}), the after-tax CAPM is written as:

$$R_{price,i} = r_f q_{debt} + \beta (R_{price,M} - r_f q_{debt})$$

where the subscripts i and M indicate the return on the share and the return on the market, respectively. If bonds and shares are taxed in the same way, and bond and share markets are not segregated, q and q_{debt} should be the same. However, where bonds and shares are taxed differently, or where different investors set prices in bond and equity markets, then q and q_{debt} can differ.

MEASURING q

Two questions that naturally arise are: How do you measure q, and is it likely to vary much across stocks? Addressing the second question first, q might vary across stocks if the prices of different stocks are set by different types of investor. However, it seems unlikely that q will vary greatly across stocks in a given tax jurisdiction. This is because substantial variation in q across stocks would create opportunities for profitable arbitrage. Substantial variation in q across stocks therefore requires different dividend clienteles to hold different stocks and also calls for substantial barriers to arbitraging the valuation differences created by these clienteles.

Several methods exist for measuring q, and improved methods are being developed. One common approach is to look at the change in the price when the stock changes from trading cum-dividend to trading ex-dividend. Since the dividend detaches from the stock on the ex-dividend day, the change in the value of the stock is a measure of the market value of the dividend. Unfortunately, however, several other factors influence the price change, so this measurement can often be inaccurate as an estimate of dividend value. For example, the stock trades one day at the cum-dividend price and then trades the next day at the ex-dividend price. Thus, the price change reflects both the detaching of the dividend and the effect of news items released in the time between the observations of the two prices.

The price impact of the news often swamps the price impact of the stock going ex-dividend. It is, therefore, much better to simultaneously observe stock prices with and without entitlement to the dividend. One case where this happens is when a company makes a new share issue and the new shares are not entitled to the current dividend.

CASE STUDY

A Measurement of q

In mid-1995 Coca-Cola Amatil, an Australian company, made a rights issue in which the newly issued shares were not entitled to the next dividend. The dividend had a face value of AU$0.095. Figure 1 plots the prices of the old and the new shares, which were matched to be no more than one minute apart. It was possible to observe these prices from 26 July to 30 August. After this time, the old shares went ex-dividend and the old and the new shares became identical.

As can be seen from Figure 1, movements in the price of the old and new shares follow each other closely and there is a more or less constant difference in the price of the two shares. This difference represents the market value of the dividend. Over the cases where each trade involved at least 100 shares, the average difference was 1.53 times the dividend. In other words, q was 1.53 and the average price difference was about AU$0.145. The dividend had a market value greater than its face value because it had tax credits attached. The tax credits had a face value of AU$0.049 per share, so adding the tax credit to the dividend gives a grossed up value of AU$0.144, which is very close to the estimated market value. Clearly, a big difference in valuation would result from assuming $q = 1$, as against the value of $q = 1.53$ that is suggested by the data.

CONCLUSION

The errors in valuations that arise from assuming $q = 1$ when this is not the case are highly variable depending on the pattern of project cash flows, the life of the project, the cost of capital, and how the project is financed. However, even small deviations from a value of $q = 1$ can result in substantial changes to project value for some projects. The most benign cases arise when the project is funded from retained earnings. In this case there are errors that tend to offset each other. For, example if $q = 0.75$ but is assumed equal to one, the market value of each cash flow is overstated by 25%. However, the cost of financing the investment with retained earnings is also overstated by 25%. Consequently, the overstatement of the cash flows is to some extent balanced by the overstatement of the cost of the investment. Unfortunately, we can't rely on these offsetting errors to always be of similar magnitude.

The moral for senior executives is clear: Whether the market value of dividends is equal to the face value is important. If you believe that the face value and market value of dividends are equal ($q = 1$), carry on using the traditional models; if not, use the q method. If you are uncertain about the magnitude of q, use the valuation equations in this chapter to analyze the sensitivity of the valuation to the size of q.

MAKING IT HAPPEN

- The first step is for top management to consider whether the market value and face value of dividends are likely to differ for the firm. In other words, is q for dividends equal to one? For some firms, as in the mini-case for Coca-Cola Amatil above, there will be direct evidence on the value of q for the firm. In other cases, published research may provide evidence on market-wide values of q. In most cases the firm value for q is likely to be close to the market-wide value. In some cases management may need to commission a special study to estimate q.
- A precise estimate of q may be difficult to obtain, but imprecise estimates are a common feature of many of the input variables in valuation and capital budgeting. Consequently, imprecision is not a reason for ignoring the impact of q. It is a reason for doing a sensitivity analysis.
- Given a value of q not equal to one, then capital budgeting and valuation procedure manuals need to be updated to include the formulae presented in this chapter. Treasury staff and divisional mangers will need to be trained in the use of these formulae. Top management should provide divisional managers with the value of q, or the range for q to be used in sensitivity analysis. This will eliminate the temptation for managers to use varying estimates of q in gaming the budget.
- It should be emphasized that q impacts not only on the value of cash flows and the cost of capital, but also on the cost of using retained earnings. It also feeds into the measurement of performance using techniques such as EVA, since such techniques rely on measuring the capital invested and the cost of capital.

MORE INFO

Book:

Armitage, Seth. *The Cost of Capital: Intermediate Theory*. Cambridge, UK: Cambridge University Press, 2005.

Articles:

Dempsey, Mike. "The cost of equity capital at the corporate and investor levels allowing a rational expectations model with personal taxations." *Journal of Business Finance and Accounting* 23:9–10 (December 1996): 1319–1331. Online at: dx.doi.org/10.1111/1468-5957.00082

Dempsey, Mike. "The impact of personal taxes on the firm's weighted average cost of capital and investment behaviour: A simplified approach using the Dempsey discounted dividends model." *Journal of Business Finance and Accounting* 25:5–6 (June/July 1998): 747–763. Online at: dx.doi.org/10.1111/1468-5957.00210

Dempsey, Mike. "Valuation and cost of capital formulae with corporate and personal taxes: A synthesis using the Dempsey discounted dividends model." *Journal of Business Finance and Accounting* 28:3–4 (April/May 2001): 357–378. Online at: dx.doi.org/10.1111/1468-5957.00377

Dempsey, Mike, and Graham Partington. "Cost of capital equations under the Australian imputation tax system." *Accounting and Finance* 48:3 (September 2008): 439–460. Online at: dx.doi.org/10.1111/j.1467-629X.2007.00252.x

NOTES

1 Miller, Merton H., and Franco Modigliani. "Dividend policy, growth, and the valuation of shares." *Journal of Business* 34:4 (October 1961): 411–433. Online at: www.jstor.org/stable/2351143

2 For a rigorous exposition of the *q* method, see the early work of Dempsey (1998) and the later work of Dempsey and Partington (2008). Full citations of both works are given above.

3 The stock goes ex-dividend on a particular date, and shares bought after this date are not entitled to the current dividend. Shares bought prior to this date are referred to as cum-dividend and are entitled to the current dividend.

4 In deriving the project valuation model, the interest payments are initially scaled by qdebt, but this term cancels out in the derivation and so does not appear in the cash flow.

WACC versus APV Valuation: Financial Policy and the Discount Rate
by Antoine Hyafil

EXECUTIVE SUMMARY
The article uses a simple numerical example to illustrate that:
- Weighted average cost of capital (WACC) and adjusted present value (APV) valuation yield identical results in the (hypothetical) situation when expected cash flows are constant over time;
- The equivalence depends crucially on using the right discount rates;
- Such discount rates are different when the debt is constant over time, or when it is only expected to be constant over time;
- The equivalence between WACC and APV disappears in the more realistic situation when expected cash flows are nonconstant, unless the financial structure remains stable;
- The formula most often used by practitioners to relate the beta of equity and the beta of the assets of a corporation is inconsistent with WACC valuation.

INTRODUCTION

Franco Modigliani and Merton Miller's (1958) Propositions I and II have generated two valuation methodologies, hereafter referred to as WACC (weighted average cost of capital) and APV (adjusted present value) valuation. Briefly, Proposition I states that the value of a firm does not depend on its capital structure, and Proposition II states that a firm's value depends on three things: the required rate of return on its assets; its cost of debt; and its debt/equity ratio. Both valuation methodologies are equivalent provided that the discount rates are chosen appropriately and consistent assumptions are made regarding the corporation's financial policy. They are not equivalent otherwise, and both may lead to inappropriate valuation if used with insufficient care.

Modigliani and Miller's (MM) Proposition II addresses the relationship between the cost of equity of a levered firm and the cost of equity of its unlevered equivalent. Whenever financial markets are frictionless, such a relationship reflects an equilibrium generated by investors' arbitrage activities. A consequence is that, in the absence of market imperfections, neither the value nor the the cost of capital of a corporation vary with its financial structure: the value of the firm is equal to the present value of the free cash flows, discounted at a constant weighted average cost of capital.

Conversely, as emphasized in many ways by contemporary corporate finance, when imperfections exist a firm's financial structure may impact its valuation. The most familiar imperfection is the tax advantage of debt implied by the tax deductibility of interest. MM

Proposition I shows that the value of a levered firm is equal to the present value of the free cash flows discounted at the unlevered cost of capital, plus the present value of the tax savings. This is the basis for APV valuation. WACC valuation remains valid if an adjustment is made for a world where borrowing has a tax advantage; the value is equal to the present value of the free cash flows discounted at a weighted average cost of capital, with the latter now incorporating the impact of the tax shield:

$$\text{WACC} = \text{Cost of debt} \times w(1 - t) + \text{Cost of equity} \times (1 - w)$$

where w is the ratio, D/EV, of debt to enterprise value, and t is the tax rate.

The WACC and the APV approaches are equivalent to the extent that the return requirements used for discounting reflect the arbitrage-implied structure of return requirements. However, practitioners using both methodologies usually arrive at different valuations. This article shows that such differences are the consequence of different implicit assumptions regarding the firm's debt policy, and it attempts to draw conclusions on the methodological precautions that must be taken. An example will illustrate this.

VALUATION WITH CONSTANT FREE CASH FLOWS: A COMPUTATIONAL EXAMPLE

Base Case: Debt Level Is Fixed over Time

Consider a company with capital employed (CE) of 270, earnings before interest and taxes (EBIT) of 66, and beta (β_u) of the assets = 1.00; initial debt (D), with a beta (β_d) of 0.3, is set at 77.81, and the tax rate, t, is 1/3. We shall assume that the capital asset pricing model applies, with risk-free rate, $R_p = 5.7\%$ and market risk premium, R_p, = 6.0%. As a consequence, the required return on assets, COE_u, is 11.7%, and the cost of debt, COD, is 7.5%. (COE_u is the cost of *unlevered* equity, i.e. the return shareholders would require if the assets were 100% equity financed.)

We shall start by assuming an expected growth rate of 0% and that debt remains constant over time at 77.81.

Table 1 shows that APV valuation yields an enterprise value (EV) of 402.30, and therefore a market value of equity (MVE) of 323.60. With free cash flows to the firm (FCFFs) discounted at COE_u, and tax savings (TS) discounted at COD, the terminal value of the FCFFs equals

$FCFF_4/COE_u$ and the terminal value of the tax savings equals TS_4/COD. Note that using COD to discount the tax savings does not imply that the latter are assumed to be riskless, but, as in Modigliani and Miller's seminal paper, they are assumed to carry the same risk as the debt itself.

Table 2 shows that WACC valuation yields the same result as APV, with FCFF now discounted at WACC = 10.9370% and residual value at the end of the third year equaling $FCFF_4/WACC$. The WACC computation, and therefore the equivalence between the two methodologies, depends critically on the cost of equity (COE) being consistent with the arbitrage-implied structure of return requirements. In the case of debt remaining constant over time, the classical formulae used by practitioners applies:

Table 1. Adjusted present value (APV) valuation

	Today	Year 1	Year 2	Year 3	Residual value
Growth		0%	0%	0%	0%
EBIT		66.00	66.00	66.00	66.00
Tax (33%)		22.00	22.00	22.00	22.00
Net operating profit after tax		44.00	44.00	44.00	44.00
Variation in capital employed		—	—	—	—
Free cash flows to the firm (FCFF)		44.00	44.00	44.00	44.00
Discount factor @ COE_u (11.70%)		0.90	0.80	0.72	0.72
DCFF @ COE_u		39.39	35.27	31.57	269.84
Market value of assets	376.07	376.07	376.07	376.07	
Debt	78.71	78.71	78.71	78.71	
Interest @ COD (7.50%)		5.90	5.90	5.90	5.90
Tax savings @ tax rate (33.33%)		1.97	1.97	1.97	1.97
Discount rate		7.50%	7.50%	7.50%	7.50%
Discount factor		0.93	0.87	0.80	0.80
Present value of each annual tax savings		1.83	1.70	1.58	21.12
Present value of all annual tax savings	26.24	26.24	26.24	26.24	
Enterprise value (EV)	402.30	402.30	402.30	402.30	
Debt	78.71	78.71	78.71	78.71	
Market value of equity (MVE)	323.60	323.60	323.60	323.60	

Table 2. Weighted average cost of capital (WACC) valuation

	Today	Year 1	Year 2	Year 3	Residual value
Growth		0%	0%	0%	0%
FCFF		44.00	44.00	44.00	44.00
WACC		10.94%	10.94%	10.94%	10.94%
Discount factor @ WACC		0.90	0.81	0.73	0.73
DCFF @ WACC		39.66	35.75	32.23	294.66
Enterprise value (EV)	402.30	402.30	402.30	402.30	
Debt	78.71	78.71	78.71	78.71	
Market value of equity (MVE)	323.60	323.60	323.60	323.60	

$COE = R_f + \beta_e \times R_p$

and

$\beta_e = \beta_u[1 + (1 - t) \times D/EV]$

with computation of D/EV based on the debt of 77.81 and the enterprise value of 402.30 implied by the APV valuation. The latter formula is the one that prevails in a Modigliani–Miller setting in a world *with* taxes. In this case β_e =1.1135 and COE = 12.3810%.

Modified Case: Debt Varies with the Value of the Assets
Impact on the Discount Rates
Continue to assume an expected growth of 0%, but now replace the assumption that the firm will maintain a fixed debt level equal to 77.81 over time by the assumption that it will maintain a constant proportion of debt to enterprise value (D/EV) equal to 20%, whatever the actual deviation from expected growth. The consequences are as follows:

• Tax savings beyond year 1 are now a function of the actual debt levels realized in the future, which are themselves a function of the actual free cash flows. This implies that tax savings beyond year 1 have the same probability distribution, and therefore the same risk, as the value of the assets. As a consequence, from year 2 onwards an APV valuation now needs to discount them at the rate COE$_u$, which reflects the risk of the assets, rather than at the cost of debt, COD.

• Equity is no longer partially protected in a downturn by a fixed level of the tax shield, since the latter adjusts to the lower value of the assets; it benefits more than before in an upturn, but, given investors' risk-aversion, this does not compensate. As a result, equity holders now require a higher return, COE. The latter can be derived using the following formulae:

$COE = R_f + \beta_e \times R_p$

and

$\beta_e = \beta_u(1 + D/EV)$

with computation of D/EV based on the target D/EV ratio of 20%. In this case β_e = 1.1709 and COE = 12.7256%. Note that the formula for the β_e computation is no longer the same as before but is now identical to the one which would prevail in a Modigliani–Miller setting in a world *without* taxes.

Impact on Valuation
Table 3 shows APV valuation. Applying the D/EV target ratio of 20% yields D = 77.81 *as before*. Enterprise value (EV) is 393.54, and market value of equity (MVE) is 314.83, lower than when debt is assumed to remain constant whatever happens, even though *expected* debt is assumed to remain constant. FCFFs and the terminal value of the FCFFs, discounted at COE$_u$, yield the same value as before, but tax savings (TS), as well as the terminal value of the tax savings

Table 3. Adjusted present value (APV) valuation

	Today	Year 1	Year 2	Year 3	Residual value
FCFF		44.00	44.00	44.00	44.00
Discount factor @ COE$_u$ (11.70%)		0.90	0.80	0.72	0.72
DCFF @ COE$_u$		39.39	35.27	31.57	269.84
Market value of assets	376.07	376.07	376.07	376.07	
Debt	78.71	78.71	78.71	78.71	
Interest @ COD (7.50%)		5.90	5.90	5.90	5.90
Tax savings @ tax rate (33.33%)		1.97	1.97	1.97	1.97
Discount rate		7.50%	11.70%	11.70%	11.70%
Discount factor		0.93	0.83	0.75	0.75
Present value of each annual tax savings		1.83	1.64	1.47	12.54
Present value of all annual tax savings	17.48	17.48	17.48	17.48	
Enterprise value (EV)	393.54	393.54	393.54	393.54	
Debt	78.71	78.71	78.71	78.71	
Market value of equity (MVE)	314.83	314.83	314.83	314.83	

Analysis • Best Practice

Table 4. Weighted average cost of capital (WACC) valuation

	Today	Year 1	Year 2	Year 3	Residual value
FCFF		44.00	44.00	44.00	44.00
WACC		11.18%	11.18%	11.18%	11.18%
Discount factor @ WACC		0.90	0.81	0.73	0.73
DCFF @ WACC		39.58	35.60	32.02	286.36
Enterprise value (EV)	393.54	393.54	393.54	393.54	
Debt	78.71	78.71	78.71	78.71	
Market value of equity (MVE)	314.83	314.83	314.83	314.83	

(equal to TS_4/COE_u), are now discounted at COD for one year only and at COE_u thereafter, which yields a lower overall value of the tax savings.

Table 4 shows that WACC valuation yields the same result as APV, with FCFF now discounted at WACC (11.1805%) higher than before, and a residual value at the end of the third year equaling $FCFF_4/WACC$.

VALUATION WHEN CASH FLOWS VARY OVER TIME

Introducing a non-zero growth rate adds to the complexity: WACC and APV valuation continue to yield the same outcome under a financial policy of a constant proportion of debt; they do *not* yield the same outcome under a policy of a constant level of debt, since such a debt level is now *expected* to be a variable proportion of the enterprise value.

- If we assume a D/EV of 20%, a 3% perpetual yearly growth of the free cash flows increases debt capacity from 77.81 to 87.77; both APV and WACC valuations yield an enterprise value (EV) = 438.85.
- On the other hand, fixed debt of 77.81 with a 3% growth of the free cash flows yields EV = 451.56 with WACC valuation, but EV = 456.51 with APV valuation. The latter correctly reflects the evolution of the financial structure over time, while the former contradictorily assumes that financial structure remains constant.

CONCLUSION

Practitioners often compute the equity beta of an unlisted corporation from the asset betas for comparable listed peers, using the formula which includes tax savings, and then discount the free cash flows at the cost of capital, thereby making the implicit assumption that the financial structure will remain constant. The latter assumption is inconsistent with the beta computation. If the financial structure is expected to remain constant, the beta computation should not incorporate tax savings into the formula. If debt is expected not to increase with the enterprise value but to remain stable or decrease over time, WACC valuation is not appropriate.

APV valuation on the other hand will always give the correct value, to the extent that the asset beta has been computed correctly and tax savings are discounted at the proper rate. In particular, and contrary to popular belief, using the formula which incorporates the tax shield when applying APV and discounting tax savings at the cost of debt *does not overestimate* the value as long as the debt level is expected to remain constant. In the case of leveraged finance, where debt levels are scheduled to decrease through time, it overestimates the beta, and therefore *underestimates* the value. From a purely methodological point of view, approaches that apply APV using the levered formula for the asset beta and cost of unlevered equity to discount tax savings are therefore overly conservative.

MAKING IT HAPPEN

- The emphasis in this article on methodological rigor may seem excessive to practitioners, given the uncertainty about many other parameters; however, in our eyes this does not justify using a wrong methodology unknowingly.
- Practitioners willing to make the methodological effort should be careful in their computation of the asset beta when using APV in leveraged finance situations.
- Computing industry beta by unleveraging peer corporations' equity beta first implies assessing, for each corporation, whether its financial policy is closer to (1) maintaining a stable target debt to enterprise value ratio or (2) maintaining a stable debt level.
- The same applies when computing the asset beta from the firm's equity beta prior to a leveraged recapitalization.
- The unlevered beta formula crucially depends on the above assumption, and may therefore vary from one peer corporation to another.
- When industry betas have been carefully computed as above, discount the tax savings at the (pretax) cost of debt.
- Do not forget to take into account the expected costs in case of default to balance the positive valuation impact of the tax savings.

MORE INFO

Books:

Note that books on this subject usually relate asset beta to equity beta using the formula that incorporates tax savings. They do not point out that this is only valid when financial structure is assumed to be constant through time.

Articles:

Harris, R. S., and J. J. Pringle. "Risk-adjusted discount rates—Extensions from the average-risk case." *Journal of Financial Research* 8 (Fall 1985): 237–244.

Miles, James A., and John R. Ezzell. "The weighted average cost of capital, perfect capital market and project life: A clarification." *Journal of Financial and Quantitative Analysis* 15:3 (September 1980): 719–730. Online at: dx.doi.org/10.2307/2330405

Modigliani, Franco, and Merton H. Miller. "The cost of capital, corporation finance and the theory of investment." *American Economic Review* 48:3 (June 1958): 261–297. Online at: www.jstor.org/stable/info/1809766

Forecasting Default Rates and the Credit Cycle by Martin S. Fridson

EXECUTIVE SUMMARY

The benefit to corporate bond investors of staying a step ahead of the credit cycle has stimulated interest in models for forecasting one of the cycle's best markers, the default rate.

- A market-based forecasting model can complement actuarial and econometric models, which have inherent limitations.
- This article describes a market-based default-rate forecasting model, based on the distribution of outstanding high-yield bonds between the distressed and non-distressed categories, and the respective, historical default rates of those categories.
- The actual default rate tracks the market-based model's year-ahead forecast fairly closely, although the forecast can overshoot under extreme market conditions.

THE NATURE AND IMPORTANCE OF THE CREDIT CYCLE

Cycles play a major role in analysis aimed at achieving superior investment returns. Stock market participants base their valuations on corporate earnings, which fluctuate with the business cycle. The interest rate cycle strongly influences the performance of high-quality fixed-income assets, such as government bonds and mortgage-backed securities. Similarly, investors in corporate bonds, for which the risk of default is a material factor, can benefit from anticipating turns in the credit cycle.

At the beginning of the credit cycle, lenders perceive the risk of default to be low. They gladly extend loans even to low-quality borrowers, and accept small risk premiums (measured by yield differentials over risk-free rates). Inevitably, some borrowers incur more debt than they are able to support when the business cycle turns down. They consequently default on their obligations, which causes lenders to turn more conservative in their credit extension policies. As it becomes more difficult to borrow, other borrowers fail as a result of being unable to refinance their maturing debts. Finally, as the default wave subsides, lenders regain confidence and a new cycle begins.

The link between the comparative liberality of credit extension risk and premiums on debt is illustrated in Figure 1. In a quarterly survey conducted by the Federal Reserve, senior loans officers of major money center banks indicate whether they are currently raising or lowering the quality standards that corporate borrowers must satisfy to obtain loans. As banks make it harder to qualify for loans, the average risk premium rises in the investment grade corporate bond market.

Figure 1. Bank lending standards and risk premium, quarterly, Q2 1990–Q2 2009. (*Source*: Merrill Lynch & Co. and US Federal Reserve)

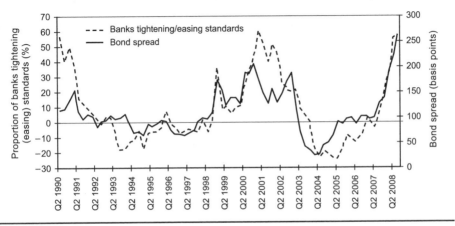

Figure 2. Default rate and risk premium: default rate (global speculative grade, by issuer) and high-yield spread vs. Treasuries, quarterly, Q1 1989–Q3 2009. (*Source*: Merrill Lynch & Co. and Moody's Investors Service)

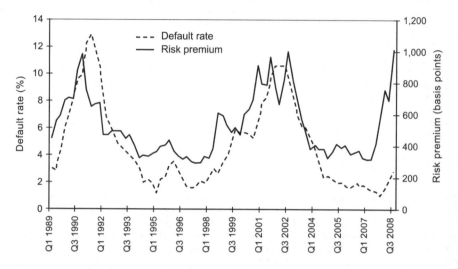

Risk premiums, in turn, are closely connected with default rates. Figure 2 documents this linkage over the past two US credit cycles. The trailing 12-months default rate on speculative grade issuers reached cyclical highs in June 1991, January 2002 and November 2009. Corresponding to these peaks were the cyclical maximum points of the option-adjusted spread on the Merrill Lynch High Yield Master II Index, in January 1991, June 2002 and December 2008.

APPROACHES TO FORECASTING THE DEFAULT RATE

One outgrowth of investors' interest in understanding the credit cycle is an effort to develop a model for forecasting one of its best markers, the default rate.[1] Credit market analysts have worked extensively on this problem since the early 1990s (see More Info for key articles). Three types of default rate forecasting models have emerged from the research—actuarial, econometric, and market-based.[1]

The actuarial approach derives from empirical data documenting the relationship between bond ratings and the historical incidence of default over stated periods. For example, based on statistics compiled for the period 1983–2008, Moody's Investors Service reports that on average, issuers rated Aa had a 0.019% probability of defaulting within one year and a 0.247% cumulative probability of defaulting within five years. The corresponding figures

for issuers rated Caa are 13.730% and 43.747%. Actuarial models apply the rating-specific default rates to the distribution of speculative grade issuers within the rating categories (Ba, B, Caa, and Ca-C), to generate forecasts of the default rate for the speculative grade category as a whole.

A fundamental limitation of the actuarial method is that rating-specific default rates vary substantially from year to year, as a function of variation in economic and credit market conditions. For instance, the B category had a 1.983% default rate in 1997 and a 9.340% default rate in 2001. Actuarial models do not capture this effect, although they typically take into account another period-related variance, namely that an issue's probability of default within a given year is partly a function of the number of years elapsed since issuance. (The curve rises for the first three to four years, then declines thereafter.)

The econometric approach models the speculative grade category's default probability as a function of several variables. These may include indicators of aggregate economic activity, for example, interest rates, measures of credit market conditions, and the variables employed in actuarial models. Generally, the economic indicators employed in such models are forecast, rather than historical, variables. Accordingly, the accuracy of the default rate forecast depends on the accuracy of the forecasts of such items as gross domestic product (GDP) and factory utilization. To put it mildly, errors are not uncommon in macroeconomic forecasting.

THE MARKET-BASED PREDICTOR

Both actuarial and econometric forecasts shed light on the credit cycle, but additional insight into the future default rate can be obtained from the debt market. Day by day, bond investors gauge the default risk of each outstanding issue. To the extent that their consensus assessments are accurate, a cyclical rise or fall in the proportion of issuers judged to be at high risk of default will be followed by a corresponding rise or fall in the actual incidence of default.

The author of this study introduced a now widely used definition of distressed bonds as those with risk premiums greater than 1,000 basis points (10 percentage points) above the rate on default risk-free US Treasuries. He subsequently introduced the distress ratio, or percentage of issues within the high-yield bond index quoted at distressed levels, a gauge of prevailing corporate credit risk. With his colleagues, the author later calculated the average one-year default rate on distressed bonds (Fridson, Covey, and Sterling, 2008). This finding confirmed that, separate from the judgments of the rating agencies, the market was effective in subdividing the universe of speculative grade credits into a higher-risk group (distressed, with a median one-year default probability of 23.53%), and a lower-risk group (non-distressed, with a median one-year default probability of 1.23%). These tools can be combined to create a one-year default rate forecasting model.

As in the actuarial approach, the year-ahead forecast is a function of expected default rates for specified categories, and the universe's breakdown among those categories. The difference is that, unlike rating categories, which are deliberately not fully adjusted to reflect cyclical variation in economic and financial market conditions, market assessments shift in response to short-term changes in issuer-specific default risk. Consequently, the default probability of an individual bond deemed distressed by the market is fairly high in any given year, regardless of the economy-wide level of default risk. As for how it differs from the econometric approach, the market-based predictor's accuracy does not depend on accurate predictions of difficult-to-forecast underlying economic variables.

DETAILS OF THE MODEL

To generate a year-ahead forecast of the trailing 12-months default rate, we calculate a weighted average of the distressed and nondistressed default rates, as shown in Table 1. In addition, a positive or negative adjustment factor is required, based on whether the default rate series is in the rising or declining phase of the cycle. This factor is the average amount by which the simple weighted average underestimates the default rate on the way up (1.60 percentage points), and overestimates it (0.75 percentage points) on the way down. These systematic, but correctable, errors arise from the fact that as the distress ratio rises from the preceding month, the number of expected defaults also rises. Some of the incremental expected defaults will probably occur within the 12-month forecast period of the previous month's forecast. This dynamic reverses itself in the default rate cycle's downleg.

Figure 3 confirms that the market is astute in estimating default rates one year in advance. The actual default rate series tracks the year-earlier forecast fairly closely. Comparatively large divergences partly reflect spikes and dips in the series arising from the required switchovers from positive to negative (or vice versa) adjustment factors. On average, the predicted default rate varies from the actual rate by 23.3%. For example, the model's average divergence from Moody's long-run average annual default rate of 4.35% would be from 3.34% to 5.36%. From a practitioner's standpoint, this degree of accuracy makes the market-based default rate predictor a useful tool for analyzing the credit cycle.

A caveat is that, under extreme conditions, the predictor may overstate the prospective default rate. Retrofitting the analysis to November 1990, we find that the prevailing distress ratio indicated that the default rate would escalate to 16%. As it turned out, the rate rose no higher than 13% in the succeeding 12 months. The probable explanation was forced selling by high-yield mutual bond funds as a consequence of large and persistent redemptions by fund shareholders. These liquidations evidently pushed prices down to distressed levels on a number of issues that did not truly have a one-year default probability in the neighborhood of 23.53%. Chaotic market conditions in 2008 caused a similar overshoot for the 2009 default rate.

CONCLUSION

The default rate predictor is useful to investors in projecting future returns, which are influenced by fluctuations in default rates and risk premiums. Market timers can exploit it as well, because peaks and troughs in the default rate can represent major turning points in performance of the high-yield asset class. Finally, the default rate predictor can be used as a valuation tool. When the predictor indicates a default rate higher than the rates forecast by econometric models, a possible inference is that some issues are undeservedly priced at distressed levels. That may signal an opportunity to scoop up bargains, in the form of bonds with greater risk premiums than their risk truly warrants.

Table 1. One-year default rate forecast, December 7, 2009. (*Source*: Merrill Lynch & Co.)

		Distribution of high yield universe (%)		Annual default rate (%)		Weighted average (%)
Distressed		18.78%	×	25.53%	=	4.42%
Non-distressed	+	81.22%	×	1.23%	=	1.00%
Error correction term	+			−0.75%	=	−0.75%
Default rate forecast					=	**4.67%**

* Discrepancies in the default rate forecast due to rounding

Figure 3. Default rate predictor: actual vs. forecast, annually, 1997–November 30, 2009. (*Source*: Merrill Lynch & Co. and Moody's Investors Service)

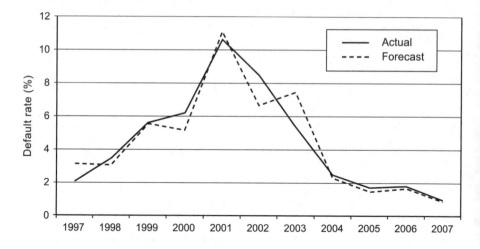

MAKING IT HAPPEN

- The market-based model helpfully corroborated early 2009 econometric forecasts of a rise in the default rate to a level not observed since the Great Depression, a conclusion that many market participants found difficult to accept.
- During the financial crisis that began in 2008, comparing the market-based and econometric models became a way to determine when risk premiums were overstated, making speculative-grade corporate bonds attractive on a risk-reward basis.
- The practical benefits of the market-based default rate forecasting model have parallels elsewhere in the investment world, for example, election markets, and bookmakers' odds on events expected to affect security prices.

MORE INFO

Books:

Fridson, Martin, M. Christopher Garman, and Sheng Wu. "Real interest rates and the default rates on high yield bonds." In Theodore M. Barnhill, Jr, William Fr. Maxwell, and Mark R. Shenkman (eds). *High Yield Bonds: Market Structure, Portfolio Management, and Credit Risk Modeling.* New York: McGraw Hill, 1999; pp. 164–174.

Moyer, Stephen G. *Distressed Debt Analysis: Strategies for Speculative Investors.* Boca Raton, FL: J. Ross Publishing, 2005.

Articles:

Fridson, Martin S., Kevin P. Covey, and Karen Sterling. "Performance of distressed bonds." *Journal of Portfolio Management* 34:3 (Spring 2008): 56–62. Online at: dx.doi.org/10.3905/jpm.2008.706243

Helwege, Jean, and Paul Kleiman. "Understanding aggregate default rates of high yield bonds." *Journal of Fixed Income* 7:1 (June 1997): 55–61. Online at: dx.doi.org/10.3905/jfi.1997.408202. (Also published in *Current Issues in Economics and Finance* (May 1996): 1–6. Online at: tinyurl.com/65mqnwo)

Jónsson, Jón G., and Martin S. Fridson. "Forecasting default rates on high yield bonds." *Journal of Fixed Income* 6:1 (June 1996): 69–77. Online at: dx.doi.org/10.3905/jfi.1996.408166

Reports:

Fons, Jerome S. "An approach to forecasting default rates." Moody's Special Report. August 1991.

Keegan, Sean C., Jorge Sobehart, and David T. Hamilton. "Predicting default rates: A forecasting model for Moody's issuer-based default rates." Moody's Special Comment. August 1999. Online at: ssrn.com/abstract=1020303

Metz, Albert, and Richard Cantor. "A cyclical model of multiple horizon credit ratings transactions and default." Moody's Investors Service. August 2007.

NOTES

1 Forecasting the aggregate default rate is distinct from estimating individual default probabilities for individual bond issuers, a problem that has generated an extensive literature in its own right.

Carrying Out Due Diligence on Hedge Funds by Amarendra Swarup

EXECUTIVE SUMMARY

- Due diligence should be the cornerstone of any hedge fund investment program.
- Hedge funds are a complex and volatile asset class, and poor selection will greatly increase the chances of fraud and poor performance.
- Due diligence is about identifying the best hedge fund manager for your investment goals and risk appetite.
- Due diligence is proactive risk management that seeks to generate superior returns while minimizing risk.
- Performance alone is meaningless.
- You need to understand how and why a hedge fund makes money.
- Dig deep and understand all the risks in all possible markets.
- If in the slightest doubt about a fund, just walk away.

INTRODUCTION

Hedge funds have often been cited as valuable additions to any institutional portfolio, thanks to their typically uncorrelated returns to traditional asset classes over the long term, and superior risk-adjusted returns. However, they are also a complex and volatile asset class, and since their ascent onto the investment podium, both institutional and private investors have found themselves burned at regular intervals by embarrassing and costly blowups. The oft-cited collapse of Long-Term Capital Management in 1998 and Amaranth Advisers in 2006, the litany of hedge fund managers wrong-footed by the credit crunch, and, most recently, the uncovering of the US$50 billion Ponzi scheme run by Bernie Madoff are but some of the stark reminders of the minefield investors navigate in their quest for absolute and consistent returns.

The reason is simple: Today's increasingly complex asset markets make it more difficult than ever for investors to peer under the bonnet and select the best hedge funds. Many make the naïve decision to invest based solely on a strong track record, little realizing that the simple effort of conducting a thorough investigation into the fund prior to investment can often save them considerable financial pain in the future.

Due diligence is the most important aspect of investing in hedge funds, and often also the most ignored part. It's a bizarre oversight—most people would not buy a house without learning first about the area, local schools, and amenities, conducting structural surveys, investigating the state of the housing market, and so on. Yet when most institutional investors allocate to hedge funds, the lack of simple questions as to honesty, competence, and future potential reduces most investments to the ignoble status of a crapshoot.

DUE DILIGENCE: A DEFINITION

Due diligence is the process of identifying the best hedge fund manager for your investment goals and thereafter continually reevaluating them at regular intervals to ensure that they continue to meet your requirements. In doing so, it looks across the entire gamut of the fund—its investment strategy, performance, personnel, legal structure, risk management, documentation, operational infrastructure, service providers, counterparties, and client base. In essence, it is a proactive risk management approach that successfully balances the twin goals of any investment: generating superior returns while minimizing risk.

Looking at past performance alone is often meaningless in the hedge fund world. Performance tells you nothing about the underlying strategy, its advantages and disadvantages, management's skill, the use of leverage, the impact of different market conditions, and so on. Further, selection bias means that most investors will naturally gravitate toward those strategies and funds that have performed well in the past. Any successful hedge fund strategy will seek in principle to deliver targeted returns within the confines of some defined risk constraints. Yet, while quantitative measures such as volatility capture the riskiness of performance, it does not tell investors how robust the fund's underlying risk management is and how it may react to leaner times in the future.

In contrast, careful due diligence provides a valuable insight into the quality of the fund's strategy, personnel, systems, and, vitally, their risk management. Investors know what to expect in good and bad times, and are able to approach their investment in a rational manner without worrying over every inevitable jitter.

The questions you ask are driven ultimately by your investment goals and the constraints on your balance sheet, such as your investment horizon and the need to maintain an optimal liquidity profile commensurate with your cash flow requirements. While no two investors are likely to have the same set of questions, there are fundamental areas that any proper due diligence process needs to cover.

INVESTMENT STRATEGY

There are over 8,000 hedge funds today, and most claim to have a unique edge over the rest. Further, they are scattered among a myriad of strategies and substrategies—all with very different risk and return profiles that profit during varying market conditions. For example, long/short equity funds are very liquid and target absolute performance irrespective of stock market direction, by going both long and short shares. In contrast, event-driven strategies are more catalyst-driven, focusing on changing corporate structures, mergers and acquisitions, and distressed investing. Arbitrage funds might exploit perceived pricing anomalies to eke out small, steady gains, while strong commodity, currency, and interest rate trends could be harvested by momentum-driven strategies such as those used by CTAs (commodity trading advisers) and global funds. There is no shortage of managers playing across different financial instruments, different sectors, and different geographies—all with their own unique traits, opportunities, and risks.

It's a daunting prospect for any investor looking to pick the right funds, and the two key questions in any due diligence process are:

• How does the fund make its money?
• Why does the fund make its money?

It may seem almost facile, but true outperformance and differentiation from the crowd comes from identifying trading talent and potential, and knowing how to time those investments.

To answer the first question, you need to understand and document the hedge fund's basic investment strategy and trading style. What markets does the manager operate in, and what instruments are used? What are the potential returns, and what is the downside if

someone makes the wrong call? What is the outlook given today's markets?

Finding a strategy that matches your investment needs and risk appetite is important. Changing market conditions favor different instruments and strategies. For example, CTAs invest in listed financial and commodity markets as well as in currency markets through options and futures, giving them a wide and often highly liquid market. They are highly directional as they pick trends in momentum-driven markets, and can also lose significantly when these suddenly reverse.

The strategy also needs to sit well within your broader portfolio and balance sheet. For example, despite their volatility, CTAs can be a valuable addition to a broadly diversified portfolio, providing stability and an often rare stream of positive returns at times of negative market stress. Equally, if a company is involved in the energy sector, it is unlikely to want to invest in a long/short equity hedge fund specializing in natural resources.

MORE QUESTIONS TO ASK

The first hurdle crossed, we come on to a more troubling question—what edge does the manager have, if any? Manager selection will contribute far more to your portfolio's performance than broad strategy allocation. True talent lies not in doubling your money in a bull market but in consistently growing it in all markets—good and bad. And ultimately, that's what you're paying those hefty fees for.

Two managers operating the same strategy may look ostensibly the same in terms of style and performance. But one may simply be lucky—a beta jockey riding some market wave for all it's worth, with an inevitable and costly crash looming somewhere on the horizon—while the other may be genuinely skilled, capable of producing consistently good returns irrespective of the wider market (or "alpha" in hedge fund parlance).

How do you tell the difference? The answers are all hidden within their portfolios and in how they generate and implement their ideas.

• Who are the people? A veteran manager who has proven his ability to make consistent money in many different environments is often preferable to the newbie who's churned out spectacular returns using an otherwise unfamiliar strategy for the last couple of years.
• Where do the ideas come from? A manager who grabs ideas off golfing buddies and follows the herd means that you could find

yourself in the same position as many others, greatly increasing the chances of large losses in stressed situations.

- Are the people who developed the strategies and models still there? Or is the fund now relying solely on a mysterious oracle for guidance? Models may work fantastically, but they all have limitations—and inevitably stop working without constant research.
- How is the investment process implemented? Ideas need to be robustly examined and debated to ensure not only that the potential rewards are worth the risk, but that the downside is amenable. They also need to be compared to what's already there—a portfolio with 20 great pharmaceutical stocks probably doesn't need a twenty-first.
- How have they performed? Were all their returns based on a couple of great trades, or do they consistently make money on the majority? Astoundingly good performance may be just as suspicious as bad performance.
- What's the capacity of the strategy? Every strategy has an optimal size beyond which returns will begin to suffer as the market gets too crowded. Some strategies, such as global macro, invest around the world across many asset classes—their limitations are likely in the billions. Others, such as those investing in niche emerging markets, may find the constraints considerably tighter.
- Is the manager a jack of all trades? The best managers are those who stick to what they know. Sticking your finger into every pie that comes by is likely to become very messy—both for managers and their investors.
- What happens when the markets turn? Does the trading strategy have the ability to adapt? Knowing how the fund might perform when the environment suddenly changes is vital. Every strategy will inevitably make losses, but the extent, duration, and how the manager bounces back says a lot about their skill. But going down in the past whenever the broader market does is a worrying sign—that's not what you signed up for, and perhaps that perceived skill was just an extended lucky run at the roulette wheel.

RISK MANAGEMENT
Implicit in the answers to the last two questions is the quality of risk management at the hedge fund. A dynamic risk-monitoring process aimed at reviewing positions and reallocating precious capital is the key to ensuring that portfolios are nimble and always a step ahead of any downturn.

The more comprehensive the risk process, the more comfortable you can feel about your assets.

Most importantly, the risk management needs to be independent, with the right of veto. A fund where management can choose to overrule or ignore risk warnings is one that's not worth investing in, no matter how good the returns are. Once past that, there are innumerable other questions regarding the strength of the control framework around the compelling investment strategy that is presented to you.

- How are positions and exposures sized? Are there any limits? It's a simple question, but many an eager manager has been caught out by betting the bank on a guaranteed winner—right up to the point where they failed.
- How is risk actually measured? Volatility is one measure, value-at-risk another, stress tests a third. Does the manager attempt to capture the unique risks within the investment strategy and actively watch out for them?
- What are the fund's exposures on the long and short sides? An equity long/short with mostly long positions and token shorts is likely to be a closet long-only fund, looking to make a bit extra from fees by masquerading as a hedge fund, and unlikely to do well in a downturn.
- How large is the leverage? Are there limits, and is it secured on a long-term basis? Some strategies, such as arbitrage, need leverage, but in a downturn this can quickly magnify losses. Equally, with too much leverage, returns could be due to leveraging substandard returns rather than any genuine talent.
- What about noninvestment risks such as liquidity? Are there plans in place if this suddenly dries up? If positions need to be liquidated quickly, this may impact the fund adversely and significantly, as shown by the experience of hedge funds trading asset-backed securities during the recent credit crunch.
- What about counterparties with whom the fund trades or relies on for derivative contracts? Are there safeguards against defaults, and are contracts watertight?

FINAL HURDLES
Assuming that these questions are all answered to your satisfaction, the due diligence can move on to more mundane but equally important topics, such as the fund's operational infrastructure and checking the legalese in the fund prospectus. Many a brilliant fund manager

Asset Management: Tools and Strategies

Analysis • Best Practice

has been undone by a sloppy pricing process and poor systems, and many a fraud has been perpetrated on an unsuspecting investor who didn't check the clauses in the contract until after they had signed.

- Are the fund managers invested in the fund themselves? Nothing brings manager and client together as close as knowing you're both rowing the same boat.
- How long have the people been there? Having staff on a revolving door policy is likely to cause instability and poor performance.
- What are the fees? Talented managers have their price but, no matter how brilliant, there is always a point where you may feel that what you pay to access their skill is simply too high to justify. Moreover, if you're handing over enough cash, you may well be able to negotiate more advantageous fees.
- How long will your money be locked up for, and how quickly can you get it back? It is important that the liquidity offered by the fund is consonant with your own circumstances and investment horizons. Equally, the liquidity of the investments made by the manager needs to match or be better than that offered to investors. Otherwise, there may be problems if the fund hits a lean patch and everyone rushes for the exits—as happened with many hedge funds in 2008.
- Does the manager have reliable references who can tell you honestly about their past experiences? Ultimately, you have to trust the people you hand your money over to.
- Visit their offices. See how they work and interact. Try out some of their systems for yourself.

Potentially, there are hundreds of minor questions. The selection—in both qualitative and quantitative terms—of a successful fleet of hedge fund managers is an exhausting process, at the heart of which is an attempt to best capture trading talent. And even when complete, it's an exercise that is worth repeating every year for every hedge fund you choose to invest in.

CONCLUSION

The ultimate aim of the due diligence process is to convince you that the fund you select is genuinely suited to your investment needs. If

there is any niggling doubt, the answer is simple: No matter how good it may seem in other respects, walk away.

The catastrophic demise of Amaranth is a case in point. Amaranth performed in stellar fashion for several years, and its reputation as a stable multi-strategy fund with attractive risk-adjusted returns attracted many institutional investors.

Yet its collapse in September 2006 was not the result of some unavoidable fraud. Rather, the warning signs were there for those investors who chose to look, particularly in the last year or two. Amaranth began to unilaterally change its liquidity terms to make it harder for investors to exit quickly, adopted a burdensome fee structure that passed expenses through to the investor, and morphed into a complex corporate structure which included self-administration.

Strong performances throughout the summer of 2005 flagged a rapidly increasing exposure to volatile energy markets such as natural gas futures. The size of this grew to the extent that to all intents and purposes, Amaranth effectively became the market.

Trapped eventually in a liquidity vice of its own making, its failure serves as a salient example of how active due diligence can avoid these market events. The management of Amaranth was always forthcoming in explaining strategies and exposures, and investors received exposure information continuously through the website and monthly letters. Thorough due diligence would have identified the problems, as well as revealed style drift, operational changes, and inadequate risk systems, all failing to control concentration of exposures and an ever increasing value-at-risk.

It's a powerful lesson. The hedge fund industry thrives because of the freedom offered by the lack of constraints on its activities. However, this freedom is also a double-edged sword that can make the allocation of assets to hedge funds a hazardous exercise.

A thorough due diligence process offers the best chance of avoiding fraud and incompetence, while identifying the best hedge fund managers for your investment goals. Properly carried out, due diligence gives a high probability that the managers you choose will live up to your investment goals and provide a bulwark against the inevitable downturn.

MORE INFO
Websites:
Alternative Investment Management Association (AIMA): www.aima.org
Chartered Alternative Investment Analyst (CAIA) Association: www.caia.org

QFINANCE

Carrying Out Due Diligence on Private Equity Funds by Rainer Ender

EXECUTIVE SUMMARY

- Private equity fund due diligence is the first step in an investment process. The goal of due diligence is to identify the risk–return profile of a fund offer.
- A well-structured due diligence process contains a top-down macro and a bottom-up manager analysis, allowing the investor to filter the most promising funds.
- A consistent framework for fund and fund-manager assessment is essential. This assessment must address quantitative and qualitative aspects, and focus on the manager's "ingredients for success".
- At first sight, fund offerings may appear attractive from a pure return perspective. It is crucial that the investment has an attractive risk–return balance.

INTRODUCTION

The term "due diligence" covers a broad range of different due diligence types. These can be grouped into three major types; financial, legal/tax, and business due diligence. The goal of this article is to shed light on business due diligence for investing in private equity funds. Due diligence is commonly defined as "the process of investigation and evaluation, performed by investors, into the details of a potential investment, such as an examination of operations and management, the verification of material facts".[1] "It is a requirement for prudent investors and the basis for better investment decisions."[2] Private equity fund evaluation faces specific challenges; the private character of the industry makes it inherently difficult to obtain the relevant information; furthermore, the investment decision reflects a commitment to a fund manager to finance future investments rather than a straightforward purchase of specific assets. Therefore, common evaluation techniques used to assess public equity investments are not appropriate within the private equity asset class.

The private equity market has enjoyed extraordinary growth rates in the past, and private equity investments showed strong returns, supported by a booming economy and an expanding debt market. The current financial crisis will have a significant impact on the private equity market; a shake-out of fund managers is to be expected over the coming years. Managers who can demonstrate how they created value in the past, beyond just benefiting from favorable market developments, and who are able to make a compelling case for future value creation will continue to raise capital successfully.

Before investing in a private equity fund, an investor should have sufficient comfort regarding:

- Strategy perspective: the investment strategy of the fund.
- Return perspective: evidence that the manager stands out compared to his/her peer group.
- Risk perspective: assurance that risk is mitigated to the level required by the investor.

The relative youth of the private equity industry, data paucity, as well as benchmarking difficulties within and across asset classes are just a few elements that indicate why the investor has to rely on qualitative aspects and judgment during the due diligence process of private equity funds.

STRUCTURAL SET-UP OF A DUE DILIGENCE PROCESS

The Overall Framework

A solid due diligence framework contains a top-down review as a first step. This review must assess the attractiveness of the various private equity sub-segments and regions. The assessment includes various evaluation criteria, such as investment opportunities in the segment, capital demand and supply, the quality of the fund manager universe, entry and exit prices, and the future development potential of the sub-segments. Furthermore, it is important that the investment strategy of a fund manager is not only attractive on a stand-alone basis, but also within the overall context of the investor's total portfolio.

Generating a complete overview of the relevant fund manager universe is the second step. Worldwide, there are about 3,000 private

Figure 1. Example of a proven due diligence process structure

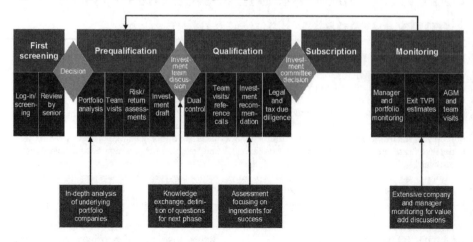

equity fund managers to be considered, making the creation of this overview a very demanding task. It is crucial not to assess the managers who provide you with their fund offering passively, but proactively to benchmark all relevant fund managers for a proper peer-group comparison.

The third step of the framework is to ensure that risks related to the potential commitment are mitigated through an in-depth due diligence process. For all identified issues, due diligence steps must be taken in order to clarify the situation. An investment should only be considered if a sufficient level of comfort is achieved on all issues.

Example of a Due Diligence Process
A clear, well-structured due diligence process, which is tailored to the context of the fund manager, with concrete steps and tools, is an important prerequisite for a comprehensive and consistent fund-manager evaluation. Below, we describe a process structure that is the result of continuous improvements over the past 25 years

The first screening of the fund offering addresses the track record, strategy, team, and fit with the portfolio. This analysis can be performed by junior professionals, but it is important to have an experienced senior professional reviewing the screening and taking the final decision whether to conduct further due diligence. This ensures that the senior has the full picture of the deal flow and the market dynamics.

The prequalification phase starts with a detailed portfolio analysis of all past investments made by the fund manager. Interactions with the fund manager are used to clarify the impact on the

value contribution of the manager to past and future investments. Putting these insights into a structured risk–return framework (see next section detailed below), combined with peer-group benchmarking, allows the identification of fund offerings with a promising risk–return potential. It is beneficial broadly to discuss fund offerings within the investment team to identify critical aspects, residual risks, and external referencing possibilities. This knowledge exchange defines questions for the qualification phase.

The qualification phase is divided into four steps:

1 Dual control: the project worker starts working with an independent devil's advocate. The goal of this step is to identify all potential weaknesses that could be discovered by a pair of fresh eyes, and to ensure the quality of the process. It also helps specify further tailored action steps that need to be addressed, and to clarify open issues.

2 The second step is to review the fund manager's governance structures and processes, with the goal of identifying operational and team dynamic risks.

3 The third step is the verification of the self-assessment through third-party referencing. Well-prepared reference calls with past and present key people from underlying companies are an extremely helpful resource for verifying your current impression of the fund manager. Reference calls provide the opportunity to check the contribution of the fund manager to the value creation and the investment sourcing. If external referencing confirms the current assessment and does not lead to new

Best Practice • Analysis

questions, the investment opportunity fulfils all three evaluation levels: appealing strategy, return potential, and controlled risk.

4 The last step is the legal and tax due diligence. The investment decision and subscription: having a formalized investment approval mechanism, for example through an investment committee, rounds off the due diligence process, which, as a last step, includes the subscription process to the fund.

Thorough monitoring must be put in place once a long-term investment is made. Monitoring is needed to ensure that active measures can be taken where needed, in order to maximize value for the investor. Monitoring is also an integral part of the due diligence for the investment decision regarding the fund manager's next fund (typically after three to four years). Due diligence represents a deep monitoring effort on prior fund investments.

Risk–Return Framework

A clear fund-manager evaluation framework provides consistency among different manager evaluations, and allows for proper benchmarking of managers within a specific peer group. A scoring system that is appropriate for the qualitative and quantitative analyses on a fund manager has proven useful. By constantly applying the system, the scoring becomes well calibrated. Furthermore, it allows for best-practice manager benchmarking across geographies and segments. Due to the qualitative nature of private equity, the focus of the assessment must be on the "ingredients for success" within the future competitive landscape.

In order to enable the ranking of fund managers within a peer group, a quantitative benchmarking that looks at the return and risk aspects helps to put the full due diligence findings into an aggregate picture. We have applied the following framework during the past decade.

Table 1. Framework for a manager evaluation addressing risk and return aspects with a scoring system

Return assessment criteria	Score	Risk assessment criteria	Score
Historical performance • Quality of past performance • Aggregate deal performance over time	X.XX	**Historical performance** • Quality of past performance • Deal by deal volatility	X.XX
Deal sourcing • Quality of deal flow • Involvement in deal origination	X.XX	**Operations/team risk** • Governance structure • Process quality	X.XX
Value creation • Operational competence • Level of active involvement in deals	X.XX	**Investment strategy risk** • Investment discipline • General risk elements	X.XX
Exit capacity • Track based on many deals vs. single hit • Corporate buyers network	X.XX	**Aggregate company financing risk** • Milestone vs. upfront financing • Quality of syndication partners	X.XX
Portfolio return considerations • Common characteristics of individual companies supporting return potential	X.XX	**Portfolio return considerations** • Common characteristics of individual companies supporting risk potential	X.XX
Total return score	X.XX	Total return score	X.XX

CASE STUDY

Fund Due Diligence for the MCAP Fund[3]

MCAP is a newly formed, European, first-time fund manager launching a €250 million fund specialized in development capital and small buyout investments in a single industry. The key person for the fund has deep industry experience. He successfully founded and grew a company operationally superior to more mature, competitive companies. Subsequently, the company was acquired by an international corporation, where he then became the CEO. After stepping down, he formed MCAP. Besides him, there are two other partners who also left their high caliber jobs to launch MCAP. The additional team members previously worked together in various positions; however, none of them has a track record as an investment professional.

A standard due diligence process focused mainly on the historic performance of the fund would pass on this fund after the first screening. The risk–return framework has a different approach:

- The industry targeted by the fund is not covered by existing fund managers. The industry appears to be attractive for backing small, flexible, and dynamic companies with high technological and operational excellence. MCAP could, therefore, be a promising complementary investment.
- The fund manager's ingredients for success from a deal-sourcing and value-creation perspective are in place through the extensive networks of MCAP's partners, and their in-depth industry expertise. Exit capability has only been proven in the sale to the international corporation; there is neither a proven track record, nor an established competitor. Nevertheless, the risk–return assessment framework can be applied to benchmark this new fund against other funds with a single industry focus. Reference calls are important sources for validating the reputation and the competency of MCP's team.
- Risk mitigation for the investor is the most challenging aspect of the due diligence in this case. The management firm is in formation, and the concept is to operate like an industry holding company, managing five investments with deep operational involvement. It is evident that the fund operation will be loss-making, and that the partners are pre-financing this initiative substantially. They are well aligned with the investors in the fund. Close interaction with the manager, and legal terms allowing intervention by investors, should MCAP drift off course, are prerequisites for reaching the level of comfort needed to make a fund commitment.

CONCLUSION

Private equity fund due diligence is a work-intensive undertaking. It requires a clear top-down assessment of investment segments and geographies that, based on fundamental drivers, appear attractive for investment. For the bottom-up fund manager evaluation, a proper due diligence process with clear milestones must be established. This process must be supported by tools that allow a structured assessment of a fund offering, and ensure comparability of different funds. When working in a broad team, special attention is also needed to make certain that all professionals apply the same framework, and that evaluations by different people lead to comparable results.

Finally, it must be emphasized that, while there appear to be many promising investment opportunities, the most important element for due diligence is to identify the risk behind each opportunity.

MAKING IT HAPPEN

The foundation of a successful due diligence process is a structured process, a proven evaluation framework, and an experienced team. Some valuable aspects are:

- In-depth knowledge of past fund investments, their business and investment performance, and the fund manager's value creation is crucial for the evaluation and the understanding of a private equity fund's offering.
- Broad sharing of the investment project work among all investment team members ensures the quality of the due diligence process, and a consistent investment philosophy across the firm.
- Well-prepared reference calls provide an excellent perspective on how a fund manager creates value.
- An experienced senior professional acting as devil's advocate on an investment project provides valuable, internal challenging and risk mitigation.

MORE INFO

Books:

Mayer, Thomas, and Pierre-Yves Mathonet. *Beyond the J-Curve: Managing a Portfolio of Venture Capital and Private Equity Funds*. Chichester, UK: Wiley, 2005.

Probitas Partners. *The Guide to Private Equity Investment Due Diligence*. London: PEI Media, 2005.

Report:

Kreuter, Bernd, and Oliver Gottschalg. "Quantitative private equity fund due diligence: Possible selection criteria and their efficiency." Working paper. November 7, 2006. Online at: ssrn.com/abstract=942991

NOTES

1 Sood, Varun. "Investment strategies in private equity." *Journal of Private Equity* 6:3 (Summer 2003): 45–47. Online at: dx.doi.org/10.3905/jpe.2003.320050

2 Mayer and Mathonet, 2005.

3 Fictitious fund example, based on actual cases.

Private Equity Fund Monitoring and Risk Management by Rainer Ender

EXECUTIVE SUMMARY

- Private equity fund monitoring is a continuous screening of the fund manager's development and the fund's progress, within the context of a top-down and bottom-up market analysis.
- Once implemented, a well-structured private equity monitoring framework, composed of qualitative and quantitative elements, facilitates an assessment addressing two dimensions; the manager and the fund.
- A consistent set of monitoring and benchmarking elements is essential for a coherent assessment of both the single funds and the aggregate portfolio, forming the basis for risk management.
- A functioning monitoring process enables investors to keep control over their private equity portfolio, and take appropriate action where needed. Early risk identification and active involvement are crucial in order to secure maximum value for their investments.

INTRODUCTION

Private equity fund commitments tend to be long-term investments of approximately 12 years. The fund's life consists of three general phases:

- Investment phase: deal origination, due diligence, investments;
- Value creation phase: (re-)positioning the investments for success;
- Harvesting phase: divesting portfolio companies.

Private equity monitoring is a continuous process of tracking the fund's progress and the fund manager's development. The goal of the process is to maximize the investment value and the relationship with the fund manager. Monitoring the current investment is an integral part of due diligence for the investment decision regarding the fund manager's next fund. Due diligence also has a deep monitoring effort on prior fund investments.

An effective private equity monitoring framework is a fine-tuned combination of quantitative and qualitative monitoring elements, based upon the systematic gathering of information and intelligence, supported by a robust IT platform. The information gathering and evaluation must be embedded in an overall monitoring framework. That framework must address concern/comfort levels with regards to funds and fund managers, and trigger which related actions are to be taken by the investor.

A MULTI-DIMENSIONAL PRIVATE EQUITY MONITORING FRAMEWORK

The monitoring process of private equity fund commitments is at the fund level, and is focused on the progress of the portfolio companies and financial performance. At the fund manager level, the investor concentrates on the manager's structural and behavioral developments, such as adherence to the strategy, governance structures, compliance with the terms of the partnership agreement, and the value contribution to the underlying portfolio companies.

It is important to highlight that monitoring involves far more than simple performance control. Monitoring identifies needs for action, and takes the measures needed to secure the best interest for the investor. A simple "traffic lights" concept relating to fund and fund manager illustrates the structured monitoring approach.

Figure 1. "Traffic lights" monitoring concept relating to fund and fund manager development

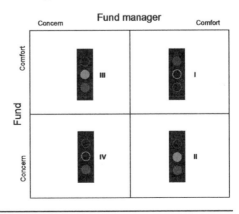

Four different monitoring situations can emerge from a private equity fund investment.

1 There is no reason for concern on both fund and fund manager level. The fund is developing on or above plan, and there are no disturbing developments from the manager side. The investor has a sufficient level of comfort on both aspects.

2 Concern about the fund but comfort with the fund manager. This situation can emerge due to negative external market effects/ shocks. The impact of the negative effects on the underlying portfolio has been identified, analyzed, addressed, and communicated proactively by the fund manager in a timely manner. Nevertheless, a first escalation level for the monitoring activity is appropriate in such a situation, and can be summarized as follows. Actively support the fund manager to correct deviation. An intense dialogue with the manager and corrective measures are needed. When close interaction with the fund manager provides sufficient assurance that the required measures are taken, no special action may be needed beyond closer monitoring of the development.

3 Comfort with the fund, concern with the fund manager. This often occurs in the context of team issues at manager level, or deviation from the strategy (as a fund or as a manager). The future of the fund is at risk; this triggers the second level of escalation. Put pressure on the fund manager to take corrective actions.

4 Concern with the fund, concern with the fund manager. This development represents the worst situation. The fund appears to develop below plan, and the investor has clear indications that the manager does not cope with the situation properly. The third escalation level is the most rigorous escalation step. Mitigate open risks and reduce exposure, for example join forces with a sufficient base of investors, and limit the fund size.

During a fund's lifetime, the emphasis and focus of the monitoring process shifts through phases, due to the changing information requirements and the change in options for actions.

Investment phase: the main focus is on the current and future investments, and whether they are aligned with the declared strategy and value contribution concept of the fund manager. Furthermore, the developments of the fund manager (such as team broadening), and the progress in the older portfolio are important elements for fund-manager monitoring.

Value creation phase: the fund monitoring emphasis shifts towards the progress in the portfolio companies, their valuations, and the resulting interim performance. Manager monitoring focuses on value contribution to the portfolio companies, and the resources made available to support the companies.

Harvesting phase: during the fund's lifetime, this is the real "moment of truth." Fund monitoring focuses on the success of the divestment process for portfolio companies, and related up- or down-valuations relative to the book value. Manager monitoring during this phase concentrates on the peer-group comparison, especially on performance benchmarking in a risk/return context.

KEY FUND MONITORING AND BENCHMARKING ELEMENTS

The key fund monitoring elements can be structured along the value chain of a single company investment.

Figure 2. Key elements for fund and fund monitoring and benchmarking

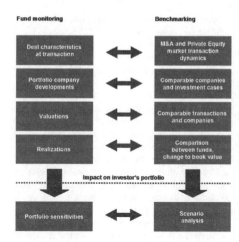

- Deal characteristics are evaluated and compared to the overall mergers and acquisitions (M&A) market (for example, entry price, debt financing structure, new investment themes), the private equity market (such as source of transaction) and the declared strategy of the fund manager (for example, proprietary sourcing from network to family businesses and entrepreneurs).
- Development of the portfolio companies (such as sales, margins, etc.) must be compared to public companies where

Figure 3. Illustrative recurring due diligence and monitoring activity loop

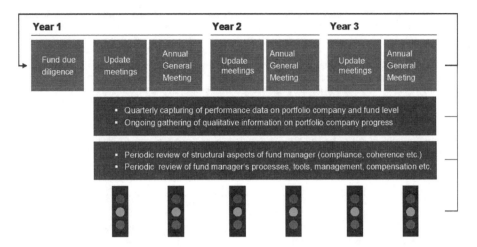

Best Practice • Analysis

applicable, to similar investments of fund managers in the peer group, and to the original investment plan and strategy. Interim valuations as reported on a quarterly basis are typically not directly comparable between managers. The investor must convert valuations into a standardized format to enable comparisons with similar transactions, public company valuations, or comparable investments of other private equity fund managers.

- In order to review the fund manager's valuation practice, realizations must be tracked against book values prior to the sale. Realizations are the "moment of truth" for a fund performance. Although benchmarking should be applied with caution on unrealized values (see above), the development of fund distributions can be compared to competitive funds.

- In addition to fund monitoring, it is also crucial to control the aggregate portfolio. Sensitivities of the overall portfolio with regards to single macro risk factors (for example, leverage ratios, commodity prices, behavior of US consumers) are critical in turbulent markets. Key data derived from bottom-up monitoring allows for scenario analyses and risk-sensitivity analyses for the complete portfolio. This perspective provides the investor with the required knowledge and information to assess potential rebalancing or risk-mitigating activities within the overall

private equity investment program (such as through secondary sales).

THE FUND AND MANAGER MONITORING PROCESS

A best practice is for fund and fund-manager monitoring to be a continuous process with semi-annual, in-depth review across the portfolio.

Figure 3 shows a recurring three-year timeline of a due diligence and monitoring activity loop, based on the assumptions that the fund manager launches a successor fund every three years.

Process and interaction responsibilities must be defined and assigned for all existing fund manager relationships in order to ensure ongoing monitoring and risk management. The monitoring requirements must be clearly specified with regards to bottom-up information needed to create the aggregate view of the overall portfolio. The responsible professionals continuously monitor developments at the level of both the fund manager and the underlying portfolio companies. Information is compiled from various sources including quarterly reports from the fund, presentations from the annual general meeting (AGM), information from commercial information providers, and broad intelligence activity from interaction with market participants. An aggregate portfolio review should be performed semi-annually, based on the outcome from well-prepared, open, one-on-one meetings with individual fund managers.

QFINANCE

CASE STUDY

A well-established venture-capital fund manager with an IT focus started to show below-standard portfolio progress in a subsector, which triggered concern with respect to fund level monitoring. More in-depth analysis provided clear indications that the two persons responsible for the subsector were underperformers compared to their peer group. The rest of the firm had a strong portfolio in the firm's core industry. The concern was actively addressed with the managing partner of the firm, and led to a constructive process resulting in the firm refocusing on its core and separating from the two underperforming partners way before the fund was fully invested. In this case, the fund manager reacted responsively and rigorously. In other cases, the investors would face the following options to push harder for corrective action:

- Indicate plan to decline follow-on fund if there is no change;
- Attempt to pool investors behind the concern and to increase pressure for change on fund manager;
- Enforce an investment stop or a fund size reduction, in line with the legal agreement of the fund through sufficient investor votes, and avoid throwing good money after bad money.

CONCLUSION

The fund commitments typically lock in a 12-year business relationship with a fund manager. Therefore, it is not a luxury but a bare necessity to actively monitor developments at both the fund manager and the fund portfolio level. A well-functioning monitoring concept, framework, and process are indispensable for an investor to keep watch over their private equity portfolio. Taking action as specified through the monitoring framework enables the investor to minimize risks and maximize future performance.

MAKING IT HAPPEN

The following are a few aspects that have proven beneficial to the overall monitoring work of a private equity investor.

- Monitoring requires a coherent concept, framework, and process that serves as day-to-day guidance for the monitoring work.
- Adequate internal or external resources are needed for the start, implementation, and execution of a continuous monitoring process.
- An investor should willingly take action in case of any concern, in order to effectively manage the risk identified through the monitoring work performed.
- Regular interaction with the fund manager is key for the long-term business relationship with the fund manager, and to ensure a proper monitoring outcome.
- Being a value-adding investor with constructive feedback and criticism to the fund manager is part of monitoring. Providing help and support to the fund manager contributes to a positive impact on the fund result for the investor.

MORE INFO

Books:

Mayer, Thomas, Pierre-Yves Mathonet. *Beyond the J Curve: Managing a Portfolio of Venture Capital and Private Equity Funds*. Chichester, UK: Wiley, 2005.

Müller Kay. *Investing in Private Equity Partnerships. The Role of Monitoring and Reporting*. Heidelberg, Germany: Gabler Verlag, 2007.

Measuring Country Risk
by Aswath Damodaran

EXECUTIVE SUMMARY

- As companies and investors globalize and financial markets expand around the world, we are increasingly faced with estimation questions about the risk associated with this globalization.
- When investors invest in Petrobras, Gazprom, and China Power, they may be rewarded with higher returns, but they are also exposed to additional risk.
- When US and European multinationals push for growth in Asia and Latin America, they are clearly exposed to the political and economic turmoil that often characterize these markets.
- In practical terms, how, if at all, should we adjust for this additional risk? We review the discussion on country risk premiums and how to estimate them.

INTRODUCTION

Two key questions must be addressed when investing in emerging markets in Asia, Latin America, and Eastern Europe. The first relates to whether we should impose an additional risk premium when valuing equities in these markets. As we will see, the answer will depend upon whether we view markets to be open or segmented and whether we believe the risk can be diversified away. The second question relates to estimating an equity risk premium for emerging markets.

SHOULD THERE BE A COUNTRY RISK PREMIUM?

Is there more risk in investing in Malaysian or Brazilian equities than there is in investing in equities in the United States? Of course! But that does not automatically imply that there should be an additional risk premium charged when investing in those markets. Two arguments are generally used against adding an additional premium.

Country risk can be diversified away: If the additional risk of investing in Malaysia or Brazil can be diversified away, then there should be no additional risk premium charged. But for country risk to be diversifiable, two conditions must be met:

1. The marginal investors—i.e., active investors who hold large positions in the stock—have to be globally diversified. If the marginal investors are either unable or unwilling to invest globally, companies will have to diversify their operations across countries, which is a much more difficult and expensive exercise.
2. All or much of country risk should be country-specific. In other words, there should be low correlation across markets. If

the returns across countries are positively correlated, country risk has a market risk component, is not diversifiable, and can command a premium. Whereas studies in the 1970s indicated low or no correlation across markets, increasing diversification on the part of both investors and companies has increased the correlation numbers. This is borne out by the speed with which troubles in one market can spread to a market with which it has little or no obvious relationship—say Brazil—and this contagion effect seems to become stronger during crises. Given that both conditions are difficult to meet, we believe that on this basis, country risk should command a risk premium.

The expected cash flows for country risk can be adjusted: This second argument used against adjusting for country risk is that it is easier and more accurate to adjust the expected cash flows for the risk. However, adjusting the cash flows to reflect expectations about dire scenarios, such as nationalization or an economic meltdown, is not risk adjustment. Making the risk adjustment to cash flows requires the same analysis that we will employ to estimate the risk adjustment to discount rates.

ESTIMATING A COUNTRY RISK PREMIUM

If country risk is not diversifiable, either because the marginal investor is not globally diversified or because the risk is correlated across markets, we are left with the task of measuring country risk and estimating country risk premiums. In this section, we will consider two approaches that can be used to estimate country risk premiums. One approach builds on historical risk premiums and can be viewed as the *historical risk premium plus approach*. In the other approach, we estimate the equity risk premium by looking at how the market prices stocks and expected cash flows—this is the *implied premium approach*.

Historical Premium Plus

Most practitioners, when estimating risk premiums in the United States, look at the past. Consequently, we look at what we would have earned as investors by investing in equities as opposed to investing in riskless investments. With emerging markets, we will almost never have access to as much historical data as we do in the United States. If we combine this with the high volatility in stock returns in such markets, the conclusion is that historical risk premiums can be computed for these markets, but they will be useless because of the large standard errors in the estimates. Consequently, many analysts build their equity risk premium estimates for emerging markets from mature market historical risk premiums.

$$\text{Equity risk premium}_{\text{Emerging market}} = \text{Equity risk premium}_{\text{Mature market}} + \text{Country risk premium}$$

To estimate the base premium for a mature equity market, we will make the argument that the US equity market is a mature market and that there is sufficient historical data in the United States to make a reasonable estimate of the risk premium. Using the historical data for the United States, we estimate the geometric average premium earned by stocks over treasury bonds of 4.79% between 1928 and 2007. To estimate the country risk premium, we can use one of three approaches:

Country Bond Default Spreads

One of the simplest and most easily accessible country risk measures is the rating assigned to a country's debt by a ratings agency (S&P, Moody's, and IBCA all rate countries). These ratings measure default risk (rather than equity risk), but they are affected by many of the factors that drive equity risk—the stability of a country's currency, its budget and trade balances and its political stability for instance.[1] The other advantage of ratings is that they can be used to estimate default spreads over a riskless rate. For instance, Brazil was rated Ba1 in September 2008 by Moody's and the ten-year Brazilian ten-year dollar-denominated bond was priced to yield 5.95%, 2.15% more than the interest rate (3.80%) on a ten-year US treasury bond at the same time.[2] Analysts who use default spreads as measures of country risk typically add them on to the cost of both equity and debt of

every company traded in that country. If we assume that the total equity risk premium for the United States and other mature equity markets is 4.79%, the risk premium for Brazil would be 6.94%.[3]

Relative Standard Deviation

There are some analysts who believe that the equity risk premiums of markets should reflect the differences in equity risk, as measured by the volatilities of equities in these markets. A conventional measure of equity risk is the standard deviation in stock prices; higher standard deviations are generally associated with more risk. If we scale the standard deviation of one market against another, we obtain a measure of relative risk.

$$\text{Relative standard deviation}_{\text{Country X}} = \text{Standard deviation}_{\text{Country X}} \div \text{Standard deviation}_{\text{US}}$$

This relative standard deviation when multiplied by the premium used for US stocks should yield a measure of the total risk premium for any market.

$$\text{Equity risk premium}_{\text{Country X}} = \text{Risk premium}_{\text{US}} \times \text{Relative standard deviation}_{\text{Country X}}$$

Assume, for the moment, that we are using a mature market premium for the United States of 4.79%. The annualized standard deviation in the S&P 500 between 2006 and 2008, using weekly returns, was 15.27%, whereas the standard deviation in the Bovespa (the Brazilian equity index) over the same period was 25.83%.[4] Using these values, the estimate of a total risk premium for Brazil would be as follows:

$$\text{Equity risk premium}_{\text{Brazil}} = 4.79\% \times 25.83\% \div 15.27\% = 8.10\%$$

The country risk premium can be isolated as follows:

$$\text{Country risk premium}_{\text{Brazil}} = 8.10\% - 4.79\% = 3.31\%$$

While this approach has intuitive appeal, there are problems with comparing standard deviations computed in markets with widely different market structures and liquidity. There are very risky emerging markets that have low standard deviations for their equity markets because the markets are illiquid. This approach will understate the equity risk premiums in those markets.

Default Spreads and Relative Standard Deviations

The country default spreads that come with country ratings provide an important first step, but still only measure the premium for default risk. Intuitively, we would expect the country equity risk premium to be larger than the country default risk spread. To address the issue of how much higher, we look at the volatility of the equity market in a country relative to the volatility of the bond market used to estimate the spread. This yields the following estimate for the country equity risk premium.

$$\text{Country risk premium} = \text{Country default spread} \times \sigma_{Equity} \div \sigma_{Country\ bond}$$

To illustrate, consider again the case of Brazil. As noted earlier, the default spread on the Brazilian dollar-denominated bond in September 2008 was 2.15%, and the annualized standard deviation in the Brazilian equity index over the previous year was 25.83%. Using two years of weekly returns, the annualized standard deviation in the Brazilian dollar-denominated ten-year bond was 12.55%.[5] The resulting country equity risk premium for Brazil is as follows:

$$\text{Additional equity risk premium}_{Brazil} = 2.15\% \times 25.83\% \div 12.55\% = 4.43\%$$

Unlike the equity standard deviation approach, this premium is in addition to a mature market equity risk premium. Note that this country risk premium will increase if the country rating drops or if the relative volatility of the equity market increases. It is also in addition to the equity risk premium for a mature market. Thus, the total equity risk premium for Brazil using this approach and a 4.79% premium for the United States would be 9.22%.

Both this approach and the previous one use the standard deviation in equity of a market to make a judgment about country risk premium, but they measure it relative to different bases. This approach uses the country bond as a base, whereas the previous one uses the standard deviation in the US market. It also assumes that investors are more likely to choose between Brazilian government bonds and Brazilian equity, whereas the previous approach assumes that the choice is across equity markets.

Implied Equity Premiums

There is an alternative approach to estimating risk premiums that does not require historical data or corrections for country risk but does assume that the market, overall, is correctly priced. Consider, for instance, a very simple valuation model for stocks:

$$\text{Value} = \text{Expected dividends next period} \div (\text{Required return on equity} - \text{Expected growth rate})$$

This is essentially the present value of dividends growing at a constant rate. Three of the four inputs in this model can be obtained externally—the current level of the market (value), the expected dividends next period, and the expected growth rate in earnings and dividends in the long term. The only "unknown" is then the required return on equity; when we solve for it, we get an implied expected return on stocks. Subtracting out the risk-free rate will yield an implied equity risk premium. We can extend the model to allow for dividends to grow at high rates, at least for short periods.

The advantage of the implied premium approach is that it is market-driven and current, and it does not require any historical data. Thus, it can be used to estimate implied equity premiums in any market. For instance, the equity risk premium for the Brazilian equity market on September 9, 2008, was estimated from the following inputs. The index (Bovespa) was at 48,345 and the current cash flow yield on the index was 5.41%. Earnings in companies in the index are expected to grow 9% (in US dollar terms) over the next five years, and 3.8% thereafter. These inputs yield a required return on equity of 10.78%, which when compared to the treasury bond rate of 3.80% on that day results in an implied equity premium of 6.98%. For simplicity, we have used nominal dollar expected growth rates[6] and treasury bond rates, but this analysis could have been done entirely in the local currency. We can decompose this number into a mature market equity risk premium and a country-specific equity risk premium by comparing it to the implied equity risk premium for a mature equity market (the United States, for instance).

- Implied equity premium for Brazil (see above) = 6.98%.
- Implied equity premium for the United States in September 2008 = 4.54%.
- Country specific equity risk premium for Brazil = 2.44%.

This approach can yield numbers very different from the other approaches, because they reflect market prices (and views) today.

Asset Management: Tools and Strategies

Analysis • Best Practice

CONCLUSION

As companies expand operations into emerging markets and investors search for investment opportunities in Asia and Latin America, they are also increasingly exposed to additional risk in these countries. While it is true that globally diversified investors can eliminate some country risk by diversifying across equities in many countries, the increasing correlation across markets suggests that country risk cannot be entirely diversified away. To estimate the country risk premium, we considered three measures: the default spread on a government bond issued by that country, a premium obtained by scaling up the equity risk premium in the United States by the volatility of the country equity market relative to the US equity market, and a melded premium where the default spread on the country bond is adjusted for the higher volatility of the equity market. We also estimated an implied equity premium from stock prices and expected cash flows.

MORE INFO

Book:

Falaschetti, Dominic, and Michael Annin Ibbotson (eds). *Stocks, Bonds, Bills and Inflation*. Chicago, IL: Ibbotson Associates, 1999.

Articles:

Booth, Laurence. "Estimating the equity risk premium and equity costs: New ways of looking at old data." *Journal of Applied Corporate Finance* 12:1 (Spring 1999): 100–112. Online at: dx.doi.org/10.1111/j.1745-6622.1999.tb00665.x

Chan, K. C., G. Andrew Karolyi, and René M. Stulz. "Global financial markets and the risk premium on US equity." *Journal of Financial Economics* 32:2 (October 1992): 137–167. Online at: dx.doi.org/10.1016/0304-405X(92)90016-Q

Indro, D. C., and W. Y. Lee. "Biases in arithmetic and geometric averages as estimates of long-run expected returns and risk premium." *Financial Management* 26:4 (Winter 1997): 81–90. Online at: www.jstor.org/stable/3666130

Report:

Damodaran, Aswath. "Equity risk premiums (ERP): Determinants, estimation and implications." October 2008. Online at: www.stern.nyu.edu/~adamodar/pdfiles/papers/ERPfull.pdf

NOTES

1 The process by which country ratings are obtained is explained on the S&P website at www2.standardandpoors.com/aboutcreditratings

2 These yields were as of January 1, 2008. While this is a market rate and reflects current expectations, country bond spreads are extremely volatile and can shift significantly from day to day. To counter this volatility, the default spread can be normalized by averaging the spread over time or by using the average default spread for all countries with the same rating as Brazil in early 2008.

3 If a country has a sovereign rating and no dollar-denominated bonds, we can use a typical spread based upon the rating as the default spread for the country. These numbers are available on my website at www.damodaran.com

4 If the dependence on historical volatility is troubling, the options market can be used to get implied volatilities for both the US market (about 20%) and for the Bovespa (about 38%).

5 Both standard deviations are computed on returns: returns on the equity index and returns on the ten-year bond.

6 The input that is most difficult to estimate for emerging markets is a long-term expected growth rate. For Brazilian stocks, I used the average consensus estimate of growth in earnings for the largest Brazilian companies which have ADRs listed on them. This estimate may be biased as a consequence.

QFINANCE

Measuring Company Exposure to Country Risk by Aswath Damodaran

EXECUTIVE SUMMARY

- Following the piece on "Measuring Country Risk" (pp. 159–162), we focus on a related question: Once we have estimated a country risk premium, how do we evaluate a company's exposure to country risk?
- In the process, we will argue that a company's exposure to country risk should not be determined by where it is incorporated and traded.
- By that measure, neither Coca-Cola nor Nestlé are exposed to country risk. Exposure to country risk should come from a company's operations, making country risk a critical component of the valuation of almost every large multinational corporation.

INTRODUCTION

If we accept the proposition of country risk, the next question that we have to address relates to the exposure of individual companies to country risk. Should all companies in a country with substantial country risk be equally exposed to country risk? While intuition suggests that they should not, we will begin by looking at standard approaches that assume that they are. We will follow up by scaling country risk exposure to established risk parameters such as betas (β), and complete the discussion with an argument that individual companies should be evaluated for exposure to country risk.

THE BLUDGEON APPROACH

The simplest assumption to make when dealing with country risk, and the one that is most often made, is that all companies in a market are equally exposed to country risk. The cost of equity for a firm in a market with country risk can then be written as:

Cost of equity = Risk-free rate + β (Mature market premium) + Country risk premium

Thus, for Brazil, where we have estimated a country risk premium of 4.43% from the melded approach, each company in the market will have an additional country risk premium of 4.43% added to its expected returns. For instance, the costs of equity for Embraer, an aerospace company listed in Brazil, with a beta[1] of 1.07 and Embratel, a Brazilian telecommunications company, with a beta of 0.80, in US dollar terms would be:

Cost of equity for Embraer = 3.80% + 1.07 (4.79%) + 4.43% = 13.35%

Cost of equity for Embratel = 3.80% + 0.80 (4.79%) + 4.43% = 12.06%

Note that the risk-free rate that we use is the US treasury bond rate (3.80%), and that the 4.79% figure is the equity risk premium for a mature equity market (estimated from historical data in the US market). It is also worth noting that analysts estimating the cost of equity for Brazilian companies, in US dollar terms, often use the Brazilian ten-year dollar-denominated rate as the risk-free rate. This is dangerous, since it is often also accompanied with a higher risk premium, and ends up double counting risk.

THE BETA APPROACH

For those investors who are uncomfortable with the notion that all companies in a market are equally exposed to country risk, a fairly simple alternative is to assume that a company's exposure to country risk is proportional to its exposure to all other market risk, which is measured by the beta. Thus, the cost of equity for a firm in an emerging market can be written as follows:

Cost of equity = Risk-free rate + β (Mature market premium + Country risk premium)

In practical terms, scaling the country risk premium to the beta of a stock implies that stocks with betas above 1.00 will be more exposed to country risk than stocks with a beta below 1.00. For Embraer, with a beta of 1.07, this would lead to a dollar cost of equity estimate of:

Cost of equity for Embraer = 3.80% + 1.07 (4.79% + 4.43%) = 13.67%

Asset Management: Tools and Strategies

Analysis • Best Practice

For Embratel, with its lower beta of 0.80, the cost of equity is:

Cost of equity for Embratel = 3.80% + 0.80 (4.79% + 4.43%) = 11.18%

The advantage of using betas is that they are easily available for most firms. The disadvantage is that while betas measure overall exposure to macroeconomic risk, they may not be good measures of country risk.

THE LAMBDA APPROACH

The most general, and our preferred, approach is to allow for each company to have an exposure to country risk that is different from its exposure to all other market risk. For lack of a better term, let us term the measure of a company's exposure to country risk to be lambda (λ). Like a beta, a lambda will be scaled around 1.00, with a lambda of 1.00 indicating a company with average exposure to country risk and a lambda above or below 1.00 indicating above or below average exposure to country risk. The cost of equity for a firm in an emerging market can then be written as:

Expected return = $R_f + \beta$ (Mature market equity risk premium) + λ (Country risk premium)

Note that this approach essentially converts our expected return model to a two-factor model, with the second factor being country risk, with λ measuring exposure to country risk.

Determinants of Lambda

Most investors would accept the general proposition that different companies in a market should have different exposures to country risk. But what are the determinants of this exposure? We would expect at least three factors (and perhaps more) to play a role.

1 *Revenue source*: The first and most obvious determinant is how much of the revenues a firm derives from the country in question. A company that derives 30% of its revenues from Brazil should be less exposed to Brazilian country risk than a company that derives 70% of its revenues from Brazil. Note, though, that this then opens up the possibility that a company can be exposed to the risk in many countries. Thus, the company that derives only 30% of its revenues from Brazil may derive its remaining revenues from Argentina and Venezuela, exposing it to country risk in those countries. Extending this argument to multinationals, we would

argue that companies like Coca-Cola and Nestlé can have substantial exposure to country risk because so much of their revenues comes from emerging markets.

2 *Production facilities*: A company can be exposed to country risk, even if it derives no revenues from that country, if its production facilities are in that country. After all, political and economic turmoil in the country can throw off production schedules and affect the company's profits. Companies that can move their production facilities elsewhere can spread their risk across several countries, but the problem is exaggerated for those companies that cannot move their production facilities. Consider the case of mining companies. An African gold mining company may export all of its production but it will face substantial country risk exposure because its mines are not movable.

3 *Risk management products*: Companies that would otherwise be exposed to substantial country risk may be able to reduce this exposure by buying insurance against specific (unpleasant) contingencies and by using derivatives. A company that uses risk management products should have a lower exposure to country risk–a lower lambda– than an otherwise similar company that does not use these products.

Ideally, we would like companies to be forthcoming about all three of these factors in their financial statements.

Measuring Lambda

The simplest measure of lambda is based entirely on revenues. In the last section, we argued that a company that derives a smaller proportion of its revenues from a market should be less exposed to country risk. Given the constraint that the average lambda across all stocks has to be 1.0 (someone has to bear the country risk!), we cannot use the percentage of revenues that a company gets from a market as lambda. We can, however, scale this measure by dividing it by the percentage of revenues that the average company in the market gets from the country to derive a lambda.

$(\lambda_i - \%$ of revenue in country$_{Company}) \div \%$ of revenue in country$_{Average\ company\ in\ market}$

Consider the two large and widely followed Brazilian companies–Embraer, an aerospace company that manufactures and sells aircraft to many of the world's leading airlines, and Embratel, the Brazilian telecommunications

QFINANCE

Best Practice • Analysis

giant. In 2002, Embraer generated only 3% of its revenues in Brazil, whereas the average company in the market obtained 85% of its revenues in Brazil.[2] Using the measure suggested above, the lambda for Embraer would be:

$$\lambda_{Embraer} = 3\% \div 85\% = 0.04$$

In contrast, Embratel generated 95% of its revenues from Brazil, giving it a lambda of

$$\lambda_{Embratel} = 95\% \div 85\% = 1.12$$

Following up, Embratel is far more exposed to country risk than Embraer and will have a much higher cost of equity.

The second measure draws on the stock prices of a company and how they move in relation to movements in country risk. Bonds issued by countries offer a simple and updated measure of country risk; as investor assessments of country risk become more optimistic, bonds issued by that country go up in price, just as they go down when investors become more pessimistic. A regression of the returns on a stock against the returns on a country bond should therefore yield a measure of lambda in the slope coefficient. Applying this approach to Embraer and Embratel, we regressed monthly stock returns on the two stocks against monthly returns on the ten-year dollar-denominated Brazilian government bond and arrived at the following results:

$$Return_{Embraer} = 0.0195 + 0.2681\ Return_{Brazil\ dollar\text{-}bond}$$

$$Return_{Embratel} = -0.0308 + 2.0030\ Return_{Brazil\ dollar\text{-}bond}$$

Based upon these regressions, Embraer has a lambda of 0.27 and Embratel has a lambda of 2.00. The resulting dollar costs of equity for the two firms, using a mature market equity risk premium of 4.79% and a country equity risk premium of 4.43% for Brazil are:

$$Cost\ of\ equity\ for\ Embraer = 3.80\% + 1.07\ (4.79\%)$$
$$+ 0.27\ (4.43\%) = 10.12\%$$

$$Cost\ of\ equity\ for\ Embratel = 3.80\% + 0.80\ (4.79\%)$$
$$+ 2.00\ (4.43\%) = 16.49\%$$

What are the limitations of this approach? The lambdas estimated from these regressions are likely to have large standard errors; the standard error in the lambda estimate of Embratel is 0.35. It also requires that the country have bonds that are liquid and widely traded, preferably in a more stable currency (dollar or euro).

Risk Exposure in Many Countries

The discussion of lambdas in the last section should highlight a fact that is often lost in valuation. The exposure to country risk, whether it is measured in revenues, earnings, or stock prices, does not come from where a company is incorporated but from its operations. There are US companies that are more exposed to Brazilian country risk than is Embraer. In fact, companies like Nestlé, Coca-Cola, and Gillette have built much of their success on expansion into emerging markets. While this expansion has provided them with growth opportunities, it has also left them exposed to country risk in multiple countries.

In practical terms, what does this imply? When estimating the costs of equity and capital for these companies and others like them, we will need to incorporate an extra premium for country risk. Thus, the net effect on value from their growth strategies will depend upon whether the growth effect (from expanding into emerging markets) exceeds the risk effect. We can adapt the measures suggested above to estimate the risk exposure to different countries for an individual company.

We can break down a company's revenue by country and use the percentage of revenues that the company gets from each emerging market as a basis for estimating lambda in that market. While the percentage of revenues itself can be used as a lambda, a more precise estimate would scale this to the percentage of revenues that the average company in that market gets in the country.

If companies break earnings down by country, these numbers can be used to estimate lambdas. The peril with this approach is that the reported earnings often reflect accounting allocation decisions and differences in tax rates across countries.

If a company is exposed to only a few emerging markets on a large scale, we can regress the company's stock price against the country bond returns from those markets to get country-specific lambdas.

CONCLUSION

A key issue, when estimating costs of equity and capital for emerging market companies relates to how this country risk premium should be reflected in the costs of equities of individual companies in that country. While the standard approaches add the country risk premium as a constant to the cost of equity of every company in that market, we argue for a more nuanced approach where a company's exposure to country

QFINANCE

Analysis • Best Practice

risk is measured with a lambda. This lambda can be estimated either by looking at how much of a company's revenues or earnings come from the country—the greater the percentage, the greater the lambda—or by regressing a company's stock returns against country bond returns—the greater the sensitivity, the higher the lambda. If we accept this view of the world, the costs of equity for multinationals that have significant operations in emerging markets will have to be adjusted to reflect their exposure to risk in these markets.

MORE INFO

Book:

Falaschetti, Dominic, and Michael Annin Ibbotson (eds). *Stocks, Bonds, Bills and Inflation*. Chicago, IL: Ibbotson Associates, 1999.

Articles:

Booth, Laurence. "Estimating the equity risk premium and equity costs: New ways of looking at old data." *Journal of Applied Corporate Finance* 12:1 (Spring 1999): 100–112. Online at: dx.doi.org/10.1111/j.1745-6622.1999.tb00665.x

Chan, K. C., G. Andrew Karolyi, and René M. Stulz. "Global financial markets and the risk premium on US equity." *Journal of Financial Economics* 32:2 (October 1992): 137–167. Online at: dx.doi.org/10.1016/0304-405X(92)90016-Q

Damodaran, Aswath. "Country risk and company exposure: Theory and practice." *Journal of Applied Finance* 13:2 (Fall/Winter 2003): 64–78.

Godfrey, Stephen, and Ramon Espinosa. "A practical approach to calculating the cost of equity for investments in emerging markets." *Journal of Applied Corporate Finance* 9:3 (Fall 1996): 80–90. Online at: dx.doi.org/10.1111/j.1745-6622.1996.tb00300.x

Indro, Daniel C., and Wayne Y. Lee. "Biases in arithmetic and geometric averages as estimates of long-run expected returns and risk premium." *Financial Management* 26:4 (Winter 1997): 81–90. Online at: www.jstor.org/stable/3666130

Stulz, René M. "Globalization, corporate finance, and the cost of capital." *Journal of Applied Corporate Finance* 12:3 (Fall 1999): 8–25. Online at: dx.doi.org/10.1111/j.1745-6622.1999.tb00027.x

Report:

Damodaran, Aswath. "Measuring company risk exposure to country risk: Theory and practice." September 2003. Online at: www.stern.nyu.edu/~adamodar/pdfiles/papers/CountryRisk.pdf

NOTES

1 We used a bottom-up beta for Embraer, based upon an unlevered beta of 0.95 (estimated using aerospace companies listed globally) and Embraer's debt-to-equity ratio of 19.01%. For more on the rationale for bottom-up betas, read the companion paper on estimating risk parameters, "Measuring Country Risk" (pp. 159–162).

2 To use this approach, we need to estimate the percentage of revenues both for the firm in question and for the average firm in the market. While the former may be simple to obtain, estimating the latter can be a time-consuming exercise. One simple solution is to use data that are publicly available on how much of a country's gross domestic product comes from exports. According to the World Bank data in this table, Brazil got 23.2% of its GDP from exports in 2008. If we assume that this is an approximation of export revenues for the average firm, the average firm can be assumed to generate 76.8% of its revenues domestically. Using this value would yield slightly higher betas for both Embraer and Embratel.

ERM, Best's Ratings, and the Financial Crisis by Gene C. Lai

EXECUTIVE SUMMARY
- The objective of ERM should be to maximize the wealth of all stakeholders, including stockholders, policy-holders, creditors, and employees.
- To have a successful ERM process, a company needs to have an effective risk culture, and have the support of the CEO and other executive officers, such as the CRO or CFO.
- The ERM process should include capital modeling tools, and hold high-quality and sufficient capital.
- An effective ERM will have a positive impact, not only on the best capital adequacy ratio (BCAR) but also on Best's overall ratings.
- In addition to the traditional ERM, and recent improvements such as dynamic hedging models, an effective ERM needs to consider the systemic risks that made some insurance companies insolvent in the recent financial crisis.

INTRODUCTION

The recent financial crisis has raised some questions, such as why enterprise risk management (ERM) was not able to prevent some large insurance companies from either becoming insolvent (for example, AIG) or from suffering large losses of their market value (for example, Lincoln National), and whether rating agencies properly perform their jobs.[1] It is critical that insurance companies have effective ERM programs, and that rating agencies provide adequate ratings to protect insurance companies from bankruptcy. Initially, many insurance companies adopt ERM because rating agencies consider ERM as part of their rating. Adopting ERM for the sole purpose of fulfilling the requirements of a rating agency may not be the best practice. A recent survey conducted by Towers Perrin showed that 32% of companies name identifying and quantifying risk as their main purpose. We believe these companies are moving in the right direction, but more improvements to the current ERM process are needed.

EFFECTIVE ERM

To have an effective ERM, a company needs to have an effective risk culture. To achieve an effective risk culture, a company needs to start from the chief executive officer (CEO) and other senior executive officers (including the chief financial officer (CFO) and/or the chief risk officer (CRO)).

ERM usually involves a process that identifies and assess risks, determines a response strategy and techniques, and implements and monitors the risk-management program for the enterprise.

The objective of an ERM program is to maximize the wealth of the stakeholders – including stockholders, policy-holders, creditors, and employees—sustainably over the long term. It should be noted that wealth maximization is not equivalent to risk minimization. Risk and return are trade-offs. Insurance companies need first to establish their risk tolerance level and minimize unnecessary risk.

Some major categories of risk are credit risk, market risk, underwriting risk, operational risk, and strategic risk. Detailed items for each category of risk can be found in one of Best's articles.[2] In terms of credit risk, insurance companies should pay special attention to counterparty risk if they hold credit default swaps (CDSs). The recent collapse of AIG provides a good lesson for insurance companies that do not know the counterparty risk.

As a result of recent events such as September 11, 2001, the financial crisis which started in 2008, and major hurricanes in 2004 and 2005 (including Katrina, Rita, and Wilma), longevity issues have increased the risk profile of insurance companies. Insurance companies have to take action to deal with the increased uncertainty and volatility that they face. In addition, the regulatory changes regarding EU Solvency II and principles-based requirements have also resulted in improvements to the traditional risk management programs. Recent developments in ERM include catastrophe modeling, dynamic hedging modeling, and an enterprise-wide view of risk for insurance companies. Catastrophe modeling aims to deal with the rapid escalation of natural disasters caused by global warming, because it has been more difficult to predict

QFINANCE

catastrophic events. While the retirement of the baby-boomer generation presents opportunities for insurance companies to manage retirement savings, it also creates capital market-based risk. Insurance companies have developed some products that guarantee certain returns on the invested assets. The guarantees create additional risks related to capital market performance. To reduce the risk of the guarantees, insurance companies have developed and implemented sophisticated hedging models to protect both the policy holders and these companies against adverse movements in the capital markets. The recent financial crisis has shown that the hedging programs are far from perfect. Many insurance companies have suffered from rating downgrades and potential bankruptcy. The new emphasis on ERM today is a heuristic approach, rather than a silo approach. Not only the risk of an individual unit, but also the risk correlations among the units, are critical to the success of ERM. More importantly, ERM today should pay more attention to systemic risk, which can be defined as the risk of collapse of an entire financial system or capital market. One reason for the recent failure of the financial systems is that ERM does not consider the systemic risk.

ERM, BCAR, AND AM BEST RATINGS
There are different rating agencies that rate insurance companies. Among them, AM Best is deemed as one of the most important. This chapter therefore focuses on the relationship between ERM and AM Best ratings. AM Best expects each insurance company to customize its ERM process to their integrated risk profile and risk management needs in order to maintain acceptable ratings. The ERM process should include capital modeling tools (such as dynamic financial analysis) to maintain appropriate capital. The process also needs to include a discussion of the impact of the company's ERM on its rating in its annual meetings.

The objective of AM Best's rating system is to "provide an opinion of an insurer's financial strength, and ability to meet ongoing obligations to policyholders." One of the most important factors of Best's rating is balance sheet strength. Best uses the BCAR to proxy balance sheet strength. BCAR is defined as the ratio of adjusted surplus to net required capital (NRC). The main components of adjusted surplus are reported surplus, equity adjustments, debt adjustments, and other adjustments. NRC includes fixed-income securities, equity securities, interest rate, credit risk, loss and loss-adjustment-expense reserves, net written premiums, and

off-balance-sheet items. The BCAR formula also contains an adjustment for covariance reflecting the correlation between individual components. BCAR is similar to the calculation of the National Association of Insurance Commissioners' (NAIC's) risk-based capital but BCAR includes some important risk factors that are not considered by the NAIC's risk-based capital. BCAR can make adjustments to respond to various market issues such as rate changes, the stage of underwriting cycles, and reinsurance. It should be noted that more than two-thirds of an insurance company's gross capital requirements of BCAR comes from the company's loss reserve and net premiums written. Less than one-third of the gross capital requirements comes from investment risk, interest risk, and credit risk. After Best calculates a company's initial BCAR, it performs various sensitivity tests including the catastrophe and terrorism stress tests.

While BCAR is a critical quantitative model to measure financial strength and serve as a consistent baseline for Best ratings, it is not the sole basis for determining the final ratings. A corporate culture of risk awareness and accountability in daily operations, operating performance, business profile, and the quality of capital are also very important considerations for Best's ratings. ERM has an impact on a company's financial strength, operating performance (such as relative earnings and loss-ratio volatility), business profile (for example, catastrophe and terrorism risk exposures), and the quality of capital. Thus, an effective ERM has an important impact on the Best rating. An insurance company with a strong ERM can be allowed to lower its BCAR, compared with another company with a relatively weak ERM. It is even possible that an insurance company can keep its BCAR lower than the guideline level, on a case-by-case basis, and vice versa.

ERM AND THE FINANCIAL CRISIS
This section does not intend to examine the causes of the recent financial crisis, but to discuss whether an effective ERM can mitigate the negative impact of the financial crisis on insurance companies. In the insurance industry, AIG is now 80% owned by the US government. MetLife and Prudential, among other insurance companies, may seek aid from the government. Why did ERM fail to prevent these companies from near collapse? Here are some possible answers. First, even though the concept of ERM has been popular for more than 10 years, insurance companies had not very seriously implemented ERM until recently. The current

process is not perfect; while it considers the correlations among individual risks, it fails to consider the systemic risk facing the whole financial system, and the counterparty risk of derivative securities. To prevent future failures, the ERM approach needs to recognize that the solvency approach may not be appropriate in a financial crisis environment. Insurance companies need to have more capital than BCAR requires, because additional capital is difficult to obtain during a financial crisis. Second, CROs need to resist the temptation to sell complex products without really understanding the consequences of selling those products. The CDSs of AIG are an example. Finally, insurance companies should focus on their core business—underwriting business—rather than investing in exotic derivatives.

CASE STUDY

ERM and the Ratings of USAA and its Subsidiaries

In December 2008, AM Best confirmed it had given USAA and its subsidiaries (hereafter USAA) the financial strength rating (FSR) of A++ (superior) rating, issuer credit rating (ICR) of "aaa," and the debt rating of "aaa." The ratings reflect "USAA's superior capitalization and strong operating results through focused business and financial strategy." Diversified sources of earnings, capital accumulation, and strong ERM are also key factors for superior ratings. In addition, good catastrophe management, a sound reinsurance program to preserve the finance capital, and a conservative investment strategy were mentioned. The USAA case demonstrates that Best's ratings reflect the effectiveness of USAA's ERM.

CONCLUSION

ERM has become more and more important in recent years. The recent financial crisis makes ERM even more critical to the success and survival of an enterprise. To have a successful ERM process, a company needs to have support from the CEO and other executive officers such as the CRO or CFO. The ERM process should include capital modeling tools, and hold sufficient high-quality capital. An effective ERM will have a positive impact not only on the BCAR but also on Best's overall ratings. In addition to traditional ERM, and recent improvements such as dynamic hedging models, an effective ERM needs to consider the systemic risks that made many insurance companies insolvent in the recent financial crisis.

MORE INFO

Book:

Moeller, Robert. *COSO Enterprise Risk Management: Understanding the New Integrated ERM Framework*. Hoboken, NJ: Wiley, 2007.

Articles:

Kenealy, Bill. "Sifting through the ashes to assess ERM's value." *Insurance Networking News* (January 7, 2009). Online at: tinyurl.com/5ukt6zu

Mueller, Hubert, Eric Simpson, and Edward Easop. "The best of ERM." *Emphasis* 2008/3: 6–9. Online at: tinyurl.com/6b9m989

Reports:

AM Best. "Risk management and the rating process for insurance companies." Methodology. January 25, 2008. Online at: www.ambest.com/ratings/methodology/riskmanagement.pdf

Mosher, Matthew C. "A.M. Best comments on enterprise risk management and capital models." Special Report. AM Best, February 2006. Online at: www.ambest.com/ratings/methodology/enterpriserisk.pdf

Website:

A collection of essays from the Society of Actuaries, *Risk Management: The Current Financial Crisis, Lessons Learned and Future Implications*: www.soa.org/library/essays/rm-essay-2008-toc.aspx

NOTES

1 In addition, Prudential Financial Inc. and Hartford Financial Services Group Inc. reported losses of more than US$1 billion in the second half of 2008.

2 See AM Best (2008).

The Impact of Index Trackers on Shareholders and Stock Volatility
by Martin Gold

EXECUTIVE SUMMARY

Indexes and index-tracking strategies are an increasingly important feature of the contemporary investment environment.

Index tracking has become a risk-averse strategy for institutional investors, and its popularity has grown strongly, especially within developed capital markets where it is considered difficult to outperform the market reliably.

- Indexes (and indexed portfolios) are actively managed instruments which are constructed according to objective criteria. Their performance typically depends on the market capitalization (size) of stocks.

- Index membership literally confers "investment grade" on firms because numerous managed funds are benchmarked to, or directly invested in, these stocks. Index membership also increases institutional investor ownership levels, trading liquidity, and research coverage by market analysts.

- Index changes can have dramatic effects on stock prices and trading volumes, especially over the short to medium term; longer-term effects remain unclear.

INTRODUCTION

Stock indexing, where investment portfolios mimic or replicate market indexes, has profound implications for both firms and investors. The practice stems from theoretical research which suggests that markets are informationally efficient. Since security prices generally reflect all public information, there is no point in employing active fund management and paying for investment research if there is no prospect of reliably beating the market. Whether or not you believe that beating the market is achievable—and this remains a perennial debate within academic and practitioner circles—the reality is that institutional investors make portfolio allocations with close reference to market indexes. The essential issue for investors and financial managers, therefore, is to be aware of how indexes are managed and to understand the implications for stocks arising from index tracking.

WHAT IS THE "MARKET"? A PRIMER ON INDEXES

This is a seemingly innocuous question, but one that is seldom asked by investors, financial managers, and consumers alike, although they closely scrutinize the fortunes of the Dow Jones in New York or the FTSE100 in London. These important yardsticks affect decision-making in financial markets and also in the real economy. Every day trillions of dollars in capital expenditure/project evaluation, risk modeling,

and executive remuneration are all directly linked by market indexes. Investment managers also frequently use index derivatives as a simple and efficient alternative to buying and selling physical constituents.

In financial literature and everyday usage, indexes are given the status and importance of scientific instruments although they are far from being the precise or universal constants which exist in fields such as engineering or physics. A market index simply measures the performance of a basket of securities that is constructed in accordance with the index publisher's methodology. Consequently, an index is a "branded" measure of market performance, where the "market" is whatever the publisher deems it to be.

Although index publishers operate in a competitive marketplace, their index construction methodologies are often similar. Commonly, indexes are weighted according to market value (or capitalization) of their constituent stocks. This weighting scheme is generally regarded as the most accurate reflection of the economic outcomes experienced by all investors in a stock market. This means that once the firms are selected as being representative of the industries in the stock market covered, index performance is calculated using a sum of the individual stocks' returns weighted according to their size. For example, a stock which has a 5% return and represents 10%

of the market capitalization will generate 0.5% of the index return for the period. Other schemes which can be used are equally weighted (where each stock has the same weight and performance contribution to the index return) or price weighted (where higher-priced stocks of have a larger index impact, and vice versa).

Although the performance of competing market indexes may appear to be correlated, these outcomes can mask significant differences in the index construction methodologies used. For example, although the S&P500 Index and the Dow Jones Industrial Average may show similar performance for the US stock market, the former is a capitalization-weighted, broad market index comprising 500 constituents, while the latter is a price-weighted index covering only 30 stocks.

Indexes are typically rebalanced periodically to reflect changes to the stock market and corporate actions which can affect constituent firms (known as "index events"). For example, if an index constituent is acquired by another firm, it will be removed from the index and replaced with a new constituent. The index publisher may review the composition of the index to make sure it remains representative of the market it covers. Indexes are also subject to ad hoc changes arising from market events: for example, when a firm goes into bankruptcy.

In the early 2000s, most global index publishers introduced a "free float" calculation methodology. This reduces a stock's weighting in an index (and therefore its contribution to the market's performance) where the availability (or "float") of securities is restricted due to cross-holdings (a corporation's holdings of another company's stock), or untraded ownership stakes held by governments or founders. The adoption of a free float methodology (originally used by the International Finance Corporation for the calculation of its emerging markets indexes in the 1990s) was in part precipitated by the dot com market crash. At that time, many new issues were being included in indexes at their full market capitalization, despite the reality that sometimes less than 20% of the issued shares were actually available to investors for trading in the market.

HISTORY AND RATIONALE FOR INDEXING-TRACKING STRATEGIES

Since the late 1960s, researchers have been examining the performance of professional fund managers using risk-adjusted measures, and they have found that the majority have not outperformed the market averages, even before management fees are taken into account.[1] This empirical literature, known as the "active versus passive debate" in academic and practitioner circles, provides persuasive evidence of the concept of market informational efficiency. The consensus emerging from this work provides an important validation of orthodox economic theory, which asserts that financial markets generally function rationally and that security prices reflect fair value.

These research findings also spawned the development of so-called passive or index tracking strategies in the 1970s. The first index-tracking strategy was created in 1971 by Wells Fargo (now Barclays Global Investors) for a single pension sponsor (Samsonite) and used an equally weighted portfolio. In 1973, it created a comingled fund for its trust department clients which tracked the S&P500 Index. In 1976, the Vanguard Group launched the first US index mutual fund (the Vanguard S&P500 Index Fund). Today there are numerous indexes and index-tracking products, covering stock markets, industry sectors, hedge funds, and commodities. According to Standard & Poor's, US$4.85 trillion was benchmarked to its US indexes at December 31, 2007: This figure includes US$1.5 trillion directly indexed to the S&P500.

The prudent investment standards which govern many pension funds and institutional investors in Anglo-Saxon economies have, since the late 1980s, largely endorsed the benefits (broad diversification with lower operating costs) of investment indexation compared to active portfolio management. In fact, the general intellectual acceptance of market efficiency has effectively reversed the traditional onus on pension fund trustees and other financial fiduciaries to employ active portfolio management strategies that seek to outperform the market while minimizing risks to capital.

Although index publishers disclaim indexes as being measures of investment merit, market pundits and academic researchers have paid surprisingly little attention to the suitability of market indexes for investment purposes, concerning themselves instead with tests of market efficiency. It is also important to note that indexes are themselves actively managed instruments: Index tracking is therefore not a passive, "buy-and-hold" investment strategy, familiar to most personal investors.

MARKET IMPACTS: PRICE AND VOLUME EFFECTS OF INDEX CHANGES

Although indexes have evolved as market measures, they form the underlying basis for index-tracking strategies whose portfolios are managed mechanistically using either full replication (where all constituents are held in their index proportions) or partial replication (a subset of stocks) techniques. Index-tracking strategies are compelled to alter portfolio holdings in accordance with changes announced by index publishers. Significant trading costs (as distinct from operating costs such as brokerage and taxes)—also known as market impact or frictions—can also arise from constituent changes when index funds (and many funds have active managers who also track market benchmarks for active portfolios) rebalance their portfolios.

Because index-tracking strategies involve no judgment or market timing, unlike active portfolio management disciplines, their transactions are price-insensitive. Thus, the growth in the scale of indexed portfolio assets has brought opportunities for arbitrageurs to profit from the potential volatility and liquidity imbalances which are caused by index reconstitution events. For example, arbitrageurs may purchase (or sell) securities due to be included in (or removed from) the index prior to the date of the index event. Index-tracking funds are compelled to buy (or sell) "at any cost" to rebalance their portfolios to the revised index composition.

The direct implications of index reconstitution events have been examined in the academic literature since the mid-1980s. In 1986, Harvard economist Andre Shleifer highlighted the price and volume effects' implications for stocks in the S&P500 Index.[2] He concluded that index tracking created downward sloping demand curves due to the price inelasticity of demand created for these stocks. Several subsequent studies in the United States and the United Kingdom have also documented significant price and volume effects for stocks added and deleted from stock market indexes. Other research, however, has found that prices subsequently reverse over longer time horizons. These findings do not acknowledge the costs of price volatility experienced by investors.

In response to the practical concerns of clients and stakeholders, index publishers announce index changes in advance of the actual index reconstitution events. This has had the effect of bringing forward the volatility associated with these changes from the actual index event date.

CASE STUDY
News Corporation's Inclusion in the S&P500 Index

News Corporation is an integrated and diversified media company with assets of approximately US$62 billion as at September 30, 2008. The company has global operations but earns the bulk of its income in the United States. In April 2004, its chairman and CEO Rupert Murdoch announced that the company was seeking shareholder approval to consolidate the ownership of its Australian businesses and to move the company's legal domicile from Australia to the US state of Delaware.

In explaining the change of domicile to shareholders, the directors highlighted the important benefits that were expected to accrue from inclusion of the company in the leading US equity benchmarks, especially the S&P500 Index. They noted that this would:

- correct the "under investment" by US institutions, which only held approximately 52% of its shares compared to peer firms such as Disney (72%), Time Warner (78%), and Viacom (87%);
- increase demand from US institutions that were currently prevented from buying non-US stocks;
- increase trading in the company's shares, which should narrow the gap between the prices of its voting common stock and nonvoting common stock;
- lower the costs of raising equity in a deeper market: the S&P500 Index's total market capitalization exceeded US$10 trillion, 20 times larger than the Australian market benchmark, the S&P/ASX 200 Index.

On November 3, 2004, the company announced that its reincorporation had received court approval and that the New York Stock Exchange would become its primary listing. On November 17, 2004, Standard & Poor's preannounced that News Corporation would be included in the S&P500 index (at the close of trading on December 17, 2004) and that the stock would be removed from its Australian indexes in three additional equal installments. On the date of News Corporation's reincorporation announcement, and on the days it was phased out of the Australian market benchmark, over 195 million shares worth approximately AU$4.6 billion were traded on the Australian Stock Exchange—approximately one-third of this turnover occurring on the day of the reincorporation announcement alone. Since changing its domicile, the company has raised US$5.15 billion in debt securities and started a US$6 billion stock repurchase program.

CONCLUSION

Indexes are an essential tool for measuring financial market performance characteristics. Because there has been a dramatic increase in the scale of funds that directly track market indexes and relative performance monitoring by actively managed portfolios, gaining and maintaining membership of an "index club" is a critically important goal for financial executives.

Compared to nonconstituents, firms included in market indexes have the potential for preferential access to capital, significantly greater research coverage in the investment community, and trading liquidity. Index inclusion can increase demand and stock prices. On the downside, firms excluded from indexes typically lose institutional ownership and can experience considerable price declines in their stocks especially in the short term. The case study shows how the phenomenon of index events creates substantial stock turnover and volatility, despite the reality that no significant changes have occurred in a company's business operations.

MAKING IT HAPPEN

- Be index-aware: Membership of the "index club" is important because it confers higher demand for stocks and trading liquidity arising from institutional ownership.
- Find out which stock market indexes cover your firm or your market. What are the inclusion and exclusion criteria used by the publishers, and how is your firm classified in terms of its market value and industry representation? Even if your stock is not included in a broad market index, it may be a potential constituent in an industry-specific or customized index.
- Financial managers need to make sure that index publishers are well informed about their business operations and ownership structures. They should also be aware that index publishers are generally reluctant to delete firms from indexes because this creates excessive index turnover.
- Given that indexes are generally market capitalization-weighted, are profitable merger and takeover opportunities available which will increase the equity base (and thus index size) of the firm?

MORE INFO

Books:

Ali, Paul, Geof Stapledon, and Martin Gold. *Corporate Governance and Investment Fiduciaries.* Pyrmont, Australia: Lawbook, 2003.
Levy, Haim, and Thierry Post. *Investments.* Harlow, UK: FT Prentice Hall, 2005.
Malkiel, Burton G. *A Random Walk Down Wall Street: The Time-Tested Strategy for Successful Investing.* 9th ed. New York: WW Norton & Company, 2007.

Report:

Gold, Martin. "Fiduciary finance and the pricing of financial claims: A conceptual approach to investment." PhD thesis, University of Wollongong, 2007.

Websites:

FTSE Group/Financial Times indices: www.ftse.com/Indices
Morgan Stanley Capital International indexes: www.msci.com
Standard & Poor's indexes: www.sandp.com

NOTES

1 For a review of this literature and the debate, see Gold (2007).
2 Shleifer, Andrei. "Do demand curves for stocks slope down?" *Journal of Finance* 41:3 (July 1986): 579–590. Online at: www.jstor.org/stable/2328486

Checklists

Investments

The Bond Market: Its Structure and Function

DEFINITION
The bond market is the market for debt securities in the form of bonds where buyers and sellers determine their prices and therefore their accompanying interest rates. It is also known as the fixed-income or debit or credit market.

In purchasing a bond you are effectively lending money to a government, corporation, or municipality, known as the issuer, which agrees to pay you a certain rate of interest during the lifetime of the bond and repay its principal or face value when it matures or becomes due.

The international bond market is estimated to have a size of almost US$47 trillion. The US bond market is the largest in the world, with an outstanding debt of more than US$25 trillion. In 2007, the volume of trade in the US bond market was US$923 billion.

Since 2000, the international bond market has doubled in size as a result of the activity of big multinational companies. According to the International Capital Market Association, about US$10 trillion worth of bonds were outstanding in 2007.

The individual government bond markets have a high level of liquidity and considerable size—these are included in the international bond market. They are noted for their low credit risk and are unaffected by interest rates.

Trading generally takes place over the counter (known as OTC) between broker dealers and big institutions. The stock exchanges list a small number of bonds too.

The largest centralized bond market is the New York Stock Exchange (NYSE), which mainly represents corporate bonds. In contrast to this, most governments have bond markets that lack centralization, mostly due to the fact that bond issues vary widely and there is a large choice of different securities by comparison.

Most outstanding bonds are in the hands of institutions: pension funds, mutual funds, and banks. This is because individual bond issues are so specific and a large number of smaller issues lack liquidity.

The volatility of the bond market is in direct proportion to the monetary and economic policy of the country of the participant.

The main difference between corporate and government bonds is that the latter are guaranteed and thus carry a low risk of investment, albeit at a lower rate of return. Corporate bonds generally offer a higher rate of return on investment, but carry more risk—if the company fails, the bondholder risks losing their investment.

ADVANTAGES
* It is considered a wise move to invest in bonds as part of a considered diversified investment portfolio that also consists of stocks and cash. They are considered to be a relatively safe investment for increasing capital and receiving a reliable interest income. The principal and interest are set at the time the bond is purchased. If the owner collects the coupon and holds it to maturity, the market is irrelevant to final payout. As a long-term investment, bonds may be considered a wise choice—bearing in mind the disadvantages.

DISADVANTAGES
* Bonds are not advisable for short-term savings for the individual participant in the market.
* Long-term commitment is essential as the participant who cashes in before maturity is open to the risk of fluctuations in interest rates. Whenever there is an increase in interest rates, there is a corresponding decrease in the value of existing bonds. Conversely, a decrease in interest rates will correspond to a rise in the value of existing bonds. This is due to the fact that new issues pay out a lower yield. The basic concept of bond market volatility is that the value of bonds and changes in interest rates run inversely to each other.
* When interest rates drop, investors have to reinvest their interest income and return of principal at lower rates.
* The final purchasing power of an investment in bonds is reduced by a corresponding increase in inflation, which also results in higher interest rates and correspondingly lower bond prices.
* If there is a decline in the bond market as a whole, individual securities also fall in value.
* Timing is crucial: a security may in the future unexpectedly underperform relative to the market.
* A bond may perform poorly after purchase, or it may improve after you sell it.
* Corporate bonds have relatively low liquidity compared with government bonds, which usually have a short lock-in period (i.e. they can be cashed in quickly).

Asset Management: Tools and Strategies

ACTION CHECKLIST

✓ Make sure that you can afford to invest in long-term savings before you commit yourself to taking out bonds.

✓ Have another form of savings as an emergency fund in case you meet with an unexpected financial problem in the future.

✓ Read all the available literature and take advice from an impartial financial consultant before making a final commitment.

DOS AND DON'TS

DO

• Be sure to choose a security that is approved by a financial expert.

DON'T

• Don't rush into a transaction or pay over the odds for it.

MORE INFO

Books:

Adams, Tom. *Savings Bond Adviser: How U.S. Savings Bonds Really Work—With Investment, Tax, and Estate Strategies*. 5th ed. New York: Alert Media, 2007.

Pederson, Daniel J. *Savings Bonds: When to Hold, When to Fold and Everything In-Between*. 4th ed. Detroit, MI: TSBI Publishing, 1999.

Website:

Investopedia introduction to bonds: www.investopedia.com/university/bonds

Fund of Hedge Funds: Understanding the Risks and Returns

DEFINITION

Generally, a fund of funds is a fund that invests in other funds in order to provide investors with a lower-risk product through exposure to a larger number of vehicles, often of different types and with different regional focuses.

A hedge fund of funds is one that invests in a pool of hedge funds, instead of just investing in an individual fund. It is any fund of funds that pools capital together, while employing two or more submanagers that invest in two or more funds, and which is not dictated to by the underlying investment of such funds.

Funds of funds are set up as limited partnerships, which offer advantages to the investor. Due diligence is a primary benefit, because managers can use their time and expertise to evaluate strategies and analyze individual fund performance—a task that would be a difficult undertaking for an individual investor. The fund of funds tries to avoid untoward risk because of the different investment strategies employed by the principal fund managers. Funds of funds can be invested in, for example, a venture fund, a long/short fund, a distressed fund, and/or a private equity fund. Investors assign assets to a fund of funds mainly to limit their risk to exposure.

However, funds of funds do have some disadvantages, such as the double layer of fees and the issue of transparency. When investing in a fund of funds, a backer must pay not only the fees of the pool of funds, but also the fees of the fund of funds manager. Transparency about the fund of funds manager's background and reputation, not to mention the nature of the investments made, are issues of primary importance.

ADVANTAGES

- Funds of hedge funds normally offer a lower risk than single funds, because they are invested in a wider variety of sectors, with national and international focuses.
- Because managers can devote all of their time to evaluating strategies and analyzing individual fund performance, they are more likely to achieve a better return than an individual investor.
- Because principal fund managers are specialists in their investment areas, funds

of funds benefit from the different specialist investment strategies employed.

DISADVANTAGES

- When investors buy into a fund of funds, they are charged management fees twice: First by the fund of funds manager, and then by the individual fund managers.
- Funds of hedge funds are inevitably very secretive, which makes it difficult for an investor to assess the fund manager's performance on a daily basis.
- The Securities & Exchange Commission (SEC), the Financial Services Authority (FSA), and other securities supervisory bodies generally have limited powers to check on hedge fund activities.

ACTION CHECKLIST

✔ Find out what you will be paying in total fees: after you have deducted the double fees, it might prove wiser to select less risky investments.

✔ Check the long-term track record of the fund of funds: an experienced manager, who delivers a consistent (though perhaps lower) return, is probably a better bet than a new start-up. The manager's skills, background, and reputation, and the type of investments made, are very important issues.

DOS AND DON'TS

DO

- Research the different funds and their tactics, and make sure that you have analyzed your real return on investment after fees and expenses.
- Engage your lawyers and accountants in the evaluation of the risks and possible benefits of investing in funds of hedge funds.

DON'T

- Don't take your investment in funds of hedge funds for granted; market and legislative developments can mean that the playing field changes. Just because a risk, area, market, or country has been stable in the past is no guarantee that it will be the same in the future.

MORE INFO

Books:

Drobny, Steven. *Inside the House of Money: Top Hedge Fund Traders on Profiting in the Global Markets.* Hoboken, NJ: Wiley, 2006.

Jaeger, Robert A. *All About Hedge Funds: The Easy Way to Get Started.* New York: McGraw-Hill Professional, 2002.

Jaffer, Sohail. *Funds of Hedge Funds: For Professional Investors and Managers.* London: Euromoney Books, 2003.

Nicholas, Joseph G. *Hedge Fund of Funds Investing: An Investor's Guide.* New York: Bloomberg Press, 2004.

Articles:

Chen, Peng. "Hedge funds: Are they worth it?" *On Wall Street* (August 1, 2006). Online at: tinyurl.com/6j562cx

Jones, Bernard. "Hedge funding." *Investors Chronicle* (May 25, 2007). Online at: tinyurl.com/5reogza

Mackintosh, James. "German bank puts hedge fund unit up for sale." *Financial Times* (March 6, 2009). Online at: tinyurl.com/62qgelt

Websites:

Financial Services Authority (FSA; UK): www.fsa.gov.uk
Hedge fund research from Morningstar: www.morningstar.com
HedgeFund.net: www.hedgefund.net

Hedge Funds: Understanding the Risks and Returns

DEFINITION

Although hedge funds seem to have hit the headlines only recently, the first of these funds was actually started in 1949.

Hedge funds are normally run by small teams of portfolio managers, traders, and analysts, investing private pools of capital with few restrictions as to the areas in which they can speculate. Hedge funds benefit from limited regulation and are not required to make periodic reports to the Securities & Exchange Commission (SEC) under the Securities and Exchange Act of 1934. In order to be exempt from direct regulation, a hedge fund must be open to a limited number of accredited investors.

Hedge funds use a wide array of strategies, and sometimes are not "hedged" against the market at all. Many, but not all, of these funds aim to produce much higher returns than other investment vehicles, and markets with high volatility are often preferred, as they sometimes yield the highest returns (but also the greatest risks).

Hedge funds have the advantage that they can employ a large number of strategies and can invest in more areas than other investments. They may use leverage, short-selling, asset-backed lending, arbitrage, or a variety of other techniques in order to gain maximum returns for investors.

Hedge fund managers normally earn both a management fee and a performance or incentive fee. Performance fees are intended to be an inducement for the investment managers to produce the greatest returns they can. Typical fees are a management fee of 2% of the fund's net asset value per annum and a performance fee of 20% of the fund's profits. Fees are payable from the fund to the investment manager, and are taken directly from the assets that the backer holds in the fund.

A hedge fund can apply a high watermark to an investor's money, where the manager will only receive performance fees, on the invested money, when its value is greater than its previous greatest value.

ADVANTAGES

- Hedge funds can make use of a larger number of strategies and can invest in many more areas than with traditional investment products.
- Performance fees, calculated as a percentage of the fund's profits, act as an incentive for managers to perform above average.

DISADVANTAGES

- To make money and not disclose strategies, hedge funds are of necessity very secretive, with few public disclosure requirements. This makes it difficult for investors to assess how well or badly their fund managers are doing.
- Some, though not all, hedge funds borrow and speculate with (leverage) sums that are many times larger than the initial investment. This is fine when the investment works, but it can mean that the fund folds if it doesn't.
- When a hedge fund uses short selling as an investment strategy, rather than as a hedging strategy, it can experience very high losses if the market turns against it.
- The SEC and other securities regulators generally have limited ability to check routinely on hedge fund activities.

ACTION CHECKLIST

✔ Before investing in hedge funds, you should be aware of the risks as well as the rewards: Leverage amplifies profits but also losses; short selling opens up new investment opportunities; riskier investments typically provide higher returns but, as in poker, you shouldn't sit down at the table if you can't afford to lose.

✔ Qualify and quantify in financial terms how the failure of the fund could impact on your life or business.

✔ Seek the advice of specialists and always ask for a second opinion. There are over 10,000 hedge funds in existence, with close to $3 trillion in assets under management; separating the wood from the trees can be a difficult and risky process.

DOS AND DON'TS

DO

- Seek advice, preferably from a specialist in the industry who has some years of experience and has seen both the good and the bad.
- Involve your lawyers and accountants in the evaluation of both the risks and the potential benefits of investing in a hedge fund.

Asset Management: Tools and Strategies

DON'T

- Don't jump or be pushed into a decision. Take time to do your research before deciding.
- Don't follow tips or the sheep—sleep on it before you make your move.

MORE INFO

Books:

Black, Keith H. *Managing a Hedge Fund: A Complete Guide to Trading, Business Strategies, Operations, and Regulations*. New York: McGraw-Hill Professional, 2004.

Lhabitant, François-Serge. *Handbook of Hedge Funds*. Chichester, UK: Wiley, 2006.

Nicholas, Joseph G. *Investing in Hedge Funds*. New York: Bloomberg Press, 2005.

Ridley, Matthew. *How to Invest in Hedge Funds: An Investment Professional's Guide*. London: Kogan Page, 2004.

Article:

Sender, Henny, and Javier Blas. "Hedge funds turn to gold." *Financial Times* (March 8, 2009). Online at: tinyurl.com/bux3hl

Websites:

Hedge fund database from BarclayHedge: www.barclayhedge.com
HedgeWorld: www.hedgeworld.com
Securities and Exchange Commission (SEC; US): www.sec.gov

Investments • Checklists

QFINANCE

182

Identifying and Investing in Niche (Alternative) Investments: Art, Wine, and Coins

DEFINITION

When it comes to investing, alternative investments have risen in popularity. If hedge or mutual funds, real estate, and bonds don't fill you with enthusiasm, there are plenty of other places to invest. And those with an interest in collecting works of art, wine, or coins may find that their investments, apart from giving pleasure, yield higher profits than the stock market.

Art may be a matter of personal taste, but the markets treat it like any other commodity, and the business of investing in it is based on a very simple principle—you buy something and hope its value increases. Success in the art marketplace is not easy: The proliferation of artists and the sheer quantity of works, media, periods, and styles can make collecting an intimidating prospect, and values can rise and fall terrifyingly. Nevertheless, for those who are prepared to do their homework, investing in art can be lucrative.

As the laws of supply and demand are on its side, good wine offers first-rate opportunities for the investor, making for a solid protective asset in times of uncertainty and market turbulence. High-quality wines are one-offs that can never be replaced. Therefore, it is often better to spend on a small number of good wines than to spread your investment too thinly; any wine of a good vintage offers a lower risk.

Coins can also be considered a form of investment. Their value will depend on a number of factors, including the age and availability of the coin, its condition (for example, whether it is dented, scratched, or stained), and trends in the market for precious metals. There are also bullion coins, such as the Krugerrand, which are composed mainly of precious metals and have little value beyond that of the metal itself.

ADVANTAGES

- *Art*: High-quality pieces with good provenance make for good long-term investments.
- *Wine*: A strong, defensive asset in times of uncertainty, and, if all else fails, you can drink your assets!
- *Coins*: Have always been valued for their rarity and portability.

DISADVANTAGES

- *Art*: Making a speedy profit on a piece of art is a comparative rarity, if only because transaction costs—dealers' margins and auction house fees—tend to eat up margins.
- *Wine*: It is vital that the wine is correctly stored, as it is not always simple to realize wine investments rapidly.
- *Coins*: Well-established dealers, who have a key role in determining the value of coins, control the market.

ACTION CHECKLIST

✓ Only enter a specialty area if you have a genuine interest in the subject and will get real satisfaction from the process of collecting, buying, and selling.

✓ To maximize your chances of success, you will have to do a lot of research in your field of interest.

✓ Join associations or investment clubs and consider seeking professional help before taking the plunge.

DOS AND DON'TS
DO

- Go into your primary area of interest with the aim of enjoying yourself rather than making money.
- Research your area of interest and then specialize in a specific area, region, or time period.

DON'T

- Don't believe that you are going to make your fortune; there are plenty of other, safer places to invest your hard-earned cash.
- Don't overreach: Success in the marketplace is not easy for the amateur, and enthusiasm often takes over from common sense.

MORE INFO

Books:

Rush, Richard H. *Art as an Investment*. New York: Prentice-Hall, 1961.

Sokolin, David, and Alexandra Bruce. *Investing in Liquid Assets: Uncorking Profits in Today's Global Wine Market*. New York: Simon & Schuster, 2008.

Temple, Peter. *Superhobby Investing: Making Money from Antiques, Coins, Stamps, Wine, Woodland and Other Alternative Assets*. Petersfield, UK: Harriman House, 2004.

Articles:

Bolitho, Nigel. "Noble coining it in." *Investors Chronicle* (November 5, 2007). Online at: tinyurl.com/yk9qx8c

Malaviya, Nalini S. "Investing in art." *Economic Times (New Delhi)* (January 11, 2009). Online at: tinyurl.com/yzct8cs

Websites:

Christie's: www.christies.com

Sotheby's: www.sothebys.com

Investing in Employee Pension Plans: Understanding the Risks and Returns

DEFINITION

As baby boomers have reached retirement age, many have found that those much anticipated leisure years have eluded them. They have had to carry on working because company pension plans that were meant to deliver a comfortable retirement have often done anything but.

There are basically two types of pension plan: a defined-contribution (DC) scheme and a defined-benefit (DB) scheme.

In a DC scheme the employee takes on the investment risk and the pension received depends on, among other things, the performance of the fund into which the employee and employer have paid. Most workers have little or no knowledge of financial schemes, and those extending over long periods of a working lifetime tend to generate apathy among those who are not well informed. To save for your retirement, you need to be able to make accurate, well-informed decisions. However, very few people have the skills, patience, or interest to sit down and work out what they will need to retire comfortably. An even larger dilemma is that the level of contributions from both employers and employees into DC schemes is not always sufficient and, if less money goes in, generally less money comes out. Added to that is that the costs of running DC schemes are, on average, higher than for a DB scheme, having expense ratios of more than 1%.

In a DB scheme, the employer takes on most of the burden by promising employees a retirement income based on their pay and length of service. When these schemes were first introduced 50 years ago, their costs were manageable and they were often used as a bargaining chip, so that employers could avoid paying higher wages. However, with rising wages and the depredations of inflation, the promises of a DB pension became more expensive and burdensome for companies to keep. The soaring costs of DB pensions have encouraged many employers to switch to DC schemes. The argument is often that DB schemes place too heavy a burden on company management and, in effect, require companies to wager money on the financial markets in order to meet their pension commitments.

ADVANTAGES

- DC schemes allow businesses to get on with business and not waste their time and skills on running pensions.

- DB schemes promise employees a retirement income based on their pay and length of service, with the employer taking the risk.

DISADVANTAGES

- DC schemes leave many employees facing a retirement income well short of their expectations.
- DB schemes tend to discourage mobility and reward those who spend their whole career at a single firm.
- In a DC scheme the employee takes on the investment risk and the pension received depends on the investment performance of the fund.

ACTION CHECKLIST

✔ What type of pension plan does your company have, and is it open to new employees?

✔ Check the pension forecasts and see, after taking into account inflation, what percentage of your final salary you will receive as a pension.

✔ Lower contributions almost inevitably mean lower pensions. Therefore, if in doubt, invest in a private pension plan to make up what you estimate will be the shortfall.

DOS AND DON'TS

DO

- Check if you can take your pension rights with you if you change companies.
- If you invest in a private pension, plan ahead, assess what income you will need, and link your yearly contributions to that target.

DON'T

- Don't take your pension plan for granted. Complacency may mean that you have to carry on working instead of retiring comfortably.

MORE INFO

Books:

Hill, Michael. *Pensions*. Bristol: Policy Press, 2007.

McGill, Dan M., Kyle N. Brown, John J. Haley, Sylvester J. Schieber, *et al. Fundamentals of Private Pensions*. 9th ed. Oxford: Oxford University Press, 2005.

Munnell, Alicia Haydock. *The Economics of Private Pensions*. Washington, DC: Brookings Institution Press, 1982.

Articles:

Bellers, Chris. "Investment spotlight—deregulation of pensions—or dilution." *Pensions Management* (December 2007).

Money Management. "Tools for pension investment." March 2007.

Websites:

Pension Benefit Guaranty Corporation (PBGC; US): www.pbgc.gov

An Overview of *Shariah*-Compliant Funds

DEFINITION

Shariah-compliant funds are investment vehicles which are fully compliant with the principles of Islam. The funds are prohibited from making investments in industries categorized as morally deficient, such as those related to gambling or alcohol. Because Islam does not permit any form of exploitation, any kind of investment in conventional banking is outlawed. With the concept of debt also contrary to the principles of Islam, investment in highly leveraged companies is also not permitted for *shariah*-compliant funds. The exclusions extend to potential investments in other funds which offer guaranteed returns. Any use of futures and options, either by the fund managers or by companies in which the funds invest, is also likely to attract close scrutiny by the funds' supervisory *shariah* boards.

Due to the rapid growth in Islamic finance over recent years, the available range of *shariah*-compliant funds has expanded as financial services providers seek to tap into the increasing demand for investment products that respect the principles of Islam. The most common forms of *shariah*-compliant funds are described below.

Ijarah

Ijarah (also transliterated *ijara*) is a leasing-type fund that acquires assets such as real estate or equipment and then leases them out to another party in return for a regular rental payment. In all cases the fund retains ownership of the asset and must ensure that usage of the asset is at all times in accordance with Islamic principles.

Murabahah

Murabahah (or murabaha) is a kind of development fund that acquires assets and then sells them to a client at a predetermined price which reflects the fund's cost of acquiring the asset plus a profit margin. Sometimes described as "cost-plus" funds, *murabahah* investment vehicles do not hold long-term ownership of the assets, but instead generate a financial return from the payment obligations taken on by clients for a pre-agreed period.

Equity

Equity funds invest directly in companies through the purchase of shares. Given the difficulties involved in scrutinizing every aspect of how a company operates to verify *shariah*-compliance, this new, more progressive attitude allows investment in companies that operate in permitted industries, with the proviso that a proportion of the returns generated for the fund from any interest-bearing deposits held by the company must be donated to charity.

Commodity

Commodity funds invest in physical commodities, although speculative activities such as short selling are not permitted. However, the fund manager may make use of *istisna'a* contracts, pre-agreeing the price of goods to be manufactured and delivered at a specified future date, with the manufacturer benefiting from advance receipt of the agreed sale price. Commodity fund managers can also use *bai salam* contracts. These can be compared to conventional forward contracts, though the key *shariah*-compliant differentiator is that the seller's position is protected because payment is passed to the seller on agreement of the contract rather than on its completion. However, in return for the effective transfer of contract risk, the buyer is compensated by the fact that the agreed delivery price is set at a discount to the physical spot price.

ADVANTAGES

- *Shariah*-compliant investment funds provide a means of investing while still honoring the high morals and principles of Islam.
- *Shariah*-compliant funds promote large-scale investment along lines similar to the niche ethical funds available to Western consumers.

DISADVANTAGES

- The funds can be more expensive to develop and administer than mainstream funds due to the need for greater verification of compliance with *shariah* principles.

ACTION CHECKLIST

✔ Assess the full range of available *shariah*-compliant investment products before selecting the type you wish to use.

✔ Consider how much risk you are prepared to assume before investing.

✔ Mainstream investors may wish to consider potential investments in *shariah*-compliant funds.

QFINANCE

Asset Management: Tools and Strategies

DOS AND DON'TS

DO
- Compare fund management charges between different providers.
- Consider using index products such as exchange-traded funds to gain exposure to Islamic investment indices.

DON'T
- Don't feel you have to verify the compliance of a fund yourself—contact a fund provider for advice.
- Don't expect guaranteed attractive returns, even from the most ethical forms of investment.

MORE INFO

Books:
Anwar, Habiba, and Roderick Millar (eds). *Islamic Finance: A Guide for International Business and Investment*. London: GMB Publishing, 2008.

Jaffer, Sohail (ed). *Islamic Asset Management: Forming the Future for Shari'a-Compliant Investment Strategies*. London: Euromoney Books, 2004.

Vogel, Frank E., and Samuel L. Hayes, III. *Islamic Law and Finance: Religion, Risk, and Return*. The Hague: Kluwer Law International, 1998.

Articles:
Feinberg, Phyllis. "Seeking pension money: Mutual fund family follows Islamic law." *Pensions and Investments* (October 30, 2000). Online at: tinyurl.com/6zugr7a

Siddiqi, Moin A. "Growing appeal of Islamic investment funds." *Middle East* (July–August 1997).

Overview of Tax Deeds

DEFINITION

A tax deed is usually entered into upon an acquisition of the majority shares in a company. The tax deed is concerned with the tax affairs of the business and the company acquired. Under the tax deed, the seller agrees to pay to the buyer any tax liability and charge resulting from an event occurring before the buyer acquired the company. This includes any reasonable costs and expenses which were properly incurred and payable by the company or the buyer in connection with any reasonable action to avoid or settle a tax claim or liability. In any tax deed, the sellers will seek to limit their liability in such an undertaking to a maximum agreed amount. For example, the undertaking will not be given and the seller will not be liable to the extent that any provision or reserve in respect of the liability to taxation was taken into account in the accounts of the company. Also the seller will not be made to pay if the amount has already been recovered by the buyer under the sale and purchase agreement. The tax deed will also deal with the procedure to be followed by the parties in the event of a tax claim which the seller is not aware of. The deed will also cover how the payments, if any, will be made and scheduled. The undertaking by the seller will usually be valid for a period of seven years from the date of acquisition of the company but this can vary depending upon the laws of the applicable jurisdiction.

ADVANTAGES

- A tax deed sets out the terms and conditions under which the buyer of a company will be compensated for any tax liability that he/she must pay after the acquisition as a result of an event which occurred before the date of the acquisition.
- Because a tax deed is an agreement, it can be negotiated and agreed by the two parties, the buyer and the seller.
- Tax deeds protect buyers from unnecessary and unforeseen tax liabilities they may have as a result of acquiring a company. In general, they are reasonably standard and accepted as a necessary document by the parties of an acquisition of a majority of shares in a company.

DISADVANTAGES

- Negotiating a tax deed can be complex and time consuming. It involves thorough knowledge of the documentation and requires specialist legal, accounting, and tax advice and can therefore be an expensive process.

ACTION CHECKLIST

✓ Carefully study any tax deed which you might sign. Obtain as much information from as many sources as you can before committing to expensive liabilities. Do not sign a document that you do not understand.
✓ Through your advisers try and limit your exposure of liabilities to an amount you feel comfortable with. If your company has had its tax affairs in order you do not have much to worry about.

DOS AND DON'TS

DO

- Choose your advisers carefully. Make sure that you understand the undertakings you are giving. Involve your tax advisers and accountants in the negotiation process.
- Involve your solicitors in the evaluation of both the risks and potential benefits of entering into a tax deed.
- If you know of any tax liabilities that are due before the completion of your sale, disclose them and try to sort them out with the relevant authorities.

DON'T

- Don't make the mistake of ignoring the importance of the undertakings you will give in a tax deed. They can come back to haunt you.
- Don't overlook the importance of negotiating undertakings and indemnities that you could give with confidence. Make sure that if you know of anything that may go against these warranties, you disclose them to the buyer.

MORE INFO

Books:

CCH Tax Law Editors. *US Master Sales and Use Tax Guide*. Chicago, IL: CCH, 2007.

Reuvid, Jonathan. *Mergers and Acquisitions: A Practical Guide for Private Companies and their UK and Overseas Advisers*. Philadelphia, PA: Kogan Page, 2008.

Articles:

Gustafson, Jeanne. "GenPrime signs big distribution agreement." *Journal of Business* (October 2000).

Quinn, Robert M. "Florida tax deed sales are getting risky." *Florida Bar Journal* 81:7 (July/August 2007). Online at: tinyurl.com/6kjs6fk

Stock Markets: Their Structure and Function

DEFINITION

A stock market is a private or public market for the trading of stocks and shares in companies and derivatives of company stocks at an agreed price. These include securities listed on a stock exchange as well as those traded privately. A stock market is sometimes also known as an equity market.

The estimated size of the world stock market is around US$51 trillion. Even larger, it is estimated that the world derivatives market is worth about US$480 trillion face, or nominal, value; that is well over ten times the size of the whole world economy. However, the derivatives market is stated in terms of notional values and therefore cannot be directly compared to stocks, which refer to an actual value.

Stock markets specialize in bringing buyers and sellers of stocks and securities together. Famous stock exchanges include the New York Stock Exchange, the London Stock Exchange, the Deutsche Börse, and the Paris/Amsterdam Euronext.

A stock market is an important way for a company to raise money. It allows businesses to be publicly traded, or to raise extra capital for expansion by selling shares in the company in a public market. Share owners then have a share of ownership of that company. A stock market provides liquidity to give investors the chance to sell securities rapidly and easily. This makes investing in stocks attractive compared with, for example, real estate, which is less liquid.

The price of shares and other assets plays an important part in the economic activity of a country. It can influence or reflect the social mood of a country. A stock market is often taken as a primary indicator of a country's economic well-being as it enables the efficient allocation of capital. Stock prices reflect where capital is being invested, or should be. If share prices are rising, this is usually coupled with increased business investment, and vice versa. Share prices also have an influence on the wealth of households, and thus on how much they spend. Central banks watch the movement of the stock market closely and also the smooth operation of financial system functions. This was highlighted in September 2008, when stock markets plunged in response to failing financial institutions—particularly in the United States—and central banks stepped in to try to arrest the slide.

Stock exchanges act as a clearing house for each transaction made on them. This means that they guarantee payment to the seller of the security and collect and deliver the shares. In this way there is no risk to a buyer or seller of a default on the transaction.

With these activities functioning smoothly, economic growth is enhanced because lower costs and enterprise risks help to promote the production of goods and services, and employment. As such, financial systems contribute to increased prosperity.

ADVANTAGES

- Trading in stock and shares can be done rapidly and easily, making them an attractive liquid investment.
- A rising stock market helps to boost prosperity in a country and promote a confident social mood.
- Stock markets allow anyone to participate in the growth of any listed company.

DISADVANTAGES

- Share prices can change very quickly in today's electronic markets, driven by trading by very large institutions.
- A falling stock market creates an unhappy mood in a country and can lead to difficult economic times and unemployment.
- Prices of stocks and shares can fall as well as rise.

ACTION CHECKLIST

✓ Check the history of a stock market. How long ago was it established? How stable is it? How does its average performance rate compared with other exchanges?

✓ Check the risks involved in a particular stock market. Is it easy to buy and sell on your chosen stock market? What fees are involved? How well is it regulated? Some countries regulate less well than others, increasing your risk.

✓ Check how easy it is to find current prices on your chosen stock market.

Asset Management: Tools and Strategies

DOS AND DON'TS
DO
* Understand the volatility and risk of a stock market before investing.
* Understand the risks involved. Some emerging markets have higher growth potential, but much higher risks too.

* Keep an eye on the progress of the stocks and shares you have purchased.

DON'T
* Don't rush into stock market investments.
* Don't buy when the price is high.
* Don't sell when the price is low.

MORE INFO
Books:

Becket, Michael, and Yvette Essen. *How the Stock Market Works: A Beginner's Guide to Investment*. 4th ed. London: Kogan Page, 2011.

Chapman, Colin. *How the Stock Markets Work*. 9th ed. London: Random House Business Books, 2006.

Gough, Leo. *How the Stock Market Really Works*. 5th ed. Financial Times Guides Series. Harlow, UK: FT Prentice Hall, 2011.

Websites:

Financial Times markets news: www.ft.com/markets
London Stock Exchange: www.londonstockexchange.com
New York Stock Exchange: www.nyse.com
Wall Street Journal: online.wsj.com

Structured Investment Vehicles

DEFINITION

A structured investment vehicle, or SIV, is a limited-purpose operating company or "virtual bank" that undertakes arbitrage activities by purchasing mostly highly rated medium- and long-term fixed-income assets. These assets are funded though the issue of short-term, highly rated commercial paper or medium-term notes, which traditionally offer a rate close to the London Interbank Offered Rate (Libor). The SIV thus makes its profits from the spread between the short-term borrowing rate and long-term returns. A SIV has an open-ended and rollover business structure whereby it buys new assets as the old ones mature.

The costs of running a SIV are balanced by the economic returns: that is, the net spread to pay subordinated note-holder returns and the generation of management fee income. Most SIVs are administered or sponsored by banks, but a number are managed independently. The number of SIVs has proliferated in recent years and they control assets worth hundreds of billions of dollars. SIVs are generally quite opaque, invest in complex securities, and often do not need to be displayed on a bank's balance sheet.

The subprime crisis has caused a widespread liquidity crunch in the commercial paper markets and, given that SIVs rely on making their profits from the spread between the short-term borrowing rate and long-term returns, many SIVs have seen their business drastically reduced. Although the Federal Reserve and the European Central Bank have injected billions of dollars and euros into the market, a number of independent SIVs have closed, while other SIVs are being supported by their sponsoring banks.

ADVANTAGES

- SIVs offer good returns in highly liquid markets.
- Most SIVs are sponsored by banks, which back them when they have liquidity problems.

DISADVANTAGES

- Most SIVs issue a mixture of commercial paper or of medium-term notes, and their weighted-average liability to maturity is normally from four to six months, but the assets in the vehicle will have significantly longer average maturities.
- SIVs suffer from the credit risks associated with assets and hedges and the market risk linked to the cost of liquidating assets and hedges. There is the potential for defaults due to a lack of liquidity in world financial markets.
- Some of the SIV's assets may entail due diligence by potential purchasers, thus increasing the sale period for these assets.
- Losses can result from unhedged changes in currencies and interest rates.

ACTION CHECKLIST

✓ In the current illiquid market conditions, make sure that the SIV has a portfolio of highly liquid assets and less liquid, higher-yielding investments.

✓ Ensure that the SIV is exposed to a range of fixed-rate and currency assets and that the portfolio is conservatively hedged.

DOS AND DON'TS

DO

- Use the rating agencies (Moody's, Standard & Poor's, and Fitch IBCA) to check on the SIV. Whatever their faults in the past, rating agencies have tightened up their criteria and will give a good guide to the viability of a particular asset.
- Check who the principal backers are.

DON'T

- Don't forget that although many SIVs are administered or sponsored by banks, a number are managed independently, which might make them more likely to have liquidity problems.

MORE INFO

Books:

de Servigny, Arnaud, and Norbert Jobst (eds). *The Handbook of Structured Finance*. New York: McGraw-Hill, 2007.

El-Erian, Mohamed. *When Markets Collide: Investment Strategies for the Age of Global Economic Change*. New York: McGraw-Hill, 2008.

Tavakoli, Janet M. *Collateralized Debt Obligations and Structured Finance: New Developments in Cash and Synthetic Securitization*. Hoboken, NJ: Wiley, 2003.

Article:

Dolbeck, Andrew. "SIV survival: The fate of structured investment vehicles." *Weekly Corporate Growth Report* (November 5, 2007).

Websites:

Use search options on these websites to look up "structured investment vehicles."
Bank of Montreal: www.bmo.com
Citigroup: www.citi.com

Trading in Commodities: Why and How

DEFINITION

In contrast to other kinds of investment, such as stocks or bonds, when you trade in commodities or futures you do not in fact buy or own anything. You are speculating on the future direction of the price of the commodity. The terms "commodities" and "futures" are often used to describe commodity trading or futures trading. *Commodities* are the actual physical goods, such as corn, soybeans, gold, or crude oil. *Futures* are contracts for those commodities, which are traded at a futures exchange such as the Chicago Board of Trade.

Futures are standardized contracts among buyers and sellers of commodities, specifying the amount of a commodity, grade/quality, and delivery location. Each futures exchange has producers and consumers who want to hedge their risks of future price changes. In between them are the traders, who do not actually buy and sell the physical commodities but are there to help maintain an organized market and provide liquidity. Futures markets are generally very actively traded, so typically there is a large daily price range and trading volume.

Futures contracts have now expanded beyond just physical commodities, and there are futures contracts on financial markets such as the S&P500, treasury notes, currencies, etc.

Futures markets can be traded in both up and down. If a trader expects the market to move upwards, he will make a long trade by buying a contract and leave the trade by selling a contract. Conversely, if a trader expects the market to move downwards, he will make a short trade by selling a contract and leave the trade by buying a contract. By being able to trade in both directions, traders can make a profit or loss regardless of which direction the market is moving. In order to make decisions about when to trade commodity futures, traders tend to use price-activity charts that show futures movements and which are easily understood when tackling historical and current price movements.

ADVANTAGES

- Futures markets are available with a wide variety of underlying instruments, which in turn offer a wide range of price movements and liquidity. Some are available for day-trading 24 hours per day.
- Futures markets can be day-traded without any restrictions, which makes them preferable to stock markets that have day-trading restrictions.
- Futures markets are offered with trades in currencies such as the euro to US dollar exchange rate, stock indexes such as the Dow Jones and DAX, and commodities such as gold, silver, and oil.

DISADVANTAGES

- Unforeseen events such as floods, droughts, government currency interventions, and crop reports can cause sudden and unpredictable losses.
- Risk and reward go hand in hand. It is ridiculous to expect to be able to earn above-average profits without above-average risks.

ACTION CHECKLIST

✓ Learn about and specialize in a particular commodity before you begin trading. Every commodity has different trading guidelines and a profile that includes the basics of contract specifications, market reports, and charts.

✓ Begin trading with small amounts until you learn the ropes; trades on some exchanges are available for as little as $100.

DOS AND DON'TS

DO

- Do your homework and start by trading in small amounts until you are thoroughly familiar with your chosen commodity.
- Use price-activity charts before making decisions about when to trade in futures.

DON'T

- Don't forget that, although the risks can be managed, they can never be eliminated. Keep in mind that the high returns are available only because the trader is being paid to take risk away from others.
- Don't forget that losses are part of the process and that the best traders lose money, but over time they make even more.

Asset Management: Tools and Strategies

MORE INFO

Books:

Buckley, John (ed). *Guide to World Commodity Markets: Physical, Futures and Options Trading*. 7th ed. London: Kogan Page, 1996.

Chicago Board of Trade. *Commodity Trading Manual*. London: Lessons Professional Publishing, 1998.

Gregoriou, Greg N., Vassilios N. Karavas, François-Serge Lhabitant, and Fabrice Rouah. *Commodity Trading Advisers: Risk, Performance Analysis, and Selection*. Hoboken, NJ: Wiley, 2004.

Articles:

Chong, Sidney. "Commodity investment." *Australasian Business Intelligence* (July 27, 2006).

M2 PressWIRE. "Maximizing returns through fundamental analysis in commodity investing." *M2 PressWIRE* (March 10, 2008).

Websites:

Commodity Futures Trading Commission (CFTC; US): www.cftc.gov
Financial Services Authority (FSA; UK): www.fsa.gov.uk

Investments • Checklists

QFINANCE

Trading in Corporate Bonds: Why and How

DEFINITION

The term "corporate bond" is, from time to time, used to refer to all bonds except those issued by governments in their own currencies. However, it should actually be applied only to longer-term debt instruments that are issued by corporations.

Corporate bonds promise a higher return than some other investments, but the higher return comes at a cost. Most corporate bonds are debentures, which means that they are not secured by collateral. Investors in these bonds must take on not only the interest rate risk but also the credit risk, which is the chance that the corporate issuer will default on its debt. It is important that investors in corporate bonds know how to weigh up credit risk and its possible payoffs. Rising interest rates can reduce the value of your bond investment, and a default can almost eliminate it. The *total yield* on a bond is all gains from coupons and price appreciation, and *current yield* is that from coupon payments.

Corporate bonds are like no other bonds in that they carry an implied risk. Takeovers, corporate restructuring, and leveraged buyouts can change a corporate bond's credit rating and price. Institutional investors use credit rating agencies such as Moody's, Standard & Poor's, and Fitch IBCA to check credit risk. However, many investors also use interest-coverage ratios and capitalization ratios. The *interest-coverage ratio* tells one how much money the company generates each year to fund the annual interest on its debt. The higher the ratio the better, but a company should at least generate enough earnings to service its annual debt. The *capitalization ratio* shows the company's degree of financial leverage. The lower the capitalization ratio, the better the company's financial leverage.

There are also other risk factors. If the bond is *callable*, the company has the right to buy it back after a period of time, while the *poison pill provision* permits shareholders to buy stock at a heavily discounted price to prevent or hinder takeovers. *Putable* bonds have a feature designed to protect against interest rate fluctuations, which allows the holder to return, or "tender," the bond to the issuer at par before the bond's maturity date. With junk bonds (i.e. those rated below S&P's BBB) the risk of losing everything is high and investors should consider the diversification of a high-yield bond fund, which can support a few defaults while still giving high returns.

ADVANTAGES

- Corporate bonds offer higher yields than their treasury equivalents. If you can spot the right investment, the compounding interest over the life of the bond can be quite astounding.
- The default risk on corporate bonds can be quantified using spread analysis, which seeks to determine the difference in yield between a given corporate bond and a risk-free treasury bond of the same maturity.

DISADVANTAGES

- Corporate bonds have an implied event risk. Takeovers, corporate restructuring, and even leveraged buyouts can penalize a bond's credit rating and price.
- Rising interest rates can reduce the value of your bond investment; a default can almost eliminate it.

ACTION CHECKLIST

✓ Assess the bond's credit risk rating in lists published by Standard & Poor's, Moody's, and Fitch IBCA.

✓ Analyze the credit risk and remember that bonds may have multiple issuances; each of these issues will receive different ratings from the credit agencies due to the fact that they have different repayment structures and conditions.

DOS AND DON'TS

DO

- Use interest-coverage ratios and capitalization ratios to back up the ratings given by Standard & Poor's, Moody's, and Fitch IBCA.
- Think about investing in a high-yield bond fund, which can support a few failures yet still provide high returns.

DON'T

- Don't take on credit risk or default from a single corporate bond issue unless you are receiving enough extra yield to cover the risk.

Investments • Checklists

MORE INFO

Books:

Crabbe, Leland E., and Frank J. Fabozzi. *Managing a Corporate Bond Portfolio*. New York: Wiley, 2002.

Swensen, David F. *Unconventional Success: A Fundamental Approach to Personal Investment*. New York: Simon & Schuster, 2005.

Wilson, Richard S., and Frank J. Fabozzi. *Corporate Bonds: Structures & Analysis*. New York: Wiley, 1995.

Article:

Investment Adviser. "The complete James Bond guide to investing." (May 21, 2007). Online at: tinyurl.com/64brvgj

Website:

Standard & Poor's: www.standardandpoors.com

QFINANCE

Trading in Equities on Stock Exchanges

DEFINITION

Equity trading is the buying and selling of company stocks and shares. Stocks and shares in publicly traded companies are bought and sold through one of the major stock exchanges, which serve as managed auctions for stock. A stock exchange, share market, or bourse is a company, corporation, or mutual organization that provides facilities for stockbrokers and traders to trade stocks and other securities. Stock exchanges also provide facilities for the issue and redemption of securities, trading in other financial instruments, and the payment of income and dividends. To be traded on a stock exchange, a company has to be listed on it. Some international companies are listed on more than one exchange.

A share is one of a finite number of equal portions in the capital of a company, and a person owning shares is called a shareholder. Shares entitle the owner to a proportion of distributed, non-reinvested profits known as dividends, and to a proportion of the value of the company in the event of liquidation. Shares are classed as voting (Class A), with the right to vote on the board of directors, or non-voting (Class B). This right can often affect the value of the share.

The value of a publicly traded company is called its market capitalization. This is calculated as the number of shares outstanding (as opposed to those authorized but not necessarily issued) times the price per share. A company's market capitalization should not be confused with the fair market value of the company, as the price per share can be influenced by factors such as the volume of shares traded.

A stockbroker is a qualified and regulated professional who buys and sells shares and other securities on his or her own behalf or on behalf of investors. Equity trading can be performed by the owner of the shares or by a stockbroker authorized to buy and sell on behalf of the owner (in return for a commission). Most trading is carried out on electronic networks, which offer the advantages of up-to-the-second prices and information on the number of shares bought or sold, together with speed and a low transaction cost. The initial public offering (IPO) of stocks and shares to investors is done on the primary market and any subsequent trading is done in the secondary market.

ADVANTAGES

- Holding shares allows an investor to spread investment risk and participate in some of the world's premier companies.

- As a general rule, shares as an investment vehicle have, over the long run, outperformed all other types of investment.

DISADVANTAGES

- Share prices can be very volatile, and the value of shares depends on a number of external factors over which the investor has no control.
- Different shares can have different levels of liquidity, i.e. demand from buyers and sellers. Normally, blue-chip stocks have greater depth and liquidity. The lower the market capitalization, the lower the liquidity, which may affect the ease with which the shares can be sold. Liquidity also affects share prices because, if the shares have low liquidity, it is sometimes more difficult to convert them into cash.

ACTION CHECKLIST

✓ To trade shares, you must have an account with a stockbroker or a licensed intermediary (financial planner, accountant, etc.). This is to ensure that the trading environment is secure. Many new investors start using stockbrokers but others prefer to do their own research and use online brokers.

✓ Most brokers require you to have an account to ensure that you have the funds to cover orders. Some online brokers require you to have an account with an associated financial institution before you can begin trading.

✓ When placing a buy or sell order, there are two ways you can trade. Shares can be traded at *market order*, which means buying at the prevailing market price. The alternative is the *limit order*, where you set the minimum or maximum price.

DOS AND DON'TS

DO

- Research the company, and take into account any risks you feel might arise. If in doubt, use a *stop loss* to help protect your investment.

DON'T

- Don't invest on the basis of tips unless you are extremely confident of the source. More often than not, tipped shares—like tipped horses—will end up as "also-rans."

MORE INFO

Books:

Maginn, John L., Donald L. Tuttle, Jerald E. Pinto, and Dennis W. McLeavey. *Managing Investment Portfolios: A Dynamic Process.* 3rd ed. CFA Institute Investment Series. Hoboken, NJ: Wiley, 2007.

Mobius, Mark. *Equities: An Introduction to the Core Concepts.* Singapore: Wiley, 2006.

Morris, Virginia B., and Kenneth M. Morris. *Standard & Poor's Guide to Money and Investing.* New York: Lightbulb Press, 2005.

Articles:

Investment Adviser. "Worldwide equity trading portal comes to the market." November 5, 2007. Online at: tinyurl.com/698evb3

Mehta, Nina. "TradeWeb eyes equity expansion in 2008." *Traders* (December 2007). Online at: www.tradersmagazine.com/issues/20_275/100087-1.html

Websites:

E*TRADE trading (US): www.etrade.com

Interactive Investor share dealing (UK): www.iii.co.uk/sharedealing

Trading in Government Bonds: Why and How

DEFINITION

A government bond is a bond issued by a national government, denominated in the country's own currency. Sovereign bonds are those issued by foreign governments in their own currencies. Government bonds are usually thought of as risk-free, because even if a government has problems it can always raise taxes or simply print more money to redeem the bond. The maturities of sovereign bonds vary and will depend on the issuing government. The US government is the largest seller of government or treasury bonds in the world. Its bonds are auctioned in February and August, and have 30-year maturities.

In the *primary market*, bonds are sold in auctions. Bids are divided into competitive and noncompetitive bids. Competitive bids are restricted to primary government dealers, while noncompetitive bids are open to individual investors and small institutions.

Secondary market trading in bonds occurs in the over-the-counter (OTC) market. All US government securities are traded OTC, with the primary government securities dealers being the largest and most important market participants. In the secondary market a wide variety of investors use bonds for investing, hedging, and speculation. These investors include commercial and investment banks, insurance companies, pension funds, mutual funds, and retail investors.

While some electronic bond trading is available to retail investors, the entire bond market remains very much an OTC market. The bond market, unlike the equity markets (where electronic dealing and transparency have leveled the playing field for individual and institutional investors), lacks price transparency and liquidity, except in the case of government bonds. For the independent bond investor who would prefer to spread his or her risk and not pay the high fees for a managed fund, a good alternative is an *exchange-traded fund* or an *index bond fund*, which will track government bond indices and, given the high liquidity of these bonds, will present fewer problems than corporate bonds.

ADVANTAGES

- Price transparency and liquidity for government bonds are comparatively high, providing a safe platform for a wide range of investors to hedge and speculate. These investors include commercial and investment banks, insurance companies, pension funds, mutual funds, and retail investors.
- Government bonds are generally referred to as risk-free bonds, because governments can simply raise more taxes or print more money to pay for them.
- Government bonds are highly liquid and investors can recover some of their investment quickly if necessary.

DISADVANTAGES

- There is foreign-exchange risk for investors when the currency of the bonds in which they have invested declines in relation to their own.
- The risks of trading in government bonds stem, above all, from changes in interest rates, which can cause fluctuations in prices for bonds.
- Bond prices are influenced by economic data such as employment, income growth/decline, and consumer and industrial prices. Any information that implies rising inflation will weaken bond prices, as inflation reduces the income from a bond.

ACTION CHECKLIST

✓ If you are investing in sovereign funds, how safe is the government or region? Don't forget that in 1998 the Russian government defaulted on its debt.

✓ What are interest rates going to do? Investors who buy and sell bonds before maturity are exposed to many risks, most importantly changes in interest rates. When interest rates increase, new issues will pay a higher yield and the value of existing bonds will fall. When interest rates decline, the value of existing bonds will rise as new issues pay a lower yield.

DOS AND DON'TS

DO

- Before you buy, check how quickly you will be able to sell if necessary, and at what discount and dealing fee.

DON'T

- Don't unless you are completely confident, invest in only one type of bond. An exchange-traded fund or an index bond fund might be a much safer bet.

MORE INFO

Books:

Faerber, Esmé. *All About Bonds and Bond Mutual Funds: The Easy Way to Get Started*. 2nd ed. New York: McGraw-Hill, 1999.

Rini, William A. *Mathematics of the Securities Industry*. New York: McGraw-Hill Professional, 2003.

Wong, M. Anthony, in collaboration with Robert High. *Trading and Investing in Bond Options: Risk Management, Arbitrage, and Value Investing*. New York: Wiley, 1991.

Articles:

Pensions Management. "Comment: Investment—Getting the best from bonds." April 2008.

Rodier, Melanie. "The massive growth of electronic bond trading." *Wall Street and Technology* (April 15, 2008). Online at: www.wallstreetandtech.com/articles/207200781

Websites:

Bloomberg current government bond prices: tinyurl.com/2dbqurw

FTSE Global Bond Index Series: www.ftse.com/Indices/FTSE_Global_Bond_Index_Series

Understanding and Using the Repos Market

DEFINITION

A repo, or repurchase agreement, is an agreement between two parties whereby one party sells the other a security at a specified price with a commitment to buy the security back at a later date. A repo is economically similar to a secured loan, with the buyer receiving securities as collateral to protect against default. Virtually any security can be used as a repo: treasury and government bills, corporate and government bonds, and stocks or shares can all be used as securities to back a repo. Although the transaction is similar to a loan, it differs in that the seller repurchases the legal ownership of the securities from the buyer at the end of the agreement. Also, while the legal title to the securities passes from the seller to the buyer, coupons that are paid while the repo buyer owns the securities are normally passed directly to the repo seller.

Repos are contracts for the sale and future repurchase of a financial asset, normally treasury securities. The annualized rate of interest paid on the loan is known as the repo rate. Repos can be of any duration, but are most commonly overnight loans, or *overnight repos*. Repos longer than this are known as *term repos*. There are also *open repos*, which can be terminated by either side on a day's notice. The lender normally receives a margin on the security, meaning that it is priced below market value, typically by 2% to 5%, depending on maturity. Repos are normally not for the smaller investor: in the primary market dealers frequently transact hundreds of millions of dollars, and in the secondary market repos of one million dollars are not uncommon.

The Federal Reserve Bank also uses repos in its open-market operations as a method of fine-tuning the money supply. To expand the supply of money temporarily, the Federal Reserve arranges to buy securities from non-bank dealers, which deposit the proceeds in their commercial bank accounts, thereby adding to reserves. The repos usually last 1 to 15 days, or whatever length of time the Federal Reserve needs to make the adjustment. When it wishes to reduce the money supply, it reverses the process using a "matched sale purchase transaction": it sells securities to dealers, who either draw on bank balances directly or take out a bank loan to make the payment, thereby withdrawing reserves.

ADVANTAGES

- Repos allow investors to keep surplus funds invested without losing liquidity or incurring price risk or credit risk because the collateral is more often than not in high-class securities.
- Repos can be used for investing surplus funds in the short term, or for short-term borrowing against collateral. Corporations can use repos to help manage their liquidity and short-term financing of their inventories.

DISADVANTAGES

- Overnight changes in interest rates or currency fluctuations can affect the value of a dealer's securities holding, and a dealer who holds a large position takes a risk.
- Repos are normally not for the smaller investor: in the primary market dealers frequently transact hundreds of millions of dollars, and in the secondary market repos of one million dollars are not uncommon.
- The seller could default on his or her obligation and fail to repurchase the securities.

ACTION CHECKLIST

✓ What type of repo are you buying, and in which international market? Will risk and return be affected by currency fluctuations, credit risk, the type and liquidity of the security, or third-party involvement?

✓ Does the securities dealer have a special repo account at a clearing bank to settle his or her trades?

✓ Primary dealers must be authorized by the Federal Reserve Bank to bid on newly issued treasury securities for resale on the markets.

DOS AND DON'TS

DO

- Check on any repos in equity securities. Complications can arise sometimes because of greater complexity in the tax rules on dividends.

DON'T

- Don't fail to check on the credit risk associated with the repo, i.e. type and liquidity of security, other parties involved, etc.

Asset Management: Tools and Strategies

MORE INFO

Books:

Fabozzi, Frank J., and Moorad Choudhry (eds). *The Handbook of European Fixed Income Securities.* Frank J. Fabozzi Series. Hoboken, NJ: Wiley, 2004.

Levinson, Marc. *Guide to Financial Markets.* 4th ed. London: Profile, 2006.

Mathieson, Donald J., and Garry J. Schinasi. *International Capital Markets: Developments, Prospects, and Key Policy Issues.* Washington, DC: International Monetary Fund, 2001.

Articles:

de Teran, Natasha. "Euribor swap a boost for repo market." *Financial News* (September 15, 2003).

Wright, Ben. "Growth of European repo market stalls." *Financial News* (March 16, 2003).

Websites:

European Central Bank (ECB): www.ecb.int

Federal Reserve (US): www.federalreserve.gov

Understanding Private Equity Strategies: An Overview

DEFINITION

Private equity firms generally want to buy companies or parts of companies for their portfolios, repair them, enhance them, and sell them on. The investment period is seldom less than a year and can be as long as 10 years, but the objective is always to sell the business on at a substantial profit. Private equity investors have three main investment strategies:

1 *Venture capital* is a broad class of private equity that normally refers to equity investments in less mature companies. Venture capital is often subdivided according to the phase of maturity of the company, ranging from capital used for the launch of start-up companies to later-stage and growth capital. It is often used to fund the expansion of an existing business that is generating revenue but may not yet be profitable or generating sufficient cash flow to fund future investment.

2 *Growth capital* refers to equity investments (most often minority investments) in more mature companies that are looking for capital to expand or restructure operations, enter new markets, or finance a major acquisition without a change in the control of the business.

3 The *leveraged buyout* (LBO) is a strategy of equity investment whereby a company, business unit, or business asset is acquired from the current shareholders, typically with the use of financial leverage. The companies involved in these buyouts are generally more mature and generate cash flows.

Occasionally, investments are made in *distressed* or *special* situations, where the equity or debt securities of a distressed company are unlocked as a result of a one-off opening, such as market turmoil or changes in financial regulations.

ADVANTAGES

- Private equity can provide high returns, with the best private equity investments significantly outperforming the public markets. The potential benefits for successful investors can be annual returns of up to 30%.

- An important perceived advantage of private equity is that the agency problem is reduced, because the owners have direct contact with the managers and can do detailed monitoring.
- Because private equity firms focus on just a few investments, their due diligence is much more solid (and costly) than that of the investor in a public company.
- Not only is a far larger share of executive pay tied to the performance of the business, but top managers may also be required to put a major chunk of their own money into the deal and have an ownership mentality rather than a corporate mentality.
- With LBOs, management can focus on getting the company right without having to worry about shareholders.

DISADVANTAGES

- Most private equity investments have significant entry requirements, stipulating a considerable initial investment (normally upwards of $1,000,000), which can be drawn upon at the manager's discretion.
- Private equity investment is for those who can afford to have their capital locked in for long periods of time and who are able to risk losing it.

ACTION CHECKLIST

✓ Bankers are much more wary of leveraged financing nowadays, and they should be included at the beginning of the planning, as well as during the negotiation stages.

✓ Carefully analyze any business you might be proposing to acquire. Does its portfolio fit the characteristics required to mount an LBO? Can you revamp it, enhance it, and sell it? What time-frame will you be looking at?

✓ Use specialist financial researchers and advisers. Remember that any undiscovered potential liabilities might cost more in the long run.

DOS AND DON'TS

DO

- In the primary stages, involve your lawyers and accountants in the evaluation of both the risks and the potential benefits of an acquisition.
- When the company has been acquired, use incentives to engage the onboard key business managers in helping with the turnaround process.
- Involve key stakeholders, and spell out in clear terms the risks the organization may be facing, their probability, and their potential impact, whether positive or negative.

DON'T

- Don't put the cart before the horse and make the mistake of being drawn to a business that has not been thoroughly investigated. Consider not only whether it can be turned around, but also whether you can get the financing.

MORE INFO

Books:

Fraser-Sampson, Guy. *Private Equity as an Asset Class*. Chichester, UK: Wiley, 2007.

Maginn, John L., Donald L. Tuttle, Jerald E. Pinto, and Dennis W. McLeavey (eds). *Managing Investment Portfolios: A Dynamic Process*. 3rd ed. CFA Institute Investment Series. Hoboken, NJ: Wiley, 2007.

Morris, Virginia B., and Kenneth M. Morris. *Standard and Poor's Guide to Money and Investing*. New York: Lightbulb Press, 2005.

Articles:

Dewar, Sally. "Private equity." *Australasian Business Intelligence* (June 2007).

McKellar, Peter. "An appetite for private equity." *Investment Adviser* (April 21, 2008). Online at: tinyurl.com/5s5l3wk

Website:

British Private Equity and Venture Capital Association (BVCA): www.bvca.co.uk

Using Investment Funds (Unit and Investment Trusts)

DEFINITION

Unit investment trusts (UITs) are companies that are registered to make investments on behalf of their clients. They buy and hold a portfolio of stocks and bonds, which they then sell to investors. These portfolios are known as "units." The purchasers of units are known as unit holders, and they receive interest on the investment that they make in this way.

UITs have a termination date according to the investment units they offer. Long-term bonds may be held for as long as 20 to 30 years. When the termination date arrives, unit holders may choose to receive the proceeds or reinvest them in another trust.

Units are bought and sold through the fund manager. The value of the units may rise or fall according to the overall value of the fund. This value moves according to the underlying share prices in the fund.

In investment trusts, the buyer invests directly in the shares of different companies rather than indirectly through shares in a pooled fund. This is the main difference between investment trusts and unit trusts. The value of these trusts can fluctuate more often and more significantly than that of unit trusts, as share prices are more directly affected by supply and demand.

The companies offering these trusts are diverse in terms of risk, and the buyer can choose among high and low-risk investments, as is also the case with unit trusts.

ADVANTAGES

- The main advantage of a UIT is its diversification. The UIT buys various types of stocks or bonds, which helps its investors to reduce their risk. The risk is mitigated by potential gains in some securities that offset the risk of loss in others. The idea here is that some of the purchased securities will always show gains, even if others do not.
- UITs provide the average investor with more possibilities in terms of investments than would otherwise be the case. In other words, UIT investments can be much less costly than constructing a portfolio of individual securities.
- A further advantage is the two different types of UIT, offering the investor even further choices. Fixed-income and equity UITs provide the buyer with almost any level of risk and investment objective desired.

DISADVANTAGES

- First-time investors might be tempted to take risks for which they are unprepared. It is therefore important to take great care to investigate all the markets involved. Diversifying investments means diversifying risks. While this may be an advantage, it can also bring certain disadvantages. There is always the risk, for example, that losses in some securities may outweigh the gains in others. However, with the necessary precautions, UITs and investment trusts offer perhaps the best opportunity for investors to enter the market.

ACTION CHECKLIST

✔ Ensure that you have enough funds to invest your chosen amount in a UIT or investment trust.

✔ Obtain the trust's prospectus, which will contain specific information about your investment.

✔ Make sure that you are fully informed of the level of risk you are taking and that you are comfortable with this risk level.

DOS AND DON'TS

DO

- Consult experienced financial advisers and investment brokers before investing.
- Look carefully at the variety of choices within the UIT and investment markets.
- Ensure that you are aware of the legislation relating to the company and investment you choose.
- Ensure that you receive an annual report from your UIT as it will contain valuable information about your investment.

DON'T

- Don't invest if you have not carefully considered and discussed your options with your financial advisers.
- Don't make an investment if you are not sure that you can handle the risks involved.
- Don't invest without having sufficient funds to do so; your current financial security is as important as your wealth in the future.

QFINANCE

Asset Management: Tools and Strategies

Investments • Checklists

MORE INFO

Books:

Investments • Checklists

MORE INFO

Books:

Burton, H., and D. C. Corner. *Investment and Unit trusts in Britain and America*. London: Elek, 1968.

Downes, John, and Jordan Goodman. *Finance and Investment Handbook*. 8th ed. Hauppauge, NY: Barron's, 2010.

Duddington, John. *Equity and Trusts*. 3rd ed. Law Express Series. Harlow, UK: Pearson Education, 2010.

Edwards, Richard, and Nigel Stockwell. *Trusts and Equity*. 10th ed. Foundation Studies in Law Series. Harlow, UK: Pearson Education, 2011.

QFINANCE

Checklists
Analysis

Analysis Using Monte Carlo Simulation

DEFINITION
The Monte Carlo method of simulation uses repeated random sampling to obtain results and is generally used for simulating physical and mathematical systems. It is best suited to calculations using a computer, due to the reliance on repetitive computations and its use of random (or pseudo-random) numbers. It is most often used when it is not possible to reach an exact result using a deterministic algorithm. Monte Carlo simulation is useful for modeling situations that have a good deal of uncertainty in the inputs, and this includes calculations of risks in business.

There is no single Monte Carlo method—the term covers a wide range of approaches to simulation. However, these approaches use a certain pattern in which:

1 A domain of possible inputs is defined;
2 Inputs are randomly generated from the domain;
3 Using the inputs, a deterministic computation is performed;
4 The results are aggregated from the individual computations to give a final result.

Monte Carlo simulation randomly samples inputs to produce many thousands of possible outcomes, rather than a few discrete scenarios as produced, for example, by deterministic modeling using single-point estimates. Monte Carlo results also give probabilities for different outcomes. Lay decision-makers can use Monte Carlo to determine confidence levels for a graphical representation.

In finance, Monte Carlo methods are used in the following areas:

- By financial analysts in corporate finance, project finance, and real option analysis to construct probabilistic financial models.
- To generate many possible price paths to value options on equity.
- To value bonds and bond options.
- To evaluate a portfolio.
- In personal finance planning.

Monte Carlo methods are flexible and can take many sources of uncertainty, but they may not always be appropriate. In general, the method is preferable only if there are several sources of uncertainty.

ADVANTAGES
- Using Monte Carlo simulation is quite straightforward.
- It can provide statistical sampling for numerical experiments using a computer.
- In optimization problems, Monte Carlo simulation can often reach the optimum and overcome local extremes.
- It provides approximate solutions to many mathematical problems.
- Monte Carlo analysis produces a narrower range of results than a "what if" analysis.

DISADVANTAGES
- Monte Carlo simulation is not universally accepted in simulating a system that is not in equilibrium (i.e. in a transient state).
- A large number of samples is required to reach the desired results. This can be time-consuming compared to using a spreadsheet program, such as Excel, which can generate a simple calculation fairly quickly.
- A single sample cannot be used in simulation; to obtain results there must be many samples.
- The results are only an approximation of the true value.
- Simulation results can show large variance.

ACTION CHECKLIST
✓ Consider the problem. Does it have many sources of uncertainty?
✓ Is there an analytical solution? If so, use that.
✓ Choose the software you will use for Monte Carlo simulation.
✓ Decide on the inputs and generate the results.

DOS AND DON'TS
DO
- Use Monte Carlo simulation where an analytical solution either does not exist or is too complicated.
- Use it where there are lots of uncertainties.

DON'T
- Don't use Monte Carlo simulations that might require months or years of computer time—it is not worth it.
- Don't use Monte Carlo simulations where an analytical solution exists and is simple. In this case it is easier to use the analytical solution to solve the problem.

Analysis • Checklists

MORE INFO

Books:

Fishman, George S. *Monte Carlo: Concepts, Algorithms, and Applications*. New York: Springer, 2003.
McLeish, Don L. *Monte Carlo Simulation and Finance*. Hoboken, NJ: Wiley, 2005.
Mooney, Christopher Z. *Monte Carlo Simulation*. Thousand Oaks, CA: Sage Publications, 1997.

Website:

Monte Carlo simulation basics from Vertex42:
www.vertex42.com/ExcelArticles/mc/MonteCarloSimulation.html

Applying the Gordon Growth Model

DEFINITION

The Gordon growth model is a tool that is commonly used to value stocks. Originally developed by Professor Myron Gordon and also known as Gordon's growth model, the aim of the method is to value a stock or company in today's terms, using discounted cash flows to take into account the present value of future dividends.

The model requires three inputs:
- D: The expected level of the stock's dividend one year ahead
- R: The rate of return the investor is seeking
- G: The assumed constant rate of future dividend growth in perpetuity.

The formula is as follows:

Gordon growth stock valuation per share = $D \div R - G$

ADVANTAGES

- The main strength of the Gordon growth model is that the valuation calculation is easily performed using readily available or easily estimated inputs.
- The model is particularly useful among companies or industries where cash flows are typically strong and relatively stable, and where leverage patterns are also generally consistent.
- The model is widely used to provide guideline fair values in mature industries such as financial services and in large-scale real-estate ventures. The model can be particularly appropriate in the valuation of real-estate investment trusts, given the high proportion of income paid out in dividends and the trusts' strictly defined investment policies.

DISADVANTAGES

- Although the model's simplicity can be regarded as one of its major strengths, in another sense this is its major drawback, as the purely quantitative model takes no account of qualitative factors such as industry trends or management strategy. For example, even in a highly cash-generative company, near-future dividend payouts could be capped by management's strategy of retaining cash to fund a likely future investment. The simplicity of the model affords no flexibility to take into account projected changes in the rate of future dividend growth.

- The calculation relies on the assumption that future dividends will grow at a constant rate in perpetuity, taking no account of the possibility that rapid near-term growth could be offset by slower growth further into the future. This limitation makes the Gordon growth model less suitable for use in rapidly growing industries with less predictable dividend patterns, such as software or mobile telecommunications. Its use is typically more appropriate in relatively mature industries or stock-market indices where companies demonstrate more stable and predictable dividend growth patterns.

ACTION CHECKLIST

✔ The Gordon growth model is generally more effective among companies and industries where dividend payments tend to be high—ideally, close to free cash flow to equity (FCFE). FCFE is a measure of how much cash a company can afford to pay out to shareholders after allowing for factors such as debt repayments and various expenses. Consider whether the entity to be valued exhibits such high dividend payments before making use of the model.

✔ Take into account other company-specific factors before applying the model to particular stocks. For example, consider how changes to the regulatory environment could affect a company's prospects.

✔ In the case of individual company valuations, consider whether a shift in the management's geographical horizon or major investment programmes could affect cash flow and future dividend patterns. Remember that the Gordon growth model does not take into account possible fluctuations in future dividend growth rates.

DOS AND DON'TS

DO

- Understand the underlying characteristics of the company, industry, or market index before deciding whether to use this model.
- If appropriate, use the model for easily calculated outline valuations.
- Consider the benefits of using other valuation tools in conjunction with or as alternatives to the Gordon growth model.

DON'T
- Don't use the model for companies, industries, or market indices where growth rates are rapid or leverage is subject to sudden swings.

- Don't make the mistake of blindly applying the model to companies in isolation.
- Don't totally ignore nonquantitative factors that could have a major bearing on future valuations.

MORE INFO

Books:

Gordon, Myron J. *The Investment, Financing, and Valuation of the Corporation*. Westport, CT: Greenwood Press, 1982.

Hitchner, James R. *Financial Valuation: Applications and Models*. 2nd ed. Hoboken, NJ: Wiley, 2006.

Articles:

Jackson, Marcus. "The Gordon growth model and the income approach to value." *Appraisal Journal* 62:1 (Spring 1994): 124–128.

Kiley, Michael T. "Stock prices and fundamentals: A macroeconomic perspective." *Journal of Business* 77:4 (October 2004): 909–936. Online at: dx.doi.org/10.1086/422629

Website:

Myron J. Gordon's homepage: www.rotman.utoronto.ca/~gordon

Calculating a Company's Net Worth

DEFINITION

The net worth of a company (sometimes referred to as its net assets) is measured by subtracting the total assets of the company from its total liabilities. Thus, net worth represents the liquidation proceeds a company would fetch if its operations were to cease immediately and the firm were sold off. For example, if a company has total assets of US$80 million and total liabilities of US$40 million, its net worth would amount to US$40 million. In this example, the company might own a factory worth US$40 million, machinery valued at US$20 million, and a fleet of vans valued at a further US$20 million. Its liabilities might consist of a loan of US$40 million used to fund the purchase of the machinery and vans. The net worth of a company is also known as the shareholders' equity.

Net worth can be easily identified by referring to the company's balance sheet, which will detail its total assets and liabilities, as well as its net worth. Of course, the balance sheet does not necessarily reflect the current market value of a firm but simply expresses the value at a particular point in time, i.e. when the balance sheet was drawn up. It is also important to remember that net worth does not take any account of how profitable the company is. It may be worth more or less if sold as a going concern.

ADVANTAGES

- It is easy to find out the net worth of a company—simply refer to its latest balance sheet.
- Net worth provides a simple and straightforward way of measuring a company's breakup value if it were to cease trading.

DISADVANTAGES

- The balance sheet does not necessarily reflect the current market value of a firm but simply expresses the value at a particular point in time, i.e. when the balance sheet was drawn up.

- It is also worth remembering that a company may have a different value if it is sold as a going concern. Net worth may underestimate or overestimate the true value of a company by a considerable extent. It does not take into account intangible assets such as goodwill, copyright, patents, and intellectual property. It also ignores how much revenue and profit (or loss) a company is generating.

ACTION CHECKLIST

✓ Obtain the company's net worth from its latest balance sheet.
✓ Obtain as much other financial information as possible, including figures for revenue and profit (or loss).
✓ Look at other indicators, such as the firm's order book, and try to assess nonfinancial factors such as goodwill and the competitiveness of the company's goods and services.

DOS AND DON'TS

DO

- Obtain an estimate of the intangible assets of a company, such as intellectual property.
- Look at other measures of corporate health, such as revenues, costs, and profits (or losses), as well as forward indicators such as order books.
- Try to obtain estimates of the current value of the company's assets and liabilities, rather than rely on figures from the balance sheets, which may be considerably out of date in volatile market conditions.

DON'T

- Don't assume that net worth provides an accurate guide to the current value of a company.

MORE INFO

Books:

Baker, H. Kent, and Gary E. Powell. *Understanding Financial Management: A Practical Guide.* Malden, MA: Blackwell Publishing, 2005.

Bandler, James. *How to Use Financial Statements: A Guide to Understanding the Numbers.* Burr Ridge, IL: Irwin, 1994.

Dickie, Robert B. *Financial Statement Analysis and Business Valuation for the Practical Lawyer.* 2nd ed. Chicago, IL: American Bar Association, 2006.

Articles:

Cummins, Jason G., Kevin A. Hassett, and Stephen D. Oliner. "Investment behavior, observable expectations, and internal funds." *American Economic Review* 96:3 (June 2006): 796–810. Online at: dx.doi.org/10.1257/aer.96.3.796

Halliwell, Leigh J. "ROE, utility, and the pricing of risk." *CAS Forum* (Spring 1999). Online at: www.casact.org/pubs/forum/99spforum/99spf071.pdf

Huberman, Gur. "Familiarity breeds investment." *Review of Financial Studies* 14:3 (Fall 2001): 659–680. Online at: dx.doi.org/10.1093/rfs/14.3.659

Website:

VentureNavigator: www.venturenavigator.co.uk

Calculating Total Shareholder Return

DEFINITION

When assessing the performance of stocks, inexperienced investors risk falling into the trap of looking purely at stock price movements, in the process ignoring the value of dividends which may be paid. Total shareholder return (TSR) over a period is defined as the net stock price change plus the dividends paid during that period. While it is possible that a stock could deliver a negative price performance over a certain period yet still generate a positive total shareholder return should the dividend paid outweigh the stock price fall, in practice this happens only rarely. In most markets, the dividend yield indicators are low, with the result that stock prices are generally the key driver of TSR. However, the importance of the dividend component of the total return calculation is typically more significant in traditionally higher-yielding areas of the stock market such as utilities, tobacco companies, and beverage producers.

Total shareholder return over a period can be calculated as follows:

$$\text{Total Shareholder Return \%} = \text{Stock price}_{\text{end of period}} - \text{Stock price}_{\text{start of period}} + \text{Dividends paid} \div \text{Stock price}_{\text{start of period}}$$

Importantly, when calculating TSR, we must take account of only the dividends that our period of ownership of the stock entitles us to receive, so we need to take account of the stock ex-dividend date rather than the dividend payment date. It could be that we own the stock on the day when the dividend is actually payable, yet we would only be entitled to receive the dividend had we owned the stock on the ex-dividend day.

An alternative ways of thinking of total shareholder return is the internal rate of return of all cash flows paid to investors during a particular period. However, whichever method we choose to calculate total shareholder return, the result essentially represents an indication of the overall return generated for stockholders, expressed in percentage terms. In all cases, the "dividends paid" element of the calculation should also include any special cash payments returned to stockholders, as well as any stock buyback programs. The figure should also take account of any special one-off dividend payments, as well as regular dividend payouts.

ADVANTAGES

* TSR represents a readily understood figure of the overall financial benefits generated for stockholders.
* The figure can be interpreted as a measure of how the market evaluates the overall performance of a company over a specified period.
* Given that TSRs are expressed in percentage terms, the figures are readily comparable between companies in the same sector.

DISADVANTAGES

* TSRs can be calculated for publicly traded companies at the overall level, but not at a divisional level.
* The calculation is not "forward looking" in that it reflects the past overall return to shareholders, with no consideration of future returns.
* TSR is externally focused in that it reflects the market's perception of performance; it could, therefore, be adversely impacted should a share price of a fundamentally strong company suffer excessively in the short term.

ACTION CHECKLIST

✓ Calculate the share price change over the specified period plus any dividends paid to generate a simple TSR calculation.
✓ If necessary, be prepared to make adjustments for special events such as share buybacks and/or splits in stocks' prices.
✓ Investors can use TSR percentages to make comparisons against industry benchmarks.
✓ From a company perspective, remuneration packages can be linked to TSR.

DOS AND DON'TS

DO

* Consider how TSR calculations might be applied to mutual funds as well as company stocks, thus taking account of income paid out by yield-orientated funds when looking at their annual performance.
* However, remember that TSR reflects past performance rather than a perception or indication of future returns.

Asset Management: Tools and Strategies

DON'T
- Don't forget that past performance shouldn't be taken as the best guide to future returns.
- Don't look to calculate TSR for privately held companies as the calculation requires stock price inputs.

MORE INFO
Books:
Ward, Keith. *Marketing Strategies: Turning Marketing Strategies into Shareholders Value.* Burlington, MA: Butterworth-Heinemann, 2004.
Young, David S., and Stephen F. O'Byrne. *EVA and Value Based Management.* New York: McGraw-Hill, 2000.

Articles:
Elali, Wajeeh. "Contemporaneous relationship between EVA and shareholder value." *International Journal of Business Governance and Ethics* 2:3–4 (October 2006): 237–253. Online at: dx.doi.org/10.1504/IJBGE.2006.011157
Gardner, Tim, and Eric Spielgel. "Total shareholder return: Planning a perfect future." *Public Utilities Fortnightly* (January 2006): 45–50. Online at: tinyurl.com/5wdc5no [PDF].

Analysis • Checklists

QFINANCE

218

How to Use Credit Rating Agencies

DEFINITION

A credit rating agency is a company that assigns credit ratings to issuers of debt instruments and to the debt instruments themselves. A wide variety of organizations may issue debt in the primary market and thus come under the scrutiny of the credit rating agencies. These include companies, national, and local governments, and government and semi-government entities. Their debt instruments are then traded on a secondary market. Credit rating agencies assign ratings that seek to determine how creditworthy the issuer is, i.e. to gauge the level of risk that they will be unable to repay the loan.

An entity with very strong finances will be given the highest rating, often described as AAA, while the least creditworthy will receive the lowest rating, normally D, which applies to debt that is already in arrears. An entity with low credit ratings will have to pay a premium in terms of the interest on loans in order to compensate the lender for the higher risk that the loan may not be repaid. The rating agencies constantly monitor all the instruments they rate and will issue upgrades or downgrades if an issuer's creditworthiness has changed.

Ratings are an invaluable tool for investors, providing a convenient way to identify the creditworthiness of a potential investment. Issuers use credit ratings to provide an independent analysis of their own creditworthiness, thus helping to determine the value of the instruments they issue. Government regulators and other agencies also use credit ratings to gauge the health of their financial system. Thus, regulators allow banks to use credit ratings from certain approved ratings agencies when calculating their net capital reserve requirements. Regulators could, for example, allow banks to include highly rated, liquid bonds when calculating their net capital reserve requirements.

The three largest credit rating agencies are Standard & Poor's, Moody's, and Fitch. All have come under fire as a result of the global credit crunch that developed in 2007. In July 2008, a damning report from the US Securities and Exchange Commission identified "serious shortcomings" in the rating of securities related to subprime mortgages, the products that triggered the crisis. Credit rating agencies have also come under fire for problems in structured finance products that they have rated, particularly in assigning AAA ratings to structured debt, which in a large number of cases has subsequently been downgraded or defaulted. There is thus increasing pressure to introduce greater regulation of the credit rating agencies.

ADVANTAGES

- The ratings assigned by credit rating agencies allow investors to quickly, cheaply, and conveniently identify the risk involved in buying a particular debt instrument or in developing a business relationship with a particular organization.
- The use of ratings opens capital markets to entities such as new companies.
- Credit ratings give you an insight into an entity from an independent expert analyst.

DISADVANTAGES

- The rating agencies have come under criticism as a result of the credit crunch. Many AAA-rated companies were downgraded to very low levels within a very short space of time.
- Credit rating agencies have come under fire for failing to downgrade companies quickly enough, with some companies faltering despite being assigned relatively good ratings.
- Credit rating agencies have been criticized for developing too close a relationship with the management of the companies that they rate.
- Credit rating agencies have been criticized for their role in rating structured finance products, and in particular for large losses in the collateralized debt obligation (CDO) market that occurred despite being assigned top ratings by the agencies.

ACTION CHECKLIST

✓ Look at the ratings from as many credit rating agencies as possible.
✓ Gather as much other information as you can on a potential investment or business partner.

DOS AND DON'TS

DO

* Be aware that issuers pay the rating agencies a fee. Critics say that this creates a potential conflict of interest.
* Conduct your own research as well as looking at the analysis supplied by the agencies.

DON'T

* Don't forget that the ratings agencies are not infallible.
* Don't forget that entities are subject to constant monitoring by the credit rating agencies. Ratings can and do change over time.

MORE INFO

Books:

Beder, Sharon. *Suiting Themselves: How Corporations Drive the Global Agenda*. London: Earthscan, 2005.

Brooks, Chris. *Introductory Econometrics for Finance*. 2nd ed. Cambridge, UK: Cambridge University Press, 2008.

Ganguin, Blaise, and John Bilardello. *Fundamentals of Corporate Credit Analysis*. New York: McGraw-Hill, 2005.

Articles:

Goodhart, C. A. E. "The background to the 2007 financial crisis." *International Economics and Economic Policy* 4:4 (February 2008): 331–346. Online at: dx.doi.org/10.1007/s10368-007-0098-0

Maxwell, James. "Ratings agencies eye ERM for all industries." *Financial Executive* (March 2008): 44–46. Online at: tinyurl.com/68ju22f [PDF].

Wray, L. Randall. "Lessons from the subprime meltdown." *Challenge* 51:2 (March–April 2008): 40–68. Online at: www.challengemagazine.com/extra/040_068.pdf

Website:

VentureNavigator: www.venturenavigator.co.uk

Mean–Variance Optimization: A Primer

DEFINITION

Mean–variance optimization (MVO) is a quantitative tool used to spread investment across different assets within a portfolio by assessing the trade-off between risk and return in order to maximize the return while minimizing any risks. The concept was devised by economist Harry M. Markowitz, who developed an algorithm to calculate optimized returns over a specified period. MVO is part of Markowitz's modern portfolio theory (MPT), which assumes that investors will optimize their investment portfolios through diversifying their investments on a balanced risk–return basis. Markowitz's concept of efficiency as laid out in MVO contributed to the development of the capital asset pricing model (CAPM).

The Markowitz algorithm relies on inputting three data sets on a graph: expected return per asset, standard deviation of each asset (a metric for risk), and the correlation between the two. Together these produce what Markowitz named the "efficient frontier," or those assets expected to produce better returns than others that carry the same or fewer risks, and, conversely, a smaller risk than those expected to produce the same or a higher rate of return. Investors should ensure the three data sets, or inputs, represent their expectations of probability for the specified period, as well as include possible outcomes, each with a return per asset and probability of occurrence. The expected return, standard deviation, and correlations can then be calculated with standard statistical formulae.

ADVANTAGES

- Because MVO assumes that investors are risk-averse and will choose a less-risky investment among any assets that offer similar expected returns, it is a useful tool for identifying assets that have the most favorable risk–return profile.

DISADVANTAGES

- MVO treats return as a future expectation and uses volatility as a proxy for risk, the flaw being that volatility is a historical parameter and you cannot assume that today's prices provide an accurate forecast for the future.

ACTION CHECKLIST

✔ Be aware of the risks of using only historical data for your inputs—you

✔ may prefer to use your own estimates for a given asset's future performance in the specified period.

✔ Watch out for something called mean reversion. This occurs when an asset performs extremely well for a period and then performs spectacularly badly in the following period, or vice versa. If you have used historical data for your inputs, your outputs will indicate a strong (weak) future performance, but if mean reversion occurs, you will have results opposite to what you expected in the specified period.

DOS AND DON'TS

DO

- Make careful decisions about which data sets to use as inputs.
- Pay extra attention when calculating the expected returns, as your choices will determine the actual returns that you assign to each asset in the investment portfolio.

DON'T

- Don't assume that historical data are an accurate reflection of future performance.

MORE INFO

Book:
Markowitz, Harry M. *Portfolio Selection*. 2nd ed. Malden, MA: Blackwell Publishers, 1991.

Article:
Markowitz, Harry. "Portfolio selection." *Journal of Finance* 7:1 (March 1952): 77–91. Online at: www.jstor.org/stable/2975974

Website:
Full text of Markowitz book: cowles.econ.yale.edu/P/cm/m16

Obtaining an Equity Value Using the Weighted Average Cost of Capital (WACC)

DEFINITION

Equity value is a market-based measure of the value of a company. In mergers and acquisitions, equity value is a more accurate measure of the value of a company than is market capitalization because equity value incorporates all equity interests in a firm. In contrast, market capitalization is calculated by multiplying the number of common shares currently outstanding by the share price.

WACC influences the calculation of equity value because the cost of financing any debt will reduce the company's nominal value. Valuation of a business using WACC means using the market value of equity, not its book value.

The example below shows how using WACC to calculate the debt value actually reduces the value of the debt and therefore reduces the company's overall equity value.

Example

Let us assume that a company has five million shares outstanding and that each share has a current market value of $8. The market capitalization of this company is thus 5,000,000 × $8 = $40,000,000.

Now let us assume the company has a debt value of $10 million and a WACC of 15%. The WACC equity value is calculated as follows:

Equity value = Market capitalization
$$+ [\text{Debt value} \times (1 - \text{WACC})]$$
$$= \$40,000,000 + [\$10,000,000 \times (1 - 0.15)]$$
$$= \$40,000,000 + \$8,500,000$$
$$= \$48,500,000$$

If WACC were not used in this calculation, the equity value of the company would simply be the sum of market capitalization and the debt value—that is, $50 million.

WACC is particularly used in acquisitions or financing business operations, and is also the method used to determine the discount rate for valuing a company using the discounted cash flow method.

ADVANTAGES

- Calculating equity value using WACC takes into account the market capitalization *plus* the debt *plus* the cost of financing that debt.

DISADVANTAGES

- WACC is not easy to obtain because of the different types of data that have to be found. It is a complicated measure that requires a lot of detailed company information.

ACTION CHECKLIST

✓ A company with an investment return that is greater than its WACC is creating value. Conversely, a company with a return less than WACC is losing value and investors should look elsewhere.

✓ WACC should be recalculated annually in order to maintain correct figures.

DOS AND DON'TS

DO

- Use the market value of equity to value a business.
- Use the WACC if you are considering buying a business or if you are a value investor.

DON'T

- Don't use the book value of the equity to value a business.
- Don't invest in a company with a rate of return less than the WACC.

Asset Management: Tools and Strategies

MORE INFO

Books:

Loos, Nicolaus. *Value Creation in Leveraged Buyouts: Analysis of Factors Driving Private Equity Investment Performance*. Wiesbaden, Germany: Deutscher Universitäts-Verlag (DUV), 2006.

Stewart, G. Bennett, III. *The Quest for Value: A Guide for Senior Managers*. 27th ed. New York: HarperCollins, 1991.

Articles:

Miles, James A., and John R. Ezzell. "The weighted average cost of capital, perfect capital markets and project life: A clarification." *Journal of Financial and Quantitative Analysis* 15:3 (September 1980): 719–730. Online at: dx.doi.org/10.2307/2330405

Yee, Kenton K. "Earnings quality and the equity risk premium: A benchmark model." *Contemporary Accounting Research* 23:3 (Fall 2006): 833–877. Online at: dx.doi.org/10.1506/8M44-W1DG-PLG4-8E0M

The Efficient Market Hypothesis

DEFINITION

The efficient market hypothesis (EMH) is a controversial economic theory that states that it is impossible for investors to purchase undervalued stocks or sell stocks for inflated prices because share prices always reflect all relevant information. It is therefore impossible to beat the market except by chance. According to the EMH, expert stock selection or market timing is of no value. Indeed, the only way an investor can possibly obtain higher than average returns is by purchasing riskier investments.

The EMH led to the argument that a blindfolded chimpanzee throwing darts at the *Wall Street Journal* would perform as well as highly-paid investment managers. The inevitable conclusion was that investors would be better off placing their money in broad-based index or tracker funds, which reflect the overall composition of the market and charge very low fees. These funds are known as passive funds, as opposed to actively managed funds, which aim to outperform the market by identifying undervalued stocks.

The EMH was developed by Professor Eugene Fama at the University of Chicago Business School in the 1960s. The theory was widely accepted until the 1990s, when behavioral economists began to question its validity. They argued that markets were far from perfect in terms of processing information and that other factors such as investor confidence have to be taken into account. They reasoned that it was indeed possible for investors to outperform the market by identifying undervalued stocks.

Empirical evidence can be used to support both sides of the argument. Many point to a wealth of data showing that few active managers consistently outperform the overall index. But there is other evidence that undermines the EMH. For example, it can be argued that markets do behave irrationally, with stock prices overshooting during bull markets and falling back excessively in bear markets, in the latter case allowing shrewd investors to buy undervalued stocks. There are also some investors—such as Warren Buffett—who appear able to beat the market consistently, which should not be possible if the EMH is correct.

ADVANTAGES

- If the EMH is correct there is no need for investors to pay the high fees charged by investment managers and their armies of analysts, researchers, and fund managers. They can simply put their money in tracker or index funds, which mirror the overall performance of the market.
- Investing in a tracker or index fund reduces risk since the investor is exposed to an entire market, rather than a selected number of stocks. It also eliminates the risk that a manager of an actively managed fund could simply make a mistake and invest in the wrong firm.
- Selecting passive over active fund management also means that the investor does not incur the high transaction costs resulting from the frequent trading undertaken by active managers.

DISADVANTAGES

- Actively managed funds aim to outperform the market. Thus, if an investor chooses only index funds, he will miss out on the opportunities for extra returns that an active manager can potentially generate.
- By avoiding actively managed funds, an investor will also fail to benefit from the other advantages that investing in such a fund can bring. During an economic downturn, for example, an active manager can focus on defensive stocks and sectors, which should outperform more cyclical stocks. The converse is true when the economy is performing well.

ACTION CHECKLIST

✓ Look at the performance of actively managed and passive funds to make your own assessment of the merits of the EMH.

✓ Decide whether it is worth paying the extra money required to invest in an actively managed fund compared to a passive fund.

DOS AND DON'TS

DO

- Consider investing in index or tracker funds if you believe that the EMH is true—i.e. that active managers cannot outperform the market on a sustained basis.
- Remember that if an active manager does beat the benchmark index, this may simply be due to chance rather than skill—unless, of course, the manager can outperform it consistently over a number of years.

Analysis • Checklists

DON'T

- Don't ignore the benefits that actively managed funds can bring in terms of risk reduction and the potential to outperform the overall market.

- Don't ignore the benefits of investing in both actively managed and passive funds.

MORE INFO

Books:

Graham, Benjamin, and David L. Dodd. *Security Analysis*. 6th ed. New York: McGraw-Hill, 2009.

Malkiel, Burton G. *A Random Walk Down Wall Street: The Time-Tested Strategy for Successful Investing*. 10th ed. New York: WW Norton & Company, 2011.

Mandelbrot, Benoit, and Richard L. Hudson. *The (Mis)behavior of Markets: A Fractal View of Risk, Ruin, and Reward*. London: Profile, 2004.

Articles:

Eom, Cheoljun, Gabjin Oh, and Woo-Sung Jung. "Relationship between efficiency and predictability in stock price change." *Physica A* 387:22 (15 September 2008): 5511–5517. Online at: dx.doi.org/10.1016/j.physa.2008.05.059

Ozdemir, Zeynel Abidin. "Efficient market hypothesis: Evidence from a small open-economy." *Applied Economics* 40:5 (March 2008): 633–641. Online at: dx.doi.org/10.1080/00036840600722315

Yen, Gili, and Cheng-few Lee. "Efficient market hypothesis (EMH): Past, present and future." *Review of Pacific Basin Financial Markets and Policies* 11:2 (June 2008): 305–329. Online at: dx.doi.org/10.1142/S0219091508001362

Website:

A personal website on the academic background to EMH: www.e-m-h.org

QFINANCE

Understanding Portfolio Analysis

DEFINITION

Portfolio analysis is a tool which helps managers assess how best to identify opportunities and to allocate resources across a set of products or businesses. The portfolio analysis framework seeks to first identify individual business units' growth cycle stages. The tool then examines these business units in the context of the overall growth of their respective industries, with a view to optimizing resources and maximizing overall portfolio performance. As an example, the technique seeks to identify resource-hungry units in sectors with the potential for dynamic growth and then shows how highly profitable cash-generative units in more mature industry sectors could be exploited to meet the resource needs of the growing businesses in such a way as to maximize overall portfolio returns. Portfolio analysis can also be used to identify business units or products that have already fulfilled their potential and could therefore be sold to free up resources for more productive investment elsewhere.

Though there are many different portfolio analysis tools, many approaches assess business units on the basis of market share and the growth rate of the industry or sector in which they operate. The technique is founded on the basis that increasing market share should generate higher earnings, while a higher rate of overall market growth typically requires higher levels of investment if the business is to capitalize on the available opportunities. Portfolio analysis also seeks to evaluate the strength of a company's competitive franchise within an industry or sector, using inputs such as its rate of change of market share, cost base, and product factors such as cost per unit and the strength of its new product pipeline. Using these inputs, portfolio analysis can help to promote success by highlighting areas with the potential to deliver the most attractive future profits, while flagging other areas with limited prospects, thus helping management to steer resources toward areas where they can best be invested.

ADVANTAGES

- Portfolio analysis simplifies complex situations and provides a valuable overview of the strengths and weaknesses of a company's mix of businesses and products.
- The technique is forward looking and can play an important role in delivering improved overall returns for shareholders over the medium to long terms.
- Portfolio analysis can help understanding of diversification and identify risks in a company's portfolio, for example by drawing attention to an overemphasis on particular areas.
- The technique underlines the need to understand business and product lifecycles and emphasizes the importance of achieving the breakthrough to profitability early, long before an industry or a product begins to mature.
- The analysis can help to overcome the danger that managers favor their pet projects and industries with extra resources, particularly if some inputs to analysis, such as industry growth projections, can be sourced independently.
- Portfolio analysis also encourages a view of businesses as collections of diversified cash flows and investments and so shows how corporate strategy integrates with individual business strategy at the business unit level.

DISADVANTAGES

- Portfolio analysis relies heavily on estimates of future patterns. Even a slight change in a forecast can significantly impact the results of the analysis.
- Excessively short-term use of portfolio analysis can lead to frequent and expensive switches of company resources.
- Acquiring or divesting businesses can be complex and time-consuming. One should take these costs into account before acting on marginal recommendations on portfolio changes.
- Most businesses are actually "average" but should still be kept. For example, Apple's laptop business is not growing and the market for laptops isn't growing, but it is still important to keep it in the firm.
- Market share is not the same as profitability: firms with low market share can be quite profitable (e.g. mail order catalogs have low market share but are highly profitable).
- There may be better places to put your money than in your surplus cash cows (e.g. the open market).
- Portfolio analysis techniques do not generally consider synergies across businesses or products.

ACTION CHECKLIST

✓ Before applying portfolio analysis, managers should achieve some understanding of all business units/products and the challenges/ opportunities they face.

✓ Consider using particular forms of portfolio analysis, such as the Boston Consulting matrix. This places business units into readily understandable categories (cash cow, stars, problem child, dogs) according to factors such as market share and industry growth rate.

✓ Use the technique to emphasize the goal of portfolio balance and the need to achieve a "pipeline" of future income streams, rather than relying on the hope of any single blockbuster product resulting from a R&D success.

DOS AND DON'TS

DO

• Whenever possible, include statistical inputs from external sources to avoid the risk that internal company-specific assumptions may be inaccurate.

• Be prepared to question and challenge assumptions during the process.

DON'T

• Don't rely totally on any one strategic planning technique.

• Don't plan for every conceivable eventuality as it is not practical to do this—even the best analysis can come unstuck should a highly improbable "freak" event happen. For example, as a result of the recent credit crunch, a reliance on bank finance to fund future product development costs has been a weakness against the backdrop of tighter credit conditions.

MORE INFO

Books:

Wheelen, Thomas L., and David J. Hunger. *Strategic Management and Business Policy: Concepts and Cases*. 11th ed. Upper Saddle River, NJ: Prentice Hall, 2007.

Wilson, Richard M. S., and Colin Gilligan. *Strategic Marketing Management: Planning, Implementation & Control*. 3rd ed. Oxford: Elsevier Butterworth-Heinemann, 2005.

Articles:

Eng, Teck-Yong. "Does customer portfolio analysis relate to customer performance? An empirical analysis of alternative strategic perspective." *Journal of Business and Industrial Marketing* 19:1 (2004): 49–67. Online at: dx.doi.org/10.1108/08858620410516736

Wind, Yoram, and Susan Douglas. "International portfolio analysis and strategy: The challenge of the 80s." *Journal of International Business Studies* 12:2 (June 1981): 69–82. Online at: dx.doi.org/10.1057/palgrave.jibs.8490579

Websites:

Tutor2u guide to portfolio analysis (including Boston Consulting grid and McKinsey/GE matrix): tutor2u.net/business/strategy/ge_matrix.htm

Value Based Management.net guide to McKinsey/GE matrix: www.valuebasedmanagement.net/methods_ge_mckinsey.html

Understanding Price Volatility

DEFINITION

In a free market, prices are effectively set by the relative levels of supply and demand for the underlying asset. Thus, prices are naturally impacted by rapid changes in the levels of confidence and conviction of market participants, both over short and long terms. Though price fluctuations are part of normal free market activity, at times unexpected major events can have a significant impact on the market's confidence. During such periods, normal price movements can give way to greater price swings, as market prices gyrate according to the participants' rapidly changing view of fair value. These price swings are exacerbated in periods of sharp market declines, partly because liquidity can also fall as fewer market participants are willing to attempt to underpin tumbling markets hit by panic selling. In contrast, rising markets typically enjoy higher levels of liquidity, but can, nevertheless, also suffer from rapid price swings, although these are frequently less dramatic in nature than in sudden market slides. Nevertheless, all kinds of market uncertainty can breed volatility.

Though the general concept of volatility is widely understood, in statistical terms volatility represents the relative rate at which the price moves up or down, as defined by the daily price movement's annualized standard deviation. Thinking in terms of the "bell curve" image associated with the mention of statistical calculations, one standard deviation represents the maximum daily movement we can expect 68% of the time, while the range of two standard deviations should cover 95% of daily net changes. However, it's important to recognize that by utilizing the input of past data, we are calculating *historical volatility*. Another way of expressing volatility is *implied volatility*, which uses the prices of market instruments, such as options, to evaluate investors' forecasts of future volatility. Though the models developed for options pricing can be highly complex, it is predictable that options prices are likely to be higher at a time of greater perceived uncertainty and elevated volatility, than at other times when investors' expectations of market conditions are more benign.

ADVANTAGES

- Volatility calculations allow comparisons of market conditions during different eras.

- The pricing of derivative instruments, such as options, relies on some form of volatility variable.
- Elevated levels of market volatility can create opportunities for longer-term investors.

DISADVANTAGES

- Volatility-related calculations can be complex, particularly when related to advanced options pricing models.
- High levels of volatility can add to existing levels of market uncertainty, creating a vicious circle for inexperienced market participants.

ACTION CHECKLIST

- Visualize the basic "bell curve" image of past price movement outcomes to help introduce the concept of volatility to inexperienced investors.
- Acknowledge that volatility in itself is not a guide to market direction, as volatility can move independently of market sentiment.
- Consider how derivative instruments, such as options, caps, and collars, could help you towards your volatility and wider risk management objectives.

DOS AND DON'TS

DO

- Recognize the difference between historical (backward-focused) and implied volatility (based on future perceptions).
- Appreciate that volatility isn't a "bad thing" or a "good thing" as such—it's part and parcel of free markets.

DON'T

- Don't waste resources crunching the numbers manually—use spreadsheets or specialized volatility/options pricing packages for calculations.
- Don't mistake calculations based on historical data as any definitive guide to the market's future movements—more stocks can be subject to movements beyond the "predicted" standard deviations than the numbers might suggest.

Analysis • Checklists

MORE INFO

Books:

Knight, John, and Stephen Satchell. *Forecasting Volatility in the Financial Markets*. 3rd ed. Quantitative Finance Series. Woburn, MA: Butterworth-Heinemann, 2007.

Taylor, Stephen J. *Asset Price Dynamics, Volatility and Prediction*. Princeton, NJ: Princeton University Press, 2007.

Articles:

Garman, Mark B., and Michael J. Klass. "On the estimation of security price volatility from historical data." *Journal of Business* 53:1 (1980): 67–78. Updated version online at: tinyurl.com/28o42u [PDF].

Mazzucato, M., and W. Semmler. "The determinants of stock price volatility: An industry study." *Nonlinear Dynamics, Psychology, and Life Sciences* 6:2 (April 2002): 197–216. Online at: oro.open.ac.uk/9463

Website:

Volatility and option price calculator: www.option-price.com

Using Dividend Discount Models

DEFINITION

Dividend discount models are essentially tools that have been developed to value a stock on the basis of estimated future dividends, discounted to reflect their value in today's terms.

Many variations of dividend discount models exist, but their central basis is the following formula:

Estimated valuation = $D \div (R - G)$

where D is present dividend per share, R is discount rate, and G is dividend growth rate.

Variations on the standard model can be used, depending on the company's stage in the growth cycle, but the common theme of dividend discount models is that the resulting estimated valuation is compared with the share's prevailing market price to determine whether the share is presently trading above or below its fair value.

ADVANTAGES

- Dividend discount models attempt to put a valuation on shares, based on forecasts of the sums to be paid out to investors. This should, in theory, provide a very solid basis to determine the share's true value in present terms.
- Dividend discount models can be of great use over the short to medium term, making use of widely available company research over timescales of up to five years.
- In stable industries, dividend discount models can still be of value over the longer term if investors are prepared to make the assumption that current dividend payout policies will remain in place.

DISADVANTAGES

- Standard dividend discount models are of no value in determining the estimated value of companies that don't pay dividends. This is typically not a problem in mature industries such as utilities and food, but the models are generally of less value in industries such as technology and mobile telecoms, where investors commonly look for share price appreciation rather than high dividend payments.
- The ability of a company to maintain a certain rate of dividend growth over the longer term can be extremely difficult to forecast accurately. Dividend discount models rely heavily on the validity of the data inputs, making them of questionable value given the challenges associated with accurately forecasting growth rates beyond five or so years.
- When used for longer-term analysis, the valuations provided by dividend discount models take no account of the possibility of a deliberate change to a company's dividend policy. This can further compromise the usefulness of dividend discount models over the longer term.

ACTION CHECKLIST

✓ Make every effort to establish the integrity and validity of the data to be input into a dividend discount model. The calculation relies on the accuracy of the source data, making the result very susceptible to inaccurate inputs.

✓ Consider using a dividend discount model as a screening tool, such that stocks that are apparently undervalued according to the model could scrutinized more closely using alternative valuation techniques.

DOS AND DON'TS
DOS

- Recognize the limitations imposed by the assumption made by standard dividend discount models that dividend growth rates will be fixed in perpetuity.
- Consider whether a multistage dividend discount model would be more appropriate. These models take account of the various stages in a company's development, from growth to maturity.

DON'TS

- Don't attempt to use standard dividend discount models for growth-orientated companies that have yet to establish dividend payouts.
- Don't invest purely on the basis of the result of a single dividend discount model calculation in isolation. Given the total reliance on the data inputs, using a wider range of valuation tools could result in better investment decisions.

Analysis • Checklists

MORE INFO

Books:

Correia, Carlos, David Flynn, Enrico Uliana, and Michael Wormald. *Financial Management*. 6th ed (spiral-bound). Lansdowne, South Africa: Juta, 2007.

Pinto, Jerald E., Elaine Henry, Thomas R. Robinson, and John D. Stowe. *Equity Asset Valuation*. 2nd ed. Hoboken, NJ: Wiley, 2010.

Articles:

Beneda, Nancy L. "Estimating free cash flows and valuing a growth company." *Journal of Asset Management* 4:4 (December 2003): 247–257. Online at: dx.doi.org/10.1057/palgrave.jam.2240106

Foerster, Stephen R., and Stephen G. Sapp. "The dividend discount model in the long-run: A clinical study." *Journal of Applied Finance* 15:2 (Fall/Winter 2005): 55–75. Online at: ssrn.com/abstract=869545

Report:

Harris, Robert S., Kenneth M. Eades, and Susan J. Chaplinsky. "The dividend discount model." Darden case no. UVA-F-1234. Darden Business School, University of Virginia, 1998. Online at: ssrn.com/abstract=909419

Using Multistage Dividend Discount Models

DEFINITION

Conventional dividend discount models attempt to value a company based on projections of future dividends discounted to reflect their present value. However, the main drawback of these models is their assumption that dividends will grow in perpetuity at a constant rate that can be determined at the time of the calculation. In practice this assumption is frequently unrealistic, with companies typically undergoing different stages of growth:

- *High growth:* Fast growth is typical early in the company's development as it capitalizes on exciting opportunities in a new market segment or uses a new approach to aggressively gain a share of an existing market. With the overall market expanding, new clients may be relatively easy to attract, and revenues grow rapidly.
- *Transition:* The company's initial growth spurt slows as the "market grab" period ends. Typically, the overall market may grow at a slower pace or the market may become more competitive, reducing scope for dynamic revenue growth.
- *Maturity:* Revenue growth slows as the market moves closer to saturation. New clients become more difficult to attract and companies may have to compete more aggressively on price or service to persuade new clients to switch from a competitor.

Recognizing the different phases of the growth of companies, multistage dividend models typically focus on forecast cash flows for the high-growth and transition stages. Only when the maturity phase is reached would this approach advocate using a constant dividend growth projection, often employing the Gordon growth model to assess a company's longer-term value.

ADVANTAGES

- The multistage approach to companies' development makes intuitive sense, recognizing and addressing the limitations of fixed-growth assumptions, making it more readily applicable to a wider range of nonmature companies.
- Multistage discount dividend models are versatile and flexible, readily facilitating amendments to their data inputs.
- The model's flexibility extends to allowing us to test market assumptions by reversing the underlying calculation. For example, we can test the levels of growth at various time intervals implied by the prevailing share price.

DISADVANTAGES

- Dividend discount models of all kinds put heavy reliance on the quality and accuracy of their data inputs. Despite their perceived advantages over fixed-growth techniques such as the Gordon growth model, multistage dividend growth models remain vulnerable to relatively minor inaccuracies in source data.
- Multistage models are particularly prone to errors in calculations resulting from poor cash flow estimates during the high-growth phase of a company's development. At this relatively early stage, estimates of the constant dividend growth rate to be used in the maturity phase can be very difficult to make.
- For companies that are still in the early phases of growth, it can also be very difficult to accurately forecast the duration of the high-growth and subsequent transition stages. This may necessitate applying the models using a range of input parameters to help arrive at a more realistic valuation band.

ACTION CHECKLIST

✓ As with all dividend discount models, it is imperative to establish the integrity and validity of the input data as far as is possible. The models are totally reliant on the numbers fed into them, making the resulting estimated valuations very sensitive to inaccurate inputs.

✓ Apply the multistage dividend discount model to the company you are interested in, and also to some of its industry competitors. Companies within the same sector could highlight apparent valuation anomalies or unjustified differences in their implied growth rates.

DOS AND DON'TS

DO

- Realize that, despite their undoubted advantages over the fixed-growth approach, multistage discount models remain prone to inaccuracies from any one of a number of inputs.
- However, make maximum use of the model's flexibility to test the market's underlying assumptions. Use the model to ask questions, such as whether the implied growth phase timescales are too long or short, and whether the early growth rate forecasts are appropriate based on the present valuation.

DON'T

- Don't use the models in isolation; rather, combine the technique with other methods of valuation.
- Don't simply employ the model to test whether a stock is currently either under- or overvalued. Test your own assumptions on factors such as future growth rates and the duration of the growth cycle, performing "what if" analysis using variations on your initial input.

MORE INFO

Books:

Barker, Richard. *Determining Value: Valuation Models and Financial Statements*. Harlow, UK: Pearson Education, 2001.

Hitchner, James R. *Financial Valuation: Applications and Models*. Hoboken, NJ: Wiley, 2003.

Articles:

Arnott, Robert D. "Disentangling size and value." *Financial Analysts Journal* 61:5 (September/October 2005): 12–15. Online at: dx.doi.org/10.2469/faj.v61.n5.2751

Woolridge, J. Randall. "Do stock prices reflect fundamental values?" *Journal of Applied Corporate Finance* 8:1 (Spring 1995): 64–69. Online at: dx.doi.org/10.1111/j.1745-6622.1995.tb00275.x

Report:

CFA Institute. "Equity investments: Valuation models." CFA program level II study session 12. Online at: tinyurl.com/3aqtvgv [PDF].

Using Shareholder Value Analysis

DEFINITION

Shareholder value is a term that suggests that the decisive measure of a company's success is how well it enriches its shareholders. Shareholder Value Analysis (SVA) is one of a number of techniques used as substitutes for traditional business measurements. It became fashionable in the 1980s, when it was linked to Jack Welch, then CEO of General Electric.

Essentially, the idea is that shareholders' money should be used to earn a higher return than it could by investing in other assets with the same amount of risk. To calculate shareholder value, you estimate the total net worth of a company, i.e. total assets minus total liabilities, and divide this figure by the value of its shares. The result gives you the shareholder value of the company. The basic rule of SVA is that a company adds value for its shareholders only when equity returns exceed equity costs. When that value has been calculated, the company can take steps to improve its performance and also use SVA to measure the success of those actions.

Although there are some complex formulae for working out shareholder value, it can also be determined using three simpler approaches:

- Discount the expected cash flows to the present to reach an estimated economic value for the business.
- Use the appropriate cost of capital for the business to find the actual cost of investment discounted to the present.
- Work out the economic value of the business by calculating the difference between the results of the above analyses.

SVA is also known as value-based management. The principle is that the management of any company should first and foremost consider how the interests of its shareholders will be affected by any decisions it takes. This is not a new management theory; it is the legal premise upon which any publicly traded company is set up.

ADVANTAGES

- SVA holds that management should first and foremost consider the interests of shareholders in its business decisions.
- Multistage discount dividend models are versatile and flexible, readily facilitating amendments to their data inputs.
- SVA takes a long-term view and is about measuring and managing cash flows over time. It provides the user with a clear understanding of value creation or degradation over time within each business unit.
- SVA offers a common approach, which is not subject to the particular accounting policies that are adopted. It is therefore globally applicable and can be used across most sectors.
- SVA forces companies to focus on the future and their customers, with specific attention to the value of future cash flows.

DISADVANTAGES

- The concentration on shareholder value does not take into account societal needs. Shareholder value financially benefits only the owners of a corporation; it does not provide a clear measure of social factors such as employment, environmental issues, or ethical business practices. Therefore, a management decision can maximize shareholder value while adversely affecting third parties, including other companies.
- It can be extremely difficult to estimate future cash flows accurately—a key component of SVA. This can lead to the use of faulty or ambiguous figures as the basis for strategic decisions.
- The development and implementation of an SVA system can be long and complex.
- Management of shareholder value requires more complete information than traditional measures and can therefore take up management time.

ACTION CHECKLIST

✓ Before adopting SVA, it is important to understand the implications it will have for your business.

✓ You should consult professional advisers, such as accountants or consultants who specialize in this area and who can inform you of what the ramifications may be.

✓ SVA is based on the principle that creation and maximization of shareholder value is the most important measure of a business's performance.

✓ All members of the organization must be committed to the principle for it to work effectively.

DOS AND DON'TS

DO

- Consult professional advisers, such as accountants or consultants who specialize in this area. The changes required to implement SVA could be costly—even more so if you find you need to reverse them.

DON'T

- Don't take on board SVA as a system unless you are positive that your overriding concern is shareholder value.

MORE INFO

Books:

Barker, Richard. *Determining Value: Valuation Models and Financial Statements*. Harlow, UK: FT Prentice Hall, 2001.

Pike, Richard, and Bill Neale. *Corporate Finance and Investment: Decisions and Strategies*. 6th ed. Harlow, UK: FT Prentice Hall, 2009.

Report:

Chartered Management Institute. "Shareholder value analysis (Checklist 160)." April 2010. Online at: tinyurl.com/3bevp2s

Websites:

American Accounting Association (AAA): www.aaa-edu.org
Institute of Internal Auditors (IIA): www.theiia.org

Index

Index

Index